Lecture Notes in Computer Science 8184

Commenced Publication in 1973
Founding and Former Series Editors:
Gerhard Goos, Juris Hartmanis, and Jan van Leeuwen

Guorong Wu Daoqiang Zhang
Dinggang Shen Pingkun Yan
Kenji Suzuki Fei Wang (Eds.)

Machine Learning in Medical Imaging

4th International Workshop, MLMI 2013
Held in Conjunction with MICCAI 2013
Nagoya, Japan, September 22, 2013
Proceedings

 Springer

Volume Editors

Guorong Wu
Dinggang Shen
University of North Carolina at Chapel Hill, NC, USA
E-mail: {grwu,dgshen}@med.unc.edu

Daoqiang Zhang
Nanjing University of Aeronautics and Astronautics, China
E-mail: dqzhang@nuaa.edu.cn

Pingkun Yan
Chinese Academy of Sciences, Xi'an, China
E-mail: pingkun@ieee.org

Kenji Suzuki
The University of Chicago, IL, USA
E-mail: suzuki@uchicago.edu

Fei Wang
IBM Almaden Research Center, San Jose, CA, USA
E-mail: wangfe@us.ibm.com

ISSN 0302-9743   e-ISSN 1611-3349
ISBN 978-3-319-02266-6   e-ISBN 978-3-319-02267-3
DOI 10.1007/978-3-319-02267-3
Springer Cham Heidelberg New York Dordrecht London

Library of Congress Control Number: 2013947072

CR Subject Classification (1998): I.4.3, I.4.6, I.4.0-1, I.5.2-3, J.3, I.2.1, I.2.6, I.2.10, H.2.8, I.3.3

LNCS Sublibrary: SL 6 – Image Processing, Computer Vision, Pattern Recognition, and Graphics

Typesetting: Camera-ready by author, data conversion by Scientific Publishing Services, Chennai, India

Printed on acid-free paper

Springer is part of Springer Science+Business Media (www.springer.com)

Preface

The 4th International Workshop on Machine Learning in Medical Imaging (MLMI 2013) was held at Toyoda Auditorium Complex, Nagoya, Japan, on September 22, 2013, in conjunction with the 16th International Conference on Medical Image Computing and Computer Assisted Intervention (MICCAI).

Machine learning plays an essential role in the medical imaging field, including computer-assisted diagnosis, image segmentation, image registration, image fusion, image-guided therapy, image annotation, and image database retrieval. With advances in medical imaging, new imaging modalities and methodologies, such as cone-beam CT, tomosynthesis electrical impedance tomography and new machine learning algorithms/applications, come to the stage for medical imaging. Due to large inter-subject variations and complexities, it is generally difficult to derive analytic formulations or simple equations to represent objects such as lesions and anatomy in medical images. Therefore, tasks in medical imaging require learning from patient data for heuristics and prior knowledge, in order to facilitate the detection/diagnosis of abnormalities in medical images.

The main aim of this MLMI 2013 workshop is to help advance scientific research within the broad field of machine learning in medical imaging. This workshop focuses on major trends and challenges in this area, and presents works aimed to identify new cutting-edge techniques and their use in medical imaging. We hope that the MLMI workshop becomes an important platform for translating research from the bench to the bedside.

The range and level of submissions for this year's meeting were of very high quality. Authors were asked to submit full-length papers for review. A total of 57 papers were submitted to the workshop in response to the call for papers. Each of the 57 papers underwent a rigorous double-blinded peer-review process, with each paper being reviewed by at least two (typically three) reviewers from the Program Committee, composed of 62 well-known experts in the field. Based on the reviewing scores and critiques, the 32 best papers (56%) were accepted for presentation at the workshop and chosen to be included in this Springer LNCS volume. The large variety of machine-learning techniques applied to medical imaging were well represented at the workshop.

We are grateful to the Program Committee for reviewing the submitted papers and giving constructive comments and critiques, to the authors for submitting high-quality papers, to the presenters for excellent presentations, and to all the MLMI 2013 attendees who came to Nagoya from all around the world.

July 2013

Guorong Wu
Daoqiang Zhang
Dinggang Shen
Pingkun Yan
Kenji Suzuki
Fei Wang

Organization

Program Committee

Siamak Ardekani	John Hopkins University, USA
Hidetaka Arimura	Kyusyu University, Japan
Marleen de Bruijne	University of Copenhagen, Denmark
Weidong (Tom) Cai	The University of Sydney, Australia
Guangzhi Cao	GE Healthcare, USA
Guo Cao	Nanjing University of Science and Technology, China
Heang-Ping Chan	University of Michigan Medical Center, USA
Rong Chen	The University of Maryland, Baltimore County, USA
Ting Chen	Ventana, USA
Yong Fan	Chinese Academy of Sciences, China
Bram van Ginneken	Radboud University Nijmegen Medical Centre, The Netherlands
Ghassan Hamarneh	Simon Fraser University, Canada
Yong He	Beijing Normal University, China
Edward Herskovits	The University of Maryland, Baltimore County, USA
Heng Huang	University of Texas at Arlington, USA
Junzhou Huang	University of Texas at Arlington, USA
Xiaoyi Jiang	University of Muenster, Germany
Nico Karssemeijer	Radboud University Nijmegen Medical Centre, The Netherlands
Minjeong Kim	University of North Carolina at Chapel Hill, USA
Ruijiang Li	Standford University, USA
Shuo Li	GE Healthcare, Canada
Yang Li	Allen Institute for Brain Science, USA
Jianming Liang	Arizona State University, USA
Marius Linguraru	National Institutes of Health, USA
Jing Liu	University of California at San Francisco, USA
Kongkuo Lu	Philips, USA
Le Lu	National Institutes of Health, USA
Anant Madabhushi	Rutgers, The State University of New Jersey, USA
Yoshitaka Masutani	University of Tokyo, Japan

Brent Munsell   Claflin University, USA
Feiping Nie   University of Texas at Arlington, USA
Marc Niethammer   University of North Carolina at Chapel Hill,
                                 USA
Ipek Oguz   The University of Iowa, USA
Kazunori Okada   San Francisco State University, USA
Emanuele Olivetti   Fondazione Bruno Kessler, Italy
Kilian Pohl   University of Pennsylvania, USA
Daniel Rueckert   Imperial College London, UK
Mert Sabuncu   MGH, Harvard Medical School, USA
Clarisa Sanchez   Radboud University Nijmegen Medical Center,
                                 The Netherlands
Li Shen   Indiana University School of Medicine, USA
Feng Shi   University of North Carolina at Chapel Hill,
                                 USA
Jun Shi   Shanghai University, China
Min Shin   University of North Carolina at Charlotte,
                                 USA
Greg Slabaugh   City University London, UK
Ron Summers   National Institutes of Health, USA
Amir Tahmasebi   Philips, USA
Hotaka Takizawa   University of Tsukuba, Japan
Tolga Tasdizen   University of Utah, USA
Qian Wang   University of North Carolina at Chapel Hill,
                                 USA
Yalin Wang   Arizona State University, USA
Chong Yaw Wee   University of North Carolina at Chapel Hill,
                                 USA
Lin Yang   University of Kentucky, USA
Jieping Ye   Arizona State University, USA
Liang Zhan   University of California at Los Angeles, USA
Yiqiang Zhan   Siemens Medical Solutions, USA
Shaoting Zhang   Rutgers University, USA
Kevin Zhou   Siemens Corporate Research, USA
Luping Zhou   CSIRO, Australia
Sean Zhou   Siemens Medical Solutions, USA
Xiangrong Zhou   Gifu University, Japan
Dajiang Zhu   University of Georgia, USA
Hongtu Zhu   University of North Carolina at Chapel Hill,
                                 USA

Table of Contents

Unsupervised Deep Learning for Hippocampus Segmentation in 7.0 Tesla MR Images

Minjeong Kim, Guorong Wu, and Dinggang Shen

Department of Radiology and BRIC, University of North Carolina at Chapel Hill

Abstract. Recent emergence of 7.0T MR scanner sheds new light on the study of hippocampus by providing much higher image contrast and resolution. However, the new characteristics shown in 7.0T images, such as richer structural information and more severe intensity inhomogeneity, raise serious issues for the extraction of distinctive and robust features for accurately segmenting hippocampus in 7.0T images. On the other hand, the hand-crafted image features (such as Haar and SIFT), which were designed for 1.5T and 3.0T images, generally fail to be effective, because of the considerable image artifacts in 7.0T images. In this paper, we introduce the concept of unsupervised deep learning to learn the hierarchical feature representation directly from the pre-observed image patches in 7.0T images. Specifically, a two-layer stacked convolutional Independent Subspace Analysis (ISA) network is built to learn not only the intrinsic low-level features from image patches in the lower layer, but also the high-level features in the higher layer to describe the global image appearance based on the outputs from the lower layer. We have successfully integrated this deep learning scheme into a state-of-the-art multi-atlases based segmentation framework by replacing the previous hand-crafted image features by the hierarchical feature representations inferred from the two-layer ISA network. Promising hippocampus segmentation results were obtained on 20 7.0T images, demonstrating the enhanced discriminative power achieved by our deep learning method.

1   Introduction

Numerous methods have been developed for hippocampus segmentation in MR images [1-6], since accurate labeling of hippocampus is significant for study of many neurological diseases, including Alzheimer's disease. However, due to the tiny size of hippocampus ($\approx 35 \times 15 \times 7mm^3$) and also the complexity of surrounding structures, the accuracy of hippocampus segmentation is limited by the poor imaging contrast and resolution (i.e., often with the voxel size of $1 \times 1 \times 1mm^3$).

Recently, the development of high-resolution imaging technique makes a rapid progress in hippocampus segmentation. For example, in the 7.0T scanner, much more detailed hippocampal structures can be observed, compared to the 3.0T scanner [7]. However, it is not straightforward to apply the existing segmentation methods (developed for 1.5T or 3.0T) to 7.0T images, since the image content is significantly different, in terms of rich structural information and severe intensity inhomogeneity in 7.0T images. The typical examples of 7.0T and 1.5T MR images are shown in Fig. 1, where we can see the obvious difference.

G. Wu et al. (Eds.): MLMI 2013, LNCS 8184, pp. 1–8, 2013.

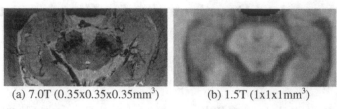

(a) 7.0T (0.35x0.35x0.35mm^3)　　　　　　(b) 1.5T (1x1x1mm^3)

Fig. 1. Large difference between 7.0T (a) and 1.5T (b) MR images

Thus, it is not difficult to notice that the conventional segmentation methods will encounter difficulties in segmenting hippocampus from 7.0T MR images, because of (1) severe intensity inhomogeneity in the 7.0T that can adversely affect the feature consistency of similar anatomical structures; (2) high signal-to-noise ratio (SNR) which brings forth plenty of anatomical details at the expense of troublesome image noise; (3) incomplete brain volume (i.e., with only a segment of brain, considering the practical issue during image acquisition).

Many learning-based methods [8-12] can be used for automatically segmenting hippocampus in 1.5T or 3.0T images. For example, Adaboost is able to learn image features by building a sequence of weak classifiers. It is assumed in this approach that the features (e.g., Haar or SIFT) are general enough to represent the input images. However, it is not straightforward to apply this approach to the 7.0T images which always have various troublesome artifacts (as shown in Fig. 1(a)). Furthermore, it is not guaranteed to obtain robust classifiers by the existing learning-based approaches, unless a large number of manual segmented samples are available for supervised learning.

Inspired by the recent success of deep learning [13, 14] in the field of computer vision and machine learning, we introduce the concept of deep learning to perform unsupervised learning directly on the 7.0T images with following reasons: (1) Deep learning is a unsupervised learning method, which leverages the plethora of unlabeled data for training; (2) Deep learning is able to provide the hierarchical feature representation for each image patch and ensure the discriminative power and robustness for the learned image features; (3) The success of deep learning in analyzing natural images also motivates us to apply it to 7.0T images with its rich image content as the natural images.

Specifically, we apply a two-layer stacked convolutional ISA [15] to learn the hierarchical feature representations from the image patches extracted from 7.0T MR images. To segment hippocampus for a new subject, we first extract image patch for each point and calculate the response of the extracted patch through the trained ISA network. The response vector is regarded as the intrinsic morphological representation for characterizing the underlying image point/patch. Then, we incorporate the learned hierarchical feature representations into a state-of-the-art multi-atlas segmentation framework to label hippocampus in the 7.0T images. Our proposed hippocampus segmentation method with unsupervised deep learning achieves more accurate labeling results than the counterpart with hand-crafted features, as it provides a better way to represent image features in the 7.0T MR images.

2 Method

The goal of learning-based hippocampus segmentation methods is to accurately label each image point $x \in \Omega$ in a new subject into either positive (i.e., hippocampus) or negative (i.e., non-hippocampus). Generally, a set of image features are extracted from a neighborhood of x, which is used as the morphological pattern to label point x.

Although 7.0T image displays plenty of image details around hippocampus, it also introduces severe noise and intensity inhomogeneity compared to the lower-resolution 1.5T or 3.0T images, which raises critical issues of using conventional hand-crafted image features for labeling. By taking Haar features as the example, we examine its discriminative power in representing image patches at different locations of 7.0T image. As shown in Fig. 2, image patches b and c belong to the hippocampus, but image patch a does not. The zoom-in views of these three patches are displayed in Fig. 2(a)-(c). Although the image contents are quite different among these patches, the responses from Haar filters are very similar, as shown in Fig. 2(d)-(f), where each column represents the responses from a set of Haar filters and each row denotes one point in the image patch. According to this observation, we can predict that the hand-crafted Haar features will be not distinctive enough to guide hippocampus segmentation in the 7.0T MR images.

Inspired by the recent success of deep learning [13, 14] in recognizing natural images, we introduce the concept of deep learning to directly extract the hierarchical feature representation of image patches in the 7.0T images (which contains the complex patterns as the natural images). Then, we incorporate the hierarchical feature representation into a state-of-the-art learning-based segmentation framework, for improving hippocampus segmentation in the 7.0T MR images.

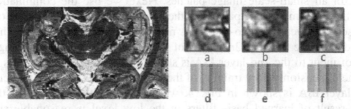

Fig. 2. Demonstration of the moderate power of the hand-crafted features (i.e., Haar features) in representing image patches in a 7.0T MR image

2.1 Learn Hierarchical Feature Representations for Image Patches by ISA

Here, we assume all observed image patches on 7.0T MR image forms a feature space. Then, independent subspace analysis is applied upon image patches, in order to (1) learn basis filters to represent the observed image patches and (2) use the representation coefficients as morphological signature in the feature space to identify the characteristics of each image point in 7.0T image.

Given M basis filters $\boldsymbol{W} = [w_i]_{i=1,\dots,M}$, we can obtain M responses for each image patch $x^t \in \boldsymbol{X}$ ($t = 1, \dots, T$) where T denotes the total number of observed image patches. Note that both x^t and w_i are the column vectors. The presence of image feature, i.e., obtained with the inner product $w_i \cdot x^t$, is termed as *response* in this paper. ISA is the unsupervised learning method to learn the basis filters $\boldsymbol{W}$ from the observations X, without requiring independency among all responses $\{w_i \cdot x^t\}$. Instead, ISA seeks for the subspaces in the entire domain of responses and allow dependencies inside each subspace, but independency between any two subspaces. Therefore, similar image features can be grouped into the same subspace to achieve the invariance. To this end, ISA uses the matrix $V = [v_{ij}]_{i=1,...,M, j=1,...,Q}$ to represent the structure of Q subspaces, where each entry v_{ij} in V indicates whether the basis filter w_i is associated with the j-th subspace. V is usually fixed in training ISA. The objective function of ISA is given by:

$$\widehat{W} = \arg\min_w \sum_{t=1}^{T} \sum_{j=1}^{Q} p_j(x^t; W, V), \quad s.t., WW' = I, \tag{1}$$

where p_j is called as the *activation* of particular image patch x^t in the j-th sub-space:

$$p_j(x^t; W, V) = \sqrt{\sum_{i=1}^{M} v_{ij}(w_i \cdot x^t)^2}. \tag{2}$$

In order to make the training of ISA efficient for high-resolution 7.0T MR images, we follow the method in [15] to construct a stacked two-layered convolutional network, as an extension of ISA by utilizing the technique of stacking and convolution in deep learning. The demonstration of ISA is shown in the bottom of Fig. 3. The input of ISA is the observed image patches, as denoted by boxes. The basis filters and the subspace learned by ISA are shown by triangles and circles, respectively. Specifically, we first extract image patches with a large scale. Then, we follow the sliding window to obtain a set of overlapped image patches but with smaller scale. Since the dimension of these cropped patches are small, we can efficiently train the ISA, thus obtain the activations for all small-scale image patches. Next, we use the combination of the activations from all small-scale patches in the large-scale patch as the input of another ISA in the second layer. The two-layer ISA network is shown in Fig. 3, with blue and red colors denote the 1st and 2nd layer of ISA, respectively. Considering that the dimension of input to the 2nd-layer ISA is still high but redundant, PCA is deployed to reduce the dimension before training of the 2nd-layer ISA. The basis filters learned by the 1st-layer ISA is shown in Fig. 4, where most of them look like the Gabor filters. The result of learned basis filters in the low level is reasonable since edge information is very rich in 7.0T images.

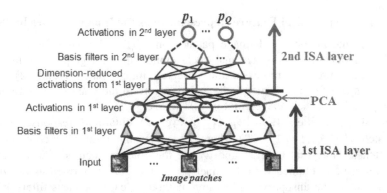

Fig. 3. Stacked convolutional ISA networks for feature extraction

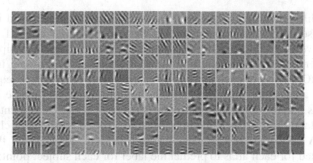

Fig. 4. The learned basis filters by 1st layer ISA

2.2 Segment Hippocampus by Learned Feature Representations

Although 7.0T imaging technique has demonstrated the superior image quality around hippocampus, few automatic segmentation methods have been proposed in the literature. As mentioned in the introduction, the characteristics of 7.0T image, e.g., severe intensity inhomogeneity and high SNR, can degrade the segmentation performance by the existing learning-based methods. Moreover, the alignment of 7.0T images is also not straightforward. Therefore, we extend auto-context model (ACM) [10], which does not require accurate alignment of training images, into a multi-atlases based segmentation framework, as demonstrated in Fig. 5.

In the *training* stage (Fig. 5(a)), totally N images $I = \{I_s(x)|x \in \Omega, s = 1, ..., N\}$ and their corresponding manual hippocampi labels $L = \{L_s(x)|x \in \Omega, s = 1, ..., N\}$ are used as atlases. In each atlas space (depicted by dashed boxes in Fig. 5), all other $N - 1$ atlases are linearly aligned onto this atlas and then a number of image features are extracted for each point, within a certain neighborhood. Note that we extract the hierarchical features learned by the stacked convolutional ISA model (as described in Section 2.1), rather than the hand-crafted features.

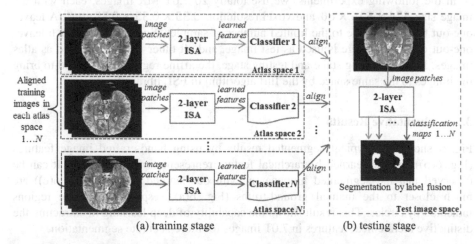

(a) training stage   (b) testing stage

Fig. 5. Schematic illustration of multi-atlases based hippocampus segmentation framework, which consists of training stage (a) and testing stage (b)

Since it is difficult to align 7.0T images, ACM method is deployed in our multi-atlases based segmentation framework. ACM utilize spatial context information, which is iteratively perceived from the probability map of segmented hippocampus at the previous iteration, without requiring the well alignment of training images. After deploying an ACM classifier sequence in each atlas, a set of classifier sequences w.r.t. the number of atlases are trained, where the training samples include not only the underlying atlas but also the linearly aligned other $N - 1$ atlases as mentioned above. In the testing stage (Fig. 5(b)), same image features (in our case, hierarchical features learned by ISA network) are extracted for each subject point. Then, the following steps are repeated for each atlas to predict the label for each subject point: (1) Map the classifiers on each atlas to the underlying subject space by using the affine registration between the atlas and subject image; (2) Predict the probabilistic labeling map by applying the trained ACM classifiers, trained w.r.t. each atlas, to each point in the subject; (3) Fuse all labeling results from all atlases to obtain the final segmentation result.

3   Experimental Results

We demonstrate the performance of hierarchical feature representation through deep learning by incorporating it into the state-of-the-art multi-atlases based segmentation framework. Specifically, we compare our method with the other method in the same multi-atlases framework but incorporating with hand-crafted image features used in [10]. We extract the smaller image patch with the size of $16 \times 16 \times 3$ to train the 1st layer ISA, and the larger image patch the size of $20 \times 20 \times 5$ to train the 2nd layer ISA network, respectively. The initial dimension for patch representation by the 1st ISA layer is 200, while the final dimension by the 2nd layer is 100. We report both qualitative and quantitative segmentation results of hippocampus by our proposed method, with comparison to other method using the hand-crafted features.

In the following experiments, we use totally 20 7.0T MR images, each with the image size $576 \times 576 \times 60$ and voxel resolution $0.35 \times 0.35 \times 0.35 mm^3$. A leave-one-out test is used due to the limited number of samples. Specifically, at each leave-one-out case, one image is used as test image, and all other images are used as atlas images. In both training stage and testing stage, the affine registration is used to bring the images to the same space by the flirt algorithm in FSL library.

3.1   Qualitative Results

Fig. 6 shows two typical segmented results by using hand-crafted image features (Fig. 6(b)) and the learned hierarchical feature representations (Fig. 6(c)). It can be observed that the segmented hippocampi with our learned features (Fig. 6(c)) are much closer to the manual ground-truths (Fig. 6(a)), especially for the regions indicated by circles. This result shows the capability of deep learning in extracting the distinctive hierarchical features in 7.0T images for more accurate segmentation.

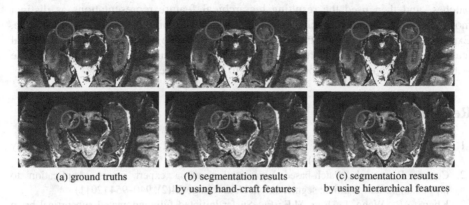

| (a) ground truths | (b) segmentation results by using hand-craft features | (c) segmentation results by using hierarchical features |

Fig. 6. Comparison of segmented hippocampus regions by (b) using hand-crafted features, and (c) using hierarchical feature representations. Compared to the manual ground truths (a), hippocampus segmentation results with our learned features gives better performance.

3.2 Quantitative Results

For quantitative evaluation of hippocampus segmentation, we use the following 4 overlap metrics: precision (P), recall (R), relative overlap (RO), and similarity index (SI), as defined below:

$$P = \frac{V(A \cap B)}{V(B)}, \quad R = \frac{V(A \cap B)}{V(A)}, \quad RO = \frac{V(A \cap B)}{V(A \cup B)} \quad \text{and} \quad SI = \frac{V(A \cap B)}{\{(V(A)+V(B))/2\}} \quad (3)$$

where $V(A)$ is the volume of ground-truth segmentation such as manual segmentation, and $V(B)$ is the volume of automatic segmentation. Table 1 shows the averaged overlap scores for these 4 above metrics for the 20 leave-one-out cases, indicating that our learned hierarchical feature representations consistently achieve better hippocampus segmentation than hand-crafted features across all 4 metrics.

Table 1. Quantitative comparisons based on the averaged 4 overlap metrics (precision (P), recall (R), relative overlap (RO), and similarity index (SI)) for the 20 leave-one-out cases, which shows the improvements by our method using learned feature representation over other method using hand-craft features in the same segmentation framework (unit: %)

	P	R	RO	SI
By hand-crafted features	84.3	84.7	77.2	86.5
By hierarchical patch representations	88.3	88.1	81.9	89.4

4   Conclusion

In this paper, we proposed using the unsupervised deep learning to extract discriminative image features for segmenting hippocampus in the 7.0T MR images. In view of abundant image details as well as image artifacts, we constructed a two-layer ISA network to seek for the intrinsic basis filters directly from the pre-observed image patches, and then used the resulting hierarchical feature representations as distinct morphological signature to characterize each image point in the 7.0T MR image. Experimental results demonstrated superior performance of our learned hierarchical features over the hand-crafted image features in substantially improving the segmentation accuracy of hippocampus in 7.0T MR images.

References

1. Zhou, J., Rajapakse, J.C.: Segmentation of subcortical brain structures using fuzzy templates. NeuroImage 28(4), 915–924 (2005)
2. Coupé, P., et al.: Patch-based segmentation using expert priors: Application to hippocampus and ventricle segmentation. NeuroImage 54(2), 940–954 (2011)
3. Khan, A.R., Wang, L., Beg, M.F.: FreeSurfer-initiated fully-automated subcortical brain segmentation in MRI using Large Deformation Diffeomorphic Metric Mapping. NeuroImage 41(3), 735–746 (2008)
4. Chupin, M., et al.: Automatic segmentation of the hippocampus and the amygdala driven by hybrid constraints: Method and validation. NeuroImage 46(3), 749–761 (2009)
5. van der Lijn, F., et al.: Hippocampus segmentation in MR images using atlas registration, voxel classification, and graph cuts. NeuroImage 43(4), 708–720 (2008)
6. Lötjönen, J.M.P., et al.: Fast and robust multi-atlas segmentation of brain magnetic resonance images. NeuroImage 49(3), 2352–2365
7. Cho, Z.-H., et al.: Quantitative analysis of the hippocampus using images obtained from 7.0 T MRI. NeuroImage 49(3), 2134–2140 (2010)
8. Wang, H., et al.: A learning-based wrapper method to correct systematic errors in automatic image segmentation: Consistently improved performance in hippocampus, cortex and brain segmentation. NeuroImage 55(3), 968–985 (2011)
9. Morra, J.H., Tu, Z., Apostolova, L.G., Green, A.E., Toga, A.W., Thompson, P.M.: Automatic Subcortical Segmentation Using a Contextual Model. In: Metaxas, D., Axel, L., Fichtinger, G., Székely, G. (eds.) MICCAI 2008, Part I. LNCS, vol. 5241, pp. 194–201. Springer, Heidelberg (2008)
10. Tu, Z., Bai, X.: Auto-Context and Its Application to High-Level Vision Tasks and 3D Brain Image Segmentation. IEEE Transactions on Pattern Analysis and Machine Intelligence 32, 1744–1757 (2010)
11. Zhang, S., Zhan, Y., Metaxas, D.N.: Deformable segmentation via sparse representation and dictionary learning. Medical Image Analysis 16(7), 1385–1396 (2012)
12. Zhang, S., et al.: Towards robust and effective shape modeling: Sparse shape composition. Medical Image Analysis 16(1), 265–277 (2012)
13. Bengio, Y.: Learning Deep Architectures for AI. Found. Trends Mach. Learn. 2(1), 1–127 (2009)
14. Shin, H.-C., et al.: Stacked Autoencoders for Unsupervised Feature Learning and Multiple Organ Detection in a Pilot Study Using 4D Patient Data. IEEE Transactions on Pattern Analysis and Machine Intelligence 99(PrePrints), 1 (2012)
15. Le, Q.V., et al.: Learning hierarchical invariant spatio-temporal features for action recognition with independent subspace analysis. In: 2011 IEEE Conference on Computer Vision and Pattern Recognition, CVPR (2011)

Integrating Multiple Network Properties
for MCI Identification

Biao Jie[1,2], Daoqiang Zhang[1,*], Heung-Il Suk[2], Chong-Yaw Wee[2],
and Dinggang Shen [2,*]

[1] Dept. of Computer Science and Engineering,
Nanjing University of Aeronautics and Astronautics, Nanjing 210016, China
dqzhang@nuaa.edu.cn
[2] Dept. of Radiology and BRIC, University of North Carolina at Chapel Hill, NC 27599
dgshen@med.unc.edu

Abstract. Recently, machine learning techniques have been actively applied to the identification of Alzheimer's disease (AD) and mild cognitive impairment (MCI). However, most of the existing methods focus on using only single network property, although combination of multiple network properties such as local connectivity and topological properties may be more powerful. Employing the kernel-based method, we propose a novel classification framework that attempts to integrate multiple network properties for improving the MCI classification. Specifically, two different types of kernel (i.e., vector-kernel and graph-kernel) extracted from multiple sub-networks are used to quantify two different yet complementary network properties. A multi-kernel learning technique is further adopted to fuse these heterogeneous kernels for MCI classification. Experimental results show that the proposed multiple-network-properties based method outperforms conventional single-network-property based methods.

1   Introduction

Alzheimer's disease (AD) is the most common form of dementia in elderly people worldwide. Diagnosis of mild cognitive impairment (MCI), i.e., the early stage of AD, is important for possible delaying the progression of the disease. At present, many researchers have investigated the connectivity properties of the brain networks in AD/MCI using between-group analysis (i.e., between two clinically different groups). Abnormal connectivity patterns have been observed in series of brain networks, including the default mode network (DMN) [1] and other resting-state networks (RSNs) [2]. Existing findings suggest that the neurodegenerative diseases, such as AD and MCI, are associated with a large-scale, highly connected functional connectivity network, rather in one single isolated region [3]. For instance, 'small-world' properties (i.e., characterized by high clustering coefficient and short average path length) have been reported to be disrupted in functional brain network of AD/MCI patients [2].

Recently, machine learning approaches have been widely used to identify AD and MCI at individual level [4]. Many connectivity-network-based classification methods

---

* Corresponding authors.

G. Wu et al. (Eds.): MLMI 2013, LNCS 8184, pp. 9–16, 2013.

have been proposed for accurate identification of AD and MCI [5, 6]. Though good performance was achieved, these methods used only single individual network property to identify patients from healthy controls (HC). In fact, many properties can be extracted from a single connectivity network, including local connectivity and global topological properties, with each of them carries different characteristics of the network. Intuitively, integration of these properties may improve the classification performance.

Accordingly, in this paper, we present a novel connectivity-network-based classification framework to accurately identify individuals with MCI from HC. The key of our proposed approach involves using kernel-based method to quantify and integrate multiple network properties. To the best of our knowledge, our current study is the first attempt that integrates different yet complementary network properties to identify individuals with MCI from HC.

2   Materials

Table 1 shows the demographic information of the participants. Informed consent was obtained from all participants, and the experimental protocols were approved by the institutional ethics board. All the recruited subjects were diagnosed by expert consensus panels. A 3T scanner was used to acquire resting-state fMRI volumes. The fMRI images of each participant were acquired with the following parameters: TR/TE=2000/32ms, flip angle=77°, acquisition matrix=64×64, FOV=256×256 mm^2, 34 slices, 150 volumes, and voxel thickness=4mm.

Table 1. Demograhic information of the subjects used in this study

Group	MCI	HC
No. of subjects (male/female)	6/6	9/16
Age (mean ± SD)	75.0 ± 8.0	72.9 ± 7.9
Years of education (mean ± SD)	18.0 ± 4.1	15.8 ± 2.4
MMSE (mean ± SD)	28.5 ± 1.5	29.3 ± 1.1

3   Method

Fig. 1 illustrates the proposed framework for MCI identification. Specifically, for each subject, we first construct a functional connectivity network from the mean time series of ROIs, each of which was computed by averaging the intensity of voxels in each ROI. Then, the connectivity network is decomposed into multiple sub-networks by thresholding the connectional weights with the predefined threshold values. From the sub-networks, we build two types of kernels, namely, vector-kernel and graph-kernel. Feature extraction and selection are preceded before the vector-kernel construction. Finally, these heterogeneous kernels are fused by means of a multi-kernel SVM for MCI identification.

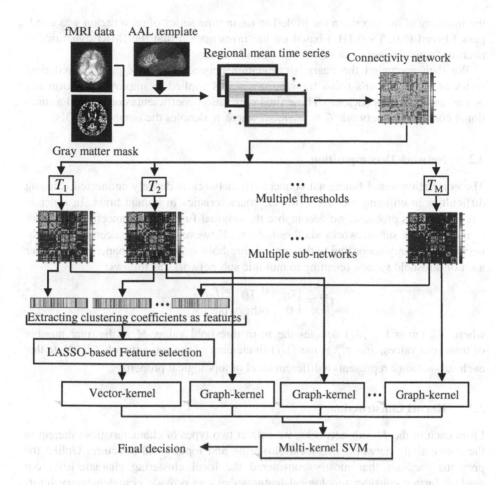

Fig. 1. The proposed classification framework

3.1 Preprocessing and Functional Connectivity Network

The fMRI images were preprocessed for slice timing and head-motion corrections using the Statistical Parametric Mapping software package (SPM8[1]). Specifically, the first 10 fMRI volumes of each subject were discarded to ensure magnetization equilibrium. The remaining 140 images were corrected for the acquisition time delay among different slices before they were realigned to the first volume of the remaining images for head motion correction. In order to reduce the effects of nuisance signals, regression of ventricle and WM signals, and six head-motion profiles was performed.

The brain space of fMRI images of each subject was then parcellated into 90 regions-of-interests (ROIs) based on the Automated Anatomical Labeling (AAL) template [7]. The mean time series of each individual ROI was computed by averaging

[1] http://www.fil.ion.ucl.ac.uk.spm

the intensity of the voxels in the ROI. The mean time series of each region was band-pass filtered (0.025 - 0.1Hz) based on the investigation that the fMRI dynamics of neuronal activities are most salient within this frequency range.

We then computed the Pearson correlation between the band-pass filtered time series of ROIs. Fisher's r-to-z transformation was applied to improve the normality of the correlation coefficients. These final correlation coefficients constructed a functional connectivity network $G = [\tau_{ij}]_{n \times n}$, where n denotes the number of ROIs.

3.2   Network Decomposition

The correlation-based functional connectivity network is densely connected, causing difficulties in utilizing the '*small-world*' characteristics in human brain. In order to circumvent this problem, we decompose the original functional connectivity network G into multiple sub-networks via thresholding. However, since the decomposed sub-networks can vary according to the applied threshold value, in this paper, we consider a set of threshold values, resulting in multiple sub-networks as follows:

$$\tau_{ij}^m = \begin{cases} \tau_{ij} & \text{if } \tau_{ij} \geq T_m \\ 0 & \text{otherwise} \end{cases} \tag{1}$$

where T_m $(m = 1, ..., M)$ denotes the m-th threshold value, M is the total number of threshold values, and τ_{ij}^m is the (i, j)-th element of the sub-network G^m. Note that each sub-network represents a different level of topological properties.

3.3   Kernel Construction

From each of the M sub-networks, we extract two types of characteristics inherent in the connectivity network, i.e., local clustering and topological structure. Unlike the previous methods that mostly considered the local clustering characteristic, our method further consider topological features that can provide complementary information. The local clustering and topological structure reflect the efficiency of local information processing and information transmission between distant nodes in a network, respectively. To this end, in this paper, we propose a kernel-based method to combine this complementary information for MCI identification.

First, for local clustering, we use the local weighted clustering coefficient defined as follows [8]:

$$c_p^m = \frac{2 \sum_{i,j} (\tau_{pi}^m \tau_{ij}^m \tau_{jp}^m)^{1/3}}{d_p(d_p - 1)} \tag{2}$$

where c_p^m is the clustering coefficient of the node p of the sub-network G^m and d_p denotes the number of neighboring nodes directly connected to the node p. The coefficients of n nodes $f^m = \left[c_p^m\right]_{p=1,\cdots,n}$, i.e., ROIs, compose a feature vector representing the local clustering characteristic of a sub-network G^m. We then concatenate the feature vectors of all the sub-networks to form a single large vector

$\mathbf{f} = [(\mathbf{f}^1)^T \cdots (\mathbf{f}^m)^T \cdots (\mathbf{f}^M)^T]^T$. In order to remove irrelevant and/or redundant features, we further perform feature selection by means of the least absolute shrinkage and selection operator (LASSO) [9], in which the sparsity or feature selection is obtained with l_1-norm regularization. We then compute a kernel function using the kernel-induced implicit mapping function $\varphi(\cdot)$ as follows:

$$k_v(\mathbf{f}, \mathbf{f}') = \langle \varphi(\mathbf{f}), \varphi(\mathbf{f}') \rangle \tag{3}$$

where $\mathbf{f}$ and $\mathbf{f}'$ denote, respectively, the dimension-reduced feature vectors from two subjects. This kernel function measures the similarity of two functional connectivity networks in terms of a local clustering characteristic. Here, we call it 'vector-kernel'.

Regarding to the topological structure of a network, we utilize a 'graph-kernel', which aims at computing the similarity between graphs. Since the connectivity network is a form of graph, where the ROIs and the connectivities between ROIs correspond, respectively, to the nodes and edges, it is natural to apply this method to our data. The graph-kernel bridges the gap between graph-structured data and the kernel-based learning algorithms. In this study, we utilize a subtree-pattern-based method [10] with Weisfeiler-Lehman test of isomorphism [11] to measure the topological similarity between two connectivity sub-networks.

Given two graphs, we first label each node in the graphs with the number of edges connected to it, and then iterate the *label-updating process* until two label sets, one for each graph, become disjoint, or it reaches the predefined number of iterations. The label-updating process operates as follows:

- For each node, we augment its label by concatenating the labels of its neighboring nodes in an ascending order;
- Then, we re-label each node with a new short one that is not used so far.

Assume that after h iterations of the label-updating process, we have h sets of labels

$$\mathbf{L} = \{L_1, \cdots, L_i, \cdots, L_h\} \tag{4}$$

where $L_i = \{l_{i1}, l_{i2}, \ldots, l_{i|l_i|}\}$, l_{in}, and $|l_i|$ denote a set of new labels, a unique label in $\mathbf{L}$, and the number of labels generated after i-th iteration, respectively. Based on the final label set $\mathbf{L}$, we define a mapping function as follows:

$$\Phi(G) = \left(\rho_0(G, l_{01}), \ldots, \rho_0(G, l_{0|L_0|}), \ldots, \rho_h(G, l_{h1}), \ldots, \rho_h(G, l_{h|L_h|})\right) \tag{5}$$

where $\rho_i(G, l_{ij})$ denotes the frequency of the label l_{ij} in the graph G after i-th iteration. This mapping function efficiently represents the topological features of a graph, i.e., a function connectivity network for our case. Then, it is straightforward to define a graph-kernel on graphs G and H as follows:

$$k_g(G, H) = \langle \Phi(G), \Phi(H) \rangle. \tag{6}$$

3.4   Kernel Combination and Classification

In this paper, we consider two types of kernels, i.e., vector-kernel and graph-kernel, and, as stated above, we believe these kernels can provide complementary information for MCI identification. In order for systematical aggregation of the heterogeneous kernels into a single model [6], we utilize a multi-kernel learning (MKL) technique via a linear combination of them:

$$k(\mathbf{x}, \mathbf{x}') = \beta_v k_v(\mathbf{f}, \mathbf{f}') + \sum_{m=1}^{M} \beta_{g,m} k_{g,m}(G_\mathbf{x}^m, G_{\mathbf{x}'}^m) \tag{7}$$

where $\mathbf{x}$ and $\mathbf{x}'$ are the input fMRI data, $\mathbf{f}$ and $\mathbf{f}'$ are their local clustering feature vectors, $G_\mathbf{x}^m$ and $G_{\mathbf{x}'}^m$ are their m-th sub-network, $k_v(\mathbf{f}, \mathbf{f}')$ is a vector-kernel, $k_{g,m}(G_\mathbf{x}^m, G_{\mathbf{x}'}^m)$ is a graph-kernel, β_v and $\beta_{g,m}$ are weight coefficients of the kernels with the constraints of $\beta_v \geq 0$, $\beta_{g,m} \geq 0$, and $\beta_v + \sum_{m=1}^{M} \beta_m = 1$, and M is the number of total sub-networks. The optimal weight coefficients are determined via grid search [6] with SVM, which is called a multi-kernel SVM.

4   Results

Leave-one-out (LOO) cross-validation strategy was adopted in this study to evaluate the generalization power of our proposed framework. Specifically, for N total number of subjects, one was left out for testing, and the remaining $N - 1$ subjects were used for training. This process was repeated for each subject. In the experiment, five sub-networks were constructed based on the thresholds of $T = [0.2, 0.3, 0.38, 0.4, 0.45]$. In the feature selection step, LASSO-based method was implemented using the SLEP package [12], and the regularization parameter λ ($\lambda \in [0\ 1]$) was determined based on the training subjects via another LOO cross-validation.

The classification performance was evaluated based on classification accuracy and area under receiver operating characteristic (ROC) curve (AUC). In this study, we compared the proposed method with the competing methods that use only a single network property. In the single-network-property based methods, only one kernel was used for classification, i.e., linear kernel (denotes as LK) or five graph kernels (denotes as GK1, GK2, GK3, GK4 and GK5, respectively). These five graph kernels, which correspond to five different levels of network topological properties, were combined using MKL technique, and is denoted as GK-C. The classification performances for all compared methods are summarized in Table 2.

The proposed multiple-network-properties based method yields a classification accuracy of 91.9%, an increment of **at least 10.8%** from other compared methods. The AUC of 0.87 indicates a good generalization power. The results indicate that the integration of two network properties (i.e., local clustering coefficient and global topological property) can significantly improve the classification performance.

Furthermore, we performed an additional experiment by comparing our MKL method with a baseline scheme, i.e., assigning a uniform weight to all kernels including vector-kernel and graph-kernels. This method achieved a classification accuracy of 86.5%, which is inferior to our MKL-based method as shown in Table 2. This result validates that the contributions of different types of kernels are different and thus different (instead of uniform) weights should be adopted in the combination.

Table 2. Classification performance of different methods

Method	Accuracy (%)	AUC
LK	81.1	0.84
GK1	73.0	0.51
GK2	73.0	0.79
GK3	70.3	0.63
GK4	73.0	0.83
GK5	75.7	0.71
GK-C	81.1	0.87
Proposed	**91.9**	**0.87**

Effect of Regularization Parameter λ

In LASSO-based feature selection, the regularization parameter, i.e., λ, is used to balance the complexity of the model and the goodness-of-fit. In the experiment, we seek to investigate the influence of different λ values on the classification accuracy. The classification accuracies with different λ values are plotted in Fig. 2. Here, the λ value varies within the range of $[0.0, 0.1, 0.2, 0.3, 0.4, 0.5]$. It is worth noting that, when $\lambda = 0$, no feature selection step was performed, i.e., all features extracted from thresholded connectivity networks were used for linear kernel construction and classification.

High classification accuracy of the proposed method is consistently observed for different λ values. The obtained classification accuracies are more than 80% for all λ values, indicating the robustness of the proposed method with respect to the regularization parameter, λ. In addition, when there is no feature selection, our method can achieve classification accuracy of 83.8%, which is still higher than the accuracies of other methods. This result again validates that the integration of multiple network properties can significantly improve the disease classification performance.

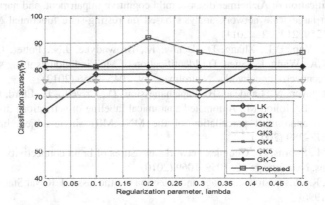

Fig. 2. Performance of different methods with respect to λ

5   Conclusion

In summary, we present a novel connectivity network-based classification framework, which fuses multiple network properties, for MCI identification. In the proposed framework, two different types of kernels are used to quantify two different yet complementary network properties, i.e., local clustering and global topological property. A multi-kernel learning technique is further adopted to fuse these heterogeneous kernels, and promising results obtained demonstrate the effectiveness of the proposed method in improving the classification performance. In the future, we will extend our current work to select the disease-related sub-networks from a connectivity network for further improving the classification performance.

Acknowledgments. This work was supported in part by NIH grants EB006733, EB008374, EB009634, and AG041721, SRFDP grant (No. 20123218110009), NUAAFRF grant (No. NE2013105), JiangsuSF for Distinguished Young Scholar, and also UNSFA grant (No. KJ2013Z095).

References

1. Agosta, F., Pievani, M., Geroldi, C., Copetti, M., Frisoni, G.B., Filippi, M.: Resting state fMRI in Alzheimer's disease: beyond the default mode network. Neurobiol. Aging 33, 1564–1578 (2012)
2. Sanz-Arigita, E.J., Schoonheim, M.M., Damoiseaux, J.S., Rombouts, S.A., Maris, E., Barkhof, F., Scheltens, P., Stam, C.J.: Loss of 'small-world' networks in Alzheimer's disease: graph analysis of FMRI resting-state functional connectivity. PloS ONE 5, e13788 (2010)
3. Xie, T., He, Y.: Mapping the Alzheimer's brain with connectomics. Front Psychiatry 2, 77 (2011)
4. Ye, J.P., Wu, T., Li, J., Chen, K.W.: Machine Learning Approaches for the Neuroimaging Study of Alzheimer's Disease. Computer 44, 99–101 (2011)
5. Chen, G., Ward, B.D., Xie, C., Li, W., Wu, Z., Jones, J.L., Franczak, M., Antuono, P., Li, S.J.: Classification of Alzheimer disease, mild cognitive impairment, and normal cognitive status with large-scale network analysis based on resting-state functional MR imaging. Radiology 259, 213–221 (2011)
6. Wee, C.Y., Yap, P.T., Zhang, D., Denny, K., Browndyke, J.N., Potter, G.G., Welsh-Bohmer, K.A., Wang, L., Shen, D.: Identification of MCI individuals using structural and functional connectivity networks. Neuroimage 59, 2045–2056 (2012)
7. Tzourio-Mazoyer, N., Landeau, B., Papathanassiou, D., Crivello, F., Etard, O., Delcroix, N., Mazoyer, B., Joliot, M.: Automated anatomical labeling of activations in SPM using a macroscopic anatomical parcellation of the MNI MRI single-subject brain. Neuroimage 15, 273–289 (2002)
8. Rubinov, M., Sporns, O.: Complex networks measures of brain connectivity: Uses and interpretations. Neuroimage 52, 1059–1069 (2010)
9. Tibshirani, R.: Regression shrinkage and selection via the lasso. J. Royal Statist. Soc. B 58, 267–288 (1996)
10. Shervashidze, N., Borgwardt, K.M.: Fast subtree kernels on graphs. In: NIPS, pp. 1660–1668 (2009)
11. Douglas, B.L.: The Weisfeiler-Lehman Method and Graph Isomorphism Testing. arXiv:1101.5211 (2011)
12. Liu, J., Ji, S., Ye, J.: SLEP: Sparse Learning with Efficient Projections, Arizona State University (2009)

Learning-Boosted Label Fusion
for Multi-atlas Auto-Segmentation

Xiao Han

Elekta Inc., St. Louis, MO, USA
xiao.han@elekta.com

Abstract. Structure segmentation of patient CT images is an essential step for radiotherapy planning but very tedious if done manually. Atlas-based auto-segmentation (ABAS) methods have shown great promise for getting accurate segmentation results especially when multiple atlases are used. In this work, we aim to further improve the performance of ABAS by integrating it with learning-based segmentation techniques. In particular, the Random Forests (RF) supervised learning algorithm is applied to construct voxel-wise structure classifiers using both local and contextual image features. Training of the RF classifiers is specially tailored towards structure border regions where errors in ABAS segmentation typically occur. The trained classifiers are applied to re-estimate structure labels at "ambiguous" voxels where labels from different atlases do not fully agree. The classification result is combined with traditional label fusion to achieve improved accuracy. Experimental results on H&N images and ribcage segmentation show clear advantage of the proposed method, which offers consistent and significant improvements over the baseline method.

Keywords: atlas-based segmentation, machine learning, label fusion, random forests, radiotherapy planning, CT image.

1 Introduction

Structure segmentation of patient CT images is an essential step for radiotherapy planning. Although manual contouring by human experts is still the common standard for high quality segmentation in clinics, it is tedious, time-consuming and suffers from large intra- and inter- rater variability.

Automated segmentation of CT images is a very challenging problem due to image noise and other artifacts, as well as limited image contrast for most soft-tissue structures. In recent years, atlas-based auto-segmentation (ABAS) methods have shown great promise in helping solve the problem and been applied in commercial products [1-2]. Although the segmentation results still need be edited manually before they can be used clinically, ABAS methods have been proven to be able to greatly reduce manual labor and improve contouring consistency [1].

The basic principle of ABAS is to perform segmentation of a novel patient image using expert-labeled images, called atlases. After aligning the new image to the atlas image through image registration, atlas structure labels can be mapped to the patient

G. Wu et al. (Eds.): MLMI 2013, LNCS 8184, pp. 17–24, 2013.

image to get the automatic segmentation result. Large anatomical variation among different subjects often limits the accuracy of ABAS if only a single atlas is used. Thus, it becomes common standard to use multiple atlases, where each atlas is first applied independently and their results are combined in the end through label fusion.

Even with multi-atlas and label fusion, accuracy of ABAS is still heavily dependent on performance of image registration. Rather than relying on image registration alone, in this work we aim to combine the strength of multi-atlas ABAS with that of learning-based image segmentation techniques in order to get much improved accuracy. In the method developed here, we apply Random Forests (RF) – a state-of-the-art supervised learning algorithm (cf. [3]) to construct a voxel classifier for each structure using the existing atlases as training data. The RF algorithm can effectively handle a large number of training data with high data dimension, which allows us to explore a large number of image features to fully capture both local and contextual image information. We also specially tailor the training of the RF algorithm to focus on structure border regions where errors in ABAS typically occur. After a standard multi-atlas label fusion is performed, the RF classifier(s) are applied to re-estimate the label probability for voxels where labels mapped from different atlases do not fully agree. The RF result is then combined with the initial label fusion to get the final structure segmentation.

There are some related works in the literature. The RF method itself has been applied for structure localization and lesion segmentation problems (cf. [3]). In [4], Powell et al used ANN-based voxel classifier to improve brain structure segmentation from a probabilistic atlas. Nie and Shen [6] designed a SVM-guided deformable surface model to refine structure surface segmentation of mouse brain images. Hao et al [5] applied a Lagrangian SVM algorithm to train massive localized voxel classifiers on the fly for hippocampus segmentation with multiple atlases. The SVM classification was directly used as final result instead of being combined with traditional label fusion. The method can be slow since one classifier is built for each voxel, and only a small number of features were used. Another recent work [7] combined multi-atlas ABAS with a simpler kNN classifier for brain image segmentation. Only six local intensity values were used as voxel features, which is unlikely to produce accurate voxel classification for CT images. Some other works [9, 11] applied machine learning driven statistical shape models for structure detection and segmentation in either CT or MR images. As a competing method, ABAS has its own advantages. For example, spatial structure relationship and full image information are implicitly taken into account during atlas registration. But shape model can also be incorporated to further improve ABAS accuracy.

2   Methods

The proposed method integrates learning-based voxel classification at the label fusion stage within a multi-atlas ABAS framework. We first present the underlying multi-atlas ABAS method and then discuss our design of RF-based voxel classification and the incorporation of it to improve the label fusion accuracy.

2.1   Multi-atlas ABAS Method

Fig. 1 summarizes the workflow of a basic multi-atlas ABAS procedure that we adopt in this work, where the segmentation of a new subject is computed by applying multiple atlases separately and then combining the individual segmentation results through label fusion.

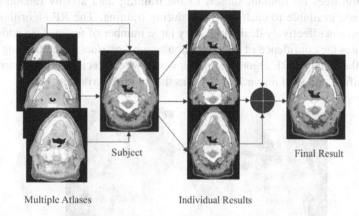

Fig. 1. Overall workflow of ABAS with multiple atlases and label fusion

The registration of each individual atlas to the subject image is performed using a hierarchical atlas registration method we previously developed in [8]. The method computes first a global mutual information (MI) linear registration followed by two non-linear registration steps with gradually increasing degrees-of-freedom. Structure surface information from the atlas is incorporated into the deformation field regularization to improve both the robustness and the accuracy of atlas registration.

The popular STAPLE method [10] is used to combine multiple structure label maps from the different atlases. Although the STAPLE method appears to have a weakness in that it does not make use of image intensity information, we found it work well for CT images. We have also tried various intensity-weighted label fusion methods but found that the improvement is minimal or none since local intensity information is often ambiguous for CT images and sensitive to common CT artifacts.

2.2   RF Voxel Classification

Learning-based classification methods offer an alternative approach for object detection and segmentation. Voxel classifiers, once trained, can predict the structure label of a new image based on discriminative features computed at each voxel location. Voxel classification alone also has its limitations, and is thus often used together with other techniques such as statistical shape models [9, 11]. In this work, we apply learning-based voxel classification to complement ABAS – a registration-based approach. The expert-labeled atlases available in multi-atlas ABAS naturally serve as training data for building the voxel classifier.

We train a RF classifier for each structure to predict the probability of a voxel as belonging to the specific structure. Although RF can easily handle multi-class classification as well, there is minimal benefit for the structures we consider in this work since they are not directly adjacent to each other. RF is a state-of-the-art supervised learning method and often considered to have better generalization power than SVM or boosting [3]. It achieves high generalization by growing an ensemble of independent decision trees on random subsets of the training data and by randomizing the features made available to each tree node during training. The RF algorithm is very efficient and can effectively deal with a very large number of features. In addition, RF also estimates the confidence of the prediction as a by-product of the training process. We apply the standard RF algorithm in this work, where decision stumps are used as weak classifiers and the Gini index is used as the impurity criterion.

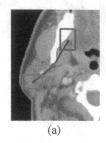
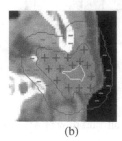

(a)   (b)

Fig. 2. Illustration of RF training. (a) contextual feature definition; (b) training samples selection.

Using image intensity alone is insufficient for accurate voxel classification. Relying on point-wise intensity comparison to predict voxel correspondence is also a major limiting factor of image registration algorithms. Instead, we employ a large set of features in order to fully capture both local and contextual information at each image point, which include:

- Image intensity values – the raw intensity value I and the smoothed ones: $G_\sigma * I$, where G_σ denotes a Gaussian filter with a kernel size (scale) of σ. Three different scales are used in this work: 1.0 mm, 1.7 mm, and 2.5 mm.
- Image gradients $(I_x, I_y, I_z) = \nabla(G_\sigma * I)$ and gradient magnitudes $\|\nabla(G_\sigma * I)\|$ computed at three different scales.
- Eigen-values of the image Hessian matrix $H = \nabla^T \nabla(G_\sigma * I)$, which are again computed at three different scales.
- Image location – the (x, y, z) coordinates of a voxel. The coordinates are normalized first with respect to a common reference frame by aligning each image to a fixed reference image through a coarse B-spline image registration.
- Generalized Haar-like features as proposed in [3], which help capture contextual information. As illustrated in Fig. 2a, each such feature is computed as the mean image property difference over two randomly displaced, asymmetric cubical regions around the voxel: $f = |R_1|^{-1} \sum_{x \in R_1} F(x) - |R_2|^{-1} \sum_{x \in R_2} F(x)$. Such features

can be computed very efficiently with the use of *integral images* (cf. [3]). In this work, $F(\mathbf{x})$ is either the raw image intensity value or the image gradient magnitude. We typically sample 200 random features of each type.

Training data are collected from the atlases with some special consideration. As illustrated in Fig. 2b, training samples are only taken within close proximity to the structure boundary, which helps the RF training focus on voxels close to the structure border – a region where ABAS segmentation error is most likely to occur. We use an 8 mm distance threshold to define the sampling region. Training of the RF classifiers is performed offline and one RF classifier is trained for each structure of interest, as mentioned earlier. The RF algorithm is very fast, and different trees can be trained in parallel. It normally takes less than 20 minutes to build a RF classifier with 50 trees. Note that the RF classifier(s) only need be trained once after the atlases are collected.

2.3   RF-Enhanced Label Fusion

The trained RF classifiers are applied after the standard multi-atlas ABAS computation as described in Section 2.1 is finished. Our goal is to combine the strengths of both techniques. Hence, the RF classifier for each structure is only applied to re-estimate the label probability of "ambiguous" voxels in the original ABAS result, which are voxels where labels mapped from different atlases do not fully agree.

The RF classification result can be combined with the initial ABAS result in different ways. For example, we can use the RF result as an extra input to the STAPLE algorithm. Since both RF and STAPLE produce a probabilistic estimation of voxel labels, we choose to compute the final structure label probability as a simple weighted sum of the RF probability (P_R) and the initial STAPLE estimation (P_S):

$$P = w_R P_R + w_S P_S, \tag{1}$$

where w_R and w_S are the relative weights of the two terms. In this work, we assign a slightly higher weight for the RF result as $w_R = 0.6$, then $w_S = 0.4$. Once the label probability is computed for every voxel of the subject image, it can be thresholded at 0.5 or the 0.5-isosurface be computed to get the final structure segmentation result.

3   Experimental Results

3.1   Head & Neck (H&N) Image Segmentation

In the first experiment, we apply the learning-enhanced multi-atlas ABAS for the segmentation of H&N cancer patient CT images. Ten randomly collected patient images with manual expert segmentation are used as the test data. All images have a voxel size of $0.9375 \times 0.9375 \times 2.5$ mm^3. The following 4 structures are considered in this study: the mandible, the brainstem, and the left and the right parotids.

We use a leave-one-out strategy to evaluate the proposed method: for each subject, the remaining subjects are considered as atlases. The Dice similarity coefficient (cf. [1]) is used to quantify the accuracy when comparing automatic segmentation results with original manual labeling.

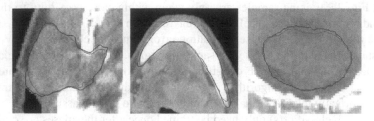

Fig. 3. Qualitative comparison of H&N segmentation results. Blue: STAPLE label fusion results; red: Learning-enhanced label fusion. From left to right: parotid, mandible, and brainstem.

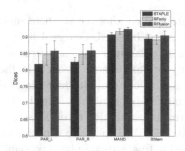

Fig. 4. Quantitative comparison: the bar plots show mean Dice values over 10 subjects for the 4 structures and the error bars indicate one standard deviation

Fig. 3 shows some qualitative comparisons of the segmentation results between the proposed method and the baseline multi-atlas ABAS method with STAPLE label fusion. It can be seen that combining the RF classification clearly improves the segmentation accuracy. Quantitative comparison results are summarized in the box plot of Fig. 4, where the mean and the standard deviation of Dice values for each structure are shown. As can be seen, the learning-enhanced label fusion consistently produces higher accuracy for all 4 structures than the STAPLE method. In addition, the weighted fusion (Eq. (1)) is also more accurate than directly using the RF results (RF-only). Note that the RF-only results still rely on ABAS since RF classification is only computed for the ambiguous voxels as mentioned earlier. It was verified through paired-t tests that the improvements of the combined label fusion over both STAPLE and RF-only are statistically significant at the 0.05 level for all 4 structures. Note that some of the remaining segmentation error is inherent to the data due to intra-observer variation, especially for structures with very low contrast such as the brainstem.

The computation time for both the original multi-atlas ABAS method and the RF-enhanced one is quite comparable. It takes about one minute to run a single atlas registration on a desktop computer with an Intel Xeon Quad-core 2.66 GHz CPU and a

NVIDIA GTX 480 graphics card. The STAPLE label fusion takes less than a minute. Computing the RF classification only adds one extra minute, which is about 1/10-th of the total computation time assuming 9 atlases are used.

3.2   Ribcage Segmentation

In the second experiment, we test the proposed method on ribcage segmentation of lung CT images. Expert labeled images from 15 different patients are used as the test data. The image resolution is about $0.9765 \times 0.9765 \times 3$ mm^3. We again use the leave-one-out strategy for the validation study, where for each patient image the other 14 are used as atlases for ABAS segmentation and RF training.

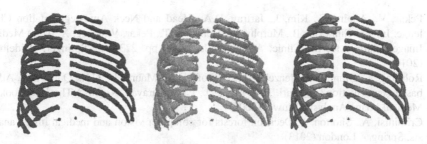

Fig. 5. Illustration of ribcage segmentation results. Left: truth; middle: STAPLE result; right: STAPLE combined with RF classification.

The ribcage segmentation is a difficult problem [12], and turns out to be very challenging for a registration-based segmentation method, i.e., ABAS. It is because the rib bones are all similar to each other and spatially clustered. After linear registration, one rib from the atlas image can partially overlap with two or more ribs from the subject image. Purely intensity-based image registration can never get out of the local optimum of the image similarity function and cause large errors in the final image matching. As a result, the segmentation accuracy is rather low even with 14-atlases, which can be seen from the STAPLE result shown as the middle figure in Fig. 5.

Applying RF-based voxel classification greatly improves the segmentation accuracy, as shown in Fig. 5. Computing the Dice statistics over all 15 patients, we found that the original multi-atlas ABAS with STAPLE label fusion produced Dice values of 0.73 ± 0.03, whereas learning-enhanced label fusion improved the Dice values to 0.86 ± 0.02. The 0.86 overlap ratio is actually very high, considering that the ribs are narrow tube-like structures. This improvement is also statistically significant as verified by the paired-t test.

4   Conclusion

We have developed a hybrid multi-atlas ABAS method that effectively combines the strengths of traditional ABAS methods and learning-based segmentation approaches.

Experimental results on H&N CT image segmentation and ribcage segmentation showed significant improvements of the proposed method over the baseline method without the learning-based enhancement. Future work will investigate extra image features such as local binary patterns and region co-variances. We also plan to construct shape priors from the atlases and investigate whether incorporating explicit statistical shape information can further improve the ABAS segmentation accuracy.

Acknowledgment. The author would like to thank Drs. Jan-Jakob Sonke and Barbara Stam from the Netherlands Cancer Institute for providing the lung CT images and the manual ribcage segmentation.

References

1. Pekar, V., Allaire, S., Kim, J., Jaffray, D.A.: Head and Neck Auto-segmentation Challenge. In: van Ginneken, B., Murphy, K., Heimann, T., Pekar, V., Deng, X. (eds.) Medical Image Analysis for the Clinic: A Grand Challenge, pp. 273–280. Springer, Heidelberg (2010)
2. Rohlfing, T., Brandt, R., Menzel, R., Russakoff, D.B., Maurer Jr., C.R.: Quo Vadis, Atlas-based segmentation? In: Suri, J., Wilson, D., Laxminarayan, S. (eds.) The Handbook of Medical Image Analysis. Kluwer (2005)
3. Criminisi, A., Shotton, J.: Decision forests for computer vision and medical image analysis. Springer, London (2013)
4. Powell, S., Magnotta, V.A., Johnson, H., Jammalamadaka, V.K., Andreasen, N.C., Pierson, R.: Registration and machine learning based automated segmentation of subcortical and cerebellar brain structures. NeuroImage 39, 238–247 (2008)
5. Hao, Y., Liu, J., Duan, Y., Zhang, X., Yu, C., Jiang, T., Fan, Y.: Local label learning (L3) for multi-atlas based segmentation. In: Proc. SPIE, vol. 8314, p. 83142E (2012)
6. Nie, J., Shen, D.: Automated segmentation of mouse brain images using multi-atlas multi-ROI deformation and label fusion. Neuroinformatics 11, 35–45 (2013)
7. Srhoj-Egekher, V., Benders, M.J.N.L., Kersbergen, K.J., Viergever, M.A., Isgum, I.: Automatic segmentation of neonatal brain MRI using atlas based segmentation and machine learning approach. In: MICCAI Grand Challenge: Neonatal Brain Segmentation (2012)
8. Han, X., Hoogeman, M., Levendag, P., Hibbard, L., Teguh, D., Voet, P., Cowen, A., Wolf, T.: Atlas-based auto-segmentation of head and neck CT images. In: Metaxas, D., Axel, L., Fichtinger, G., Székely, G. (eds.) MICCAI 2008, Part II. LNCS, vol. 5242, pp. 434–441. Springer, Heidelberg (2008)
9. Zheng, Y., Barbu, A., Georgescu, B., Scheuering, M., Comaniciu, D.: Four-chamber heart modeling and automatic segmentation for 3D cardiac CT volumes using marginal space learning and steerable features. IEEE Trans. Med. Imag. 27, 1668–1681 (2008)
10. Warfield, S.K., Zou, K.H., Wells, W.M.: Simultaneous truth and performance level estimation (STAPLE): An algorithm for the validation of image segmentation. IEEE Trans. Med. Imag. 23, 903–921 (2004)
11. Tu, Z., Narr, K.L., Dollar, P., Dinov, I., Thompson, P.M., Toga, A.W.: Brain anatomical structure segmentation by hybrid discriminative/generative models. IEEE Trans. Med. Imag. 27, 495–508 (2008)
12. Wu, D., Liu, D., Puskas, Z., Lu, C., Wimmer, A., Teitjen, C., Soza, G., Zhou, S.K.: A learning based deformable template matching method for automatic rib centerline extraction and labeling in CT images. In: Proc. CVPR 2012 (2012)

Volumetric Segmentation of Key Fetal Brain Structures in 3D Ultrasound

Mohammad Yaqub[1], Remi Cuingnet[2], Raffaele Napolitano[3], David Roundhill[4], Aris Papageorghiou[3], Roberto Ardon[2], and J. Alison Noble[1]

[1] Institute of Biomedical Engineering, University of Oxford, Oxford, UK
[2] Medisys Research Lab, Philips Research, Paris, France
[3] Nuffield Department of Obstetrics and Gynaecology, University of Oxford, Oxford, UK
[4] Philips Ultrasound, Bothell, USA

Abstract. Neurosonography is the most widely used imaging technique for assessing neuro-development of the growing fetus in clinical practice. 3D neurosonography has an advantage of quick acquisition but is yet to demonstrate improvements in clinical workflow. In this paper we propose an automatic technique to segment four important fetal brain structures in 3D ultrasound. The technique is built within a Random Decision Forests framework. Our solution includes novel pre-processing and new features. The pre-processing step makes sure that all volumes are in the same coordinate. The new features constrain the appearance framework by adding a novel distance feature. Validation on 51 3D fetal neurosonography images shows that the proposed technique is capable of segmenting fetal brain structures and providing promising qualitative and quantitative results.

Keywords: 3D ultrasound, segmentation, fetal brain, random decision forests.

1   Introduction

In the assessment of the fetal brain, volumetric measurements show great potential compared with 2D measurements if performed accurately. 2D measurement of fetal brain structures is used in currently clinical practice as it is usually easy to perform since post image capture only requires placement of two or more callipers. However, repeatability of 2D scanning is known to be variable. Depending on fetal orientation and position, finding a good 2D measurement plane requires experience. For instance, when diagnosing ventriculomegaly of a fetus, a 2D measurement plane that crosses the posterior lateral ventricle is found and to estimate the width of the atrium [1]. An atrial width greater than 10mm [2] is defined as ventriculomegaly. Fig 1 (a) shows an ultrasound image of a fetus diagnosed with this disease. Although clinical guidelines [2, 3] have been developed for acquiring good 2D image measurement plane, a 2D plane that crosses the ventricle can may be acquired in many different orientations. Each image measurement plane will result in a different apparent width of the lateral ventricle leading to measurement error. This problem is a general one, and equally a problem for measurement of other key fetal brain structures such as the head

G. Wu et al. (Eds.): MLMI 2013, LNCS 8184, pp. 25–32, 2013.
© Springer International Publishing Switzerland 2013

circumference, biparietal diameter (BPD), cisterna magna, and anterior and posterior horns of the lateral ventricles. In contrast, volumetric measurements on 3D fetal brain images could overcome this problem by estimating the complete volume of structures. Manual volumetric measurement is possible but it is tedious, time consuming, and subjective. Therefore, automatic measurement of such structures is of significant interest for clinical use.

There are a few recent publications which use Random Decision Forests (RDF) for medical image segmentation applications [4-12]. Few are targeted at ultrasound imaging [4, 5, 11, 13]. We are aware of only one publication in which the authors segment the fetal cerebellum in 3D ultrasound [11]. In that work, the cerebellum was segmented via a 3D Point Distribution Model (PDM) and a simple genetic algorithm applied to optimize an objective function. Overall, the result is promising but validation limited to 5 volumes. Authors in [13] propose a technique to detect Substantia Nigra Echogenicities in 3D US. They combine the output of two RDFs which are used to model appearance and spatial location independently. In [14], the authors investigate the problem of detecting key fetal brain structures in 3D ultrasound. The objective was to detect the centre point of each structure (detection) but not to annotate (segmentation) the whole structure as we aim to do in the current paper. Segmenting the whole structure in 3D is more challenging than locating the structure.

The RDF technique was originally proposed for natural image segmentation and has recently been adapted for medical image segmentation [4-12]. Random Forests has been also used to do regression, density estimation, and other tasks [16].

In this paper, we develop an automatic technique to segment fetal brain structures in 3D ultrasound. We build the solution within a RDF framework [15] which is a state-of-the-art machine learning technique used in classification problems. We have applied this framework to design a novel method to segment four fetal brain structures in 3D ultrasound. The novelty of the paper is twofold. First, the application itself is an interesting and very challenging problem mainly due to 1) the imaging modality; 3D ultrasound suffers from shadowing, signal attenuation, speckle, 2) variability and complexity of fetal brain structures, and 3) fetal movement. Second, novel features within the RDF are proposed to make the technique more robust to acquisition variability and artefacts that are characteristic of typical ultrasound scans in this application. In our framework, we first pre-process the 3D images to put them in a common coordinate space. We then approximate the regions which contain the targeted structures. Finally, we introduce novel features within the RDF framework to help guide the segmentation of structures.

2   Method

We formulate the segmentation as a classification problem in which we have five objects to classify; background, Choroid Plexus (CP), Lateral Posterior Ventricle Cavity (PVC), the Cavum Septum Pellucidi (CSP) and Cerebellum (CER). The four anatomical structures are four of the seven anatomical structures used in basic ultrasound examination of the fetal central nervous system [2]. For instance, the width of PVC is used to assess ventriculomegaly.

2.1   Dataset

3D ultrasound brain images from 51 fetuses were acquired with a fetal gestational age range of 18 – 26 weeks. Volumes were acquired by two sonographers following a standardized clinical image acquisition protocol. Images were acquired using the iU22 machine (Philips Healthcare). The volume size is approximately 500×256×500 voxels with mean (0.2×0.33×0.2) mm^3 voxel spacing.

The CP, PVC, CSP and cerebellum from the distal hemisphere were manually segmented on all volumes by an experienced clinician.

2.2   Finding Skull, Eyes Center, and Head Center

In recent work [17], a technique was proposed to automatically detect the fetal skull, left and right eyes' centers, the head center, and orientation of the head in 3D ultrasound. The method employs template deformation to segment the skull and random forests to detect the position of the eyes. The midsagittal plane was approximated using a weighted Hough transform on the responses of a plate detector at different scales. The neck orientation was approximated and used with the both the midsagittal plane and eye positions to find the fetal head orientation and the head center.

We used this method 1) to preprocess our images in order to find the approximate head orientation and head center; and subsequently 2) to develop novel features to be used within RDF for segmentation. These features rely on the skull, head center, and left and right eye centers.

2.3   Preprocessing

The orientation of the head is represented as a 3 × 3 matrix in which the signs of the 3 vectors indicate the three principal directions that the fetal brain is facing. We use the orientation of the head to, where necessary, flip the orientations of the fetal head to place all brains in the same coordinate space. This only means flipping upside down, left to right, or front to back.

Given we know the approximate volume of a structure from manually segmented images and the approximate head center and orientation; we can estimate the approximate volume of interest (VOI) in which the structure should be located. The VOI needs to cover the different variations in structure volumes and shapes. We define three (not four) such VOIs – one to surround the cerebellum, one for the CSP and the last one for both CP and PVC together because these two structures are adjacent to each other. Fig 1 shows a typical example of CP, PVC and CSP manual annotation and the corresponding VOIs. The VOIs are used to focus segmentation on these areas only which also considerably speeds up analysis.

Assuming that the fetal brain is symmetrical, one should expect that structures that appear on one hemisphere should also appear on the other. An anomaly of fetal neurosonography is that this is not the case always. In practice, when the ultrasound signal hits the fetal skull, the signal may experience a large attenuation in the proximal hemisphere of the fetal head which results in most of the brain structures in the proximal hemisphere becoming invisible. This can be observed from Fig 1 (b). However, structures in the distal hemisphere are visible. For this reason, analysis is focused on structures in the distal hemisphere only. Knowing the head orientation and center allows us to focus on a specific hemisphere. Without loss of generality, the segmentation on one hemisphere can be mirrored to the other hemisphere if we know the midsagittal plane which we have already found.

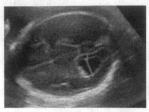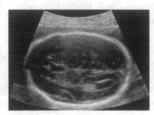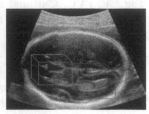

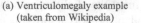

(a) Ventriculomegaly example   (b) Original 2D slice   (c) Manual segmentation and
      (taken from Wikipedia)   approximated regions

Fig. 1. (a) Ventriculomegaly example where the width of PVC is larger than normal. (b & c) an example of a 2D slice from a 3D image which contains CP (*red*), PVC (*green*) and CSP (*blue*). The two VOIs surrounding these structures are also shown. The cerebellum is not shown here as it is not visible in this image measurement plane.

Finally, we find the smallest cuboid that encloses the manual annotation of each structure as the VOI. The cuboid which contains the union of regions from all images was used as the VOI. The CP and PVC were used as one structure to create one VOI.

2.4   RDF for Fetal Brain Segmentation

The previous steps result in three regions that contain structures of interest. An independent RDF classifier is trained on the voxels from each region. These classifiers are 1) a binary classifier to distinguish cerebellum from background, 2) a binary classifier to distinguish CSP from background, and 3) a 3-class classifier to distinguish between CP, PVC and background.

Feature Sets. In medical image segmentation, classic appearance features have been pre-dominantly used. For instance, intensity, Haar, cuboid, absolute voxel positions, etc, features have showed promising results in some applications [4-6, 8, 12, 18]. However, as also found to be true for other approaches to ultrasound image segmentation, such features do not work well on ultrasound images due to classic artefacts such as the existence of shadowing, signal attenuation and speckle. In order to make the approach more robust to ultrasonic image variations, we propose to use novel geometric features which will complement the classic features within the RDF framework. In our RDF solution, we use intensity, Cuboid, and generalized Haar [4, 5, 12, 19] but in addition we employ the following distance features; 1) distance to the skull, 2) distance to the head center, 3) distance to the left eye, and 4) distance to the right eye. To calculate the distance of a voxel to the skull, we calculate the signed distance map of the voxels in the fetal brain to the skull. This distance represents the Euclidean distance between the voxel of interest and the closest skull voxel. In the distances with the head center and left and right eyes, we let RDF randomly choose between four types of distances between the voxels and the object centers. These distances are

$$Sagittal\ distance(v_i, obj_k) = X(v_i) - X(obj_k) \qquad (1)$$

$$Coronal\ distance(v_i, obj_k) = Y(v_i) - Y(obj_k) \qquad (2)$$

$$Axial\ distance(v_i, obj_k) = Z(v_i) - Z(obj_k) \qquad (3)$$

$$Euclidian\ distance(v_i, obj_k) =$$
$$\sqrt{(X(v_i) - X(obj_k))^2 + (Y(v_i) - Y(obj_k))^2 + (Z(v_i) - Z(obj_k))^2} \qquad (4)$$

Here, $X(v_i)$, $Y(v_i)$, $Z(v_i)$ and   represent position of a voxel in 3D space. k is 1, 2, 3 to represent the head center, left eye center and right eye center respectively. All distances are in millimeters.

Training the RDF. Three RDF classifiers are trained to classify voxels in the three VOIs. In each classifier, a set of trees are trained in a random fashion. Bagging was used to randomly subsample voxels for each tree to increase diversity in different trees which improves generalization during testing [20].

In each tree, every internal node is trained on a set of training examples. All internal nodes end up containing a feature which is parameterized by $\theta = \{f_{type}, \emptyset, t\}$, where f_{type} is the feature type, $\emptyset$ is the set of parameters of the chosen feature type, e.g., size and location of a feature, and t is a threshold used to binarize the feature value to either 0 or 1. This threshold is used to split the training examples to either left or right recursively down the tree. An internal node is created by finding the best feature out of a randomly chosen subset of features via maximizing a binary splitting metric. We used information gain as a metric since it worked well in other medical imaging applications [4-12, 16]. Splitting training examples proceeds in a top-down manner until either the maximum depth of the tree is reached or no more gain is achieved in splitting. At the end of tree creation, leaf nodes contain an empirical distribution of voxels over the different classes. This empirical distribution is used as voting tool during testing. All remaining trees in each RDF classifier are trained in the same way. Finally, Table 1 shows the parameters used to train each classifier.

Testing the RDF. To test an unseen 3D ultrasound of a fetal brain, the image has to first undergo the steps of finding the skull, eyes centers, head orientation and center. The three VOIs are then found. The voxels within these VOIs only need to be classified by the three RDF classifiers.

Table 1. Parameters used in our experiments

Classifier	Max tree depth	# of trees	# of candidate features	Haar & cuboid max box size[1]	Haar & cuboid search area around voxel of interest[1]
Cerebellum	10	15	400	25	-25 — 25
CSP	10	15	400	15	-15 — 15
CP and PVC	13	20	400	25	-25 — 25

---

[1] These sizes are in each image dimension.

To test a specific RDF classifier on a specific image, the testing voxels from that classifier region traverse all trees starting from the root of each tree until reaching a leaf node. The empirical distribution from all trees is averaged to generate one probabilistic prediction for each voxel. The class label for the unseen voxel is the class label of the maximum probability between classes.

Validation. 31 random volumes were selected for the training stage and the remaining 20 volumes were used for testing. We used the Dice coefficient to measure automatic segmentation accuracy. We also report the volume difference between the manual segmentation and the automatic one. Parameters of the RDF classifiers were experimentally optimized. In addition, we studied the effect of the proposed distance features on the classification accuracy. To do this we also trained the RDFs with and without the proposed features to understand their effect to the classification result.

3   Results

Fig 2 presents qualitative segmentation results on slices from a 3D volume using the RDF technique trained on the appearance features only, Fig 2 (b), and on both appearance and distance features, Fig 2 (c). Manual segmentation is also provided for visual assessment, Fig 2 (a). Quantitative assessment is provided in Table 2 where we present the Dice coefficient, volume of manual segmentation and the difference of volume with the manual segmentation for the four structures using the classis RDF approach and RDF with distance features.

4   Discussion

In this work, we developed an originally approach to segment four fetal brain structures in 3D ultrasound based on machine learning methods. The technique proposes novel features to this problem utilized within the RDF framework. The results are promising with good accuracy for some structures. However, the cerebellum requires further investigation to improve segmentation accuracy. Notice in Table 2 that the cerebellum has the largest variability relative to its size.

Our work shows the importance of using distance features which intuitively reflect the way clinicians use context in decision making. For instance, during anomaly screening, sonographers find either the trans-thalamic or trans-ventricular planes to measure important clinical characteristics like head circumference, BPD, etc. The position of the CSP is important to find both planes. In a clinical setting, the CSP is usually visible in the anterior one third of the falx cerebri; but there are structures that have similar appearance to it [2]. Therefore, without the proposed constraints, appearance features have a higher chance of not distinguishing between these similar tissues.

Notice in Fig 2 that RDF with distance features avoids several regions which have similar appearance to the structure of interest. This can be clearly seen in the results for PVC and the cerebellum. From Table 2, The Dice coefficient suggests that using the new features, we achieve a small improvement when segmenting the CP. This is because CP has good appearance inside its VOI. However, from volume measurements, the automated method under-estimates the CP volume. On the other hand, good results were obtained for the other three structures which is very encouraging. This is because other similar tissues exist within these regions, therefore appearance only features can falsely segment these tissues as structures of interest. With the aid of distance features, we can avoid some tissues.

One of the limitations of discriminative models can be their limited ability to segment the border of a structure when it is not clearly defined. Although RDF with distance features performs better at segmenting the border of a structure than the appearance RDF, both techniques are sensitive to edge clarity and strength. A possible way to address this would be to add a generative shape constraint. Our future studies will explore this.

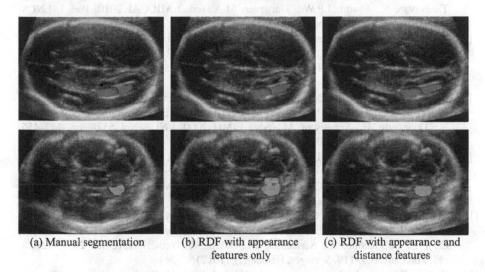

(a) Manual segmentation (b) RDF with appearance features only (c) RDF with appearance and distance features

Fig. 2. Segmentation results shown on 2D slices from a 3D image. Top row: segmentation on CP (*red*), PVC (*green*) and CSP (*blue*). Bottom row: segmentation on the cerebellum (*yellow*).

Table 2. Mean ± Standard Deviation of the dice coefficient and volume difference (defined as manual seg. volume − technique seg. Volume; in mm^3) to report the segmentation accuracy on the 4 structures using RDF with conventional features and RDF with the proposed features.

		CP	PVC	CSP	Cerebellum
Dice	RDF	78±9%	79±10%	70±11%	59±14%
	RDF with proposed features	79±9%	82±10%	74±11%	63±15%
	Volume of manual seg.	555±146	248±72	155±50	246±121
Volume	RDF	-27±38	41±44	31±16	38±20
difference	RDF with proposed features	-25±26	1±32	7±10	2±14

References

[1] Cardoza, J.D., Goldstein, R.B., Filly, R.A.: Exclusion of fetal ventriculomegaly with a single measurement: the width of the lateral ventricular atrium. Radiology 169(3), 711–714 (1988)

[2] Malinger, G., et al.: Sonographic examination of the fetal central nervous system: guidelines for performing the 'basic examination' and the 'fetal neurosonogram'. Ultrasound in Obstetrics and Gynecology 29(1), 109–116 (2007)

[3] Salomon, L.J., Bernard, J.P., Ville, Y.: Reference ranges for fetal ventricular width: a non-normal approach. Ultrasound in Obstetrics and Gynecology 30(1), 61–66 (2007)

[4] Yaqub, M., et al.: Efficient Volumetric Segmentation using 3D Fast-Weighted Random Forests. In: MLMI 2011 (2011)

[5] Yaqub, M., et al.: Weighted Voting in 3D Random Forest Segmentation. In: MIUA 2010 (2010)

[6] Geremia, E., Menze, B.H., Clatz, O., Konukoglu, E., Criminisi, A., Ayache, N.: Spatial Decision Forests for MS Lesion Segmentation in Multi-Channel MR Images. In: Jiang, T., Navab, N., Pluim, J.P.W., Viergever, M.A. (eds.) MICCAI 2010, Part I. LNCS, vol. 6361, pp. 111–118. Springer, Heidelberg (2010)

[7] Yi, Z., Criminisi, A., Shotton, J., Blake, A.: Discriminative, semantic segmentation of brain tissue in MR images. In: Yang, G.-Z., Hawkes, D., Rueckert, D., Noble, A., Taylor, C. (eds.) MICCAI 2009, Part II. LNCS, vol. 5762, pp. 558–565. Springer, Heidelberg (2009)

[8] Lempitsky, V., Verhoek, M., Noble, J.A., Blake, A.: Random Forest Classification for Automatic Delineation of Myocardium in Real-Time 3D Echocardiography. In: Ayache, N., Delingette, H., Sermesant, M. (eds.) FIMH 2009. LNCS, vol. 5528, pp. 447–456. Springer, Heidelberg (2009)

[9] Cuingnet, R., Prevost, R., Lesage, D., Cohen, L.D., Mory, B., Ardon, R.: Automatic Detection and Segmentation of Kidneys in 3D CT Images Using Random Forests. In: Ayache, N., Delingette, H., Golland, P., Mori, K. (eds.) MICCAI 2012, Part III. LNCS, vol. 7512, pp. 66–74. Springer, Heidelberg (2012)

[10] Margeta, J., Geremia, E., Criminisi, A., Ayache, N.: Layered Spatio-Temporal Forests for Left Ventricle Segmentation from 4D Cardiac MRI Data. In: Camara, O., Konukoglu, E., Pop, M., Rhode, K., Sermesant, M., Young, A. (eds.) STACOM 2011. LNCS, vol. 7085, pp. 109–119. Springer, Heidelberg (2012)

[11] Becker, B.G., et al.: Automatic segmentation of the cerebellum of fetuses on 3D ultrasound images, using a 3D Point Distribution Model. In: EMBC 2010 (2010)

[12] Zikic, D., et al.: Decision Forests for Tissue-Specific Segmentation of High-Grade Gliomas in Multi-channel MR. In: Ayache, N., Delingette, H., Golland, P., Mori, K. (eds.) MICCAI 2012, Part III. LNCS, vol. 7512, pp. 369–376. Springer, Heidelberg (2012)

[13] Pauly, O., Ahmadi, S.-A., Plate, A., Boetzel, K., Navab, N.: Detection of Substantia Nigra Echogenicities in 3D Transcranial Ultrasound for Early Diagnosis of Parkinson Disease. In: Ayache, N., Delingette, H., Golland, P., Mori, K. (eds.) MICCAI 2012, Part III. LNCS, vol. 7512, pp. 443–450. Springer, Heidelberg (2012)

[14] Yaqub, M., et al.: Automatic detection of local fetal brain structures in ultrasound images. In: ISBI 2012 (2012)

[15] Breiman, L.: Random Forests. Machine Learning 45(1), 5–32 (2001)

[16] Criminisi, A., Shotton, J., Konukoglu, E.: Decision Forests: A Unified Framework for Classification, Regression, Density Estimation, Manifold Learning and Semi-Supervised Learning. Foundations and Trends® in Computer Graphics and Vision 7(2-3) (2012)

[17] Cuingnet, R., et al.: Where is my Baby? A Fast Fetal Head Auto-Alignment in 3D-Ultrasound. In: ISBI 2013 (2013)

[18] Konukoglu, E., Glocker, B., Zikic, D., Criminisi, A.: Neighbourhood Approximation Forests. In: Ayache, N., Delingette, H., Golland, P., Mori, K. (eds.) MICCAI 2012, Part III. LNCS, vol. 7512, pp. 75–82. Springer, Heidelberg (2012)

[19] Criminisi, A., Shotton, J., Bucciarelli, S.: Decision Forests with Long-Range Spatial Context for Organ Localization in CT Volumes. In: MICCAI workshop on PMMIA 2009 (2009)

[20] Breiman, L.: Bagging predictors. Machine Learning 24(2), 123–140 (1996)

Sparse Classification with MRI Based Markers for Neuromuscular Disease Categorization

Katerina Gkirtzou[1,2], Jean-François Deux[3], Guillaume Bassez[3],
Aristeidis Sotiras[4], Alain Rahmouni[3], Thibault Varacca[3],
Nikos Paragios[1,2], and Matthew B. Blaschko[1,2,*]

[1] Center for Visual Computing, École Centrale Paris, France
[2] Équipe Galen, INRIA Saclay, Île-de-France, France
[3] Henri Mondor University Hospital, Créteil, France
[4] Department of Radiology, University of Pennsylvania, USA

Abstract. In this paper, we present a novel method for disease classification between two patient populations based on features extracted from Magnetic Resonance Imaging (MRI) data. Anatomically meaningful features are extracted from structural data (T1- and T2-weighted MR images) and Diffusion Tensor Imaging (DTI) data, and used to train a new machine learning algorithm, the k-support SVM ($k$sup-SVM). The k-support regularized SVM has an inherent feature selection property, and thus it eliminates the requirement for a separate feature selection step. Our dataset consists of patients that suffer from facioscapulohumeral muscular dystrophy (FSH) and Myotonic muscular dystrophy type 1 (DM1) and our proposed method achieves a high performance. More specifically, it achieves a mean Area Under the Curve (AUC) of 0.7141 and mean accuracy 77% $\pm$ 0.013. Moreover, we provide a sparsity visualization of the features in order to indentify their discriminative value. The results suggest the potential of the combined use of MR markers to diagnose myopathies, and the general utility of the $k$sup-SVM. Source code is also available at https://gitorious.org/ksup-svm.

Keywords: myopathies, Diffusion Tensor Imaging, k-support regularized SVM.

1 Introduction

In this paper, we tackle the problem of disease classification. More specifically, we are interested in discriminating between two different neuromuscular diseases, facioscapulohumeral muscular dystrophy (FSH) and myotonic muscular dystrophy type 1 (DM1). Myopathies result in an atrophy and weakness of the muscle, and currently require an invasive biopsy to distinguish the two. In contrast, we pursue here a comparatively non-invasive approach based on MR imaging. Our approach to discriminate between the two diseases is centered around two axes:

---

* This work was partially funded by ERC Grant 259112 and the AFM-Telethon foundation.

G. Wu et al. (Eds.): MLMI 2013, LNCS 8184, pp. 33–40, 2013.
© Springer International Publishing Switzerland 2013

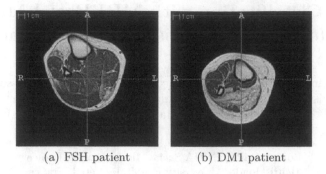

(a) FSH patient   (b) DM1 patient

Fig. 1. T1-weighted MR images of the calf from the two neuromuscular diseases. On the left, Fig. 1(a), a slice of the MR image from a patient with facioscapulohumeral muscular dystrophy (FSH) and on the right, Fig. 1(b), a slice of the MR image from a patient with myotonic muscular dystrophy type 1 (DM1). These diseases are not readily distinguishable by eye.

i) MR Imaging with particular emphasis on Diffusion Tensor Imaging, which has been successfully used in neuroimaging, and ii) a novel structured sparsity machine learning algorithm, the k-support regularized SVM.

Diffusion Tensor Imaging is an imaging modality that captures the diffusion of water in tissues, and along with it, important structural information. It has been widely used in the study of the connectivity of the human brain [1]. Nonetheless, it has also been used in different clinical scenarios. Among them, one may cite the study of the human tongue [2], the heart muscle [2] and the human calf muscle [3]. DTI can capture important structural information in the case of the muscle. This is due to the fact that muscles are highly organized structures that present an architecture of elongated myofibers. Because myopathies affect the muscles, one may expect that the diffusion properties in diseased subjects are also altered [4].

Pattern classification techniques are widely applied in medical image processing. Along with DT imaging, pattern classification has gained widespread acceptance in neuroimaging studies because of its ability to capture multivariate relationships that characterize group differences. Some important examples of their application in neuroimaging scenarios include the study of Alzheimer's disease [5], male-female or older-younger classification [6], temporal classification of block design fMRI data [7] or the study of autism spectrum disorder [8].

In this work, we are interested in verifying that different myopathies alter muscle in distinct ways. Moreover, we investigate the discriminative power of diffusion and structural MR features in distinguishing between diseases. Fig. 1 shows the T1-weighted MR images of the two myopathies under investigation. The two images are very similar, making the distinction between them a very challenging task. In order to achieve this goal, we develop a strategy that exploits the rich information that is captured by both structural data (T1- and T2-weighted MR images) and DTI data to fuel state-of-the-art machine learning techniques. The use of high dimensional pattern classification in conjuction

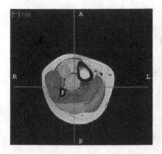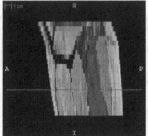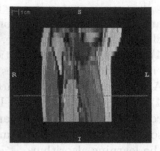

Fig. 2. An example of an T1 weighted MR image with the seven segmented muscles of the calf. Each color represents a single muscle. Yellow represents the anterior tibialis, cyan the extensor digitorum longus, magenta the peroneous longus, white the posterior tibialis, blue the soleus, green the lateral gastrocnemius, and red the edial gastrocnemius. (Figure best viewed in color.)

with DTI information has been previously investigated [9,10,8]. Nonetheless, it has been mainly applied to distinguish patients from controls in neuroimaging studies. Discriminating between patients poses additional challenges.

2   Materials and Methods

2.1   Data Description

In this study, we have used a dataset consisting of twenty five subjects, 10 subjects were affected by FSH and 15 subjects were affected by DM1. In a clinical context, this is a large sample size. The subjects were imaged in the calf using a 1.5 T MRI scanner. Diffusion weighted images were acquired using the following parameters: repetition time (TR)=3600ms, echo time (TE)=70ms, slice thickness of $7mm$ and b value of $700s/mm^2$ with 12 gradient directions and 13 repetitions. Diffusion tensors were estimated with the use of medInria software.[1] The obtained volumes had a size of 64 × 64 × 20 voxels and a voxel resolution of $3.125mm$ × $3.125mm$ × $7mm$. T1- and T2-weighted MR images were acquired at the same time. As a consequence, the image volumes are naturally co-registered.

2.2   Structural and Diffusion Features

The images were segmented by an expert in the following 7 classes/muscle groups: 1) soleus (SOL), 2) lateral gastrocnemius (LG), 3) medial gastrocnemius (MG), 4) posterior tibialis (TP), 5) anterior tibialis (AT), 6) extensor digitorum longus (EDL), and 7) peroneous longus (PL). An example of the segmented muscle can be seen in Fig. 2. It is planned to automate this process in future work. In the meantime, the approach provides a strategy to avoid an invasive biopsy.

---

[1] http://med.inria.fr/

For every anatomical region, we extracted features from both the structural and the diffusion data. From the structural data, we extracted for every muscle: 1) the absolute volume, 2) the mean T1 signal, 3) the mean T2 signal, and 4) the Signal to Noise Ration (SNR). For the diffusion, we calculated for every muscle the mean values of the following scalar measures: 1) the Fractional Anisotropy (FA), 2) the trace of the diffusion tensor, 3) the volume of the tensor, 4) the eigenvalues (L1, L2, L3), 5) the planar coefficient (Cp), and 6) the linear coefficient (Cl). These scalar measures were estimated with the use of medInria software. The resulted 84 variables were whitened and centered prior to applying the learning algorithms.

2.3 k-Support Regularized SVM

Our proposed method, the k-support regularized SVM, is a novel algorithm based on the recently introduced k-support norm by Argyriou et. al [11]. The k-support norm is a sparsity regularization method that balances the ℓ_1 and ℓ_2 norms over a linear function in order to prevent over-fitting, similar to the well known elastic net [12]. The k-support norm can be computed as

$$\|w\|_k^{sp} = \left(\sum_{i=1}^{k-r-1} (|w|_i^\downarrow)^2 + \frac{1}{r+1} \left(\sum_{i=k-r}^{d} |w|_i^\downarrow \right)^2 \right)^{\frac{1}{2}} \tag{1}$$

where $|w|_i^\downarrow$ is the ith largest element of the vector and r is the unique integer in $\{0, \dots, k-1\}$ satisfying

$$|w|_{k-r-1}^\downarrow > \frac{1}{r+1} \sum_{i=k-r}^{d} |w|_i^\downarrow \geq |w|_{k-r}^\downarrow. \tag{2}$$

In contrast to elastic net, k-support norm uses a ℓ_1 penalty only for the smallest components and ℓ_2 penalty for the largest components. We define the k-support norm regularized SVM ($k$sup-SVM) as the following optimization problem:

$$\min_{w \in \mathbb{R}^d, b \in \mathbb{R}, \xi \in \mathbb{R}^n} \lambda \|w\|_k^{sp} + \sum_{i=1}^{n} \xi_i \tag{3}$$

$$\text{s.t.} \quad y_i \left(\langle w, x_i \rangle + b \right) \geq 1 - \xi_i, \quad \xi_i \geq 0, \quad \forall i. \tag{4}$$

This learning algorithm uses the hinge loss as in a classical SVM [13], but employs the k-support norm as a structured sparsity regularizer. This enables the learning algorithm to select a sparse but correlated subset of discriminative variables. $k$sup-SVM has two input parameters, the $\lambda > 0$ regularization parameter and $k \in \{1, \dots, d\}$, where d is the dimension of the feature space, the parameter that negatively correlates with the sparsity.

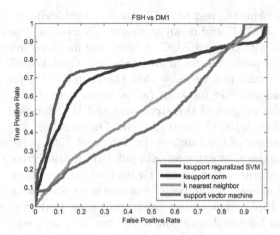

Fig. 3. Mean ROC curves for each classifier over 1000 trials. $k$sup-SVM, shown in red, outperforms the rest of the methods k-support norm regularized squared error (blue), $k$nn (green) and SVM (magenta). To the best of our knowledge, these are the first results presenting a significant discrimination between FSH and DM1 using MRI based markers. (Figure best viewed in color.)

Table 1. Classification mean accuracy (in % ± standard error) and the mean area under the curve of all methods over 1000 trials. Chance is 60%.

Method	Accuracy	AUC
$k$sup-SVM	77 ± 0.013	0.756
k-support norm	74 ± 0.006	0.726
$k$nn	61 ± 0.015	0.537
SVM	59 ± 0.015	0.494

3   Results

In order to explore the power of our proposed method we also train a number of supervised learning methods using the same features. More specifically, we examine the k nearest neighbor algorithm [14], the support vector machine (SVM) [13] for a number of different kernels, and the k-support norm with squared loss as introduced by [11]. We examine the $k$nn algorithm with Euclidean distance and $k \in \{1, 3, 5, 7, 10\}$. For the SVM, we examine the following kernel functions, i) linear, ii) polynomial of third degree, and iii) radial basis function (RBF) with a soft-margin parameter $C \in \{10^{-3}, 10^0, 10^3\}$. For the k-support regularized squared loss and for the $k$sup-SVM we examine the following combinations of parameters $\lambda \in \{1, 10, 1000\}$ and $k \in \{1, 10, 20, 40, 80\}$.

To approximate the generalization accuracy of the classification methods using the structural and DTI tensor features, we use a random splitting scheme with 1000 trials. In each trial, a random selection of 80% of the data are used to train the methods, while the remaining 20% are used to evaluate their performance. Model selection was performed in a similar fashion using only 80% of the data. We report only the generalization performance for each method.

Fig. 3 shows the mean ROC curve across all trials, while Table 3 gives the mean classification accuracy and area under the curve over 1000 trials.

$k$sup-SVM outperforms the rest of the methods by achieving a mean area under the curve (AUC) of 0.7141 and mean accuracy 77% $\pm$ 0.013. The k-support norm also performs well with a mean AUC of 0.694 and mean accuracy 72% $\pm$ 0.006, while $k$nn and SVM performances are near chance, which is 60%. Moreover, with a Wilcoxon signed rank test we show that the $k$sup-SVM is statistically significantly better than all other methods (all p-values were $\ll 10^{-9}$). Fig. 4 shows the boxplots of the weights of the structural and DTI tensor features selected by the $k$sup-SVM over 1000 bootstrap trials. On each box, the central mark is the median, the edges of the box are the 25th and 75th percentiles, while the whiskers extend to the most extreme data points that are not considered outliers. Since the MRI features are evaluated for each of the seven muscles of interest, we plot them per muscle. A number of features are systematically assigned zero weight across multiple trials (green line), indicating that they do not provide useful information for the distinction of the two diseases, while the ones with non-zero weight are considered more informative.

Toward demonstrating the added value of the DTI features, we compared the performance of the $k$sup-SVM when trained only on structural data against its previous result. The same experimental setting as before was used. In this case, $k$sup-SVM achieved a mean AUC of 0.697 and mean accuracy 73% $\pm$ 0.006. According to a Wilcoxon signed rank test, this performance is statistically significantly worse than its previous performance using both structured and DTI features (p-value was $\ll 0.05$).

4   Discussion

An analysis of variables selected by the sparsity regularizer (Fig. 4) gives an indication that discrimination varies across muscles as well as features. Increased muscle volume in AT, EDL, MG, and TP was associated with DM1, while increased volume in PL and SOL was associated with FSH. T1 and T2 signal was consistently positively associated with FSH in the EDL muscle. A broad range of statistics were discriminative for the MG muscle, while discriminative features for most other muscles were comparatively sparse.

While MRI markers, and DTI tensor features in particular, have previously been shown to differ between disease and control subjects [4, Table 2], we are unaware of previous studies that have shown significant ability to discriminate between disease conditions. Indeed, a high-dimensional analysis of MRI based markers was required to achieve non-random performance in this more challenging task. Sparsity regularization appears to be a more important property of the learning algorithm than non-linearity, as evidenced by the comparatively stronger performance of k-support norm regularized SVM or squared error, as compared to a SVM with non-linear kernels or k nearest neighbors (both non-sparse, non-linear algorithms).

In this paper, we have presented several novel methodological and clinical developments related to the use of pattern recognition methods in neuromuscular disease classification. While previous studies have focused on the comparatively

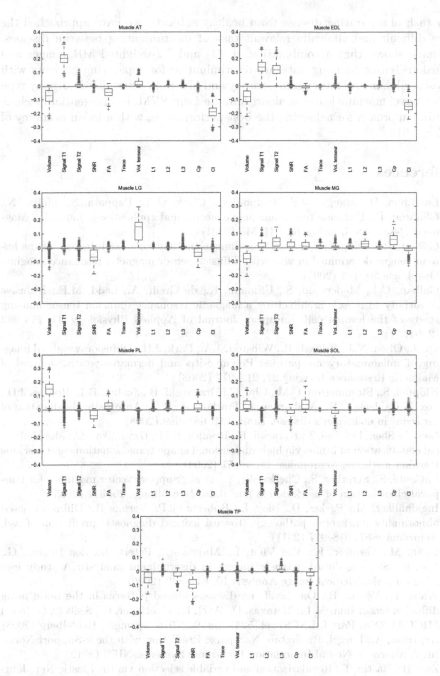

Fig. 4. Boxplot of the weights given to the structural and DTI features of the 7 muscles by the $k$sup-SVM over 1000 trials. Positive values indicate positive association with FSH, while negative values indicate positive association with DM1. Values close to zero are indicative of a lack of discriminative information between the two disease conditions.

easy task of separating disease from healthy subjects, we have approached the more difficult and clinically relevant task of discriminating between diseases. We have shown that a combination of T1- and T2-weighted MR images and Diffusion Tensor Imaging data are discriminative for separating patients with facioscapulohumeral muscular dystrophy and Myotonic muscular dystrophy type 1. Our novel machine learning algorithm, the $k$sup-SVM, is an essential machine learning approach for achieving the best performance, with a mean accuracy of $77\% \pm 0.013$.

References

1. Le Bihan, D., Mangin, J.F., Poupon, C., Clark, C.A., Pappata, S., Molko, N., Chabriat, H.: Diffusion tensor imaging: concepts and applications. Journal of Magnetic Resonance Imaging 13, 534–546 (2001)
2. Gilbert, R.J., Napadow, V.J.: Three-dimensional muscular architecture of the human tongue determined in vivo with diffusion tensor magnetic resonance imaging. Dysphagia 20, 1–7 (2005)
3. Galban, C.J., Maderwald, S., Uffmann, K., de Greiff, A., Ladd, M.E.: Diffusive sensitivity to muscle architecture: a magnetic resonance diffusion tensor imaging study of the human calf. European Journal of Applied Physiology 93, 253–262 (2004)
4. Qi, J., Olsen, N.J., Price, R.R., Winston, J.A., Park, J.H.: Diffusion-weighted imaging of inflammatory myopathies: Polymyositis and dermatomyositis. Journal of Magnetic Resonance Imaging 27, 212–217 (2008)
5. Klöppel, S., Stonnington, C.M., Chu, C., Draganski, B., Scahill, R.I., Rohrer, J.D., Fox, N.C., Jack, C.R., Ashburner, J., Frackowiak, R.S.: Automatic classification of mr scans in alzheimer's disease. Brain 131, 681–689 (2008)
6. Lao, Z., Shen, D., Xue, Z., Karacali, B., Resnick, S.M., Davatzikos, C.: Morphological classification of brains via high-dimensional shape transformations and machine learning methods. Neuroimage 21, 46–57 (2004)
7. LaConte, S., Strother, S., Cherkassky, V., et al.: Support vector machines for temporal classification of block design fmri data. NeuroImage 26, 317 (2005)
8. Ingalhalikar, M., Parker, D., Bloy, L., Roberts, T.P., Verma, R.: Diffusion based abnormality markers of pathology: Toward learned diagnostic prediction of asd. Neuroimage 57, 918–927 (2011)
9. Caan, M., Vermeer, K., Van Vliet, L., Majoie, C., Peters, B., den Heeten, G., Vos, F.: Shaving diffusion tensor images in discriminant analysis: A study into schizophrenia. Medical Image Analysis 10, 841–849 (2006)
10. Wang, P., Verma, R.: On classifying disease-induced patterns in the brain using diffusion tensor images. In: Metaxas, D., Axel, L., Fichtinger, G., Székely, G. (eds.) MICCAI 2008, Part I. LNCS, vol. 5241, pp. 908–916. Springer, Heidelberg (2008)
11. Argyriou, A., Foygel, R., Srebro, N.: Sparse Prediction with the k-Support Norm. In: Advances in Neural Information Processing Systems, NIPS (2012)
12. Zou, H., Hastie, T.: Regularization and variable selection via the Elastic Net. Journal of the Royal Statistical Society, Series B 67, 301–320 (2005)
13. Cortes, C., Vapnik, V.: Support-vector networks. Mach. Learn. 20, 273–297 (1995)
14. Wang, P., Gur, R., Verma, R.: A novel framework for identifying dti-based brain patterns of schizophrenia. In: ISMRM, Toronto, pp. 3–9 (2008)

Fully Automatic Detection of the Carotid Artery from Volumetric Ultrasound Images Using Anatomical Position-Dependent LBP Features

Fumi Kawai[1], Keisuke Hayata[1], Jun Ohmiya[1], Satoshi Kondo[1],
Kiyoko Ishikawa[2], and Masahiro Yamamoto[2]

[1] Panasonic Healthcare Co., Ltd., Yokohama, Kanagawa, Japan
{kawai.fumi,hayata.ksk,ohmiya,jun,kondo.satoshi}@jp.panasonic.com
[2] Yokohama Stroke and Brain Center, Yokohama, Kanagawa, Japan

Abstract. We propose a fully automatic method for detecting the
carotid artery from volumetric ultrasound images as a preprocessing
stage for building three-dimensional images of the structure of the carotid
artery. The proposed detector utilizes support vector machine classifiers
to discriminate between carotid artery images and non-carotid artery
images using two kinds of LBP-based features. The detector switches
between these features depending on the anatomical position along the
carotid artery. The detector narrows the search area for detection in
consideration of the three-dimensional continuity of the carotid artery
to suppress false positives and improve processing speed. We evaluate
our proposed method using actual clinical cases. Accuracies of detection
are 100 %, 87.5 % and 68.8 % for the common carotid artery, internal
carotid artery, and external carotid artery sections, respectively. We also
confirm that detection can be performed in real time using a personal
computer.

Keywords: Ultrasound, Carotid Artery, Detection, Support Vector Machine, Local Binary Pattern.

1 Introduction

Carotid ultrasonography is commonly used for the therapeutic screening, diagnosis and evaluation of arteriosclerosis. The advantages of carotid ultrasonography
include the provision of quantitative and visual information on arteriosclerosis
as well as being non-invasive and less expensive than other imaging modalities.
The presence of atherosclerotic disease is seen as a thickening of the intima-
media complex (IMC) and plaque lesions in the carotid ultrasound. It is thus
important, in carotid ultrasonography, to observe the walls of the carotid artery.

In recent years, techniques have been proposed for constructing three-
dimensional structure of the carotid wall from carotid ultrasound images [1,2].
Examiners can easily identify the thickening of the IMC or determine the presence or size of plaque in three dimensions by applying these techniques. They
can not only reduce the burden on the examiners but also improve diagnostic accuracy. When constructing a three-dimensional structure of the carotid artery,

G. Wu et al. (Eds.): MLMI 2013, LNCS 8184, pp. 41–48, 2013.

ultrasound images of the entire carotid artery are initially scanned mechanically or manually. Note that the ultrasound images are normally captured in transverse view when constructing a three-dimensional structure, unlike when measuring intima-media thickness, where the ultrasound images are captured in longitudinal view. The inside and outside boundaries of the carotid wall are then extracted from the ultrasound images by applying a contour extraction technique, such as an active contour model. Finally, the extracted contours are connected to build the three-dimensional carotid wall structure.

To extract the contours of the carotid artery from the ultrasound images, it is necessary to first identify the location of the carotid artery in each image. With conventional methods of constructing three-dimensional structures of the carotid wall, the examiner has to specify the position of the carotid artery in the ultrasound image manually [1,2], or blood flow information is used to identify its position [3]. We believe that it is difficult to use these conventional methods at busy medical sites, since they add considerably to examiners' workload.

The objective of our study is to reduce the burden on examiners during carotid artery examinations when constructing three-dimensional models of the carotid artery. We propose a fully automatic method for detecting the position of the carotid artery. Our proposed method can automatically detect the position of the carotid artery from ultrasound images by applying machine learning techniques in real time. We adopt features based on local binary patterns (LBPs) [4], which are robust to local variations in positions and shapes, in the machine learning process. We also use two types of features based on LBPs that depend on the position along the carotid artery to accurately detect those image features that change at these positions. Although our proposed method focuses on position detection, it is possible to realize the construction of the three-dimensional carotid artery structure by combining carotid contour extraction prior arts.

In a report related to our study, Golemati et al. propose a method of automatically detecting the carotid artery in a transverse view from ultrasound B-mode images using a Hough transform [5]. However, their method is evaluated only for those images that include the common carotid artery, which means that the images include only one artery. In contrast, our proposed method does not have such a limitation.

2   Classifier for Carotid Artery Detection

2.1   Characteristics of Carotid Artery Ultrasound Images

Fig. 1 is a diagrammatic illustration of the human carotid artery and a method of obtaining ultrasound images. The proposed method uses time series (volumetric) ultrasound images of the carotid artery obtained by manually scanning towards the head from the heart side using a one-dimensional ultrasonic probe. The carotid artery is depicted in transversal view in the ultrasound images. The scanning method in Fig. 1 is the standard way of observing the carotid artery in transversal view for carotid ultrasound screening.

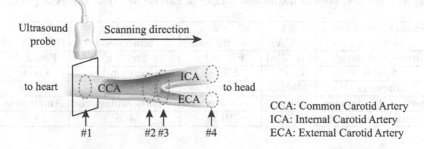

CCA: Common Carotid Artery
ICA: Internal Carotid Artery
ECA: External Carotid Artery

Fig. 1. Structure of carotid artery and typical ultrasound scanning positions

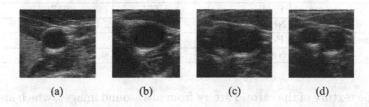

(a)   (b)   (c)   (d)

Fig. 2. Ultrasound images of carotid artery from the different scanning positions shown in Fig. 1. (a) Scanning position #1 (CCA). (b) Scanning position #2 (carotid bulb). (c) Scanning position #3 (bifurcation). (d) Scanning position #4 (ICA/ECA).

Fig. 2 (a)–(d) shows examples of ultrasound images corresponding to the scanning positions #1–#4 in Fig. 1. The characteristics of the carotid artery observed in the ultrasound images are summarized in Table 1. As shown in Fig. 1 and Table 1, the common carotid artery (CCA) is initially observed and the shape of the CCA in the transversal view is observed as a circle. As scanning proceeds towards the head, the diameter of the carotid artery increases and the shape of the carotid artery changes to an ellipse and then a snowman-like outline at the carotid bulb. Next, the artery bifurcates into the internal carotid artery (ICA) and the external carotid artery (ECA). These arteries are observed as circular shapes with diameters that are smaller than the CCA. Also, the vessel walls of the ICA and the ECA are less clear than the vessel wall of the CCA, since the ICA and the ECA are small and run deep.

2.2 Basic Configuration of Classifier Used in Our Proposed Method

The proposed method detects the carotid artery in each frame in the ultrasound image sequence, and outputs the position of the carotid artery in the frame. We have designed a classifier for detecting circular and elliptical structures, since the period where the carotid artery is observed as a snowman-like outline is short.

We use a sliding window scheme [6] with a fixed window size for detecting the carotid artery. We also use the linear support vector machine (SVM) to discriminate whether or not the scanning window includes the carotid artery. One of the features used in the classifier is local binary patterns (LBPs) [4] that can

Table 1. Characteristics of ultrasound images of carotid artery at different positions

Scanning position in Fig. 1	#1 (CCA)	#2 (carotid bulb)	#3 (bifurcation)	#4 (ICA/ECA)
Ultrasound image	Fig. 2(a)	Fig. 2(b)	Fig. 2(c)	Fig. 2(d)
Shape	Circle	Ellipse	Snowman-like	Circle
Diameter	Middle	Large	Large	Small
Vessel wall in images	Clear	Clear	Slightly ambiguous	Ambiguous
Percentage constituent	67 %	10 %	4 %	19 %

Table 2. Number of samples in data sets for training and classification image sets

		CCA data set	ICA/ECA data set
Training set	Positive sample	5,655	3,176
	Negative sample	12,112	
Classification set	Positive sample	6,330	4,004
	Negative sample	106,310	

capture the texture of the carotid artery from ultrasound images, which are much less clear than ordinary photographic images. In addition, the vessel walls of the ICA and the ECA are less clear than the vessel wall in the CCA, as mentioned in Section 2.1. Hence we also use staggered LBPs [7], which are effective for low-resolution images and noisy images, as the second feature. Staggered LBPs capture the texture more broadly by changing the angle and the distance from the pixel of interest.

The scanning window is divided into a plurality of small overlapped blocks and the feature vectors are obtained for the small blocks to allow local variations of the vessel wall. The frequency histograms of the feature patterns for the small blocks are concatenated and used for the classification.

2.3   Performance Evaluation of Proposed Classifier

We conducted an experiment to evaluate how the performance of the proposed classifier changed depending on the type of features. We prepared positive (carotid) samples, which included the carotid artery and were normalized to 64 × 64 pixels relative to the upper and lower end position of the carotid artery, and negative (non-carotid) samples. We used different image sets for the training phase and classification phases of the classifier. The samples in the training set were selected from 50 sequences. The samples in the classification set were selected from 28 sequences which were different from the sequences used in the training set. We also prepared two data sets for each image set, CCA and ICA/ECA data sets. Table 2 shows the number of images in the image sets and the data sets.

We compared the LBP and the staggered LBP used in the proposed classifier with HOG180 and HOG360 [8], which are widely used in image recognition. The size of the small blocks when dividing a scanning window is set to 16 × 16 pixels,

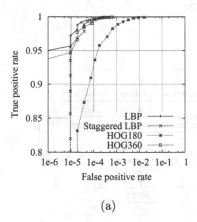
(a)

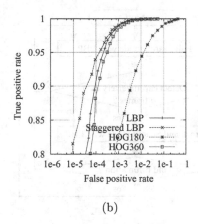
(b)

Fig. 3. Experimental results of performance evaluations of classifiers with different features. (a) Results for CCA data set. (b) Results for ICA/ECA data set.

and we obtained 49 small regions in the scanning window by shifting the small region by 8 pixels horizontally and vertically. The division method was the same for all kinds of features. We built classifiers with a linear SVM for each feature and compared the performance of the classifiers with the receiver operating characteristic (ROC) curve. The ROC curves show the performance of the classifier as the true positive rate shown in the vertical axis and the false positive rate shown in the horizontal axis. If an ROC curve for a method is located at the upper left in the graph, that means the performance of the method is high.

Fig. 3(a) shows the performance of the classifiers for the CCA data set. For the CCA data set, features other than HOG180 showed high scores, with the LBPs showing the best performance with a true positive rate of 99.7 % when the false positive rate is 1.0e-4 and a true positive rate of 97.2 % when the false positive rate is 1.0e-5. We also observed performance degradation in the low false positive rates in the staggered LBP and the HOG180.

Fig. 3(b) shows the performance of the classifiers for the ICA/ECA data set. The performance for all classifiers degrades for the ICA/ECA data set compared to the CCA data set. Staggered LBPs show the best performance, with a true positive rate of 94.0 % when the false positive rate is 1.0e-4, which is higher by nearly 4 points than other features. We believe that the characteristics of staggered LBPs, by referring to a wider area when calculating the feature vectors, act effectively on unclear vessels such as the ICA and the ECA.

3   Proposed Carotid Artery Detector

The proposed detector detects carotid artery from time-series (volumetric) ultrasound images by changing the parameters of the detector, e.g., the feature used in the classifier and the search range. Fig. 4 shows the flow chart of the proposed method. We explain the details of each process below.

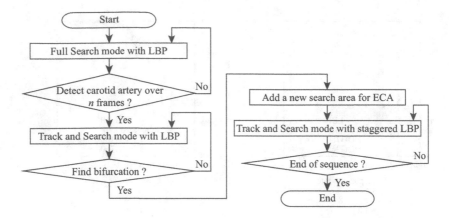

Fig. 4. Flowchart of proposed carotid artery detector

As mentioned in Section 2.1, the input data to the proposed detector comprises time series (volumetric) ultrasound images of the carotid artery, obtained by manually scanning from the heart towards the head. Initially the detector is placed in Full Search mode, in which the detection process is performed for a whole frame with a sliding window scheme [6]: it detects the CCA in each frame. The detector uses the LBP feature, since it is suitable for detecting the CCA as mentioned in Section 2.3. The detection process is also performed for multiple resolution images to cope with changes in scale. Those windows identified as including the carotid artery area are mapped onto the input image and merged into groups according to their position. The scores for windows which are obtained as outputs of the SVM detector are integrated in each group. The group with the highest score is selected as the final detection result.

If the CCA is continuously detected over several frames, the detector switches to Track and Search mode. In this mode, the proposed method narrows the search area and constrains the scales of the image pyramid based on the detection result of the previous frame. It is based on the anatomical knowledge that the positions and the sizes of the carotid artery do not change dramatically. We can at the same time suppress false positives for similarly shaped regions and improve the processing speed.

In Track and Search mode, the detector also tries to find the bifurcation. This is done by monitoring the size variation of the vessel diameter. As mentioned in Section 2.1, the diameter increases at the carotid bulb and then decreases rapidly after the bifurcation. If the difference between the maximum diameter of the carotid artery in past frames and the mean of the diameters in the latest few frames exceeds a threshold value, the detector determines that it has detected the bifurcation. The search area for the CCA is used to detect the ICA after the bifurcation. The detector also embarks on a new search area for the ECA. The topological knowledge of the carotid artery is utilized when the detector adds the new search area for the ECA.

Table 3. Experimental results used for evaluating our proposed carotid artery detector

	Number of sequences	Detection accuracy		
		CCA	ICA	ECA
Without plaque	9	100 % (9/9)	88.9 % (8/9)	66.7 % (6/9)
With plaque	7	100 % (7/7)	85.7 % (6/7)	71.4 % (5/7)
Total	16	100 % (16/16)	87.5 % (14/16)	68.8 % (11/16)

There are two search areas after the bifurcation: one for the ICA and the other for the ECA. The detection procedure is almost the same as the procedure in Track and Search mode for the CCA. The only difference is that the staggered LBP feature is used to detect the ICA and the ECA in accordance with the findings described in Section 2.3.

4   Experimental Results

We evaluated the proposed carotid artery detector using clinical cases obtained in a medical institution. The ultrasound images were obtained using a Cardio-Health Station (Panasonic Healthcare Co., Ltd., Japan). We used 16 sequences for different patients (from 30 to 89 years old) and checked if the carotid artery was detected stably for each period of the CCA, ICA and ECA. We designated detection failure if the carotid artery could not be detected for two consecutive frames even if the detection succeeded otherwise. We also measured the computational time of the detection process. The classifiers used in the detector were trained using the training set employed in the experiment mentioned in Section 2.3, selected from different sequences from the above-mentioned 16 sequences. Each sequence consisted of 256 frames. Plaques could be seen in 7 sequences.

Table 3 shows the experimental results and Fig. 5 shows an example of the detection results. The accuracies of detection were 100 % (16/16), 87.5 % (14/16) and 68.8 % (11/16) for the CCA, the ICA and the ECA sections, respectively. The accuracy for the ECA is lower than the others, we believe due to the vessel boundary of the ECA being less clear than the boundaries of the CCA and the ICA. We also confirmed that the detection accuracies are almost the same for cases with and without plaques, and that the bifurcation could be detected correctly in all sequences.

As for computational time, we measured the processing time using a computer with an Intel Core i7 3.2 GHz CPU and 24 GB memory. All the frames in the sequence were first loaded from the HDD to memory. We then measured the processing time needed for detection, including feature vector extraction for each frame as off-line processing. The average processing time was about 116 msec/frame in Full Search mode for the CCA, and about 15 msec/frame in Track and Search mode. We thus confirm that it is possible to detect the carotid artery in real time.

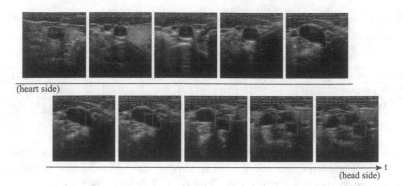

Fig. 5. An example of detection results. Red rectangles show detector outputs.

5   Conclusion

In this paper, we proposed a fully automatic method for detecting the carotid artery from volumetric ultrasound images in real time using a machine learning technique. The proposed method uses a linear SVM classifier with two types of features based on LBPs to detect the carotid arteries. The experimental results using clinical cases showed the effectiveness of the proposed method.

Items for future research are to improve the accuracy of detection of the ECA and to evaluate the performance of the construction of a three-dimensional carotid artery structure by combining the proposed method and contour extraction techniques.

References

1. Seabra, J.C.R., Pedro, L.M., Fernandes e Fernandes, J., Sanches, J.M.: A 3-D ultrasound-based framework to characterize the echo morphology of carotid plaques. IEEE Trans. Biomed. Eng. 56(5), 1442–1453 (2009)
2. Hamou, A.K., Osman, S., El-Sakka, M.R.: Carotid ultrasound segmentation using DP active contours. In: Kamel, M.S., Campilho, A. (eds.) ICIAR 2007. LNCS, vol. 4633, pp. 961–971. Springer, Heidelberg (2007)
3. Barratt, D.C., Ariff, B.B., Humphries, K.N., Thom, S.A.Mc.G., Hughes, A.D.: Reconstruction and quantification of the carotid artery bifurcation from 3-D ultrasound images. IEEE Trans. Medical Imaging 23(5), 567–583 (2004)
4. Ojala, T., Pietikainen, M., Harwood, D.: A comparative study of texture measures with classification based on feature distributions. Pattern Recognition 29(1), 51–59 (1996)
5. Golemati, S., Stoitsis, J., Sifakis, E.G., Balkizas, T., Nikita, K.S.: Using the Hough transform to segment ultrasound images of longitudinal and transverse sections of the carotid artery. Ultrasound in Medicine & Biology 33(12), 1918–1932 (2007)
6. Viola, P., Jones, M.J.: Robust real-time face detection. International Journal of Computer Vision 57(2), 137–154 (2004)
7. Cao, Y., Pranata, S., Yasugi, M., Niu, Z., Nishimura, H.: Staggered multi-scale LBP for pedestrian detection. In: IEEE ICIP, pp. 449–452 (2012)
8. Dalal, N., Triggs, B.: Histograms of oriented gradients for human detection. In: IEEE CVPR, vol. 1, pp. 886–893 (2005)

A Transfer-Learning Approach
to Image Segmentation Across Scanners
by Maximizing Distribution Similarity

Annegreet van Opbroek[1], M. Arfan Ikram[2], Meike W. Vernooij[2],
and Marleen de Bruijne[1,3]

[1] Biomedical Imaging Group Rotterdam, Departments of Medical Informatics
and Radiology, Erasmus MC - University Medical Center Rotterdam, The Netherlands
[2] Departments of Epidemiology and Radiology, Erasmus MC - University Medical
Center Rotterdam, The Netherlands
[3] Department of Computer Science, University of Copenhagen, Denmark

Abstract. Many successful methods for biomedical image segmentation
are based on supervised learning, where a segmentation algorithm is
trained based on manually labeled training data. For supervised-learning
algorithms to perform well, this training data has to be representative for
the target data. In practice however, due to differences between scanners
such representative training data is often not available.

We therefore present a segmentation algorithm in which labeled training data does not necessarily need to be representative for the target
data, which allows for the use of training data from different studies
than the target data. The algorithm assigns an importance weight to all
training images, in such a way that the Kullback-Leibler divergence between the resulting distribution of the training data and the distribution
of the target data is minimized.

In a set of experiments on MRI brain-tissue segmentation with training and target data from four substantially different studies our method
improved mean classification errors with up to 25% compared to common
supervised-learning approaches.

1 Introduction

Because of its good performance, supervised learning is a popular method to automatically segment biomedical images into different tissues and/or structures.
However, a disadvantage of supervised algorithms is that they require manually
labeled training data from the same distribution as the target data, to learn a
classification scheme that is then used for segmentation of target images. But
since images are often acquired with different scanners and different scanning
parameters, this requirement of training and target data following the same distribution hampers the use of supervised algorithms in larger studies and clinical
practice.

There is a relatively new machine-learning field called *transfer learning* which
concerns learning problems where training and target data do not necessarily

G. Wu et al. (Eds.): MLMI 2013, LNCS 8184, pp. 49–56, 2013.
© Springer International Publishing Switzerland 2013

follow the same distribution. Many transfer-learning methods weight training samples in order to increase the influence of "good" samples, while reducing the influence of "bad" samples [1]. These weights could then be used in a weighted classifier. *Sugiyama et al.* [2] presented a way to determine sample weights by minimizing the Kullback-Leibler divergence between the target probability density function (PDF) and the resulting weighted training PDF. However, the assumption made in [2] that the labeling function $P(y|\boldsymbol{x})$ is the same in training and target data, is often violated in image segmentation.

In a previous study [3] we presented a transfer-learning algorithm for medical-image segmentation by sample weighting. It uses not only training images from different studies than the target data, but also a small amount of labeled samples from the target study. This training data from the target study is used both to train a classifier and to determine the weight of the rest of the training data.

We propose a method that only requires the availability of training images from different studies than the target data, which also works if $P(y|\boldsymbol{x})$ varies between training and target data. It assigns an importance weight to the training images such that the weighted PDF of the training images best approximates the PDF of the target image. Classification is then performed by training a weighted classifier on training samples from the images, where each sample receives the weight of its image.

2   Methods

We use training data from M different images, which may be acquired with different scanning protocols. From every training image m a total of N_m training samples $\boldsymbol{x}_i^m$ ($i = 1, 2, \ldots, N_m$) are acquired, where $\boldsymbol{x}_i^m \in \mathbb{R}^n$ denotes a vector containing a value for each of the n features. Each $\boldsymbol{x}_i^m$ is given a label y_i^m by manual segmentation. From the target image we have N_{te} test samples $\boldsymbol{x}_i^{te}$, $i = 1, 2, \ldots, N_{te}$, of which we want to predict the label y_i^{te}.

We propose to assign a weight W_m to every training image m, resulting in a total weight vector $\boldsymbol{W} = [W_1, W_2, \ldots, W_M]$. Every sample $\boldsymbol{x}_i^m$ from image m will then be assigned a weight $w_i^m := W_m$, and a weighted classifier will be trained on the training samples and their weights.

We propose to determine the weights of the training images from the PDF of the samples of the image in the used feature space, $P_m(\boldsymbol{x})$ will be determined from the samples of image m, $\{\boldsymbol{x}_i^m\}_{i=1}^{N_m}$ by kernel density estimation. We first present a way to individually weight every training sample, after which a way to jointly determine weights is presented.

2.1   Individual Image Weights with Kullback-Leibler Divergence

In the individual weighting the image weights are chosen proportional to the difference between the PDF of the training image and the PDF of the target image. This assumes that the image with the most corresponding PDF is most suitable for training a classifier. For a training image m with PDF $P_m(\boldsymbol{x})$ the distance to the PDF of the target image, $P_{tar}(\boldsymbol{x})$, can be measured by the Kullback-Leibler (KL) divergence:

$$\mathrm{KL}(P_{tar}(\boldsymbol{x})\|P_m(\boldsymbol{x})) = \int_{\mathcal{D}} P_{tar}(\boldsymbol{x}) \log\left(\frac{P_{tar}(\boldsymbol{x})}{P_m(\boldsymbol{x})}\right) d\boldsymbol{x} \tag{1}$$

$$\approx \frac{1}{N_{te}} \sum_{i=1}^{N_{te}} \log P_{tar}(\boldsymbol{x}_i^{te}) - \frac{1}{N_{te}} \sum_{i=1}^{N_{te}} \log P_m(\boldsymbol{x}_i^{te}), \tag{2}$$

where Eq. 1 gives the definition of the KL divergence, and Eq. 2 follows by writing out the logarithm and approximating the whole domain $\int_{\mathcal{D}} P_{tar}(\boldsymbol{x})d\boldsymbol{x}$ by the test samples $\frac{1}{N_{te}} \sum_{i=1}^{N_{te}} \boldsymbol{x}_i^{te}$, which, since one image gives a large amount of samples, should be fairly accurate.

Note that only the second term in Eq. 2, $J_m = \frac{1}{N_{te}} \sum_{i=1}^{N_{te}} \log P_m(\boldsymbol{x}_i^{te})$, differs per $P_m(\boldsymbol{x})$, so the image weights can be set proportional to this term: $W_m = \frac{J_m - J_{min}}{\sum_{i=1}^{M} J_i - J_{min}}$, where J_{min} indicates the smallest value of all Js.

2.2 Joint Image Weights by Kullback-Leibler Minimization

Instead of determining image weights individually, they can also be determined jointly, by combining all training PDFs in such a way that the target PDF is best approximated. Compared to the individual weighting this approach gives a more local correspondence between PDFs.

By weighting each PDF $P_m(\boldsymbol{x})$ with W_m, a total training PDF is obtained:

$$P_{trn}(\boldsymbol{x}) = \sum_{m=1}^{M} \frac{W_m}{\sum\limits_{i=1}^{M} W_i} P_m(\boldsymbol{x}). \tag{3}$$

The weights W_m can be determined by minimizing $\mathrm{KL}(P_{tar}(\boldsymbol{x})\|P_{trn}(\boldsymbol{x}))$, in the same way as in Eq. 2, which equals maximizing $J = \frac{1}{N_{te}} \sum_{i=1}^{N_{te}} \log P_{trn}(\boldsymbol{x}_i^{te})$. This maximization is performed by gradient ascent, where iteratively a small step $0 < \epsilon < 1$ is taken in the direction of $\frac{dJ}{d\boldsymbol{W}}$, where

$$\frac{dJ}{dW_j} = \frac{1}{N_{te}} \sum_{i=1}^{N_{te}} \frac{\left(\sum\limits_{m=1, m \neq j}^{M} W_m\right) P_j(\boldsymbol{x}_i^{te}) - \sum\limits_{m=1, m \neq j}^{M} W_m P_m(\boldsymbol{x}_i^{te})}{P_{trn}(\boldsymbol{x}_i^{te}) \left(\sum\limits_{m=1}^{M} W_m\right)^2}. \tag{4}$$

2.3 Weighted Support Vector Machine Classification

For classification a *weighted support vector machine* (WSVM) is trained on the training samples and the corresponding weights. WSVM is an extension of the general soft-margin support vector machine (SVM) where every training sample x_i is given an importance weight w_i that indicates the importance for the classifier to correctly classify the sample [4].

Since we do multi-class classification, and an SVM can only distinguish between two classes, the SVM is extended to a multi-class classifier by one-vs-one classification (which gave better results than one-vs-rest classification).

3 Experiments

We performed a set of experiments on MRI brain-tissue segmentation through voxelwise classification. Each voxel was assigned to either white matter (WM), gray matter (GM), or cerebrospinal fluid (CSF).

Data Description. We used 56 manually segmented MRI brain images from four different studies, obtained with different scanners:

1. 6 T1-weighted images from the Rotterdam Scan Study [5], acquired with a 1.5T GE scanner with $0.49 \times 0.49 \times 0.80$ mm^3 voxel size
2. 12 HASTE-Odd images (inversion time = 4400 ms, TR = 2800 ms, TE = 29 ms) from the Rotterdam Scan Study [5], acquired with a 1.5T Siemens scanner with $1.25 \times 1 \times 1$ mm^3 voxel size
3. 18 T1-weighted images from the Internet Brain Segmentation Repository (IBSR) [6] with voxel sizes between $0.84 \times 0.84 \times 1.5$ mm^3 and $1 \times 1 \times 1.5$ mm^3
4. 20 T1-weighted images from the IBSR [6], 10 acquired with 1.5T Siemens scanner, and 10 with 1.5T GE scanner, all with $1 \times 3.1 \times 1$ mm^3 voxel size

In Fig. 1 a slice of one image from each of the four studies is shown to give an impression of the amount of variation.

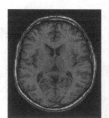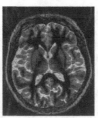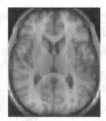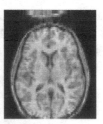

Fig. 1. Slices of images from the four different studies

We performed basic image standardization by inverting the Haste-Odd images, correcting all images for intensity non-uniformity with the N3 method [7] within a manually annotated mask, and scaling the voxels of every image in such a way that the voxels between the 4th and 96th percentile in intensity were mapped between 0 and 1.

Experimental Setup. We performed a set of four cross-validation experiments. In each experiment data from one study was selected as target data, where voxels within a manually annotated brain mask were classified, while the images from the other three studies were used as training images. In order to test the influence of the number of features on the segmentation, we tested different feature sets. First 13 features were calculated for every voxel:

- The intensity
- The intensity after convolution with a Gaussian kernel with $\sigma = 1, 2, 3$ mm^3
- The gradient magnitude of the intensity after convolution with a Gaussian kernel with $\sigma = 1, 2, 3$ mm^3
- The Laplacian if the intensity after convolution with a Gaussian kernel with $\sigma = 1, 2, 3$ mm^3
- The x, y, and z position normalized for the size of the brain.

All features were normalized to zero mean and unit standard deviation.

Feature sets of increasing dimensionality were determined in a cross-validation experiment on the training data by forward feature selection. Here in each iteration the feature is added that most improved the classification performance of a regular unweighted SVM.

The performance of the two proposed methods is compared to the performance of a regular SVM on training samples from all training images, and a regular SVM trained only on the image m with the PDF that has the largest value for J_m. For all classifications an implementation in LIBSVM [4] was used.

To enable fair comparison of methods, a total amount of 50 000 training samples was used in each of the classifiers. The weights were determined on a total of 10 000 random samples per training and target image. Classification accuracy is shown in feature curves on these 10 000 random samples per target image.

Parameter Selection. To estimate the PDFs $P_m(x)$ of the training images used in Eq. 2 we performed kernel density estimation with a multivariate Gaussian kernel with width $\Sigma_{KL}^m = \sigma_{KL}^m \cdot I$. Here σ_{KL}^m was determined by Silverman's rule:

$$\sigma_{KL}^m = \left(\frac{4}{d+2}\right)^{\frac{1}{d+4}} N_m^{\frac{-1}{d+4}} \sigma^m, \tag{5}$$

where d denotes the dimensionality of the data, N_m the number of samples, and σ^m the standard deviation of the data. This value for σ_{KL}^m is proved by *Silverman* [8] to minimize the mean integrated square error (MISE) between the actual and the estimated PDF, when a multivariate Gaussian kernel is used.

The step size in the gradient ascent was experimentally set to $\epsilon = 0.1$, in a trade-off between speed and accuracy. This way the optimal weights W can be calculated in the order of minutes.

For all classifications an SVM with Gaussian kernel was used. The SVM parameter C and the kernel parameter γ for all SVMs were determined with a grid-search experiment on the training data with a regular SVM.

3.1   Results

Fig. 2 shows the mean classification errors in each of the four studies as a function of the number of features used in the classification, for the SVM on all images, the SVM on the best image only, and the WSVMs with the individually determined weights, and the jointly determined weights. Fig. 3 shows for the latter three the 95%-confidence intervals of the percentage of improvement over the SVM on all training images, averaged over the 4 studies. Both WSVMs performed significantly better than the SVM on all training images, where the joint method also performed significantly better than the WSVM with individually determined weights. Also, the SVM trained on the single image with the lowest KL shows much more variation in performance than the other classifiers.

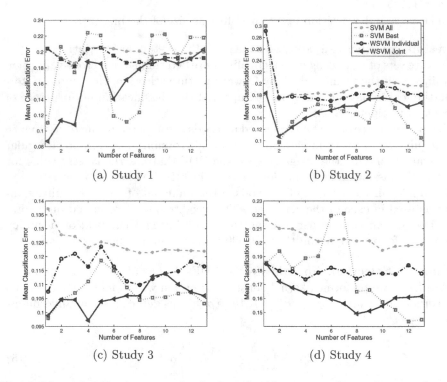

(a) Study 1   (b) Study 2

(c) Study 3   (d) Study 4

Fig. 2. Mean classification errors for the four classifiers averaged over the target images in each study, as a function of the number of features used

The figures show that WSVM with jointly optimized weights performed less well in high-dimensional feature spaces than in lower-dimensional feature spaces. However, even for 13 features this classifier significantly outperformed the conventional SVM and the individually weighted WSVM.

Fig. 4 shows the resulting segmentations of the different classifiers on an image slice from Study 1, with classification based on three features. All four classifiers under segment the amount of CSF, which is partly explained because the IBSR

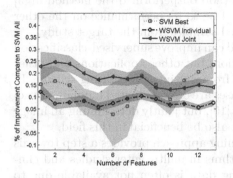

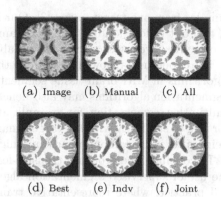

(a) Image   (b) Manual   (c) All

(d) Best   (e) Indv   (f) Joint

Fig. 3. 95%-confidence interval for the mean improvement in terms of percentage of three classifiers, compared to the baseline SVM on all training images

Fig. 4. A resulting segmentation on Study 1 with classification errors (c) 8.7%, (d) 11.7%, (e) 8.6%, (f) 8.3%

training images, which constitute the majority of training images, have no manually labeled sulcal CSF. The jointly weighted SVM yields the best segmentation.

We also obtained segmentations with SPM8 [9] on all images from the four studies. SPM8 gave mean classification errors of 12.6% on Study 1, 10% on Study 2, 20.8% on Study 3, and 24.6% on Study 4. [3] reports mean classification errors of 7% on Study 1, 6% on Study 2, 11% on Study 3, and 20% on Study 4.

4 Conclusion and Discussion

We have presented a transfer-learning algorithm to improve supervised image segmentation on images from different scanners and/or scanning parameters than the target data. In the best algorithm the different training images are weighted such that the distribution of the target samples is best approximated, and used for classification with a weighted classifier. An experiment on MRI brain-tissue segmentation showed that this algorithm greatly improved classification over a standard supervised classifier on either all training images or the single best image, even though the way several parameters were optimized favored the supervised-learning classifiers.

In the experiments we compared different numbers of features, where the proposed method appeared to be more sensitive to the used number of features than standard supervised learning. This may be due to the difficulty of estimating the PDFs in a higher-dimensional space. We therefore advise to perform feature reduction prior to determining the weights. However, even for a large number of features the proposed method outperformed standard supervised learning.

We compared the performance of our method to that of SPM8. In one study the methods performed similarly, while in three out of four studies our method outperformed SPM8, with improvements of up to 50%. We also compared our performance to that of a transfer-learning algorithm that uses labeled training samples from one target image [3]. Our method outperformed the method in [3] in two out of four studies, and was came close to its performance on the other two studies, even without the use of labeled samples from the target study.

The experiments showed that our method can improve supervised-classification algorithms in MRI brain-tissue segmentation, but other applications and other segmentation algorithms may also benefit from our image weighting scheme. In multi-atlas segmentation, for example, atlases are often weighted individually according to similarity with the target image [10], but jointly determining all image weights, as is done in our algorithm, might also be beneficial in this field.

To conclude, the proposed transfer-learning approach provides a step towards the use of supervised segmentation algorithms in multi-center studies and clinical practice, where representative training data is often not available due to population differences and the use of many different types of scanners.

Acknowledgments. This research is financed by The Netherlands Organization for Scientific Research (NWO).

References

1. Pan, S., Yang, Q.: A survey on transfer learning. IEEE Transactions on Knowledge and Data Engineering 22(10), 1345–1359 (2010)
2. Sugiyama, M., Nakajima, S., Kashima, H., Von Buenau, P., Kawanabe, M.: Direct importance estimation with model selection and its application to covariate shift adaptation. In: Advances in Neural Information Processing Systems, vol. 20, pp. 1433–1440 (2008)
3. van Opbroek, A., Ikram, M.A., Vernooij, M.W., de Bruijne, M.: Supervised image segmentation across scanner protocols: A transfer learning approach. In: Wang, F., Shen, D., Yan, P., Suzuki, K. (eds.) MLMI 2012. LNCS, vol. 7588, pp. 160–167. Springer, Heidelberg (2012)
4. Chang, C., Lin, C.: LIBSVM: a library for support vector machines. ACM Transactions on Intelligent Systems and Technology (TIST) 2(3)
5. Ikram, M., van der Lugt, A., Niessen, W., Krestin, G., Koudstaal, P., Hofman, A., Breteler, M., Vernooij, M.: The Rotterdam Scan Study: design and update up to 2012. European Journal of Epidemiology 26(10), 811–824 (2011)
6. Worth, A.: The Internet Brain Segmentation Repository (IBSR)
7. Sled, J., Zijdenbos, A., Evans, A.: A nonparametric method for automatic correction of intensity nonuniformity in MRI data. IEEE Transactions on Medical Imaging 17(1), 87–97 (1998)
8. Silverman, B.: Density estimation for statistics and data analysis, vol. 26. Chapman & Hall/CRC (1986)
9. Ashburner, J., Friston, K.: Unified segmentation. Neuroimage 26(3), 839–851 (2005)
10. Artaechevarria, X., Munoz-Barrutia, A., Ortiz-de Solorzano, C.: Combination strategies in multi-atlas image segmentation: Application to brain MR data. IEEE Transactions on Medical Imaging 28(8), 1266–1277 (2009)

A New Algorithm of Electronic Cleansing for Weak Faecal-Tagging CT Colonography

Le Lu, Bing Jian, Dijia Wu, and Matthias Wolf

Siemens Medical Solutions USA, Siemens Corporate Research
le.lu@nih.gov

Abstract. CT Colonography (CTC) has emerged as a mainstream clinical practice of colonic cancer screening and diagnosis. One of the most critical problems is to increase compliance with CTC examinations via minimal bowel preparation (i.e., weak faecal-tagging), which nevertheless causes much lower signal-noise-ratio than conventional preparation.

In this paper, we present a new algorithm pipeline of electronically cleansing tagging materials in CTC under reduced oral contrast dose. Our method has the following steps: 1, robust structure parsing to generate a list of volume regions of interest (ROIs) of tagging material (avoiding bone erosion); 2, effectively locating local tagging-air (AT) transitional surface regions; 3, a novel discriminative-generative algorithm to learn the higher-order image appearance model in AT using 3D Markov Random Fields (MRF); 4, accurate probability density function based voxel labeling corresponding to semantic classes. Validated on 26 weak faecal-tagging CTC cases from 3 medical sites, our method yields better visualization clarity and readability compared with the previous approach [1]. The whole system computes efficiently (e.g., < 40 seconds for CT images of $512 \times 512 \times 1000+$).

1 Introduction

Colorectal cancer is the second leading cause of cancer-related mortality in western countries. Computed Tomography Colonography (CTC) has become a feasible, non-intrusive clinical alternative of traditional optical Colonography, to offer good sensitivity and specificity for polyp detection via screening the whole colon. However, similar to traditional examination protocols, the colon is required to be fully cleansed manually or electronically. Electronic cleansing (eCleansing) of fecal residues by computed algorithms [1, 2] is very critical to avoid intensive manual bowel preparation, prior to the examination. The quality of electronic cleansing method directly impacts radiologist's image reading performance in 3D, as well as computer-aided diagnosis. Recently, weak faecal-tagging bowel protocol [3] has gained popularity in major research clinical sites (e.g., consuming up to 40% CTC cases) since the dose reduction largely improves patient comfort and compliance. This protocol however causes much higher imaging noises, inhomogeneous intensity patterns and lower contrast between tagging materials and surrounding soft-tissue structures. Significant challenges are imposed for radiologists and previous eCleansing methods [1,2], due to lack of precise statistical

G. Wu et al. (Eds.): MLMI 2013, LNCS 8184, pp. 57–65, 2013.

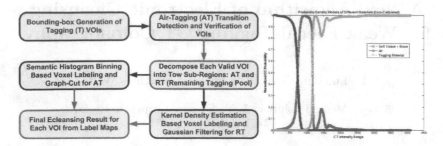

Fig. 1. (Left) The overall algorithm diagram of the proposed eCleansing approach.
(Right) Data-calibrated class probability value plots $\in [0, 4095]$. Blue for Air class F_a;
Red for (soft-tissue + bone) class F_s; and Green for tagging material class F_t.

data-driven appearance model. To address this issue, our proposed algorithm is
described as follows. The overall framework is summarized in Fig. 1 **(Left)**.

2   Materials and Method

Data-driven Intensity Calibration: To accurately model the intensity variations of three anatomical classes: air, tagging and soft-tissue (including bone) in
CT images, is an important prerequisite of eCleansing. In a data-driven manner,
we manually label > 100000 voxels per class and perform kernel density estimation (KDE) $f_a; f_s; f_t$ using these annotated voxels. The class probability values
$\in [0, 1]$ are obtained by normalization, i.e., $F_t(v) = f_t(v)/(f_a(v) + f_s(v) + f_t(v))$
where v or $v(x, y, z)$ denotes the intensity of the voxel at coordinates (x, y, z).
To achieve extremely high **efficiency** of voxel-level probability evaluation at
run-time, we convert the fitted KDE models into look-up tables of normalized $F_a(v); F_s(v); F_t(v)$ since the CT intensity value is bounded in the range
of $[0, 4095]$. Our intensity value is equal to its Hounsfield unit (HU) added with
a fixed offset, $v = HU + 1024$.

2.1   Bounding Box Generation of Tagging ROIs

We first tackle the problem of spatially detecting and bounding each tagging
material pool using a bounding box in a CT image.

Colonic Air and Bone Compartments Identification: Since the CTC
tagging materials of interest must be adjacent to air in the abdominal region,
an effective way of detecting these volume ROIs is to start from colonic air components and search around nearby regions. Air compartments can be effectively
extracted using a generic 3D region growing algorithm and the air intensity
range. However they may be from lung and other extra-colonic regions (e.g.,
small intestine, stomach) and we eliminate extra-colonic air findings, via robust
component-level structure parsing using geometric features and rank-one SVM
classification [4]. On the other hand, when searching tagging materials, we need

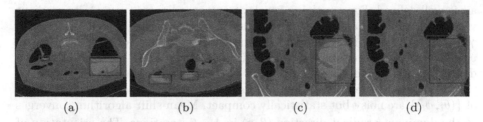

    (a)   (b)   (c)   (d)

Fig. 2. Illustration of ROI detection (in **blue**) and AT region detection (in **red**) results via 3D bounding boxes. (a,b) in axial or transverse views; (c,d) in coronal views; (d) tagging voxels are annotated in **red**.

to avoid the bone tissue voxels since they have similar Hounsfield units or CT intensity values. Anatomical bone landmarks (e.g., the centers of vertebrae) can be automatically and reliably detected using a recent cascade classifier [5] or random trees [6]. Most of bone structures in the thoracic and abdominal regions including ribs and vertebral columns can be identified by region growing from landmarks.

ROI Generation: At each transverse CT slice, run 2D connected component (CC) labeling on the labeled colonic air compartments. From each 2D air CC, we probe along the direction towards possible tagging materials (posterior if supine otherwise anterior). If a voxel $v(x, y, z)$ being probed has not been labeled (either as bone or tagging material), its CT intensity value is used to check if it can serve as a seed point of tagging material. The above tagging voxel class probability function $F_t(v(x, y, z))$ of intensity is employed. If $F_t(v(x, y, z))$ indicates high confidence (e.g., ≥ 0.85), we employ a 3D region growing algorithm from this seed to propagate a 3D connected component of tagging materials (evaluating $F_t(\cdot)$ during propagation). For each detected 3D CC (denoted as CC_t), its corresponding 3D bounding box is computed. Then we obtain a list of 3D bounding boxes $\{CC_t\}$ as ROIs per CT volume, where each box represents a cropped sub-volume containing tagging and surrounding voxels. Fig. 2 shows the volume ROI detection results, covering tagging voxel pools with various sizes or volumes. Each ROI can be "eCleansed" in parallel (for computational efficiency) since there is no logical dependency among processing them. Using region growing to link $F_t(\cdot)$ responses is more robust than running $F_t(\cdot)$ at every voxel position, which more prone to small clusters of imaging noise. Optionally, we can reject components with small volume measurements (e.g., $< 3ml$), indicating low confidence.

2.2 Efficient ROI Verification and AT Localization

This stage contains posterior or anterior directional gradient profiling and Air-Tagging (AT) transition region detection via 3D Haar feature boosting.

Dominant Air-tagging Gradient Search: For each ROI, we first mask out air-class voxels based on its intensity value since Hounsfield unit (HU) in CT for air is well defined. For remaining voxels at any coordinates (x, y, z), its gradient vector $(\Delta_x, \Delta_y, \Delta_z)$ and gradient orientation (θ, ϕ) weighted by the magnitude $\gamma = \|(\Delta_x, \Delta_y, \Delta_z)\|$ are computed. In the parameter space of $[\theta, \phi]$, each voxel v_i will cast one data sample (θ_i, ϕ_i) with weight γ_i. Then the task of finding dominant air-tagging gradient direction is essentially a mode-seeking problem that can be solved effectively by mean-shift [7]. In our case, the distributions of $\{(\theta_i, \phi_i)\}$ are noisy but statistically compact. Mean-shift algorithm converges to the dominant gradient direction $(\widehat{\theta}, \widehat{\phi})$ in $4 \sim 6$ iterations. The orientation of $(\widehat{\theta}, \widehat{\phi})$ coincides with Y-direction of $\geq 98.5\%$ probability.

Efficient AT Detection via Boosted 3D Haar Features: For each volume ROI, there can be at least one or more Air-Tagging (AT) transition regions though $\cong 65\%$ ROIs have only one AT. AT regions are labeled by one bounding box per AT for 10 CTC volumes (split evenly for training and testing). Each bounding box precisely covers the AT spatial expansion in CT coronal plane from manual annotation, which is normally a narrow-band box in Y-direction including several slices or layers of air and tagging voxels. Detecting bounding boxes in run-time is approached as a generic 3D object detection problem via Haar features boosted by Adaboost or Probabilistic Boosting Tree [8]. 3D Haar features are well capable to capture intensity contrast statistics existing from air voxel layers to tagging.

Without loss of generality, we assume that $(\widehat{\theta}, \widehat{\phi})$ is aligned with Y-coordinates (i.e., the normal of coronal plane), to eliminate the orientation degrees-of-freedom (DOF) completely. From above gradient search, we can locate Y-locations with strong gradient magnitude sums (aggregated on each coronal plane within ROI). On each XZ plane at a hypothesized Y, we can perform a 2D connected component (CC) operation on its tagging class probability response map (by evaluating $F_t(v)$) and compute the X and Z spans of the largest tagging CC as $\hat{X}, \hat{Z}$. The only remaining DOF is translation in Y within ROI. In run-time, we obtain the list of final AT bounding boxes per ROI based the detection probability rank and non-maximal suppression (to remove overlapped detections). Our detector using PBT boosted Haar feature can capture the intensity contrast of air and tagging class voxels in valid AT boxes, and achieves 99.56% sensitivity with no false positives on validation set. Only 2 very small AT boxes out of 477 annotated boxes are missed in 5 training CT volumes. Examples are shown in Fig. 2 as red boxes.

2.3 Multivariate Image Model and MRF in AT

Due to partial-volume effect in the air-tagging transition regions and air-tagging-tissue T-junctions [1, 2] in AT, there are certain amounts of air-tagging mixed, or pseudo voxels having very similar (single voxel) intensity value as soft-tissue. Therefore we formulate a high-order intensity pattern to differentiate pseudo and true soft-tissue voxels through context modeling. The motivation is that soft-tissue voxels tend to have more soft-tissue neighbors while pseudo voxels having both air and tagging voxels on both sides in Y-direction (due to gravity).

More precisely, for each voxel $v(x, y, z)$ at location (x, y, z), we form a $(2N+1)$-dimensional intensity feature vector $V(x, y, z) = [v(x, y - N, z), \ldots, v(x, y - 1, z), v(x, y, z), v(x, y+1, z), \ldots, v(x, y+N, z)]$ center at (x, y, z) where $N = 3 \sim 7$. Then $V(x, y, z)$ is classified as a supervised binary learning task. To do so, all voxels inside 36 AT boxes (Refer to Fig. 2 (d).) randomly extracted from 5 training volumes, are annotated as positive $(+)$ soft-tissue class versus negative $(-)$ tagging (including pseudo) class.

High-Order Intensity Pattern Modeling: Since KDE does not scale well with higher dimensionality $(2N+1)$ in both computation and accuracy, we propose a new method Multivariate Intensity Histograms with Adaptive Semantic Binning (*MIHASB*), via maximizing the Chernoff Information of two empirical distributions. Chernoff information [9] is defined as follows, given two discrete distributions of $\mathcal{H}(+), \mathcal{H}(-)$.

$$\mathcal{C}(\mathcal{H}(+), \mathcal{H}(-)) = - \min_{0 \leq \lambda \leq 1} \log(\sum_{b=1}^{B} \mathcal{H}^{\lambda}(+, b)\mathcal{H}^{1-\lambda}(-, b)) \tag{1}$$

When $\lambda = \frac{1}{2}$, $\mathcal{C}$ becomes Bhattacharyya coefficient [9] which is optimized here. Notations of histograms $\mathcal{H}(V^+)$ and $\mathcal{H}(+)$ are interchangeable (same for $\mathcal{H}(V^-)$, $\mathcal{H}(-)$). Histogram takes an input feature vector V to return the output value, as recoded in the corresponding bin. Histogram binning is the process on how to construct histogram by finding its associated bins while maximizing the $(+/-)$ class separability criterion of $\mathcal{C}(\mathcal{H}(+), \mathcal{H}(-))$. Maximizing $\mathcal{C}(\mathcal{H}(+), \mathcal{H}(-))$ brings the optimized classification accuracy [10, 11]. Therefore our learned models are discriminative-generative density functions. If the exhaustive histogram binning parameter search is adopted, even only 100 evenly divided intensity boundaries (CT intensity $\in [0, 4095]$) to be hypothesized and evaluated by Eq. 1, the computation complexity is already prohibitively expensive as 100^{2N+1}. Again, we draw importance samplings by leveraging the knowledge of CT intensity ranges of semantic air, soft-tissue, (weak) tagging and bone anatomies. The sampling parameters are data-calibrated similarly using normalized KDE plots as Fig. 1 **(Right)**: means $\{\mu_m\} = \{350, 750, 1100, 1400\}$ (w.r.t. air, soft-tissue, weak tagging and regular tagging voxel intensity); standard deviations $\sigma_m = \sigma_m^+ = \sigma_m^- = 40$ regardless of $m = 1, 2, 3, 4$ for simplicity. Our multivariate *MIHASB* algorithm is described in Alg. 1. Semantic Sampling Function (*SSF*) is equivalent to draw a random sample s_m from $[\mu_m - \sigma_m^-, \mu_m + \sigma_m^+]$ based on uniform sampling, or from Gaussian Distribution $\mathcal{G}(\mu_m, \sigma_m)$, $\{s\} = \{s\} \cup s_m$. In this way, *SSF* implicitly encodes the intensity patterns such as how many air, soft-tissue, bone, tagging voxels existing in the relative spatial context and makes *MIHASB* binning process very efficient in $K = 2N + 1$ dimensions. The sampling derivation σ captures the CT data variations at semantic class boundaries.

In runtime, the histograms $\mathcal{H}(V^+), \mathcal{H}(V^-)$ are normalized using likelihood ratio testing [10] per bin, to form $\mathcal{P}(+)$ (i.e., the soft-tissue class $\mathcal{P}_s$).

$$\mathcal{P}_s(V) = \frac{\mathcal{H}(V^+)}{\mathcal{H}(V^+) + \mathcal{H}(V^-)} \tag{2}$$

Algorithm 1. Adaptive Semantic Binning in Joint Multivariate Space

---

Input: Sets of positive samples $\{V^+\}$ and negatives $\{V^-\}$; K is the
dimension of the feature vector $V \in \Re^{K=9}$
Output: Trained multivariate histograms $\mathcal{H}(V^+),\mathcal{H}(V^-)$
Initialize $\mathcal{H}^0(V^+),\mathcal{H}^0(V^-)$ with one bin and $C^0_{max} = 0$;
for $t = 1, ...T$ **do**
  $\quad C^t_{max} = 0$;
  $\quad$**for** $k = 1, ..., K$ **do**
    $\quad\quad$Generate the hypothesized split set $\{s^k\}$ from semantic sampling
    $\quad\quad$function at Dimension k;
    $\quad\quad$**for** *Each* $ss \in \{s^k\}$ **do**
      $\quad\quad\quad$Update intermediate histograms $\mathcal{H}^t(V^+)$, $\mathcal{H}^t(V^-)$ by adding
      $\quad\quad\quad$the split ss into $\mathcal{H}^{t-1}(V^+)$ and $\mathcal{H}^{t-1}(V^-)$ via Cartesian data
      $\quad\quad\quad$repartitioning in $\Re^K$, respectively;
      $\quad\quad\quad$Evaluate the Chernoff Information $\mathcal{C}$ (i.e., eq. 1) given
      $\quad\quad\quad$$\mathcal{H}^t(V^+)$, $\mathcal{H}^t(V^-)$ from $\{V^+\}$ and $\{V^-\}$;
      $\quad\quad\quad$**if** $C^t_{max} < \mathcal{C}$ **then**
        $\quad\quad\quad\quad$$C^t_{max} = \mathcal{C}$; and record the current optimal split ss;
      $\quad\quad\quad$**end**
    $\quad\quad$**end**
  $\quad$**end**
  $\quad$**if** $(C^t_{max} - C^{t-1}_{max}) > \epsilon$ **then**
    $\quad\quad$Update and finalize $\mathcal{H}^t(V^+)$, $\mathcal{H}^t(V^-)$ for iteration y, by adding
    $\quad\quad$the recorded optimal split ss (according to C^t_{max}) into $\mathcal{H}^{t-1}(V^+)$,
    $\quad\quad$$\mathcal{H}^{t-1}(V^-)$ via data repartitioning;
  $\quad$**else**
    $\quad\quad$Return $\mathcal{H}^t(V^+)$, $\mathcal{H}^t(V^-)$ as the final output (converged) and exit;
  $\quad$**end**
end

Last, $\mathcal{P}_s$ is also represented as a multi-dimensional look-up table with the estimated binning boundaries where each cell stores $\mathcal{P}_s \in [0, 1]$. Our trained histogram models $\mathcal{H}(V^+), \mathcal{H}(V^-), \mathcal{P}(+)$ have 2592 bins (when $N = 4$). Longer range context of $N = 4$ improves over $N = 3$, but performance saturates after $N > 4$.

MRF Optimization: In each AT bounding box, we first evaluate every inside voxel $v(x, y, z)$ via its feature vector $V(x, y, z)$ to obtain $P_s(x, y, z)$ at the location (x, y, z). Each AT voxel is treated as a node of the 3D MRF grid and we use its negative-log form $E_{data}(x, y, z) = -log(P_s(x, y, z))$ [12] as the data term. The intensity-contrasted pairwise potential function is adopted as a spatially isotropic smoothness term (26-neighborhood is used). This energy minimization problem can be solved effectively by Max-Flow/Min-Cut algorithm [12]. The optimization output is a binary label field: $L = 1$ meaning the positive soft-tissue class (to be preserved in eCleansing); $L = 0$ indicating negative class of air, tagging and pseudo-enhanced (non soft-tissue) voxels that should be eliminated.

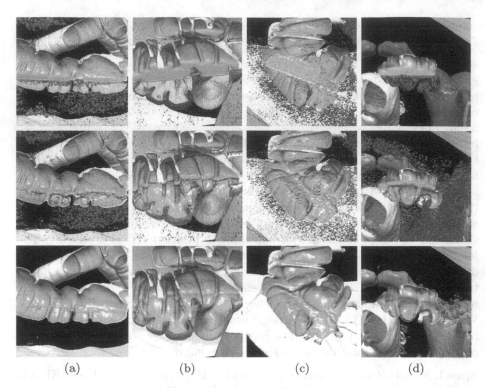

(a)　　　　　　　(b)　　　　　　　(c)　　　　　　　(d)

Fig. 3. Examples of E-cleansing results: original volume rendering **(Top)**, generated by an implementation of GMM-EM method [1] **(Middle)** and our method **(Bottom)**

2.4　Probabilistic Voxel Labeling and Smoothing in RT

Recall that in Sec. 2.1, we obtain a 3D connected component of tagging materials CC_t (guided by $F_t()$) to bound each ROI. Possible tiny holes $\in CC_t$ (e.g., created by air bubbles in the inhomogeneous tagging pool) can be filled by standard hole-filling algorithm. For each remaining voxel $v \in RT = CC_t \cap (\notin AT)$, $F_s(v) = f_s(v)/(f_a(v) + f_s(v) + f_t(v))$ is used to assign the normalized soft-tissue class probability $\in [0, 1]$. The $F_s(v)$-weighted intensity value is computed as $v_s(x, y, z) = v(x, y, z) \times F_s(x, y, z)$ for v. Finally, we apply a simple 3D isotropic Gaussian smoothing filter G (variance $= 1mm$) on $\{v_s(x, y, z)\}$ to obtain denoised $\{\mathcal{G}(v_s(x, y, z))\}$ and set label $L = 0$ for voxels satisfying $\mathcal{G}(v_s) < 350$. The threshold 350 is defined by our clinical collaborator. To prepare **CTC visualization**, all voxels with label $L = 0$ are set as 0 intensity value, thus "electronically cleansed". Voxels in the ROI but outside of CC_t remain unprocessed or "untouched".

3　Experimental Results and Discussion

Data: Twenty-six weak faecal-tagging CTC scans (15 patients) from three hospitals in Europe are used. Variations of bowel preparations with different

combinations of doses were employed. The axial image slice numbers vary from 728 to 1089 and the slice thickness ranges from 0.798 mm to 1.25 mm.

Accuracy: Tagging voxels of 10 out of 26 scans are annotated using interactive graph-cut [12] and manual touch-up. 10 volumes are split evenly for training and testing. Two performance criteria are used: *Sensitivity* (S) on the detected and removed tagging voxels versus all labeled tagging voxels; and *Accuracy* (A) on the number of removed tagging voxels versus all removed voxels. For comparison, we implement the Gaussian Mixture Model (*GMM*) based eCleansing method [1]. Our method has $S = 99.2\%$ and $A = 99.3\%$ while $S = 93.6\%$ and $A = 98.9\%$ are for our version of [1]. *The main difference is on sensitivities.* Although $S = 93.6\%$ is not low, a lot of tagging voxels at three-material (i.e., air, tagging and soft-tissue) transitional areas in AT are not effectively cleansed. There are severe artifacts "left-overs" floating in the air or adjacent to colon wall which imposes significant technical challenges for clinicians to perform 3D CTC reading. The joint use of KDE and *MIHASB* shows better intensity modeling accuracy among different voxel classes than *GMM*. Without explicit physics based three-material transition modeling [2], our data-driven approach achieves highly competitive results in less computational cost (refer "bath-tub ring" effect in Fig. 9 of [2]). We also conduct CTC 3D fly-through user study to subjectively evaluate the reader's impact on all 26 volumes, prepared by our proposed method and [1], respectively. The visualized comparison is demonstrated in Fig. 3.

Speed: *MIHASB* algorithm is compared with *GMM* [1] and random trees (RF) via random intensity testing [6]. RF-11 and RF-15 (i.e., 11 or 15 decision trees) provide comparable or slightly better accuracy than *MIHASB* (S/A: 87.5%/95.1% and 87.9%/95.4% versus 87.7%/95.5% in testing). Random trees need hundreds of arithmetic operations per voxel evaluation; *MIHASB* only requires 9-13 times of integer comparison. After MRF optimization, S/A are improved to 96.2%/98.6%. Segmenting the voxels into mixtures [1] runs as the slowest.

In summary, our main contributions are three-fold. 1), We propose a new volume ROI based algorithm pipeline in a divide-and-conquer manner, which is substantially novel from previous work [1,2]. 2), We present statistical data-driven generative and discriminative-generative models (e.g., *MIHASB*) throughout the paper that effectively cope well with the emerging minimal bowel preparation protocols. 3), Our method has been validated under various quantitative criteria and user study, using 26 CTC studies from multiple clinical sites.

References

1. Wang, Z., Liang, Z., et al.: An Improved Electronic Colon Cleansing Method for Detection of Colonic Polyps by Virtual Colonoscopy. IEEE Trans. Biomed. Engi. 53, 1635–1646 (2006)
2. Serlie, I., Vos, F., Truyen, R., Post, F., Stoker, J., van Vliet, L.: Electronic Cleansing for Computed Tomography (CT) Colonography Using a Scale-Invariant Three-Material Model. IEEE Trans. Biomed. Engi. 57, 1306–1317 (2010)

3. Liedenbaum, M., Denters, M., Zijta, F., van Ravesteijn, V., Bipat, S., Vos, F., Dekker, E., Stoker, J.: Reducing the oral contrast dose in CT colonography: evaluation of faecal tagging quality and patient acceptance. Clin. Radiol., 30–37 (2010)
4. Lu, L., Wolf, M., Liang, J., Dundar, M., Bi, J., Salganicoff, M.: A Two-level Approach Towards Semantic Colon Segmentation: Removing Extra-colonic Findings. In: Yang, G.-Z., Hawkes, D., Rueckert, D., Noble, A., Taylor, C. (eds.) MICCAI 2009, Part II. LNCS, vol. 5762, pp. 1009–1016. Springer, Heidelberg (2009)
5. Wu, T., Jian, B., Zhou, X.S.: Automated identification of thoracolumbar vertebrae using orthogonal matching pursuit. In: Suzuki, K., Wang, F., Shen, D., Yan, P. (eds.) MLMI 2011. LNCS, vol. 7009, pp. 126–133. Springer, Heidelberg (2011)
6. Lepetit, V., Fua, P.: Keypoint recognition using randomized trees. IEEE Trans. Pat. Anal. Mach. Intell. 28, 1465–1479 (2006)
7. Comaniciu, D., Meer, P.: Mean Shift: A Robust Approach Toward Feature Space Analysis. IEEE Trans. Pat. Anal. Mach. Intell. 24(5), 603–619 (2002)
8. Tu, Z.: Probabilistic boosting-tree: Learning discriminative models for classification, recognition, and clustering. In: ICCV, pp. 1589–1596 (2005)
9. Cover, T.M., Thomas, J.A.: Elements of information theory (1991)
10. Konishi, S., Yuille, A., Coughlan, J., Zhu, S.: Statistical edge detection: Learning and evaluating edge cues. IEEE Trans. Pat. Anal. Mach. Intell. 25, 57–74 (2003)
11. Lu, L., et al.: Hierarchical learning for tubular structure parsing in medical imaging: A study on coronary arteries using 3D CT Angiography. In: ICCV (2009)
12. Boykov, Y., Funka-Lea, G.: Graph Cuts and Efficient N-D Image Segmentation. Int. J. Comp. Vis. 70(2), 109–131 (2006)

A Unified Approach to Shape Model Fitting and Non-rigid Registration

Marcel Lüthi, Christoph Jud, and Thomas Vetter

Department of Mathematics and Computer Science, University of Basel

Abstract. Non-rigid registration and shape model fitting are the central problems in any shape modeling pipeline. Even though the goal is in both problems to establishing point-to-point correspondence between two objects, their algorithmic treatment is usually very different. In this paper we present an approach that allows us to treat both problems in a unified algorithmic framework. We use the well known formulation of non-rigid registration as the problem of fitting a Gaussian process model, whose covariance function favors smooth deformations. We compute a low rank approximation of the Gaussian process using the Nyström method, which allows us to formulate it as a parametric fitting problem of the same form as shape model fitting. Besides simplifying the modeling pipeline, our approach also lets us naturally combine shape model fitting and non-rigid registration, in order to reduce the bias in statistical model fitting, or to make registration more robust. As our experiments on 3D surfaces and 3D CT images show, the method leads to a registration accuracy that is comparable to standard registration methods.

1 Introduction

Statistical shape and deformation models are a well established part of many computer vision and medical image analysis pipelines. Both in building the statistical model, and in its application, the central problem is to find point-to-point correspondence between a reference (i.e. an image or surface) and a given image, such that the new image can be explained in terms of the reference. In the case where the reference is represented as an image, this is solved using image registration. The goal is to find a deformation field u^* from a space of deformations $\mathcal{F}$, which maps the corresponding points from the reference image I_R to a target images I_T. Formally, this is written as an optimization problem:

$$u^* := \arg\min_{u \in \mathcal{F}} \mathcal{D}[I_R, I_T, u] + \eta \mathcal{R}[u], \tag{1}$$

where $\mathcal{D}$ measures image similarity and the regularizer $\mathcal{R}$ how well the solution matches our prior assumptions. Given a statistical model, i.e. a generative model of the form $\mathcal{M}[\alpha](x) = \mu(x) + \sum_i \alpha_i \phi_i(x)$, which models the space of deformations in terms of a set of (learned) basis function ϕ_i, the optimization problem (1) becomes the parametric problem

$$\alpha^* := \arg\min_{\alpha \in \mathbb{R}^d} \mathcal{D}[I_R, I_T, \mathcal{M}[\alpha]] + \eta \mathcal{R}[\alpha]. \tag{2}$$

G. Wu et al. (Eds.): MLMI 2013, LNCS 8184, pp. 66–73, 2013.

It can be minimized using standard optimization techniques. The general non-rigid registration problem, is harder to solve, as there is no explicit model for the deformations available. In this case a variational approach is often employed, where the admissible deformations are specified by the regularization term $\mathcal{R}[u]$ which most often takes the form of a differential operator. A solution to the problem is obtained by solving a non-linear partial differential equation.

For building statistical models this mismatch of methodologies is unfortunate and adds considerable complexity to the modeling pipeline. In this paper we propose to unify both problems by constructing a parametric model for the general registration problem. The idea is to model the deformations as a Gaussian process $\mathcal{GP}(\mu, k)$, with mean function μ and covariance function (or kernel function) k. While this model is in general non-parametric, we can obtain a parametric approximation if we assume that the modeled deformation fields are sufficiently smooth. This is done by computing a low-rank approximation $\tilde{k}$ of the covariance function in terms of the first leading terms of its Mercer expansion $k(x, y) = \sum_i^n \lambda_i \phi_i(x) \phi_i(y)$ [11]. Under the new model $\mathcal{GP}(\mu, \tilde{k})$, each deformation can be written as

$$\mathcal{M}[\alpha](x) = \mu(x) + \sum_i \alpha_i \lambda_i \phi_i(x). \tag{3}$$

Thus, we can formulate non-rigid registration in the parametric form (2).

A main advantage of using Gaussian processes to model the deformations, is its flexibility. We can estimate its mean and covariance function from examples shapes to obtain a statistical model $\mathcal{GP}(\mu_{SM}, k_{SM})$ that incorporates shape constraints [1,12]. If we choose a zero mean and covariance function k_g that favors smooth functions, the resulting model $\mathcal{GP}(0, k_g)$ is generic and similar to models obtained by using differential operators as a regularizer [11]. The different mean and covariance functions can be combined, to construct a new Gaussian process $\mathcal{GP}(\mu_{SM}, k_D + k_{SM})$ that combines the characteristics of both models. Depending on the point of view, the resulting optimization problem can either be interpreted as a registration, which incorporates prior shape knowledge (see e.g. [17,18]) or as shape model fitting, which reduces the model bias [3,16]. In fact, this solution can be seen as an extension of the approach proposed by Wang et al. [16] for active shape models to statistical models with dense correspondence.

The use of Gaussian process models for non-rigid registration is not new. It has been extensively studied in the 90s by Grenander et al. (see the overview article [4] and references therein). Steinke et al. [13] later approached surface registration from a machine learning perspective, which led to a similar algorithm based on kernel methods. This approach was extended by Lüthi et al. [7] to a hybrid registration approach using Gaussian Process regression. The main novelty of our work is the use of the Nyström approximation to obtain a low-rank approximation of the Gaussian process. This allows us to derive an efficient numerical methods, for any covariance function that is sufficiently smooth, without requiring that the eigenfunctions are known analytically. In particular, this makes it possible to combine covariance functions for shape model fitting and non-rigid registration, which don't admit such an analytic form.

2 Background

2.1 Gaussian Processes

Stochastic processes allow us to define a probability distribution over a function space. Formally, a stochastic process is a collection of random variables $f(x), x \in \Omega$ where Ω is an index set. A Gaussian process is a stochastic process with the property that for any finite number of observations, $x_1, \ldots, x_n \in \Omega$ the values $f(x_1), \ldots, f(x_n)$ are jointly normally distributed [11]. A Gaussian process $\mathcal{GP}(\mu, k)$ is completely defined by its mean $\mu : \Omega \to \mathbb{R}$ and a covariance function $k : \Omega \times \Omega \to \mathbb{R}$. The covariance function $k(x, y)$ specifies for each pair of points x, y their covariance $E[f(x)f(y)]$. By specifying k, we define which functions are likely under the given process. Many known covariance functions imply a strong correlation between nearby values, which makes smooth functions more likely. Gaussian processes can also be used to model vector-valued functions. In this case, the covariance function becomes a matrix valued function $k(x, y) :$ $\Omega \times \Omega \to \mathbb{R}^{d \times d}$, with $k(x, y) = E[f(x)f(y)^T]$. The most simple case of matrix-valued covariance function arise when we assume that the output dimensions are uncorrelated. In this case, we can construct a matrix-valued covariance function k from a scalar-valued covariance-function l by setting

$$\mathbf{k}(x, y) = \mathcal{I}_{d \times d} l(x, y),$$

where $\mathcal{I}_{d \times d}$ is the identity matrix. While vector-valued Gaussian processes seem like an extension of the theory, it can be shown that it can be reduced to the scalar case [5]. Thus all known results for real-valued Gaussian processes carry over to this more general setting.

2.2 Mercer's Expansion and Reproducing Kernel Hilbert Spaces

Closely related to a Gaussian process $\mathcal{GP}(\mu, k)$ is the reproducing kernel Hilbert space (RKHS) spanned by its covariance function k. An easy way to construct this space is to start from the eigenfunction expansion of k. According to Mercer's theorem (see e.g. [11]), a kernel k has an expansion in terms of a orthonormal set of basis functions:

$$k(x, y) = \sum_{i=1}^{\infty} \lambda_i \phi_i(x) \phi_i(y)^T, \tag{4}$$

where (λ_i, ϕ_i) are the eigenvalue/eigenfunctions pairs of the integral operator $\mathcal{T}_k f(\cdot) := \int_{\Omega} k(x, \cdot) f(x) \, dx$. We can define a Hilbert space by taking linear combinations of these eigenfunctions: $f(x) = \sum_{i=1}^{N} \phi_i(x) \alpha_i$ with $\sum_{i=1}^{n} \alpha_i^2 / \lambda_i < \infty$. The inner product between two functions $f = \sum_{i=1} \alpha_i \phi_i$ and $g = \sum_{j=1} \beta_j \phi_j$ is defined by $\langle f, g \rangle_k = \sum_{i=1}^{\infty} \frac{\alpha_i \beta_i}{\lambda_i}$. Consequently, the norm becomes

$$\|f\|_k^2 = \langle f, f \rangle_k = \sum_{i=1}^{\infty} \frac{\alpha_i^2}{\lambda_i} \tag{5}$$

Note that the RKHS norm penalizes the eigenfunction components corresponding to small eigenvalues particularly strongly, a fact that we will use in Section 3.

2.3   The Nyström Approximation

To compute the eigenfunctions ϕ in the Mercer expansion (4), we use the Nyström approximation [11]. We randomly sample points $X = \{x_1, \ldots, x_N\}$, $x_l \in \Omega$ and perform a Monte Carlo integration of the eigenvalue equation:

$$\lambda_i \phi_i(x') = \int_\Omega k(x, x') \phi_i(x) \, dx \approx \frac{1}{N} \sum_{l=1}^{N} k(x_l, x') \phi_i(x_l),$$

which results in a matrix eigenvalue problem $K u_i = \lambda_i^{mat} u_i$. Here, $K_{il} = k(x_i, x_l)$ is the kernel matrix, u_i denotes the i-th eigenvector and λ_i^{mat} the corresponding eigenvalue. The eigenvalue λ_i^{mat} can be used as an approximation for λ_i. The eigenfunction ϕ_i in turn can be approximated using

$$\tilde{\phi}_i(x) = \frac{\sqrt{n}}{\lambda_i^{mat}} k_X(x) u_i \approx \phi_i(x)$$

with $k_X(x) = (k(x_1, x), \ldots, k(x_n, x))$.[1] In a practical implementation for image registration, it is computationally infeasible to explicitly compute $k_X(x')$ in every evaluation of ϕ_i. A suitable strategy, which we use in our method, is to pre-compute $\tilde{\phi}_i(x)$ for the points of a (possibly lower-resolution) image grid, and to use standard image interpolation to extend the values to the full image domain.

3   Registration Using a Low-Rank GP Model

The starting point for our method is the probabilistic formulation of the registration problem in [2]. The registration problem (1) is interpreted as the MAP estimation problem:

$$\arg \max_u p(u) p(I_T | I_R, u), \tag{6}$$

where $p(u) \propto \exp(-\mathcal{R}[u])$ is a Gaussian process prior over the admissible deformation fields and $p(I_T | I_R, u) \propto \exp(\eta^{-1} \mathcal{D}[I_R, I_T, u])$ is the likelihood. However, instead of specifying a regularization operator to define a Gaussian process, we model the mean μ and covariance function k directly. A MAP solution to (6) can be found by solving a minimization problem in the RKHS $\mathcal{F}_k$ defined by k (see e.g. [15] for details):

$$\arg \min_{u \in \mathcal{F}_k} \mathcal{D}[I_R, I_T, u] + \eta \|u\|_k^2, \tag{7}$$

where $\|\cdot\|_k$ denotes the RKHS norm. In the next step we construct a low-rank approximation defining an approximate kernel $\tilde{k}(x, x') = \sum_{i=1}^{n} \lambda_i \phi_i(x) \otimes \phi_i(x')$

---

[1] For the case of matrix-valued kernels, $k : \Omega \times \Omega \to \mathbb{R}^{d \times d}$, the matrices K and k_X become block matrices: $K \in \mathbb{R}^{nd \times nd}$ and $k_X \in \mathbb{R}^{nd \times d}$.

obtained as an eigenfunction expansion using the n largest eigenvalues. From (5) we see that the RKHS norm strongly penalizes components whose corresponding eigenvalue is small. Therefore, leaving out these components will have a negligible effect to the solution if the eigenvalues of the kernel k are quickly decreasing. Each deformation in the space modeled by the Gaussian process $\mathcal{GP}(\mu, \tilde{k})$ can now be written as the finite sum $u(x) = \mu(x) + \sum_{i=1}^{n} \alpha_i \phi_i(x)$. Thus, we can restate the problem in the parametric form

$$\underset{\alpha_1,\ldots,\alpha_n}{\arg\min} \mathcal{D}[I_R, I_T, \mu + \sum_{i=1}^{n} \alpha_i \phi_i] + \eta \sum_{i=1}^{n} \frac{\alpha_i^2}{\lambda_i}, \qquad (8)$$

which can be minimized using any optimization algorithm.

3.1   Surface Registration

So far we have presented our method in the context of image registration. However, the approach is more general and the Gaussian process that defines the deformation model can be defined on arbitrary domains. Thus, we can define an algorithm for surface registration, by specifying the deformation model $\mathcal{GP}(\mu, k)$ on a reference surface $\Gamma_R \subset \mathbb{R}^d$. A simple formulation of the surface registration problem, which we use in this paper, is

$$\underset{\alpha_1,\ldots,\alpha_n}{\arg\min} \sum_{x_j \in \Gamma_R} D_T(x_j + \mu(x_j) + \sum_{i=0}^{n} \alpha_i \phi_i(x_j))^2 + \eta \sum_{i=1}^{n} \frac{\alpha_i^2}{\lambda_i}, \qquad (9)$$

where D_T is a distance map defined for Γ_T.

4   Results

In this section we illustrate how our approach can be used to reduce the bias in statistical shape model fitting and show its feasibility for the use in 3D image registration. Our implementation uses the Statismo framework [8] for representing the Gaussian processes. Surface Registration is done using ITK[2] while for image registration we use Elastix [6]. Our implementation is freely available as part of Statismo[3]. For all the examples, we use a sum of squares distance metric and an LBFGS optimizer.

Shape Model Fitting. For our first experiment we used random face surfaces, which were generated using the Basel face model [10]. We sampled 60 faces as a training set to build a statistical shape model, and used 40 additional samples as a test set. We compared the fitting performance for four different models: 1) A shape model from all the samples, which we use as a ground truth, 2) A shape model obtained from the training data, which we denote by

---

[2] "The Insight Segmentation and Registration Toolkit" - http://www.itk.org

[3] "Statismo" - http://www.statismo.org

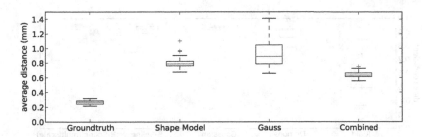

Fig. 1. Fitting results of different models to a set of 40 test surfaces. The shape model has a considerable bias. Combining it with a Gaussian with large bandwidth (which itself does not give good fitting results) helps to reduce the bias.

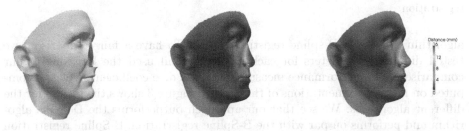

Fig. 2. A fitting result of a Gaussian model (middle) and a combined model (right) to a dataset with artifacts. Due to the shape constraint, the combined model preserves the nose shape better than the Gaussian model.

$\mathcal{GP}_{SM}(\mu_{SM}, k_{SM})$, 3) a model $\mathcal{GP}_G(0, k_G)$, with a Gaussian kernel $k_g(x, x') = \exp(\|x - x'/\sigma^2\|^2)$ ($\sigma = 100$), which is used to model the bias, 4) a combined model $\mathcal{GP}_C(\mu_{SM}, k_{SM} + k_G)$. Figure 1 shows the result of the four different fits obtained by minimizing (9). We observe that the shape model that was built from the training data only is biased and cannot accurately represent the faces. Due to the large bandwidth of the Gaussian kernel, also the Gaussian model cannot represent the faces accurately. However, combining them clearly reduces the bias of the shape model. In the second experiment we show how a registration method can be made more robust by including shape information. To simulate an artifact, we cut off the nose of one of the test faces (Figure 2a). We fit a Gaussian model (with $\sigma = 50$) and a combination of the shape model with this Gaussian model. Figure 2 shows that the combination of both models yields a smaller error around the nose, compared to using only the Gaussian model.

Registration of CT Data. In this experiment we use our method for the registration of CT images of dry femur bones, with a resolution of $176 \times 163 \times 622$. We select a reference image and perform a registration to 27 test images. As a deformation model, we used a zero mean Gaussian process with a Gaussian kernel ($\sigma^2 = 100$). We computed a low-rank approximation using the first 300 eigenfunctions. We compare the registration performance with the standard Demons

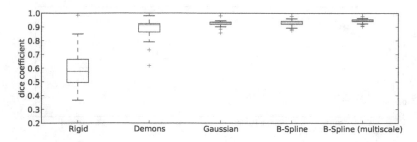

Fig. 3. Registration result achieved on a set of 27 femur images for different methods. The registration performance is measured by computing the dice coefficient of a ground-truth segmentation. As a baseline, we use a simple rigid registration (left). Our method (Gaussian) yields comparable performance to a standard B-spline and Demons registration.

algorithm [14] and a B-spline registration [12]. To have a fair comparison, we tested different parameters for each algorithm and used the best one in our comparison. As a performance measure, we use a dice coefficient, which is computed on manual segmentations of the images. Figure 3 shows the results for the different algorithms: We see that our approach outperforms the Demons algorithm and performs on par with the B-Spline registration. B-Spline registration perform, however, slightly better when a multi-scale strategy is used. This is expected, as the simple Gaussian kernel that we use only models deformations on a single scale. In order to obtain more flexible representation, more sophisticated kernels, such as e.g. the multi-scale kernel proposed in [9], can be used.

5   Conclusion

We have presented a unified approach to non-rigid registration and statistical model fitting. This is achieved by modeling the admissible deformations as a Gaussian process, which is fitted to the data. We compute a low-rank approximation using the Nyström method, and formulate registration as a parametric optimization problem. This makes our method computationally feasible even for large 3D images. We have shown that by combining kernels for non-rigid registration and shape modeling, we can reduce the bias of statistical shape models, or make non-rigid registration more robust. The main strength of our approach is that it makes it possible to use any sufficiently smooth kernel function to specify the admissible deformations. This gives us enormous flexibility to model our prior assumptions, while the algorithmic implementation remains the same. We believe that using more sophisticated prior models, such as a kernel for hybrid landmark and image registration [7], or the multi-scale kernel [9], we can obtain very powerful methods for non-rigid registration and model-fitting.

References

1. Blanz, V., Vetter, T.: A morphable model for the synthesis of 3D faces. In: SIGGRAPH 1999: Proceedings of the 26th Annual Conference on Computer Graphics and Interactive Techniques, pp. 187–194. ACM Press (1999)
2. Christensen, G.E., Miller, M.I., Vannier, M.W., Grenander, U.: Individualizing neuro-anatomical atlases using a massively parallel computer. Computer 29(1), 32–38 (1996)
3. Cootes, T.F., Taylor, C.J.: Combining point distribution models with shape models based on finite element analysis. Image and Vision Computing 13(5) (1995)
4. Grenander, U., Miller, M.I.: Computational anatomy: An emerging discipline. Quarterly of Applied Mathematics 56(4), 617–694 (1998)
5. Hein, M., Bousquet, O.: Kernels, associated structures and generalizations. Max-Planck-Institut fuer biologische Kybernetik, Technical Report (2004)
6. Klein, S., Staring, M., Pluim, J.P.: Evaluation of optimization methods for non-rigid medical image registration using mutual information and b-splines. IEEE Transactions on Image Processing 16(12), 2879–2890 (2007)
7. Lüthi, M., Jud, C., Vetter, T.: Using landmarks as a deformation prior for hybrid image registration. Pattern Recognition, 196–205 (2011)
8. Lüthi, M., Blanc, R., Albrecht, T., Gass, T., Goksel, O., Büchler, P., Kistler, M., Bousleiman, H., Reyes, M., Cattin, P.C., et al.: Statismo-a framework for pca based statistical models (2012)
9. Opfer, R.: Multiscale kernels. Advances in Computational Mathematics 25(4), 357–380 (2006)
10. Paysan, P., Knothe, R., Amberg, B., Romdhani, S., Vetter, T.: A 3D face model for pose and illumination invariant face recognition. In: Advanced Video and Signal Based Surveillance 2009, pp. 296–301 (2009)
11. Rasmussen, C.E., Williams, C.K.: Gaussian processes for machine learning. Springer (2006)
12. Rueckert, D., Frangi, A.F., Schnabel, J.A.: Automatic construction of 3D statistical deformation models using non-rigid registration. In: Niessen, W.J., Viergever, M.A. (eds.) MICCAI 2001. LNCS, vol. 2208, pp. 77–84. Springer, Heidelberg (2001)
13. Schölkopf, B., Steinke, F., Blanz, V.: Object correspondence as a machine learning problem. In: ICML 2005: Proceedings of the 22nd International Conference on Machine Learning, pp. 776–783. ACM Press, New York (2005)
14. Thirion, J.P.: Image matching as a diffusion process: an analogy with Maxwell's demons. Medical Image Analysis 2(3), 243–260 (1998)
15. Wahba, G.: Spline models for observational data. Society for Industrial Mathematics (1990)
16. Wang, Y., Staib, L.H.: Boundary finding with prior shape and smoothness models. IEEE Transactions on Pattern Analysis and Machine Intelligence 22(7) (2000)
17. Wang, Y., Staib, L.H.: Physical model-based non-rigid registration incorporating statistical shape information. Medical Image Analysis 4(1), 7–20 (2000)
18. Xue, Z., Shen, D., Davatzikos, C.: Statistical representation of high-dimensional deformation fields with application to statistically constrained 3D warping. Medical Image Analysis 10(5), 740–751 (2006)

A Bayesian Algorithm for Image-Based Time-to-Event Prediction

Mert R. Sabuncu*

A.A. Martinos Center for Biomedical Imaging, MGH, Harvard Medical School

Abstract. This paper presents a novel Bayesian algorithm for making image-based predictions of the timing of a clinical event, such as the diagnosis of disease or death. We build on the Relevance Voxel Machine (RVoxM) framework, a Bayesian multivariate prediction model that exploits the spatial smoothness in images and has been demonstrated to offer excellent predictive accuracy for clinical variables. We utilize the classical survival analysis approach to model the dynamic risk of the event of interest, while accounting for the limited follow-up-time, i.e. censoring of the training data. We instantiate the proposed algorithm (RVoxM-S) to analyze cortical thickness maps derived from structural brain Magnetic Resonance Imaging (MRI) data. We train RVoxM-S to make predictions about the timing of the conversion from Mild Cognitive Impairment (MCI) status to clinical dementia of the Alzheimer type (or AD). Our experiments demonstrate that RVoxM-S is significantly better at identifying subjects at high risk of conversion to AD over the next two years, compared to a binary classification algorithm trained to discriminate converters versus non-converters.

Keywords: Multivariate Pattern Analysis, Survival Models, Time-to-event prediction, MRI

1 Introduction

Clinical events, such as death, stroke, cardiac arrest or the diagnosis of disease, represent significant milestones in a subject's health history. Many researchers have developed methods for predicting the timing of a possible *future* event and/or examining the associations between the event and clinical risk factors *prior* to the event, e.g. [1–3]. Survival models provide a powerful framework for developing such models and identifying these associations [4].

Thanks to medical imaging, we continue to discover neuro-anatomical variation associated with clinical conditions. For example, conventional mass-univariate approaches, such as voxel-based morphometry [5] or cortical thickness analysis [6], can generate anatomical maps of atrophy associated with disease. On the other hand, multivariate pattern analysis (MVPA) methods, can dramatically increase

---

* Supported by NIH NIBIB 1K25EB013649-01 and a BrightFocus Alzheimer's pilot grant (AHAF-A2012333). Data used were obtained from the Alzheimer's Disease Neuroimaging Initiative (ADNI): http://tinyurl.com/ADNI-main.

G. Wu et al. (Eds.): MLMI 2013, LNCS 8184, pp. 74–81, 2013.

the specificity and sensitivity for predicting a clinical condition of interest by considering all voxels *simultaneously* [7–13]. Yet, most of these prior studies have focused on relating the image content to the *present* condition and not dealt with the problem of predicting the timing of a *future* event.

Survival analysis is a statistical approach that focuses on modeling the dynamic risk of an event, e.g., death (hence the term survival) [4], and includes popular methods such as proportional hazards regression [14]. It offers two advantages over more classical methods. First, in contrast with a classification formulation that would divide the data into two classes (survivors versus non-survivors), survival models explicitly account for the finite duration of the study (also called censoring). That is, subjects who haven't experienced the event yet are not arbitrarily classified as survivors, since there is still the probability that they might do so in the future. Secondly, they further model the variation in the observed survival times. Survival models have recently been employed in neuroimaging studies [15, 16] and yielded novel clinical insights.

In this paper, we present an extension of the Relevance Voxel Machine (RVoxM), a Bayesian MVPA algorithm that is designed to make image-based predictions [12]. Specifically, we replace the likelihood model in RVoxM with a classical parametric survival model. We call this extension RVoxM-S. The proposed algorithm is similar in spirit to other MVPA algorithms that employ survival models, such as [17,18]. To our knowledge, however, RVoxM-S is the first MVPA algorithm that is developed for making *image-based* predictions of the timing of a *future* (clinical) event of interest.

We tested RVoxM-S on the problem of predicting the timing of clinical diagnosis of Alzheimer's disease (AD) in subjects with Mild Cognitive Impairment (MCI). We instantiated RVoxM-S to make this prediction based on cortical thickness data obtained from a baseline structural brain MRI scan. Our experiments demonstrate that, in the considered set-up, a survival model can be more powerful than a classification model in identifying subjects that are at high risk of converting within a finite time-frame, e.g., two years from baseline.

2 Materials and Methods

2.1 Data

In our experiments, we analyzed the publicly available Alzheimer's Disease Neuroimaging Initiative (ADNI) dataset[1], which consisted of over 800 subjects. At recruitment, about a quarter of the subjects were categorized as cognitively healthy; another quarter as AD patients, and the remaining half as amnestic MCI – a transitionary, clinically defined pre-AD stage. Most subjects were clinically followed up every six months, starting from a baseline clinical assessment.

In this study, we focused on the MCI subjects, some of which were eventually diagnosed with clinical AD during the follow-up period. We processed the baseline structural MRI scans of these subjects with FreeSurfer [19, 20], which

---

[1] For detailed information, visit http://www.adni-info.org/

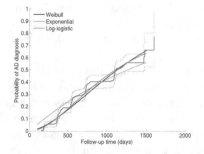

Fig. 1. Parametric and non-parametric (blue, step-like curve) estimates of the cumulative distribution function of MCI to AD conversion. Dashed lines show the 95% confidence of the non-parametric (Kaplan-Meier) curve.

Table 1. The number of converter (Conv) and non-converter (Non-conv) MCIs at each visit (mo: month). The time information is the average and standard deviation of the actual visit times as measured from baseline (in days).

Visit (mo)	Conv	Non-conv	Time
0	227	166	0
6	194	161	191 ± 43
12	177	153	373 ± 35
18	153	136	564 ± 49
24	108	106	757 ± 69
36	68	70	1115 ± 70
48	3	10	1480 ± 39

automatically computes subject-specific models of the cortical surface and thickness measurements across the entire cortical mantle [6]. Subject-level thickness measurements were then sampled on a common coordinate system, represented as a icosohedron-based triangulation of the sphere, via a surface-based nonlinear registration procedure [21], and analyzed by the MVPA models. We utilized the so-called *fsaverage5* representation, consisting of over 20,000 vertices between the two hemispheres with an inter-vertex distance of approximately 4 mm.

There were 393 MCI subjects that were classified as MCI at baseline and had MRI scans that were successfully processed with FreeSurfer. 166 of these cases converted to clinical AD during the follow-up period, which is a maximum of 4.5 years. Of the 227 non-converters, there was a significant variation in their follow-up data. For example, over 30 "non-convervter" MCI subjects were never clinically evaluated beyond the baseline and an additional 20 or so MCIs dropped out after their 6 month visit (see Table 1). Furthermore, there is a significant variation in the timing of the follow-up visits: a 6-month visit can be anywhere between 75-320 days after the baseline. Figure 1 plots the non-parametric (Kaplan-Meier) estimate of the cumulative distribution function of MCI to AD conversion.

2.2   Parametric Survival Models

Survival models provide a powerful framework for studying longitudinal follow-up data and relating independent variables to the timing of an event of interest [4]. In this study, our goal was to adopt the likelihood models commonly used in survival analysis within the Relevance Voxel Machine (RVoxM). We considered three possible parametric distributions: Weibull, exponential and log-logistic [22]. To choose the best one that was suitable for the application of interest, namely predicting MCI to AD conversion, we conducted a preliminary analysis by fitting the three models to the MCI survival data. This analysis revealed that log-logistic yielded the most appropriate model (see Fig. 1). The Akaike Information Criteria, AIC, for the three models were: 680k (Weibull), 620k(exponential) and 610k (log-logistic). Thus, we employed the log-logistic model in the RVoxM likelihood, which has the following cumulative distribution function:

$$P(T \leq t) = \frac{1}{1 + (t/a)^b},$$ (1)

where $a > 0$ is the scale parameter, $b > 0$ is the shape parameter, and T is the random variable that represents the time of the event. Note the median of T is equal to a.

2.3 The Relevance Voxel Machine Survival Model: RVoxM-S

The RVoxM [12] is a Bayesian inference algorithm that builds on Tipping's Relevance Vector Machine (RVM) framework [23] to obtain sparse solutions. To exploit the spatial smoothness in image data, RVoxM modifies the sparsity inducing prior of RVM with a Laplacian that encourages neighboring voxels to have a similar contribution to the prediction. RVoxM-S, the proposed method, replaces the RVoxM likelihood model with a parametric survival function. Let's now describe the model and inference strategy in more detail.

We assume that each subject, indexed with i, has an associated event time window, denoted with $(t_{i1}, t_{i2}]$ during which the event of interest (e.g. disease onset) occurs. For example, if we have observed the subject up to two years, and the subject has never experienced the event, the corresponding event time window is $(2y, \infty]$. On the other hand, if the subject is diagnosed at the 2 year visit and their previous visit was at year 1, the window is $(1y, 2y]$. Using the log-logistic model of Eq. 1, the log-likelihood of each subject can be written as:

$$\begin{aligned} l(t_{i1}, t_{i2}) &= \log P(t_{i1} < T_i \leq t_{i2}) \\ &= b \log(a_i) + \log(1 - t_{2i}^{-b} t_{1i}^b) - \log(a_i^b + t_{1i}^b) - \log(a_i^b t_{2i}^{-b} + 1), \end{aligned}$$ (2)

where $a_i > 0$ is a subject-specific scale parameter. Note that if the subject has not experienced the event during the finite follow-up period, i.e., $t_{2i} = \infty$, then the second and fourth terms in Eq. 2 disappear. Furthermore, if the same subject was not observed beyond the baseline, the corresponding log-likelihood is fixed to zero, i.e., $l(0, \infty) = 0$.

Each subject has an associated image, which we represent as a vector $\mathbf{x_i} = (1, x^1, \cdots, x^M)^\mathrm{T}$. Note M is the number of voxels and for notational convenience, we include an extra "voxel" to account for the bias. We define

$$a_i = \exp(\mathbf{w}^\mathrm{T} \mathbf{x_i}),$$ (3)

where $\mathbf{w} = (w^0 \cdots w^M)^\mathrm{T}$ are adjustable "weights" encoding the strength of each voxel's contribution to the prediction.

Given the subject-specific parameters, we assume each subject is independent. Given N subjects and defining $y_i = b\mathbf{w}^\mathrm{T}\mathbf{x_i}$, the total data log-likelihood can be written as:

$$\mathcal{L}(\{y_i, (t_{i1}, t_{i2}]\}, b) = \sum_{i=1}^{N} y_i + \log(1 - t_{2i}^{-b}t_{1i}^{b}) - \log(\exp(y_i) + t_{1i}^{b}) - \log(\exp(y_i)t_{2i}^{-b} + 1). \quad (4)$$

As in the RVoxM model, we assume a zero-mean Gaussian prior distribution over $\mathbf{w}$, with a precision (inverse covariance) matrix $\mathbf{P}$ that encourages sparse and spatially clustered non-zero weights. In particular, we write this prior as:

$$p(\mathbf{w}|\boldsymbol{\alpha}, \lambda) \propto \exp\left(-\frac{1}{2}\sum_{i=0}^{M}\alpha_i w_i^2 - \frac{\lambda}{2}\|\boldsymbol{\Upsilon}\mathbf{w}\|^2\right),$$

where $\boldsymbol{\alpha} = (\alpha_0, \cdots, \alpha_M)^\mathrm{T}$ and λ are *hyperparameters*, and $\boldsymbol{\Upsilon}$ is a sparse matrix in which each row corresponds to a pair of neighboring voxels in the image. For neighboring voxels $\{i, j\}$, the corresponding row has zero entries everywhere except for the ith and j^th column, which have entries -1 and 1, respectively.

2.4   Training the RVoxM-S

Given training data in the form of a set of N subjects $\{\mathbf{x}_i, (t_{i1}, t_{i2}]\}_{i=1}^N$, where $\mathbf{x}_i$ represents the ith training image and $(t_{i1}, t_{i2}]$ is the corresponding event time window, our first goal is to determine the values of the hyperparameters $\boldsymbol{\alpha}$, λ, and b. Let $\mathbf{X}$ denote the $N \times (M+1)$ matrix that concatenates the image data and $\mathbf{T} = [\mathbf{t_1t_2}]$ denote the $N \times 2$ matrix of times. Using type-II maximum likelihood, we estimate the hyperparameters by maximizing the marginal likelihood function obtained by integrating out $\mathbf{w}$:

$$p(\mathbf{T}|\mathbf{X}, \boldsymbol{\alpha}, \lambda, b) = \int_{\mathbf{w}} \exp(\sum_{i=1}^{N} l(t_{i1}, t_{i2}))p(\mathbf{w}|\boldsymbol{\alpha}, \lambda)d\mathbf{w} \propto \int_{\mathbf{w}} \exp(f(\mathbf{w}))d\mathbf{w}, \quad (5)$$

$$\approx \exp(f(\hat{\mathbf{w}}))\sqrt{\frac{2\pi}{|\mathbf{H}|}} \quad (6)$$

where $l(t_{i1}, t_{i2})$ is defined in Eq. 2, $f(\mathbf{w}) = \sum_{i=1}^{N} l(t_{i1}, t_{i2}) - \frac{1}{2}\sum_{i=0}^{M}\alpha_i w_i^2 - \frac{\lambda}{2}\|\boldsymbol{\Upsilon}\mathbf{w}\|^2$,

$$\hat{\mathbf{w}} = \underset{\mathbf{w}}{\arg\max} f(\mathbf{w}), \quad (7)$$

$\mathbf{H} = \mathbf{P} + \mathbf{X}'\mathbf{B}\mathbf{X}$, $\mathbf{B} = \mathrm{diag}\left(b^2 \exp(y_i)\left(\frac{1}{(t_{1i}^{b} + \exp(y_i))^2} + \frac{t_{2i}^{-b}}{(t_{2i}^{-b}\exp(y_i) + 1)^2}\right)\right)$ is a $N \times N$ diagonal matrix, and $|\cdot|$ denotes the matrix determinant. Note, Eq. 6 uses the Laplace approximation to compute the intractable integration over $\mathbf{w}$.

We used the numerical optimization strategies employed in the RVoxM classification algorithm [12]. The RVoxM-S training algorithm iterates between updating the hyper-parameters $\boldsymbol{\alpha}$, λ, and b by maximizing the logarithm of Eq. 6

using a coordinate-ascent strategy and solving for $\hat{\mathbf{w}}$ based on Eq. 7. Given a new training image $\mathbf{x}_{N+1}$, we predict the median time of event as $\exp(\hat{\mathbf{w}}^T \mathbf{x}_{N+1})$.

3 Experimental Results

We conducted a 5-fold cross-validation analysis on the ADNI MCI subjects. In each fold, we employed about four fifths of the MCI subjects to train two separate models, both of which used the same cortical thickness measurements computed from the corresponding baseline MRI scans as the input image data. The first method was the proposed RVoxM-S model trained to predict the time of MCI-to-AD conversion, and thus the provided target labels were the event time window for each subject: for converter MCIs, this corresponded to the timing of the visit at which the AD diagnosis happened and the timing of the previous visit. For non-converter MCIs, the event time window was input as the timing of the last clinical visit and ∞. The second model, our benchmark, was a standard binary RVoxM classification algorithm trained to discriminate converters versus non-converters. This binary discrimination strategy has been proposed in the literature to separate these two groups, e.g. [24]. Once the training was complete, we computed a prediction for each test subject. For RVoxM-S, the prediction was the median time-to-event and for the classification model it was the probability of conversion. Both these predictions can be considered to reflect the AD-risk for that individual.

We first stratified all MCI subjects into two equally-sized groups for each model based on their corresponding AD-risk scores (AD probability or predicted median time-to-diagnosis). For each of these groups, we then computed the non-parametric (Kaplan-Meier) cumulative distribution functions of AD diagnosis. As Fig. 2 illustrates, the stratification based on RVoxM-S provides a better separation between the survival curves of each group (note the significant overlap between the confidence intervals of the two groups' diagnosis functions for the classification case, shown on the left). In fact, for the RVoxM-S stratification, the fraction of high-risk subjects who converted to AD within two years from baseline was 42% as opposed to the low-risk group, which had a 28% two-year conversion rate. These numbers were 32% and 38% for the classification algorithm.

Finally, we used the AD-risk scores to predict whether a MCI subject would convert or not within the follow-up period. We assigned a binary label (converter versus non-converter) to each subject and thresholded their AD-risk score to classify. By varying the threshold we obtained the Receiver Operating Characteristic (ROC) curve for the corresponding model (see Fig. 3). The area under the curve was 0.62 for the RVoxM-S prediction and 0.59 for the RVoxM binary classifier. These results suggest that the RVoxM-S model can potentially discriminate converter and non-converter MCIs better than a binary classifier, even if it is not directly trained to achieve this goal. One reason for this improvement in prediction performance is probably because the classification algorithm might be relying on noisy labels: non-converters who are likely to convert soon but haven't done so within the follow-up period.

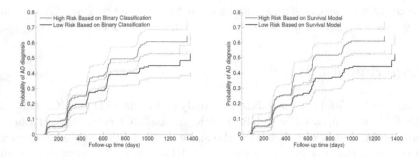

Fig. 2. Non-parametric estimates of the cumulative distribution function of MCI to AD conversion. Dashed lines show the 95% confidence of the non-parametric curve. Left: stratification based on the binary classifier, right: stratification based on RVoxM-S.

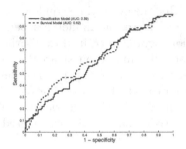

Fig. 3. ROC curves for discriminating converters versus non-converters

4   Conclusion

We proposed a novel Bayesian framework for image-based prediction of the time to a clinical event. Our method builds on the Relevance Voxel Machine framework and replaces the likelihood function with a parametric survival model. Survival models exploit the variation of the event time in non-survivors and account for the censorship in data due to finite follow-up. We instantiated the proposed algorithm, RVoxM-S, to make predictions about MCI-to-AD conversion based on cortical thickness data computed from a baseline structural brain MRI scan. Our experiments demonstrated that the survival modeling approach can improve our ability to identify subjects who are at a high risk of experiencing the event (e.g. diagnosis) within a certain time period. Future work will examine alternative approaches, such as a penalized Cox regression model, and other optimization and approximation strategies within the RVoxM framework.

References

1. Anderson, K.M., Odell, P.M., Wilson, P.W.F., Kannel, W.B.: Cardiovascular disease risk profiles. American Heart Journal 121(1), 293–298 (1991)
2. Wang, T.J., et al.: Multiple biomarkers for the prediction of first major cardiovascular events and death. New England Journal of Medicine 355(25) (2006)

3. Kamath, P.S., et al.: A model to predict survival in patients with end-stage liver disease. Hepatology 33(2) (2001)
4. Collett, D.: Modelling survival data in medical research, vol. 57. CRC Press (2003)
5. Ashburner, J., Friston, K.J.: Voxel-based morphometry–the methods. Neuroimage 11(6), 805–821 (2000)
6. Fischl, B., Dale, A.M.: Measuring the thickness of the human cerebral cortex from magnetic resonance images. PNAS 97(20), 11050 (2000)
7. Cox, D.D., Savoy, R.L.: Functional magnetic resonance imaging (fMRI) "brain reading": detecting and classifying distributed patterns of fMRI activity in human visual cortex. Neuroimage 19(2), 261–270 (2003)
8. Davatzikos, C., et al.: Detection of prodromal Alzheimer's disease via pattern classification of magnetic resonance imaging. Neurobiology of Aging 29(4) (2008)
9. Fan, Y., Batmanghelich, N., Clark, C.M., Davatzikos, C.: Spatial patterns of brain atrophy in MCI patients, identified via high-dimensional pattern classification, predict subsequent cognitive decline. Neuroimage 39(4), 1731–1743 (2008)
10. Klöppel, S., et al.: Automatic classification of MR scans in Alzheimer's disease. Brain 131(3) (2008)
11. Pohl, K.M., Sabuncu, M.R.: A unified framework for MR based disease classification. In: Prince, J.L., Pham, D.L., Myers, K.J. (eds.) IPMI 2009. LNCS, vol. 5636, pp. 300–313. Springer, Heidelberg (2009)
12. Sabuncu, M., Van Leemput, K.: The relevance voxel machine (rvoxm): A self-tuning bayesian model for informative image-based prediction. IEEE TMI 31(12) (2012)
13. Cuingnet, R., et al.: Spatial prior in SVM-based classification of brain images. In: Proceedings of SPIE, vol. 7624, p. 76241L (2010)
14. Cox, D.R., Oakes, D.: Analysis of survival data, vol. 21. Chapman & Hall/CRC (1984)
15. Desikan, R.S., et al.: Temporoparietal mr imaging measures of atrophy in subjects with mild cognitive impairment that predict subsequent diagnosis of Alzheimer disease. American Journal of Neuroradiology 30(3) (2009)
16. Vemuri, P., et al.: Time to event voxel-based techniques to assess regional atrophy associated with mci risk of progression to ad. Neuroimage 54(2) (2011)
17. Tibshirani, R., et al.: The lasso method for variable selection in the cox model. Statistics in Medicine 16(4), 385–395 (1997)
18. Gui, J., Li, H.: Penalized cox regression analysis in the high-dimensional and low-sample size settings, with applications to microarray gene expression data. Bioinformatics 21(13), 3001–3008 (2005)
19. Dale, A.M., Fischl, B., Sereno, M.I.: Cortical surface-based analysis I: Segmentation and surface reconstruction. Neuroimage 9(2), 179–194 (1999)
20. Fischl, B., Sereno, M.I., Dale, A.M.: Cortical surface-based analysis II: Inflation, flattening, and a surface-based coordinate system. Neuroimage 9(2), 195–207 (1999)
21. Fischl, B., Sereno, M.I., Tootell, R.B.H., Dale, A.M.: High-resolution intersubject averaging and a coordinate system for the cortical surface. Human Brain Mapping 8(4), 272–284 (1999)
22. Johnson, N.L., Kotz, S., Balakrishnan, N.: Continuous univariate distributions, vol. 1 (1994)
23. Tipping, M.E.: Sparse Bayesian learning and the relevance vector machine. Journal of Machine Learning Research 1, 211–244 (2001)
24. Cuingnet, R., et al.: Automatic classification of patients with Alzheimer's disease from structural mri: A comparison of ten methods using the adni database. Neuroimage 56(2) (2011)

Patient-Specific Manifold Embedding of Multispectral Images Using Kernel Combinations

Veronika A.M. Zimmer[1], Roger Fonolla[1], Karim Lekadir[1], Gemma Piella[1], Corné Hoogendoorn[1], and Alejandro F. Frangi[1,2]

[1] CISTIB, Information and Communication Technologies Department,
Universitat Pompeu Fabra, Barcelona, Spain
[2] CISTIB, Department of Mechanical Engineering,
The University of Sheffield, United Kingdom

Abstract. This paper presents a framework that optimizes kernel-based manifold embedding for the characterization of multispectral image data. The hypothesis is that data manifolds corresponding to high-dimensional images can have varying characteristics and types of nonlinearity. As a result, kernel functions must be selected from a wide range of transformations and tuned on an image- and patient-basis. To this end, we introduce a new measure to assess the quality of the kernel transformations that takes into account both local and global relationships in nonlinear manifolds. Furthermore, the calculated measures for each kernel are used to combine the different kernel transformations further highlight the tissue constituents in all regions of the image. Validation with phantom and real multispectral image data shows improvement in the visualization and characterization of the tissue constituents.

1 Introduction

With the increasing capabilities of imaging hardware and sequence designs, multispectral imaging has gained significant popularity for the characterization of biomedical tissues. By varying the acquisition parameters, one can obtain a contrast mechanism through which each image spectrum highlights different constituents and properties of the tissue. However, the obtained image stack introduces a complex high-dimensional manifold which can have varying characteristics and types of nonlinearity depending on the image, patient and pathology. Therefore, manifold embedding techniques are required such that they can adapt to each dataset, with the aim to obtain optimal tissue characterization of the multispectral images. To achieve this, kernel techniques are powerful candidates due to their ability to use different kernel transformations [2], which can be a significant benefit for patient-specific multispectral image analysis. In practice, however, the flexibility offered by kernel-techniques is not fully exploited due to the difficulty to choose an appropriate kernel for each individual dataset. As a result, the Gaussian and polynomial functions remain largely the kernels of choice in medical image computing. Yet, depending on the tissue and pathology under investigation, these kernels might not adequately discriminate all tissue

G. Wu et al. (Eds.): MLMI 2013, LNCS 8184, pp. 82–89, 2013.

constituents. Also, the associated free parameters are generally empirically defined and hard-coded for an entire application, which can potential generate suboptimal results and loss of discriminative information. A potential solution would be to measure the quality of the manifold embedding but the existing literature on the subject is limited for medical image data. Amongst recent works, a nonparametric measure of the preservation of the local relationships in the manifold was presented in [1] but it cannot detect potential global distortions of the original manifold. In contrast, the distance rank correlation measure in [4] considers the global structure of the data manifold but it is based on the Euclidean metric. Alternatively, an efficient training-based approach was proposed in [6], through which the best kernels are selected as those that optimize class separation. However, this requires labeled multispectral images which are not always available in practice. The aim of this paper is to present a workflow that addresses the limitations described above, such that the flexibility of kernel techniques is fully exploited to obtain patient-specific tissue characterization with multispectral images. We first review and implement a set of advanced kernels commonly developed in the machine learning community. We then introduce a new assessment metric that estimates the effectiveness of the kernel transformations for each individual image, such that both local and global information are taken into account. Subsequently, the calculated indices are used to combine different kernels in a single dimensionality reduction stage, with the aim to further increase the discrimination of the tissue constituents. Finally, we validate the proposed kernel optimization framework based on synthetic and real multispectral image datasets of different nature (microscopic and macroscopic) and modalities (optical, fluorescence, MRI).

2 Methods

2.1 Kernel Functions

Kernel principal component analysis (kPCA) [2] is a widely used nonlinear dimensionality reduction technique. Through the well-known kernel trick, the data points are mapped in terms of their inner products into a feature space where linear PCA can be performed. The main advantage of kPCA is its ability to use various kernel mappings and thus to potential adapt to different types of nonlinearity. In medical image computing, however, kernel manifold embedding is mostly performed using standard kernels such as the Gaussian and polynomial, which can lead to suboptimal results. In order to improve the tissue characterization, this paper presents a workflow to fully exploit the flexibility property of kPCA, by optimizing the kernel transformations on an image and patient basis. To this end, the list of kernel candidates must be exhaustive and thus we review in this section a set of advanced kernels (see Tab. 1) that can be used to unfold the nonlinear data manifold. Since the type of nonlinearity at hand is unknown

Table 1. Examples of kernel functions

Kernel name	Formula	Parameter
Translation invariant wavelet	$\prod_{i=1}^{p} h\left(\frac{x_i - y_i}{\alpha}\right)$, $h(x) = \cos(1.75x)\exp(-\frac{x^2}{2})$	α
ANOVA	$\sum_{i=1}^{p} \exp\left(-\alpha\left(x_i - y_i\right)^2\right)^{\gamma}$	α, γ
Circular	$\frac{2}{\pi}\arccos\left(-\frac{\|\mathbf{x}-\mathbf{y}\|}{\sigma}\right) - \frac{2}{\pi}\frac{\|\mathbf{x}-\mathbf{y}\|}{\sigma}\sqrt{1 - \left(\frac{\|\mathbf{x}-\mathbf{y}\|}{\sigma}\right)^2}$ if $\|\mathbf{x} - \mathbf{y}\| < \sigma$, 0 otherwise	σ
Gaussian	$\exp\left(-\frac{\|\mathbf{x}-\mathbf{y}\|^2}{2\sigma^2}\right)$	σ
Laplacian	$\exp\left(-\frac{\|\mathbf{x}-\mathbf{y}\|}{\sigma}\right)$	σ
Log	$-\log\left(\|\mathbf{x} - \mathbf{y}\|^{\gamma} + 1\right)$	γ
Multiquadratic	$\sqrt{\|\mathbf{x} - \mathbf{y}\|^2 + \beta^2}$	β
Wave	$\frac{\sigma}{\|\mathbf{x}-\mathbf{y}\|}\sin\left(\frac{\|\mathbf{x}-\mathbf{y}\|}{\sigma}\right)$	σ
Generalized histogram intersection	$\sum_{i=1}^{p} \min\left(|x_i|^{\alpha}, |y_i|^{\beta}\right)$	α, β
Linear	$\mathbf{x}^T\mathbf{y}$	
Polynomial	$\left(\alpha\mathbf{x}^T\mathbf{y} + \beta\right)^{\gamma}$	α, β, γ
Sigmoid	$\tanh\left(\alpha\mathbf{x}^T\mathbf{y} + \beta\right)$	α, β

in advance, we introduce in the next section a measure to assess the efficiency of each kernel transformation for a given multispectral image data.

2.2   Optimal Kernel Selection

Unlike existing techniques, the proposed optimal kernel selection method is unsupervised (no training or labeled data is required) and takes both local and global relationships into account. The key idea behind the introduced kernel score is that tissue similarities and dissimilarities are well preserved after the manifold embedding if the neighborhoods in the multispectral space are consistently mapped onto the low dimensional space. In other words, two distinct tissue constituents that are not adequately separated after manifold embedding would intrude each other in the new space. Let $\mathbf{x}_i$ be the coordinates of a data point p_i in the original space X^p, $\mathbf{y}_i$ its coordinates in the new space Y^q and $I_k^{\mathbf{X}}(i)$ the sets of indices of its k-NN in the original space. An ideal manifold embedding would ensure that the points corresponding to $I_k^{\mathbf{X}}(i)$ remain the k-NN of p_i in the new space. Less accurate embeddings, on the other hand, would produce local and global inconsistencies such that several points would be mapped onto neighborhoods to which they do not belong in the original manifold. To measure those intrusions, we search for the hypersphere in the new space Y^q that contains all the neighboring points in $I_k^{\mathbf{X}}(i)$. To do this, we calculate the radius $r_k^{\mathbf{X,Y}}(i)$ of this hypersphere as the distance of the point $\mathbf{y}_i$ to the farthest point among the k points that are in $I_k^{\mathbf{X}}(i)$ in the original manifold space, i.e., $r_k^{\mathbf{X,Y}}(i) = \max_{j \in I_k^{\mathbf{X}}(i)} \| \mathbf{y}_i - \mathbf{y}_j \|$. Subsequently, we derive the set of indices $\mathcal{I}_k^{\mathbf{X,Y}}(i)$ of all points that are located inside this hypersphere, i.e.,

$$\mathcal{I}_k^{\mathbf{X,Y}}(i) = \left\{ p_j | \, \| \mathbf{y}_i - \mathbf{y}_j \| \leq r_k^{\mathbf{X,Y}}(i), i \neq j \right\}.$$

This set will evidently contain all original k-NN, but depending on the quality of the embedding, points that were initially outside this neighborhood could erroneously be mapped inside it. We define the neighborhood preservation measure (NPM) by summing all point intrusions into the embedding as follows

$$\mathrm{NPM}(\mathbf{X}, \mathbf{Y}, k) = 1 - \frac{\sum_{i=1}^{N} |\mathcal{I}_k^{\mathbf{X,Y}}(i)| - k}{N(N - 1 - k)}, \tag{1}$$

where the matrix $\mathbf{X}$ is the $N \times p$ matrix of data samples in the original space and $\mathbf{Y}$ the $N \times q$ matrix of data samples in the embedding space. An ideal embedding that preserves all neighborhoods and without any local or global distortions would result in a NPM value of 1. The worst possible mapping, i.e., to a single point in the new space, would result in a value of 0. Note that NPM quantifies neighborhood intrusions, and it can thus be framed within the co-ranking matrix framework [5], which subsumes all rank errors. We also found in all experiments that the number of point intrusions increase with the neighborhood size, which allows to obtain similar NPM rankings with various values of k, which is a key advantage of the proposed technique. In the validation section we fixed k as 0.05% of the datapoints of the manifold for all datasets.

2.3 Multiple Kernel Combination

For heterogeneous multispectral datasets such as those found in biomedical applications, one can expect that a single kernel might not be sufficient to separate all tissue constituents in all regions of the image. As a result, we adapt in this paper a kernel combination approach from [8], by using the calculated NPM values to suitably weight the different kernels depending on their performance into one global kernel transformation. In other words, each kernel is assigned a weight that is proportional to its efficacy after kPCA projection as measured by the NPM. The kernel function obtained by the kernel combination is

$$K = \sum_{i=1}^{m} \mu_i K_i, \text{ with } \mu_i = \frac{\mathrm{NPM}_{K_i}}{\sum_{j=1}^{m} \mathrm{NPM}_{K_j}} \tag{2}$$

where μ_i is the weight assigned to each kernel function and NPM_{K_i} the *a priori* quality (NPM value) of kernel K_i. The μ_i's fulfill the conditions for kernel weights, because $\mathrm{NPM}_{K_i} \geq 0$, $\sum_{j=1}^{m} \mathrm{NPM}_{K_j} \geq 0$ and obviously $\sum_{i=1}^{m} \mu_i = 1$.

We also introduce an additional modification to the kernel combination to ensure that only relevant kernels that can improve the manifold embedding are used in the combination. To this end, we employ an incremental scheme where kernels are combined in the descending order of their NPM values, while updating a global NPM score after each combination. The procedure is stopped when no further improvement is noticed in the global kernel score, suggesting that an optimal manifold embedding is obtained. The approach eliminates potentially detrimental kernel combinations.

3   Results

3.1   Numerical Phantom Evaluation

The performance of the proposed kernel optimization is numerically evaluated based on a phantom dataset, which corresponds to a 24-tile colorboard scanned using a multispectral optical imaging system [3]. The multispectral dataset consists of 31 image spectra ranging from 400nm to 700nm at 10nm steps. In order to select the optimal kernel transformation for the characterization of the color tiles, kPCA was applied using the 12 kernels presented in Table 1 and the three main modes of variation were used to derive RGB images as shown in Fig. 1. Class separation (CS) of the 24 color tiles is estimated using inter-pixel distances and used as the reference measure in this experiment. Subsequently, the NPM measure and an existing distance ranking measure [4] (DR) were calculated for further quantitative comparison. Firstly, the numerical results show a strong agreement between the NPM values and the estimated CS, with a correlation coefficient equal to 0.82. In contrast, it can be seen that DR introduces inconsistencies in the ranking of the different embeddings, with a lower agreement with reference CS (i.e., 0.65). Visually, it can be seen that the extent of tile separation correlates well with the introduced NPM measure, which is well adapted to assess the preservation of the discriminative structure of such manifolds.

For parameter optimization, Fig. 2 shows an example of optimal parameter selection using the proposed technique, where it can be seen clearly that NPM scores correlate well with the visual results for different parameters.

3.2   Application to Real Datasets

Following the quantitative validation with the phantom dataset, the proposed workflow was applied to two sets of medical multispectral images. The first one is a multispectral fluorescence dataset of a rabbit carotid artery, for which 47 spectra were recorded by exciting the sample using a pulsed excitation source (an amplified and frequency-doubled Ti:Sapphire laser). The resulting fluorescence was then imaged onto a microchannel plate gated optical intensifier (GOI, gate width 400 ps). KPCA was then applied with different kernels and parameters to reduce the dimension to three for RGB image visualization. Similarly to the phantom image, the multiquadratic kernel provided the best results on this multispectral flurorescence datatset, with an NPM score of 0.75. It can be seen in Fig. 3 that poor quality manifold embeddings due to unsuitable kernel transformations (e.g., wave) are associated with a low NPM score, which then increases as the tissue discrimination improves with subsequent kernels. With

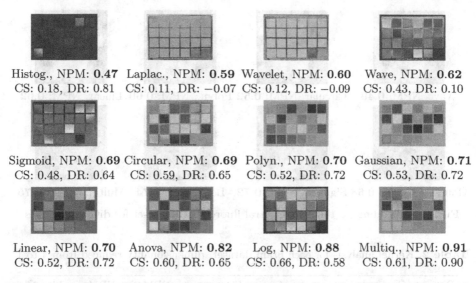

Histog., NPM: **0.47** Laplac., NPM: **0.59** Wavelet, NPM: **0.60** Wave, NPM: **0.62**
CS: 0.18, DR: 0.81 CS: 0.11, DR: −0.07 CS: 0.12, DR: −0.09 CS: 0.43, DR: 0.10

Sigmoid, NPM: **0.69** Circular, NPM: **0.69** Polyn., NPM: **0.70** Gaussian, NPM: **0.71**
CS: 0.48, DR: 0.64 CS: 0.59, DR: 0.65 CS: 0.52, DR: 0.72 CS: 0.53, DR: 0.72

Linear, NPM: **0.70** Anova, NPM: **0.82** Log, NPM: **0.88** Multiq., NPM: **0.91**
CS: 0.52, DR: 0.72 CS: 0.60, DR: 0.65 CS: 0.66, DR: 0.58 CS: 0.61, DR: 0.90

Fig. 1. Embeddings obtained from kPCA with different kernels; NPM: neighborhood preservation measure; CS: inter-class separation; DR: inter-point distance ranking

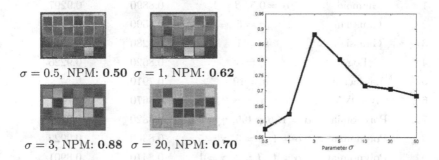

$\sigma = 0.5$, NPM: **0.50** $\sigma = 1$, NPM: **0.62**

$\sigma = 3$, NPM: **0.88** $\sigma = 20$, NPM: **0.70**

Fig. 2. Embedding results for the wave kernel for different parameters

the multiquadratic kernel projection, both large (e.g., purple area) and smaller constituents (e.g., yellow patches) are highlighted in the result.

A final experiment was carried out on the MICCAI 2012 BRATS Challenge data [7] to evaluate the specificity of kernel transformations for different patients. The dataset consists of T1, T2, FLAIR (Fluid attenuated inversion recovery) and post Gadolinium T1 MR images used as mono-channels. For each subject (12 in total), Tab. 2 summarizes the optimal kernels and parameters as selected by the proposed workflow (dimensionality reduced from 4 to 1). As expected, these vary from subject to subject, which demonstrates the importance of testing advanced kernels to achieve the best possible tissue characterization. It can be observed that even when the same kernel function is selected, the associated parameters can require specific tuning as illustrated with cases 2 and 3. Only in two cases the NPM values returned the exact same kernel and parameters (subjects 7 and 12). It is also worth noting that contrary to the phantom and fluorescence datasets,

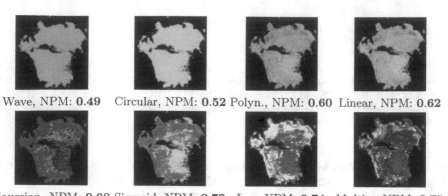

Wave, NPM: **0.49** Circular, NPM: **0.52** Polyn., NPM: **0.60** Linear, NPM: **0.62**

Gaussian, NPM: **0.68** Sigmoid, NPM: **0.72** Log, NPM: **0.74** Multiq., NPM: **0.75**

Fig. 3. Embedding for the multispectral fluorescence dataset for different kernels

Table 2. Kernel analysis for each brain dataset, dimensionality reduced from 4 to 1

Patient number	Optimal single kernel	Optimal parameter	NPM single kernel	NPM combined kernels
1	Sigmoid	$\alpha = 0.5,\ \beta = 1$	0.8890	0.9297
2	Gaussian	$\sigma = 5$	0.8590	0.9132
3	Gaussian	$\sigma = 1$	0.8280	0.8819
4	Log	$\gamma = 3$	0.8620	0.9226
5	Laplacian	$\sigma = 10$	0.7910	-
6	ANOVA	$\alpha = 1,\ \gamma = 0.5$	0.8670	-
7	Polynomial	$\alpha = 1,\ \beta = 0.5,\ \gamma = 0.5$	0.8820	0.9199
8	Polynomial	$\alpha = 1,\ \beta = 5,\ \gamma = 5$	0.8300	0.9022
9	Polynomial	$\alpha = 1,\ \beta = 2,\ \gamma = 1$	0.8410	0.8901
10	Laplacian	$\sigma = 20$	0.8770	-
11	Log	$\gamma = 5$	0.8370	-
12	Polynomial	$\alpha = 1,\ \beta = 0.5,\ \gamma = 0.5$	0.8300	0.8942

the standard Gaussian and polynomial kernels perform well for the brain images and they are identified as optimal kernel transformations in half of the datasets. On the other hand, while the multiquadratic kernel was the optimal kernel for both the multispectral optical and fluorescence images, it is not selected as such in any of the brain datasets.

Finally, the kernel combination presented in Section 2.3 was applied to all brain datasets based on the previously calculated NPM values. It can be seen from Tab. 2 (rightmost column) that the quality as estimated by NPM of the resulting manifold embedding improves for two thirds of the datasets. The NPM values increase between 5% and 8%, which can be important to better highlight subtle tissues differences in multispectral images. For the cases with no NPM

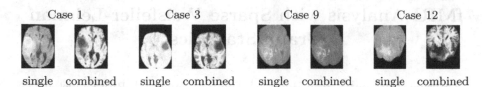

Case 1   Case 3   Case 9   Case 12

single combined   single combined   single combined   single combined

Fig. 4. Examples of improvement in manifold embedding for the brain datasets achieved by using the proposed kernel combination over a single kernel.

value for the combined kernel in Tab. 2, the combination did not outperform the best single kernel.

For visual illustration, the first principal component of the obtained kernel projections are shown in Fig. 4, where it is evident that kernel combinations improve significantly the manifold embedding results over using a single kernel transformation. In particular, the tumors and the grey matter are better highlighted by using the combined kernels in cases 1, 3 and 12.

4 Conclusions

We presented a workflow for patient- and image-specific kernel-based manifold embedding of multispectral image data. With the proposed framework, the flexibility of kernel techniques can be fully exploited to derive optimal characterization of the biomedical tissues.

References

1. Chen, L., Buja, A.: Local multidimensional scaling for nonlinear dimension reduction, graph drawing and proximity analysis. Journal of the American Statistical Association 104(485), 209–219 (2009)
2. Hofmann, T., Schölkopf, B., Smola, A.J.: Kernel Methods in Machine Learning. The Annals of Statistics 36(3), 1171–1220 (2008)
3. Hordley, S., Finalyson, G., Morovic, P.: A Multispectral Image Database and its Application to Image Rendering Across Illumination. In: Proc. 3rd Int. Conf. on Image and Graphics (ICIG), Hong-Kong, China, pp. 394–397 (2004), http://www2.cmp.uea.ac.uk/Research/compvis/MultiSpectralDB.htm
4. Kouropteva, O., Okun, O., Pietkäinen, M.: Incremental locally linear embedding. Pattern Recognition 38(10), 1764–1767 (2005)
5. Lee, J.A., Verleysen, M.: Quality assessment of dimensionality reduction: Rank-based criteria. Neurocomputing 72(7-9), 1431–1443 (2009)
6. Maaten, L.V.D., Postma, E., Herik, H.V.D.: Dimensionality reduction: a comparative review. Tech. Rep. TiCC-TR 2009-05, Tilburg University, Tilburg, The Netherlands (2009)
7. Menze, B., Jakab, A., Bauer, S., Reyes, M., Prastawa, M., van Leemput, K.: Challenge on Multimodal Brain Tumor Segmentation (MICCAI-BRATS). In: Proc. MICCAI 2012 (2012), http://www2.imm.dtu.dk/projects/BRATS2012
8. Tanabe, H., Ho, T.B., Nguyen, C.H., Kawasaki, S.: Simple but effective methods for combining kernels in computational biology. In: IEEE Int. Conf. on Research, Innovation and Vision for the Future (RIVF), pp. 71–78 (2008)

fMRI Analysis with Sparse Weisfeiler-Lehman Graph Statistics

Katerina Gkirtzou[1,2], Jean Honorio[3], Dimitris Samaras[4], Rita Goldstein[5], and Matthew B. Blaschko[1,2,*]

[1] Center for Visual Computing, École Centrale Paris, France
[2] Équipe Galen, INRIA Saclay, Île-de-France, France
[3] CSAIL, Massachusetts Institute of Technology, Cambridge, USA
[4] Computer Science Department, Stony Brook University, NY, USA
[5] Icahn School of Medicine, Mount Sinai, USA

Abstract. fMRI analysis has most often been approached with linear methods. However, this disregards information encoded in the relationships between voxels. We propose to exploit the inherent spatial structure of the brain to improve the prediction performance of fMRI analysis. We do so in an exploratory fashion by representing the fMRI data by graphs. We use the Weisfeiler-Lehman algorithm to efficiently compute subtree features of the graphs. These features encode non-linear interactions between voxels, which contain additional discriminative information that cannot be captured by a linear classifier. In order to make use of the efficiency of the Weisfeiler-Lehman algorithm, we introduce a novel pyramid quantization strategy to approximate continuously labeled graphs with a sequence of discretely labeled graphs. To control the capacity of the resulting prediction function, we utilize the elastic net sparsity regularizer. We validate our method on a cocaine addiction dataset showing a significant improvement over elastic net and kernel ridge regression baselines and a reduction in classification error of over 14%. Source code is also available at `https://gitorious.org/wlpyramid`.

Keywords: fMRI, graph kernels, Weisfeiler-Lehman, sparse regression, cocaine addiction.

1 Introduction

Functional magnetic resonance imaging (fMRI) is a wide-spread, non-invasive modality used for studying brain activity, under the objectives of localizing brain regions participating in a specific task, determining connectivity networks or making predictions about disease states. Numerous approaches have been proposed for analyzing fMRI data. Most of them select features either by a predefined set of regions of interest (ROIs) using prior knowledge [1,2], statistical methods [3,4] or thresholding [5]. Recently, there has been an exploration

---

* This work was partially funded by ERC Grant 259112 and NIA 1R21DA034954-01.

G. Wu et al. (Eds.): MLMI 2013, LNCS 8184, pp. 90–97, 2013.

of sparsity regularization methods in fMRI analysis [6,7]. fMRI analysis is particularly suited to sparsity regularization due to the intrinsic high dimensional nature of fMRI data, the small size of datasets and the lack of requirement for predefined ROIs. Although the aforementioned methods perform well in analyzing fMRI data, they tend to ignore the 3D structure of the brain. On the other hand, graph-theoretic methods can model structural information, and have also been used in fMRI analysis. The most common use is modeling the network of brain connectivity [8,9]. Graph kernel methods have also been used in fMRI connectivity graphs for brain decoding [10].

The majority of previous approaches treat prediction in fMRI as a linear combination of functions over individual voxels. Such approaches do not capture potentially complex interactions between voxels. We enrich our capacity to model such dependencies by representing fMRI recordings as graphs, and we design an algorithm that learns from the interconnections between voxels. Through efficient graph algorithms, we are able to learn in a fully exploratory fashion without restricting our prediction, e.g., to a pre-defined region of interest or a connected component. We control the complexity of our prediction while modeling non-linear interactions between voxels by adding a sparsity regularizer using the elastic net [11]. We represent fMRI data as graphs over voxels, and compare the resulting graphs with a novel method that combines elements of the Weisfieler-Lehman graph kernel [12] and the pyramid match kernel [13]. This method achieves the computational advantages of efficient graph kernels while extending the representation to continuous node labels, which represent a contrast map at a given voxel. We validate the approach on a clinically important cocaine addiction dataset [14], achieving a reduction in classification error from an elastic net baseline of over 14% with statistical significance.

2   Methods

Graphs are rich representations of networks of data, and are consequently a promising representation for neural populations. A typical approach for exploring graph representation is to consider a measure of similarity between graphs as a kernel [15,12]. The most popular strategy to define similarity over graph representations is to aggregate statistics of subgraphs and compare them. Here we agregate statistics of subtree patterns from a graph representation constructed from fMRI data. We then use these statistics with a sparsity regularizer to make predictions from graphs representing brain contrast maps. In order to make use of a graph representation for learning from fMRI data, several design choices must be made: (i) the learning algorithm, (ii) the graph construction, (iii) the graph statistics employed as a feature representation, and (iv) the node labeling. We address each of these choices in the following sections.

2.1   Sparsity Regularization

In the sequel, we will assume that we have access to a training set of data $\{(x_i, y_i)\}_{1 \le i \le n}$ of size n, where $x \in \mathcal{X}$ is a fMRI recording and $y \in \mathcal{Y} \equiv \{-1, +1\}$

Algorithm 1. The statistical learning pipeline for fMRI analysis with sparse subgraph statistics

---

Require: Training set $\mathcal{D} = \{(x_i, y_i), i = 1, \ldots, n\}$.
    Compute $\hat{\beta}_{\text{lin}}$ from the objective in Equation (1) with $\phi_{\text{lin}}(x) \equiv \text{vec}\, x$.
    Construct k-nearest neighbor graphs for all training samples from the voxels associated with non-zero $\hat{\beta}_{\text{lin}}$.
    for each level in the quantization pyramid **do**
        Label the nodes of all graphs according to the quantization of the voxel value.
        Compute the Weisfeiler-Lehman statistics for the given quantization level over all graphs and aggregate them into the feature vector $\phi_{\text{graph}}(x)$.
    end for
    Compute $\hat{\beta}_{\text{graph}}$ from the objective in Equation (1) with $\phi_{\text{graph}}(x)$.

---

is a label to be predicted (cf. Section 2.5). As our statistical estimator, we have made use of the elastic net [11]. The elastic net combines ℓ_1 with ℓ_2 regularization in order to appropriately trade off sparsity with a low variance estimator in the case of correlated signals. Formally, if $\phi(x) \in \mathbb{R}^d$ is a feature vector computed from x, the elastic net computes

$$\hat{\beta} = \arg \min_{\beta \in \mathbb{R}^d} \lambda_2 \|\beta\|_2^2 + \lambda_1 \|\beta\|_1 + \frac{1}{n} \sum_{i=1}^{n} (\langle \beta, \phi(x_i) \rangle - y_i)^2, \tag{1}$$

where $\lambda_1, \lambda_2 \geq 0$ are scalar regularization parameters. This method is particularly appropriate in fMRI where nearby voxels are likely to be correlated, and regions responsible for a given function or behavior distributed across multiple voxels. Furthermore, it is typical that the majority of voxels in the brain are not discriminative of a specific output, y. We make use of the elastic net twice in our learning pipeline (Algorithm 1). In the first instance, we use the elastic net on the raw voxel values to determine a subset of voxels on which we build a graph representation, specifically those with non-zero $\hat{\beta}_{\text{lin}}$. Our model selection step has typically chosen approximately 10^3 voxels for this stage. We subsequently compute subgraph statistics over this graph to generate a feature vector, $\phi_{\text{graph}}(x)$. Finally, we use the elastic net on these subgraph statistics in order to determine our final prediction function, with a model selection step to determine appropriate values for λ_1 and λ_2.

2.2 Graph Construction

To construct the graph representation, we have made use of k-nearest neighbor graphs on the voxels that were selected by an initial training of the elastic net. We symmetrize the k-nn relationship by considering the edges to indicate an undirected graph structure. While other models of connectivity are of interest [16,17], we have found that the use of k-nearest neighbors to determine the graph topology yields good performance in general. Furthermore, the subtree statistics considered in the next section implicitly account for longer distance connections for sufficiently deep subtree patterns. We set $k = 5$ in all experiments.

2.3   The Weisfeiler-Lehman Algorithm

The subgraph statistics considered here are subtree patterns from the Weisfeiler-Lehman algorithm [18], which has recently been employed in the construction of a graph kernel [12, Algorithm 2]. These statistics are linear-time in the number of edges in the graph, and make use of an efficient hashing scheme in order to only enumerate relevant (non-zero) dimensions of an exponentially sized feature space. In addition to these computational benefits, Weisfeiler-Lehman graph kernels have been shown to perform comparably to or better than a number of more computationally complex kernels [12]. Although Weisfeiler-Lehman statistics over subtree patterns have most recently been used in the construction of a kernel function after which ℓ_2 regularized learning is applied [12], we retain the vectors of subtree pattern counts and apply a sparsity regularizer in order to control model complexity in a high dimensional representation (Section 2.1).

2.4   Pyramid Quantized Weisfeiler-Lehman for Continuous Labels

The Weisfeiler-Lehman algorithm is efficient precisely because it makes use of a discrete labeling over nodes, which enables an efficient hashing scheme in order to scale linearly in the number of edges. This presents a problem when extending this method to continuous vector labeled graph vertices. Our vertices (fMRI voxels) are naturally labeled by their (continuous) contrast values. To retain the computational efficiencies of the graph representation, and to extend the method to continuous node labels, we consider a pyramid quantization strategy to determine a logarithmic number of discrete labelings for which we run the Weisfeiler-Lehman algorithm. This approximates a graph representation with continuous labels as a sequence of graphs with increasingly granular discrete labels. To construct our pyramid quantization, we recursively partition the space as proposed by [13]. In this manner, we have a series of nested vector quantizations of increasing granularity. We believe our method is the first to propose a pyramid quantization scheme for the efficient application of graph kernels to continuous (multi-dimensional) node labels. We expect that this will additionally be of high interest to the machine learning community, so code is available at https://gitorious.org/wlpyramid.

2.5   Cocaine Addiction Dataset

Our dataset [14] contains an approximately equal number of cocaine addicted individuals and control subjects performing a neuropsychological experiment of block design known as drug Stroop. Each subject performs six sessions with two varying conditions, a monetary reward (50¢, 25¢ and 0¢) and the cue shown (drug-related or a neutral word). We focus here on the 50¢ condition based on previous analysis of the data [5]. For the subjects that complied to motion $< 2mm$ translation, $< 2°$ rotation and at least 50% performance of the subject in an unrelated task [14], contrast maps were computed using the SPM package (http://www.fil.ion.ucl.ac.uk/spm/), which were used to determine the

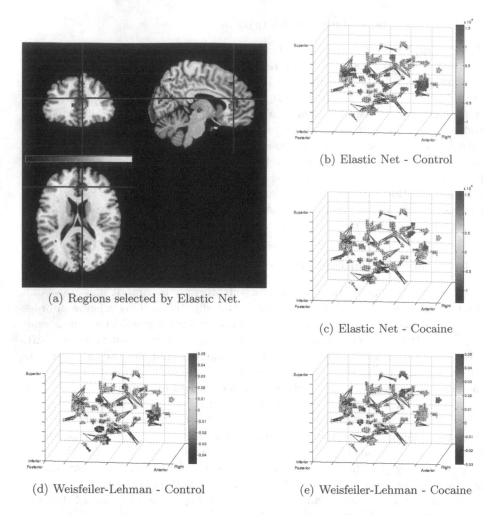

(a) Regions selected by Elastic Net.

(b) Elastic Net - Control

(c) Elastic Net - Cocaine

(d) Weisfeiler-Lehman - Control

(e) Weisfeiler-Lehman - Cocaine

Fig. 1. 1(a): A visualization of the areas of the brain selected by the elastic net. The selected regions correspond to areas previously implicated as being related to addiction [14]. 1(b)-1(c): A visualization of the function learned by Elastic net for control and cocaine subjects. 1(d)-1(e): A visualization of the function learned by the proposed system applied to control and cocaine addicted subjects.

node labels of the graphs. Finally, the task of interest is the classification of a subject as cocaine addicted or control.

3   Results

We evaluate our proposed pyramid quantized Weisfeiler-Lehman method for continuous node labels using the cocaine addiction dataset. We perform a random splitting scheme with 50 trials to estimate the classification performance.

Table 1. Mean accuracy over the hold-out data of 50 trials of the pyramid quantized Weisfeiler-Lehman algorithm for four different subtree pattern depths, $h \in \{0, 1, 2, 3\}$. Maximum performance is achieved with subtree patterns up to depth two.

Pyramid Quantized Weifeiler-Lehman				
h	0	1	2	3
Accuracy	54.00%	57.14%	**64.28%**	63.42%

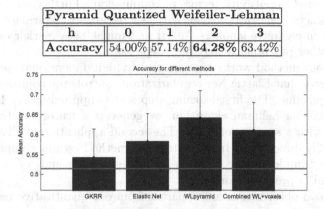

Fig. 2. Mean accuracy and standard error on the cocaine addiction dataset. The compared methods are (left to right) Gaussian kernel ridge regression (GKRR), the elastic net on raw voxels, pyramid quantized Weisfeiler-Lehman (WLpyramid), and the elastic net with a concatenation of the raw voxels and the pyramid Weisfeiler-Lehman features (Combined EN+WL). The horizontal red line indicates chance performance. The pyramid quantized Weisfeiler-Lehman features perform better than GKRR and the elastic net on raw voxels with statistical signficance.

In each trial, a random selection of 80% of the data are used for training, while the remaining 20% are used to estimate the performance. In Table 1 we show the performance of the pyramid quantized Weisfeiler-Lehman model for four different depths of subtree patterns (cf. Section 2.3). Our approach achieves a mean accuracy of 64.28% for subtree patterns up to depth two. We also compare our proposed technique with three other methods on the same dataset: (i) Gaussian kernel ridge regression, (ii) the elastic net with raw voxels as features, and (iii) elastic net with raw voxels and pyramid Weisfeiler-Lehman features concatenated in a joint feature vector. In Fig. 2 we show the mean accuracy of the final system and the standard error. Pyramid quantized Weisfeiler-Lehman outperforms the rest of the methods. With a Wilcoxon signed rank test between elastic net with raw voxels and pyramid quantized Weisfeiler-Lehman we determine that our proposed method is statistically significantly better ($p = 0.02$). Additionally, a reduction of over 14% in classification error is recorded between elastic net on the raw voxels and our method.

4   Discussion

Fig. 1 shows the areas selected by the elastic net and visualizations of the learned functions. One of the main areas is the rostral anterior cingulate cortex (rostral

ACC), which has been previously shown to deactivate in cocaine users in comparison to controls [14]. Moreover, it is an area whose activity is normalized by oral methylphenidate [19], which blocks the dopamine transporters, similar to cocaine, increasing extracellular dopamine–an escalation that has correlated with lower task-related impulsivity (errors of commission). Furthermore, this region has shown reduction in drug cue reactivity as a response to pharmacotherapeutic interventions in cigarette smokers [20,21] and might be a marker of treatment response in other psychopathology (e.g. depression).

Although our method works in an implicitly high dimensional space, we empirically observe that Elastic Net regularization controls the complexity at each stage of the pipeline. The first learning step selects approximately 1100 voxels. Using the Weifeiler-Lehman algorithm, we generate a feature vector of length 6×10^5, but with a sparsity of $\sim 2\%$. The second application of Elastic Net selects only $\sim 2K$ dimensions. In each step, the method retains complexity much lower than a "simple" linear function over tens of thousands of voxels as has been proposed in previous works.

Several broad observations are apparent from our quantitative results. From Table 1, we note that subtree patterns up to depth two seem to perform best, and that deeper subtree patterns begin to reduce average performance. This indicates that the big-$\mathcal{O}$ complexity of the graph representation is only slightly higher than using a simple linear function. The proposed method performs significantly better than the ridge regression and elastic net baselines (Table 1 and Figure 2). In our final experiment of combining the raw voxel values with the subtree pattern features, we found that performance decreased slightly from that of only considering subtree pattern features.

In this work, we have presented a fully automated, statistically sound method for classification of brain states with graph representations. It combines the Weisfeiler-Lehman graph kernel [12] with the pyramid match kernel [13], in order to learn from graphs with continuous labels through a pyramid quantization scheme. The method was evaluated on a real world dataset and outperformed other machine learning techniques with statistical significance, including kernel ridge regression and the elastic net. This validates the primary hypothesis of this work: that the interconnections between voxels can contain additional information about brain structure that is not apparent in a linear function on the raw voxel values.

References

1. Demirci, O., Clark, V., Calhoun, V.: A projection pursuit algorithm to classify individuals using fMRI data: Application to schizophrenia. Neuroimage 39 (2008)
2. Wang, X., Hutchinson, R., Mitchell, T.M.: Training fMRI classifiers to discriminate cognitive states across multiple subjects. In: NIPS (2003)
3. Mitchell, T.M., Hutchinson, R., Niculescu, R.S., Pereira, F., Wang, X., Just, M., Newman, S.: Learning to decode cognitive states from brain images. Machine Learning 57, 145–175 (2004)

4. Tahmasebi, A.M., Artiges, E., Banaschewski, T., Barker, G.J., Bruehl, R., Bchel, C., Conrod, P.J., Flor, H., Garavan, H., Gallinat, J., Heinz, A., Ittermann, B., Loth, E., Mareckova, K., Martinot, J.L., Poline, J.B., Rietschel, M., Smolka, M.N., et al.: Creating probabilistic maps of the face network in the adolescent brain: A multicentre functional mri study. Human Brain Mapping 33, 938–957 (2012)
5. Honorio, J., Tomasi, D., Goldstein, R., Leung, H., Samaras, D.: Can a single brain region predict a disorder? IEEE Transactions on Medical Imaging (2012)
6. Carroll, M., Cecchi, G., Rish, I., Garg, R., Rao, A.: Prediction and interpretation of distributed neural activity with sparse models. NeuroImage 44, 112–122 (2009)
7. Gkirtzou, K., Honorio, J., Samaras, D., Goldstein, R., Blaschko, M.B.: fMRI analysis of cocaine addiction using k-support sparsity. In: ISBI (2013)
8. Venkataraman, A., Kubicki, M., Golland, P.: From brain connectivity models to identifying foci of a neurological disorder. In: Ayache, N., Delingette, H., Golland, P., Mori, K. (eds.) MICCAI 2012, Part I. LNCS, vol. 7510, pp. 715–722. Springer, Heidelberg (2012)
9. Liu, Y., Liang, M., Zhou, Y., He, Y., Hao, Y., Song, M., Yu, C., Liu, H., Liu, Z., Jiang, T.: Disrupted small-world networks in schizophrenia. Brain 131 (2008)
10. Mokhtari, F., Hossein-Zadeh, G.A.: Decoding brain states using backward edge elimination and graph kernels in fMRI connectivity networks. Journal of Neuroscience Methods 212, 259–268 (2013)
11. Zou, H., Hastie, T.: Regularization and variable selection via the elastic net. Journal of the Royal Statistical Society Series B 67, 301–320 (2005)
12. Shervashidze, N., Schweitzer, P., van Leeuwen, E.J., Mehlhorn, K., Borgwardt, K.M.: Weisfeiler-lehman graph kernels. JMLR 12, 2539–2561 (2011)
13. Grauman, K., Darrell, T.: The pyramid match kernel: Efficient learning with sets of features. J. Mach. Learn. Res. 8, 725–760 (2007)
14. Goldstein, R., Alia-Klein, N., Tomasi, D., Carrillo, J., Maloney, T., Woicik, P., Wang, R., Telang, F., Volkow, N.: Anterior cingulate cortex hypoactivations to an emotionally salient task in cocaine addiction. PNAS 106, 9453 (2009)
15. Vishwanathan, S.V.N., Schraudolph, N.N., Kondor, R.I., Borgwardt, K.M.: Graph kernels. JMLR 11, 1201–1242 (2010)
16. Sporns, O.: Networks of the Brain. MIT Press (2010)
17. Wee, C.Y., Yap, P.T., Li, W., Denny, K., Browndyke, J.N., Potter, G.G., Welsh-Bohmer, K.A., Wang, L., Shen, D.: Enriched white matter connectivity networks for accurate identification of MCI patients. NeuroImage 54, 1812–1822 (2011)
18. Weisfeiler, B., Lehman, A.A.: A reduction of a graph to a canonical form and an algebra arising during this reduction. Nauchno-Tech. Informatsia, Ser. 2(9) (1968)
19. Goldstein, R.Z., Woicik, P.A., Maloney, T., Tomasi, D., Alia-Klein, N., Shan, J., Honorio, J., Samaras, D., Wang, R., Telang, F., Wang, G.J., Volkow, N.D.: Oral methylphenidate normalizes cingulate activity in cocaine addiction during a salient cognitive task. PNAS 107, 16667–16672 (2010)
20. Culbertson, C., Bramen, J., Cohen, M., London, E.D., Olmstead, R.E., Gan, J.J., Costello, M.R., Shulenberger, S., Mandelkern, M.A., Brody, A.L.: Effect of bupropion treatment on brain activation induced by cigarette-related cues in smokers. Archives of General Psychiatry 68, 505–515 (2011)
21. Franklin, T.R., Wang, Z., Li, Y., Suh, J.J., Goldman, M., Lohoff, F.W., Cruz, J., Hazan, R., Jens, W., Detre, J.A., Berrettini, W., O'Brien, C.P., Childress, A.R.: Dopamine transporter genotype modulation of neural responses to smoking cues: confirmation in a new cohort. Addiction Biology 16, 308–322 (2011)

Patch-Based Segmentation without Registration: Application to Knee MRI

Zehan Wang, Claire Donoghue, and Daniel Rueckert

Department of Computing, Imperial College London, UK
zehan.wang06@imperial.ac.uk

Abstract. Atlas based segmentation techniques have been proven to be effective in many automatic segmentation applications. However, the reliance on image correspondence means that the segmentation results can be affected by any registration errors which occur, particularly if there is a high degree of anatomical variability. This paper presents a novel multi-resolution patch-based segmentation framework which is able to work on images without requiring registration. Additionally, an image similarity metric using 3D histograms of oriented gradients is proposed to enable atlas selection in this context. We applied the proposed approach to segment MR images of the knee from the MICCAI SKI10 Grand Challenge, where 100 training atlases are provided and evaluation is conducted on 50 unseen test images. The proposed method achieved good scores overall and is comparable to the top entries in the challenge for cartilage segmentation, demonstrating good performance when comparing against state-of-the-art approaches customised to Knee MRI.

1   Introduction

Accurate segmentation in medical imaging plays a crucial role in many applications from patient-specific diagnosis to biomedical research. Patch-based methods for label propagation have been shown to be an effective automatic segmentation approach for many applications in medical imaging [4], [14]. In general, these approaches label each voxel of a target image by comparing the image patch centred on the voxel with patches from an atlas library and assigning the most probable label according to the closest matches. Most of these methods use affine registration rather than non-rigid registration which is often used in multi-atlas label propagation methods [8], [13], yet are still able to produce comparable results.

One advantage of patch-based approaches is that they do not assume explicit one-to-one correspondence between images, which can overcome problems for multi-atlas segmentation where the anatomical variability cannot be fully accounted for when generalised registration algorithms are used with the available atlases. However, due to computational complexity, many existing patch-based methods use limited search windows centred around the target voxel (typically around 11^3 voxels) and thus rely upon a good approximate alignment of the image to the atlases. Increasing the search window size also increases the number of

G. Wu et al. (Eds.): MLMI 2013, LNCS 8184, pp. 98–105, 2013.

patch comparisons required, which can be computationally prohibitive, limiting the potential applications of this approach. Hierarchical frameworks have been previously used to address these restrictions, such as multi-resolution solutions [6] or by combining hierarchical multi-atlas registration and patch-based segmentation [19]. Another approach uses efficient k-nearest neighbour data structures and a spatially weighted label fusion method [18].

Despite these improvements, the proposed methods still require the registration of images to establish image correspondences, albeit with affine registration rather than non-rigid. This process can still be a computationally expensive and problematic step in images with a high degree of anatomical variance and where a common template space (such as MNI space for brain images) isn't defined. Problems with affine registration of knee MRI have been previously quantified in [5] where the authors observed 4.08% of direct pairwise registrations fail without manual input in a data set of over $10,000$ knee images.

To avoid these issues, we investigate the potential to perform segmentation without registration. Our first contribution is a multi-resolution framework for patch-based segmentation which does not require image registration. This approach can quickly obtain a coarse initial segmentation in the lowest resolution which is then refined by propagating through subsequently higher resolutions. Our second contribution is an atlas selection method using a histogram approach with 3D oriented gradients to provide a fast and generic similarity measure in this context where image correspondence cannot be assumed. This is a new approach for atlas selection, but in the context of image retrieval similar approaches have been developed. We refer to [1] for a review of other potential approaches that could be utilised such as those using texture, contours or wavelets.

Our third contribution is to apply the proposed methods to knee MR images from the MICCAI SKI10 Grand Challenge [9], where 100 training atlases are provided and evaluation is conducted on 50 unseen test images. There is a high degree of anatomical variability in the cartilage and bone structures in the knee which is the primary reason why segmentation of cartilage is particularly challenging. This is the first time that a patch-based method has been developed for segmentation without requiring prior registration in addition to its application to knee images. In terms of the application to the knee MRI, the proposed method can label both bones and cartilage simultaneously, whereas many other methods require a bone segmentation first to find the bone cartilage interface as an intermediate step prior to cartilage segmentation [7].

2   Methods

2.1   Hierarchical Segmentation Strategy

A multi-resolution approach allows a coarse initial segmentation to be quickly established from the lowest resolution image which can then be refined using subsequently higher resolutions. The basic concept for our patch-based approach is a simple iterative process of atlas selection, patch selection, and then label fusion. Multiple resolutions of each image are created by constructing a Gaussian image pyramid [3]. As a pre-processing step, MR images are bias field corrected [17], re-sampled to isotropic voxel size and intensity normalised [12]. The lowest resolution is based on the findings in [16], where, motivated by the remarkable tolerance of the human visual system to degradations in image resolution, the authors reported automated segmentation tasks can be performed on images with resolutions as small as in the range of 32×32 to 16×16 depending on the size of the object. With this in mind, the sub-sampling of each image terminates if the resolution is less than $32 \times 32 \times 32$. Our initial experiments confirmed that a coarse segmentation can be performed in the lowest resolution and that a patch-based approach can be used to do so, even when the images are not registered.

Table 1. Example of a Gaussian image pyramid for an image in the SKI10 data set. Resolution levels are numbered upwards in ascending order, where level 1 denotes the highest resolution and each subsequent level is half the resolution of the previous level.

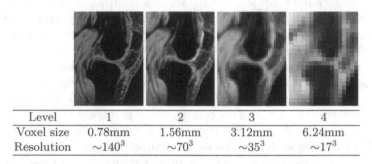

Level	1	2	3	4
Voxel size	0.78mm	1.56mm	3.12mm	6.24mm
Resolution	$\sim140^3$	$\sim70^3$	$\sim35^3$	$\sim17^3$

Given an initial segmentation from a low resolution image, only a boundary region around each, defined by the difference between the *dilation* and *erosion* of the segmentation, will need to be refined in a higher resolution. This is because a low resolution segmentation cannot represent the boundary voxels of each structure as well as a higher resolution. However, for internal voxels of each structure, the low resolution segmentation would be a sufficient, so no further refinement would be required for these voxels. Multiple iterations of this boundary refinement can be carried out at each resolution to increase the accuracy. This forms a straight-forward and computationally-efficient strategy to process images through increasing resolutions, allowing a patch-based approach to be feasibly used in all resolutions.

2.2   Atlas Selection Using Histogram of Gradients

As a trade-off between time and accuracy, only the nearest N atlas regions are used for patch-based segmentation, since linear increases in the number of atlases yields logarithmic improvements in the segmentation [18]. Without registration, existing atlas selection methods [13], [2] using voxel-to-voxel distance metrics cannot be used meaningfully as they implicitly assume correspondences between the images. One alternative is to compare images by their intensity histogram, however this discards local neighbourhood information which is relevant for patch comparisons. Instead, we propose using a histogram of oriented 3D gradients based on [10] which incorporates the local neighbourhood information of each voxel for gradient calculations.

Gradients are calculated using a 1D Sobel operator [-1, 0, 1] in each axis and binned into one of 20 orientations based on the faces of a icosahedron. Ensuring the orientation bins are equidistant in 3D is not trivial, known otherwise as the Thomson problem [15], but using the centre positions of faces on regular polyhedrons such as the icosahedron is one solution. Histograms are built by binning the gradients of all relevant voxels using the magnitude of the gradient as the value to bin. There are many distance measures that can be employed for histogram comparison such as the chi squared distance or the earth mover's distance, but in this paper the L_1 norm was found to be a sufficiently effective.

At the start of the segmentation, the atlas selection process uses a histogram of the whole image, but once an initial segmentation has been established, only the boundary region around each label are compared - since this is the focus for the refinement process. To increase specificity, histograms are calculated separately for each label within each region and then concatenated to produce an overall histogram for that region.

2.3   Spatial Information and k-NN Data Structures

k-NN data structures are constructed for each resolution of each atlas to increase the search window size without a detrimental impact to the search speed [18]. For each voxel a feature vector is constructed from spatial information as well as intensities of the patch for that voxel. The spatial information provides context to the intensity values of each patch and acts to regularise the patch selection during segmentation. A weighting, α, is applied to control its influence. These feature vectors are grouped by the voxel's label and a k-NN data structure is constructed for each label. This can also be applied for separate corresponding regions of each atlas rather than the whole image to allow more specificity in atlas selection. This allows a different set of atlases to be used for each region and also improves the search speed by decreasing the search space.

For Segmentation Initialisation. The inclusion of spatial context is not a requirement to establish an approximate segmentation, however its inclusion can improve the accuracy. Without prior image alignment, it is still possible to generalise the relative position of a patch within the image, even with varying fields of view. Rather than use exact positioning, the Euclidean distance to $n \geq 0$ reference point(s) can be used to provide weak spatial context for each voxel. The number of reference points depends on the application as increasing this would make the spatial context stronger, but assume stronger spatial correspondence which may not be the case.

For Segmentation Refinement. Once an initial segmentation is established, spatial context can then be defined relative to the segmented structures, which are invariant to their position in the image. The Euclidean Distance Transform of relevant labelled structures, which can be calculated in linear time [11], can be used to do this, as this provides the Euclidean distance to the nearest surface point for each voxel.

2.4   Patch Search and Label Fusion

Labels are calculated independently for each voxel based on euclidean distances, but in contrast to the approaches used in [4] and [14], only the k nearest patches for each possible label are used in the label fusion. Since the values providing spatial context is appended to each patch, using k-NN data structures will select the most similar patches with respect to the spatial context without any further computations. The spatial weight, α, controls the influence of the spatial context on the overall patch similarity. Let y_{l_i} represent voxels from the atlas library for label l, then the weighting for this label at voxel x is then determined by a sum of the weights, $w_l(x) = \sum_{i=1}^{k} w(x, y_{l_i})$ where

$$w(x, y) = e^{\dfrac{-\{||P(x) - P(y)||_2^2 + \alpha||S(x) - S(y)||_2^2\}}{h^2(x)}} \qquad (1)$$

$P(x)$ and $S(x)$ are, respectively, the patch intensities and the spatial context at voxel x. $h^2(x)$ provides an automatic estimation of a decay parameter to control the level of influence of patches as the distance increases [4]. This is performed for each voxel based on the minimum distance between patch $P(x)$ and the nearest k patches $\{P(y_i)\}$:

$$h^2(x) = \min\{||P(x) - P(y_i)||_2^2 + \alpha||S(x) - S(y_i)||_2^2\} \qquad (2)$$

A final label for voxel x is decided based by majority voting of the label weights. i.e. $L(x) = \arg\max_l w_l(x)$

3   Application to SKI10 Grand Challenge

3.1   Implementation and Experimentation

We implemented the framework in Python with publicly available modules such as numpy, scipy and sci-kit, using a ball tree as the k-NN data structure. During experiments, the best patch sizes to use were found to be dependent on the image resolution. At the lowest resolution, a larger patch size (7^3) is used to obtain the initial coarse segmentation and smaller patch sizes (5^3 and 3^3) are then applied to refine this before propagating it to the next resolution level. This initial segmentation provides a better initialisation for the next resolution level and therefore the rest of the segmentation process.

Table 2. Example segmentations, parameters and computation times for each resolution level. Segmentations from the proposed method are overlaid in green for the bone and yellow for the cartilage. The reference segmentation is outlined in red.

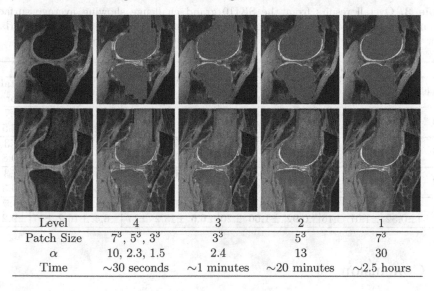

Level	4	3	2	1
Patch Size	$7^3, 5^3, 3^3$	3^3	5^3	7^3
α	10, 2.3, 1.5	2.4	13	30
Time	~30 seconds	~1 minutes	~20 minutes	~2.5 hours

In terms of spatial information, initial experiments suggested that using the centre of the image as a reference point works well for obtaining an initial segmentation in knee MRI. After this, the Euclidean distance transform of the femur and the tibia were used to provide spatial information to refine the segmentation. The weighting for the spatial information, α, is dependent on image resolution and patch size. Table 2 shows the patch sizes and spatial weighting, α, used as well as segmentation examples and computation times on an 8 core 2.7GHz CPU for each resolution. Details of the different resolution levels are shown in table 1. The k parameter for the nearest patches selected was fixed at 15 for all resolutions and 100 atlases were used for resolution levels 4 to 2, whilst 30 were used for level 1. A low value for the k parameter can provide minor speed gains but our experiments suggested $k > 10$ was a minimum requirement for accurate results. Parameters are chosen based on experiments with the training data and are not tuned to the test set.

3.2   Results

The results from the SKI10 grand challenge[1] are presented in table 3, showing promising potential for this framework and demonstrating the possibility of applying patch-based segmentation in images where accurate registration poses a challenge. The framework does not make any prior assumptions about the knees,

---

[1] See http://www.ski10.org/results.php for a full list of results from other entries.

yet achieves a good score for bone segmentation whilst the score for cartilage segmentation is comparable to the top scoring entries in the challenge.

Table 3. Overall results from the SKI10 grand challenge showing average surface distance (AvgD), root mean squared surface distance (RMSD), volumetric overlap error (VOE), volumetric difference (VD) and score (Scr) for each resolution level

	Femur Bone			Tibia bone			Femoral cartilage			Tibial cartilage			
Level	AvgD [mm]	RMSD [mm]	Scr	AvgD [mm]	RMSD [mm]	Scr	VOE [%]	VD [%]	Scr	VOE [%]	VD [%]	Scr	Total Score
4	1.72 ±0.33	2.36 ±0.68	31 ±11	1.74 ±0.68	2.40 ±1.08	8 ±6	75.7 ±3.5	−6.3 ±15.9	38 ±17	76.4 ±9.2	−2.2 ±48.1	27 ±17	25.7 ±7.5
3	1.19 ±0.48	1.91 ±1.00	49 ±15	1.17 ±0.82	1.93 ±1.42	34 ±16	56.2 ±4.3	−1.7 ±15.7	47 ±18	55.9 ±5.7	−0.8 ±24.7	47 ±17	44.3 ±9.8
2	0.96 ±0.50	1.77 ±1.04	56 ±16	0.95 ±0.92	1.84 ±1.59	44 ±18	39.3 ±5.5	0.7 ±13.8	60 ±17	40.5 ±5.5	−1.4 ±17.5	57 ±17	54.3 ±9.3
1	0.92 ±0.52	1.78 ±1.07	57 ±16	0.91 ±0.92	1.87 ±1.60	45 ±20	33.4 ±6.6	0.0 ±13.2	63 ±17	34.3 ±6.4	−1.8 ±16.2	61 ±17	56.5 ±9.2

4   Conclusion

We have presented a new multi-resolution framework for applying patch-based segmentation which is able to segment images without requiring registration, along with an atlas selection method which uses histograms of 3D gradients for image comparison in this context. Additionally, the framework allows a trade-off between segmentation accuracy and speed by selecting the resolution at which the segmentation terminates as well as the number of atlases used. We applied this approach to the MR knee images in the SKI10 grand challenge without any post-processing methods, achieving an overall score of 56.5, with average scores of 62.3 for cartilage and 50.8 for bone. This is the first time a purely patch-based method has been applied to segmenting knee images, producing results that are comparable to many of the other methods used in the challenge despite its simplicity. The scores indicate a promising first application of the proposed framework but potential improvements could be achieved by using more training images as well as as post-processing refinements. Furthermore, this framework could also be coupled with model-based approaches as well as other methods such as EM and graph cut to improve performance.

References

1. Akgül, C.B., Rubin, D.L., Napel, S., Beaulieu, C.F., Greenspan, H., Acar, B.: Content-Based Image Retrieval in Radiology: Current Status and Future Directions. Journal of Digital Imaging 24(2), 208–222 (2011)
2. Aljabar, P., Heckemann, R.A., Hammers, A., Hajnal, J.V., Rueckert, D.: Multi-atlas based segmentation of brain images: Atlas selection and its effect on accuracy. NeuroImage 46(3), 726–738 (2009)

3. Anderson, C.H., Bergen, J.R., Burt, P.J., Ogden, J.M.: Pyramid Methods in Image Processing (1984)
4. Coupé, P., Manjón, J.V., Fonov, V., Pruessner, J., Robles, M., Collins, D.L.: Patch-based segmentation using expert priors: application to hippocampus and ventricle segmentation. NeuroImage 54(2), 940–954 (2011)
5. Donoghue, C.R., Rao, A., Pizarro, L., Bull, A.M.J., Rueckert, D.: Fast and accurate global geodesic registrations using knee MRI from the Osteoarthritis Initiative. In: CVPRW, pp. 50–57 (June 2012)
6. Eskildsen, S.F., Coupé, P., Fonov, V., Manjón, J.V., Leung, K.K., Guizard, N., Wassef, S.N., Østergaard, L.R., Collins, D.L.: BEaST: brain extraction based on nonlocal segmentation technique. NeuroImage 59(3), 2362–2373 (2012)
7. Fripp, J., Crozier, S., Warfield, S.K., Ourselin, S.: Automatic Segmentation and Quantitative Analysis of the Articular Cartilages from Magnetic Resonance Images of the Knee. IEEE Transactions on Medical Imaging 29(1), 55–64 (2010)
8. Heckemann, R.A., Hajnal, J.V., Aljabar, P., Rueckert, D., Hammers, A.: Automatic anatomical brain MRI segmentation combining label propagation and decision fusion. NeuroImage 33(1), 115–126 (2006)
9. Heimann, T., Morrison, B.: Segmentation of knee images: A grand challenge. In: MICCAI Workshop on Medical Image Analysis for the Clinic, pp. 207–214 (2010)
10. Klaeser, A., Marszalek, M., Schmid, C.: A Spatio-Temporal Descriptor Based on 3D-Gradients. In: Procedings of BMVC, pp. 99.1–99.10 (2008)
11. Maurer, C.R., Rensheng, Q., Raghavan, V.: A linear time algorithm for computing exact euclidean distance transforms of binary images in arbitrary dimensions. IEEE Transactions on Pattern Analysis and Machine Intelligence 25(2), 265–270 (2003)
12. Nyúl, L.G., Udupa, J.K.: On standardizing the MR image intensity scale. Magnetic Resonance in Medicine 42(6), 1072–1081 (1999)
13. Rohlfing, T., Brandt, R., Menzel, R., Maurer, C.R.: Evaluation of atlas selection strategies for atlas-based image segmentation with application to confocal microscopy images of bee brains. NeuroImage 21(4), 1428–1442 (2004)
14. Rousseau, F., Habas, P., Studholme, C.: A Supervised Patch-Based Approach for Human Brain Labeling. IEEE Transactions on Medical Imaging 30(10), 1852–1862 (2011)
15. Thomson, J.: On the Structure of the Atom: an Investigation of the Stability and Periods of Oscillation of a number of Corpuscles arranged at equal intervals around the Circumference of a Circle; with Application of the Results to the Theory of Atomic Structure. Philosophical Magazine 7(39), 237–265 (1904)
16. Torralba, A., Fergus, R., Freeman, W.T.: 80 Million Tiny Images: a Large Data Set for Nonparametric Object and Scene Recognition. IEEE Transactions on Pattern Analysis and Machine Intelligence 30(11), 1958–1970 (2008)
17. Tustison, N.J., Avants, B.B., Cook, P.A., Zheng, Y., Egan, A., Yushkevich, P.A., Gee, J.C.: N4ITK: improved N3 bias correction. IEEE Transactions on Medical Imaging 29(6), 1310–1320 (2010)
18. Wang, Z., Wolz, R., Tong, T., Rueckert, D.: Spatially Aware Patch-based Segmentation (SAPS): An Alternative Patch-Based Segmentation Framework. In: Menze, B.H., Langs, G., Lu, L., Montillo, A., Tu, Z., Criminisi, A. (eds.) MCV 2012. LNCS, vol. 7766, pp. 93–103. Springer, Heidelberg (2013)
19. Wolz, R., Chu, C., Misawa, K., Mori, K., Rueckert, D.: Multi-organ Abdominal CT Segmentation Using Hierarchically Weighted Subject-Specific Atlases. In: Ayache, N., Delingette, H., Golland, P., Mori, K. (eds.) MICCAI 2012, Part I. LNCS, vol. 7510, pp. 10–17. Springer, Heidelberg (2012)

Flow-Based Correspondence Matching in Stereovision

Songbai Ji[1,2], Xiaoyao Fan[1], David W. Roberts[2,3],
Alex Hartov[1], and Keith D. Paulsen[1,3]

[1] Thayer School of Engineering, Dartmouth College, Hanover NH 03755
[2] Dept. of Surgery, Geisel School of Medicine, Dartmouth College, Hanover NH 03755
[3] Dartmouth Hitchcock Medical Center, Lebanon, NH 03756
(songbai.ji,xiaoyao.fan,david.w.roberts,alex.hartov,
keith.d.paulsen)@Dartmouth.EDU

Abstract. Accurate and efficient correspondence matching between two rectified images is critical for stereo reconstruction. Essentially, correspondence matching co-registers the two rectified images subject to an epipolar constraint (i.e., registration is performed along the horizontal direction). Most algorithms are based on windowed block matching that optimizes cross-correlation or its variants (e.g., sum of squared differences, SSD) between two sub-images to generate a sparse disparity map. In this work, we utilize unrestricted optical flow for a full-field correspondence matching. Relative to surface point measurements sampled with a tracked stylus as ground-truth, we show that the point-to-surface distance from the flow-based method is comparable and often superior to that from the SSD algorithm (e.g., 1.0 mm vs. 1.2 mm, respectively) but with a substantial increase in computational efficiency (5–6 sec for a full field of 41 K vs. 20–30 sec for a sparse subset of 1 K sampling points, respectively). In addition, the flow-based stereovision offers ability for feature identification based on the full-field horizontal disparity map that is directly related to reconstruction pixel depth values, whereas the vertical disparity provides an assessment of the accuracy confidence level in stereo reconstruction, which are not available with SSD methods.

1   Introduction

Stereovision is an effective intraoperative imaging tool (e.g., for brain shift compensation in image-guided neurosurgery) because of its noninvasive and unobtrusive installation and ability to provide texture-rich 3D surfaces of the surgical field at video rates. Prior to surgery, the stereovision system is calibrated by matching a set of points with known 3D coordinates to their counterparts found in the stereo image pair. A perspective projection matrix can then be established from the resulting intrinsic and extrinsic calibration parameters to reconstruct a 3D surface following image rectification and triangulation of correspondence points. Correspondence matching between two rectified images establishes the disparity map required for triangulation; therefore, its performance (accuracy and efficiency) directly determines the fidelity of the 3D surface reconstruction. Most correspondence matching algorithms are based on optimization of cross-correlation or its variants (e.g., sum of squared differences, or

G. Wu et al. (Eds.): MLMI 2013, LNCS 8184, pp. 106–113, 2013.

SSD) between two windowed sub-images [1, 2] subjected to the epipolar constraint (i.e., correspondence point pairs are restricted to a horizontal line), which essentially enforces one-dimensional block-matching registrations. The density of the disparity map depends on the window size (one disparity vector for each window) which is often a compromise between computational cost and accuracy (a smaller window results in a denser disparity map, but with considerable computational burden, whereas a larger window reduces the computational cost but may result in loss of accuracy and precision), and selection of an optimal window size is not trivial. In addition, the matching accuracy is sensitive to the lack of image features and poor illumination conditions, and correction for occluded pixels is challenging.

Optical flow, which detects apparent motion between two successive image frames based on image intensity/color, has also been employed for correspondence matching where the flow field was restricted to the horizontal direction to satisfy the epipolar constraint [1, 3]. Using a variational approach, a full-field (as opposed to selected pixels determined from windows) disparity map is possible. However, the challenges associated with regions of insufficient features or occluded pixels remain, and adoption of the technique has been limited because of its seemingly marginal advantages over traditional methods.

In this paper, we utilize *unrestricted* optical flow in correspondence matching between two rectified images without limiting the flow field to the horizontal direction. Instead, the resulting horizontal disparity is used for triangulation whereas the vertical component is used to assess the accuracy confidence level in stereo-surface reconstruction. Based on images from clinical surgeries with surface points measured via a tracked stylus serving as the ground-truth, we compare the performances (accuracy and efficiency) of the flow- and SSD-based methods in stereo surface reconstruction in the context of image-guided neurosurgery.

2   Material and Methods

A custom-designed stereovision system consisting of two C-mount cameras (Flea2 model FL2G-50S5C-C, Point Grey Research Inc., Richmond, BC, Canada) was rigidly mounted to a Zeiss surgical microscope (OPMI® Pentero™, Carl Zeiss, Inc., Oberkochen, Germany) through a binocular port. The cameras were operated at a resolution of 1024×768 and a rate of 15 fps (frames per second) and were externally triggered to ensure synchronization of the image acquisition. The position and orientation of the microscope was available from a StealthStation® navigation system via StealthLink (Medtronic, Inc., Louisville, CO) through a rigidly attached tracker.

2.1   Stereovision 3D Surface Reconstruction

Calibration of the stereovision system based on a pinhole camera model can be performed by matching point-pairs identified in the two camera images using an instrumented object with known 3D spatial positions of the matched points (e.g., [4]). The resulting intrinsic and extrinsic parameters correct radial lens distortions and generate rectified images in order to constrain the search for correspondence points along epipolar lines. In addition, these parameters fully determine the geometrical relationships required to transform image pixels into the physical space and to define the corresponding 3D point coordinates through geometrical triangulation based on the correspondence point-pairs and camera centers.

Conceptually, stereovision reconstruction determines the 3D spatial coordinate, **P**, of a given sampling point in the rectified left image, **p**:

$$P = G(p, F(p)) = G(p, p + u(p)),$$ (1)

where $F(p)$ is a functional form describing the image coordinate of the correspondence point of **p** in the rectified right image, which is readily obtained when the horizontal disparity, $u(p)$, is available, and G is the geometrical operation (including transformation and triangulation) established from calibration. Therefore, reconstructing the 3D surface in space is reduced to establishing a disparity map between the two rectified images for a given set of calibration parameters. Clearly, the quality (accuracy and density) and the computational efficiency of the disparity map directly determine the overall fidelity of the stereovision reconstruction.

2.2   Two-Frame Optical Flow

Establishing the disparity map between the rectified left ("undeformed") and right ("deformed") image pair is analogous to determining the motion field between the two images. Although the disparity map is subjected to the epipolar constraint (i.e., displacements in the vertical direction should be zero), an *unrestricted* optical flow between the two images is executed where the resulting vertical disparity is used to assess the accuracy confidence level in the horizontal disparity (i.e., pixels with vertical disparity values violating the epipolar constraint indicate possibly spurious horizontal disparity), and hence, the stereo surface reconstruction. Using a variational model [5] and assuming the image intensity of a material point, (x, y), or its corresponding pixel does not change, the gray value constancy constraint

$$I(p + w) = I(p),$$ (2)

holds in which $p = (x, y)$ and the underlying flow field, $w(p)$, is given by $w(p) = (u(p), v(p))$, where $u(p)$ and $v(p)$ are the horizontal and vertical components of the flow field, respectively. The global deviations from the gray value constancy assumption are measured by an energy term

$$E_{Data}(u, v) = \int \psi(|I(p + w) - I(p)|^2) \, dp,$$ (3)

where a robust function, $\psi(x) = \sqrt{x^2 + \varepsilon^2}$, was used to enable an L^1 minimization ($\varepsilon = 0.001$; [6]). Further, because the flow field in a natural scene is typically smooth, an additional piecewise smoothness constraint can be applied to the spatial domain, leading to the energy term

$$E_{Smooth}(u, v) = \int \phi(|\nabla u|^2 + |\nabla v|^2) dp,$$ (4)

where ϕ is a robust function chosen to be identical to ψ, and ∇ is the gradient operator where $|\nabla(u)|^2 = u_x^2 + u_y^2 \left(u_x = \frac{\partial u}{\partial x}, u_y = \frac{\partial u}{\partial y} \right)$, which is analogous for v.

Combining the gray value constancy and piecewise smoothness constraints leads to an objective function in the continuous spatial domain given by

$$E(u, v) = E_{Data} + \alpha E_{Smooth} ,$$ (5)

where α ($a{>}0$; empirically chosen as 0.02 in this study) is a regularization parameter. Computing the optical flow is then transformed into an optimization problem to determine the spatially continuous flow field (defined by u and v) that minimizes the total energy, E. Here, an iterative reweighted least squares algorithm, and a multi-scale approach starting with a coarse, smoothed image set were used to ensure global minimization [7].

2.3   Disparity Estimation Based on Optical Flow

For all flow-based stereo-surface reconstructions, the rectified images were down-sampled by 0.2 along each direction, resulting in a typical dimension of 176×232, or approximately 41 K regularly-positioned sampling points. The full-field horizontal displacements from two-frame optical flow on the two (down-sampled) rectified images served as the disparity map, $u(\mathbf{p})$, from which the texture-encoded 3D stereo surface is readily reconstructed from the geometrical operations defined in Eqn. 1. Although the flow field is spatially smooth due to the smoothness constraint applied during the optimization, spurious disparities can still occur in regions of insufficient features and/or with occluded pixels, similarly to SSD-based correspondence matching. Instead of correcting for these spurious disparities in the solution field by applying appropriate constraints in the optimization with the corresponding additional burden of algorithmic implementation and increase in computational cost [3], we detect regions of spurious disparities using values of the vertical flow field, $v(\mathbf{p})$. This strategy is possible because ground-truth values of zeros for $v(\mathbf{p})$ are known *a priori* as a direct result of the epipolar constraint where correspondence point pairs were pre-aligned on the same horizontal lines in the rectified images. Therefore, pixels with large absolute values of $v(\mathbf{p})$ (i.e., above a certain threshold) that violate the epilopar constraint would also indicate likely spurious horizontal disparities, $u(\mathbf{p})$. These pixels can simply be excluded from stereo surface reconstruction. Alternatively, the sampling pixels could be empirically filtered into regions of high, mid, or low confidence levels based on the absolute vertical disparities, abs(v). Horizontal disparity values for pixels with a high or low confidence level could be either retained or removed, while those in-between could be interpolated based on surrounding values with a high confidence level. A two-tier threshold interpolation/exclusion scheme seemed to be effective in retaining regions of sufficient disparity accuracies while removing those with insufficient features (e.g., due to specular artifacts) or occluded pixels from surface reconstruction.

2.4   Data Analysis

Stereoscopic images of the exposed parenchyma were acquired during three patient surgeries (a 38-year-old female with a mixed oligoastrocytoma, a 18-year old female with epilepsy, and a 54-year-old male with a glial neuroplasm, respectively) at five distinct procedural stages (before craniotomy, pre- and post-dural opening, and during and after tumor resection) at the lowest focal length and magnification offered by the operating microscope. Texture-encoded stereo surfaces were reconstructed using the flow-based technique as well as an SSD method [4] for comparison. For the latter method, correspondences were established for approximately 1 K uniformly distributed sampling points (regions within 50 pixels around the boundary were excluded) from which to reconstruct the surface. To objectively evaluate the accuracy in stereo surface reconstruction, ground-truth point measures were sampled on the exposed surgical surface using a tracked stylus. Distances from the stylus probe tip to the reconstructed surfaces (i.e., point-to-surface distances) were used to evaluate reconstruction accuracy. We did not use distances between the probe tip and the corresponding feature points (i.e., point-to-point distances) for accuracy assessment because the surfaces were not always sampled at uniquely identifiable feature point locations (e.g., intersection of vessels). All computations were performed on a Windows 7 computer (2.0 G Hz with 16 G memory) using MATLAB (version 2012a).

3   Results

A typical flow field in the horizontal and vertical directions (i.e., u- and v-map, respectively) is shown in Fig. 1a and b, together with an overlay of abs(u) and the rectified left image (Fig. 1c). Pixels with large abs(v) values appeared to occur in values appeared to occur in regions with no features (i.e., near the top and bottom boundaries due to zero-padding as a result of image rotation in rectification; Fig. 1b) or resulted from occluded pixels along depth transition edges (see arrows in Fig. 1b).

The reconstructed brain surface based on optical flow is shown in Fig. 2 along with its counterpart using the SSD approach. Because of the denser disparity map obtained with the flow-based technique, a much smoother depth transition was evident compared to the SSD surface (thick arrows). In addition, surface boundary areas derived from the optical flow technique appeared natural whereas their analogs were distorted with the SSD method (Fig. 2b).

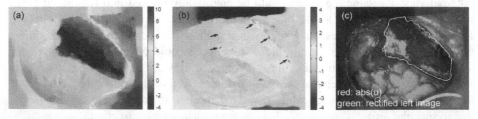

Fig. 1. Full-field u-map (a) and v-map (b) for a typical pair of rectified images at the end of tumor resection for patient 1. An overlay of abs(u) (red) and the rectified left image (green) is shown in (c), where contour lines at the level of $u=0$ are drawn that spatially corresponded to the resection cavity boundaries.

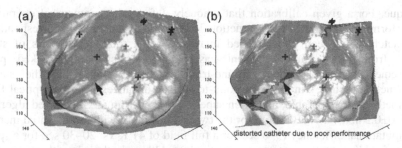

Fig. 2. Reconstructed parenchymal surfaces using the flow-based (a) or SSD (b) approach in the patient's MR space. Surface point measurement locations are also shown (black crosses).

To further illustrate the ability of the flow-based reconstruction for morphological operations such as segmentation, we show the flow field and the reconstructed 3D surface profiles of the surgical scene of patient 2 (Fig. 3), where catheters (Fig. 3) and a surgical tool (Fig. 4) were visible in the surgical scene at two surgical stages, respectively, and they could be easily segmented based on the u-map (e.g., by thresholding or region grow segmentation). Table 1 summarizes the point-to-surface distances as an accuracy measure of the reconstructed surfaces from the two correspondence matching methods based on tracked probe data at each surgical stage.

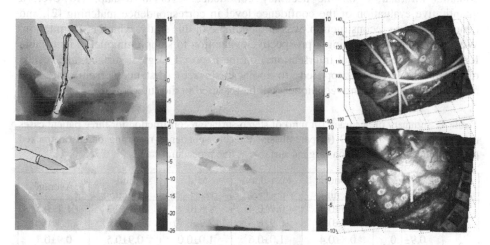

Fig. 3. Full-field u-map (left column) and v-map (mid column) for stereo-pairs showing catheters and surgical tools in view, and they can be segmented based on pixel depth values in the u-map (e.g., contour lines of segmented regions via region grow method are shown). The corresponding stereo surface profiles are shown in the right column.

4   Discussion and Conclusion

Accuracy and efficiency in stereo-surface reconstruction are critical for successful and effective deployment of stereovision as a non-invasive intraoperative imaging technique. For a given calibration that uniquely defines the geometrical operations, the performance of stereo reconstruction is directly dependent on correspondence point-matching between two rectified images. With a total of 15 pairs of stereo images from three clinical patient cases, and corresponding tracked probe measurements as independent ground-truth data, we show that the surface reconstruction accuracy in terms of point-to-surface distances from the optical flow-based method is comparable, and often superior, to that from an SSD-based algorithm (e.g., 1.0 ± 0.5 mm vs. 1.2 ± 0.6 mm for the two methods) but with a substantial increase in computational efficiency (5–6 sec for a full field of 41 K vs. 20–30 sec for a sparse subset of 1 K sampling points, respectively). Although the algorithms for both approaches can be further optimized (part of the flow-based approach was implemented in C, while the SSD method was mostly implemented in Matlab), these results do suggest a better computational efficiency with the flow-based method. In addition, the v-map allows the accuracy confidence level in stereo surface reconstruction to be assessed with the flow-based method, which is not available in the SSD algorithm. Although the v-map does not necessarily *guarantee* the level of u-map accuracy in stereo reconstruction (i.e., pixels with spurious v-values could still correspond to u-values within a tolerance, and vice versa), our results show that pixels of spurious v-values occur in regions with no/few features (e.g., due to zero-padding or specular reflection) or along surface depth transition boundaries with occluded pixels (e.g., at edges of the tumor resection cavity), suggesting the v-map contains information on the accuracy confidence level in u-map. However, a quantitative evaluation of the confidence level in correspondence matching [2], and hence, in surface reconstruction, was not available in this study, which is a limitation. We are currently conducting a prospective evaluation to sample uniquely identifiable feature points (e.g., vessel intersections) on the exposed surgical surface, and results of point-to-point (as opposed to point-to-surface) distances from the two correspondence matching techniques will be reported in the future.

Table 1. Summary of accuracy (in mm) of stereo-surface reconstruction for three patient cases using optical flow and SSD (in parenthesis) for correspondence matching based on tracked probe tip locations sampled on surgical surfaces at five procedural stages

Pat-ient	Before craniotomy	Pre-dural opening	Post-dural opening	Mid-resection	End-resection	Average
1	1.3 ± 0.1 (1.7 ± 0.4)	0.5 ± 0.4 (0.7 ± 0.8)	0.7 ± 0.4 (0.9 ± 0.3)	1.8 ± 0.7 (2.2 ± 0.7)	1.1 ± 0.3 (1.2 ± 0.8)	1.1 ± 0.5 (1.3 ± 0.6)
2	0.9 ± 1.0 (1.0 ± 1.3)	0.8 ± 0.4 (1.0 ± 0.3)	1.0 ± 0.6 (0.8 ± 0.4)	1.0 ± 0.0 (1.3 ± 0.0)	0.9 ± 0.5 (1.3 ± 0.9)	0.9 ± 0.1 (1.1 ± 0.2)
3	0.8 ± 0.9 (0.9 ± 1.0)	0.9 ± 0.6 (1.0 ± 0.6)	0.9 ± 0.9 (0.8 ± 0.8)	1.0 ± 0.6 (1.3 ± 0.8)	1.1 ± 0.6 (1.3 ± 0.9)	0.9 ± 0.1 (1.1 ± 0.2)

Because full-field disparity maps are available from the flow-based method (as opposed to a sparse subset with the SSD approach), image morphological operations are feasible with this technique based on pixel depth values. For example, segmentation of surgical cavities or identification of tools in the surgical field are possible based on u-map or pixel depth values directly because these regions usually correspond to "lower" or "higher" regions in the scene, as demonstrated in Figs. 1 and 3, for tumor cavity and surgical tool, respectively. In Fig. 1c, a simple thresholding method was used to localize the tumor resection cavity area, which may not be feasible using image color or texture information alone (e.g., the upper left corner of the resection cavity could be mistakenly identified as the intact area due to its similar color with the exposed cortical surface). With an automatic segmentation of the region of interest (ROI) being possible, improvement in surface reconstruction accuracy and precision through a multi-resolution approach may also be desirable by successively increasing the image resolution of the ROI used for reconstruction.

To summarize, we have successfully demonstrated the use of unconstrained optical flow for correspondence matching between two rectified images in stereo-surface reconstruction. By comparing with a traditional SSD correspondence matching algorithm, the flow-based technique is not only comparable (and often superior) in the accuracy of reconstructing the surface, but it is also substantially more efficient computationally. By decomposing the full-field disparity map into horizontal and vertical components, image morphological operations can be performed on the disparity maps based on pixel depth values from which confidence levels in the surface reconstruction accuracy can be inferred, which is typically not available with SSD methods. As illustrated in two clinical patient cases, we anticipate wide application of the flow-based technique in stereo-surface reconstruction, which is important for effective deployment of stereovision in the operating room.

Acknowledgement. This work was supported, in part, by the National Institutes of Health grant numbers R01 CA159324–01 and R21 NS078607 awarded by the NCI and NINDS, respectively.

References

1. Roma, N., Santos-Victor, J., Tome, J.: A comparative analysis of cross-correlation matching algorithms using a pyramidal resolution approach. In: Christensen, H.I., Phillips, P.J. (eds.) Empirical Evaluation Methods in Computer Vision, pp. 117–142. World Scientific Press, Singapore (2002) ISBN 981-02-4953-5
2. Hu, X., Mordohai, P.: A Quantitative Evaluation of Confidence Measures for Stereo Vision. IEEE Transactions on Pattern Analysis and Machine Intelligence 34(11), 2121–2133 (2012), doi:10.1109/TPAMI.2012.46
3. Hatzitheodorou, M., Karabassi, E.A., Papaioannou, G., Boehm, A., Theoharis, T.: Stereo Matching Using Optic Flow. Real-Time Imaging 6, 251–266 (2000)
4. Sun, H., Lunn, K.E., Farid, H., Wu, Z., Roberts, D.W., Hartov, A., Paulsen, K.D.: Stereopsis-guided brain shift compensation. IEEE Trans. Med. Imag. 24(8), 1039–1052 (2005)
5. Brox, T., Bruhn, A., Papenberg, N., Weickert, J.: High accuracy optical flow estimation based on a theory for warping. In: Pajdla, T., Matas, J. (eds.) ECCV 2004. LNCS, vol. 3024, pp. 25–36. Springer, Heidelberg (2004)
6. Black, M.J., Anandan, P.: The robust estimation of multiple motions: parametric and piecewise-smooth flow fields. Comput. Vision and Image Understanding 63(1), 75–104 (1996)
7. Liu, C.: Beyond Pixels: Exploring New Representations and Applications for Motion Analysis. Doctoral Thesis. Massachusetts Institute of Technology (May 2009)

Thickness NETwork (ThickNet) Features for the Detection of Prodromal AD

Pradeep Reddy Raamana[1,*], Lei Wang[2], and Mirza Faisal Beg[1]
for The Alzheimer's Disease Neuroimaging Initiative[**]

[1] School of Engineering Science, Simon Fraser University
[2] Feinberg School of Medicine, Northwestern University
pkr1@sfu.ca

Abstract. Regional analysis of cortical thickness has been studied extensively in building imaging biomarkers for early detection of Alzheimer's disease (AD), but not its inter-regional covariation. We present novel features based on the inter-regional co-variation of cortical thickness. Initially the cortical labels of each patient is partitioned into small patches (graph nodes) by spatial k-means clustering. A graph is then constructed by establishing a link between two nodes if the difference in thickness between the nodes is below a certain threshold. From this binary graph, thickness network (ThickNet) features are computed using nodal degree, betweenness and clustering coefficient measures. Fusing them with multiple kernel learning, we demonstrate their potential for the detection of prodromal AD.

Keywords: thickness, network, fusion, mild cognitive impairment, alzheimer.

1 Introduction

Today, Alzheimer's disease (AD) is the most common type of dementia, accounting for 60%−80% of the cases [1], for which definitive diagnosis can only be made with the histopathological confirmation of amyloid plaques and neurofibrillary tangles. Recent reports suggest that the alzheimer pathology begins decades before any clinical symptoms appear [2], highlighting the importance and challenge in early detection of AD. Cortical thickness has been studied extensively [3,4]. These studies show that early-stage cortical thickness by itself using only baseline MRI scans proved to be useful for the early detection of AD, but with limited utility, as was shown in [3]. Cuingnet et al., 2011 performed a comparison of the predictive performance of published image processing methods, on a common

---

[*] Corresponding author.
[**] Data used in preparation of this article were obtained from the Alzheimers Disease Neuroimaging Initiative (ADNI) database (adni.loni.ucla.edu). As such, the investigators within the ADNI contributed to the design and implementation of ADNI and/or provided data but did not participate in analysis or writing of this report. A complete listing of ADNI investigators can be found at: http://adni.loni.ucla.edu/wp-content/uploads/how_to_apply/ADNI_Acknowledgement_List.pdf

G. Wu et al. (Eds.): MLMI 2013, LNCS 8184, pp. 114–122, 2013.
© Springer International Publishing Switzerland 2013

dataset, to predict conversion to AD in MCI patients. They observed that no existing method using baseline cortical thickness is able to accurately predict conversion to AD in MCI subjects.

There has been plethora of research in ROI-based analysis of cortical thickness [3], but only few studies analyzed the co-variation of thickness in different regions of the brain [5]. We would like to capture the nature of the pair-wise changes to characterize the topographical gradient in cortical thickness as associated with the progression of AD. Establishing links (akin to edges in a graph) using cortical thickness or gray matter density extracted from structural MRI are only beginning to be explored, limited to either studying the small world properties of such a graph [6], or any group differences that exist between patient and control (CN) groups [7,8]. These studies have not, to date, constructed any features from such inter-regional co-variation, or performed evaluation of its diagnostic utility.

We propose to utilize differential changes in cortical thickness, as the progression of AD generally follows a stereotypical spatial pattern and hence pair-wise changes between cortical surface patches will likely complement existing features for early detection based on cortical thickness. We construct novel features based on the network properties of interregional links in the brain defined using cortical thickness. Further, we fuse these thickness network (ThickNet) features using probabilistic multiple kernel learning approach and investigate their predictive utility in the detection of prodromal AD (MCI converters) on a large cohort from ADNI dataset.

2 Methods

2.1 Dataset

Data used in the preparation of this article were obtained from the Alzheimer's Disease Neuroimaging Initiative (ADNI) database (adni.loni.ucla.edu). For up-to-date information, see www.adni-info.org. Cuingnet et al., 2011 [3] compared the performance of various published classification methods on fixed training and testing sets resulting in a comparable set of performance metrics. To enable comparison to a large set of similar methods, we utilized the same subset of 509 participants as studied in [3], except for a few exclusions (28 subjects in total) whose cortical parcellation did not meet our quality control metrics. We refer the reader to [3] for the complete description of the participants and demographics for the study cohort. Briefly, our study consists of 481 T1-weighted MR scans acquired at 1.5T. MRI scans from the baseline visit were used when available (and from the screening visit otherwise). This gave MR images from 159 CN subjects, 56 MCIc subjects (who had converted to AD within 18 months), 130 MCI non-converters (MCInc) subjects and 136 AD subjects. In this paper, we use the term prodromal AD to denote MCIc, and the two terms are used interchangeably.

2.2   Thickness Measurement and Processing

Cortical thickness was computed for each subject using the topology-aware thickness computation method described in [9]. Each subject is then registered to the surface of a common atlas (derived from averaging over 100 healthy subjects) and smoothed with a 10-mm full width at half height Gaussian kernel to improve the signal-to-noise ratio and statistical power, using the tools from [10].

Each cortex surface contained 327684 vertices in the whole brain and we have a limited number of subjects. To avoid the curse of dimensionality, we partitioned each cortical label (such as posterior cingulate etc. from the 68 Freesurfer-derived parcellation) containing thousands of vertices into a small number (say 10) of partitions by clustering vertices, within each label, using k-means clustering of vertex coordinates. Note that clustering is done within each Freesurfer label, which prohibits linking vertices across different labels. Moreover, the vertex density of Freesurfer parcellation is sufficiently high and uniform to satisfy the k-means assumptions [11], and visual verification of partitioning confirmed the desired outcome. The thickness feature for each sub-partition is defined as the average thickness across vertices in that partition.

Visualization of such a subdivision of the cortex into 680 partitions is shown in Figure 1. As they are all registered to a common atlas, this subdivision of the cortex is propagated into the cortical surface of each subject to establish correspondence for proper analysis. It is worth noting that certain trade-offs exist in deciding the total number of partitions (TNP) for this method. Hence we study the performance of this method for different values of TNP = 340, 680, 1020, 1360 and 1700, to avoid making an arbitrary choice.

2.3   Thickness Network (ThickNet) Features

Once the pial surface is partitioned into large number of small sub-partitions (thought of as nodes), a network (graph) is constructed by establishing a link between two nodes if the absolute difference in thickness is below a specified threshold. The term *network* is used here in the abstract sense to mean a mathematical graph and not a functional/structural network connected by physical fiber tracts or connections. From this binary undirected graph, we compute thickness network measures - we term them *ThickNet* features - such as nodal degree, betweenness centrality and clustering coefficient to represent each individual brain. Thicknet measures are *intrinsic* to each subject and offer insight into regional correlations in cortical thinning.

Suppose N is the set of all nodes in the network (the number of nodes $n = NPP * 68$, NPP=number of partitions per freesurfer label in each of the 68 freesurfer labels) and L is the set of all links in the network (l=number of links). Note N equals TNP, which is the total number of partitions in each subject's cortical surface. Let (i, j) be a link between nodes i and j $(i, j \in N)$ and a_{ij} is the link status between i and j: $a_{ij} = 1$ when link (i, j) exists; $a_{ij} = 0$ otherwise. A link is defined between i and j, if $|MT_i - MT_j| <= \alpha$, where MT_x represents the mean thickness in the node $x, x \in N$. Here α is the threshold to establish a link. A lenient threshold ($\alpha > 0.5mm$) allows large number of links in the cortex, whereas a stringent threshold ($\alpha \leq 0.5mm$) allows relatively few links. It is important to note that spatial distance or spatial adjacency is not a criteria, as the method searches all possible pairwise links between all cortical sub-partitions.

We chose to utilize nodal degree (measure of how connected each node is), betweenness centrality (measure of centrality) and clustering coefficient (measure of segregation) from the binary graph as properties to describe the network [12]. In brief, for a given node i, these are defined as

$$\text{nodal degree } k_i = \sum_{j \in N} a_{ij} \tag{1}$$

$$\text{betweenness centrality } b_i = \frac{1}{(n-1)(n-2)} \sum_{h,j \in N, h \neq j, h \neq i, j \neq i} \frac{\rho_{hj}(i)}{\rho_{hj}} \tag{2}$$

$$\text{clustering coefficient } C_i = \frac{1}{n} \sum_{i \in N} \frac{2t_i}{k_i(k_i - 1)} \tag{3}$$

where $t_i = \frac{1}{2} \sum_{j,h \in N} a_{ij} a_{ih} a_{jh}$ is the number of triangles around node i; ρ_{hj} is the number of shortest paths between h and j and $\rho_{hj}(i)$ is the number of shortest paths between h and j that pass through i. Please note k_i in Eq. (3) is the nodal degree defined in Eq. (1).

Intuitively, the *degree* of an individual node is equal to the number of links connected to that node, which therefore reflects the level of interaction of that node in the network. It is hypothesized that there are *central nodes* which participate in many short paths in the brain network. *Betweenness centrality* measures the fraction of all shortest paths in the network that pass through a given node. It is also known that human brain segregates specialized processing into interconnected groups of brain regions (clusters) - *clustering coefficient* measures the clustering connectivity around a given node. The ThickNet features for the CN and MCIc classes, in the form of group-differences, are visualized in Figure 1.

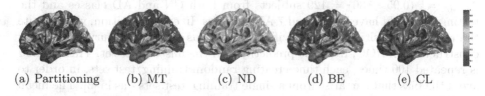

(a) Partitioning   (b) MT   (c) ND   (d) BE   (e) CL

Fig. 1. (a) Visualization of the partitions. (b) to (f) Visualization of the differences in group means, i.e. mean(CN)-mean(MCIc) at each partition, of the thicknet features when total number of partitions (TNP)=680 and α=0.30. Here MT denotes mean thickness, ND denotes nodal degree, BE denotes betweenness centrality and CL denotes clustering coefficient. Each feature in (b) to (f) are normalized to [0,1] to enable comparison across features. It can be easily seen that nodal degree exhibits largest differences followed by betweenness and then clustering coefficient. High resolution visualizations in multiple views are included in the *supplementary material*.

3   Evaluation of Predictive Utility

The ThickNet features reveal different properties of the regional links in thickness in the human brain. In order to maximize their utility for the early detection of AD, these features can be fused via Multiple kernel learning (MKL). We chose to utilize Variational Bayes probabilistic MKL (VBpMKL) [13] which has been successfully applied to protein fold recognition with attractive properties such as probabilistic estimates, automatic tuning of parameters as well as estimating the significance of individual features. Prior to fusion, further feature selection is done (within each feature *set* separately), by ranking each partition by its two-sample t-statistic computed from the training set alone.

Largest reduced dimensionality to avoid over fitting: There is an empirical relationship between the number of features (K) used to train the classifier and the minimum size of the *training* sample needed to avoid the curse of dimensionality, which is that for K number of features and small probability of error p(e), the minimum sample size required $N_{min} \geq \frac{K}{2p(e)}$ [14]. If one would like to keep $p(e)$ below 5% with K features, we need atleast $N_{min} = K/(2*0.05) = K*10$ subjects for training. We use this relation to determine the maximum number of features that can be used to train the classifier with an N_{train} number of samples in the training set i.e. $K_{max} =\downarrow (N_{train}/10)$. This would give a $K_{max} = 12$ and 5 for the experiments AD/CN and MCIc/CN respectively. We propose novel application of this approach derived from analytical results to set the largest dimensionality to avoid the possibility of over-fitting.

Repeated Hold-out, Stratified Training set (RHsT): We evaluate its predictive utility using a novel repeated stratified holdout method. It is stratified in the sense that each class has an equal number of subjects in the training set to eliminate any class imbalance that may arise for typical uses of popular cross-validation methods. In each repetition, we hold out N_{train} subjects from each class for training and the rest for testing the classifier. Here N_{train} is determined by 95% of the smallest class in the experiment. For example, in the CN (n=159) vs. AD (n=136) experiment, training set would consist of $N_{train} =\downarrow (0.95 * 136) = 129$ subjects from both CN and AD classes and the testing set would have 30 CN and 7 AD subjects. In each repetition, we compute the accuracy, sensitivity and specificity as well as area under curve (AUC) by constructing an ROC, from the predictions on the unseen test set. This method is repeated 100 times, each time creating random training/test sets, in order to avoid the bias that can arise from a single training/test sets - as in [3]. The mean performance metrics, and their standard deviations, from the 100 repetitions are reported.

4   Results and Discussion

The evaluation method as described in Section 3 is applied to the fusion of the following four feature sets: mean thickness, nodal degree, betweenness centrality and clustering coefficient at each partition. From preliminary trials in AD/CN classification, we observed the best performance from VBpMKL using a polynomial kernel (3rd degree) for each feature set and thereby fixing it as the kernel of choice for this study. The performance of the fusion method is evaluated in the following four binary classification experiments: CN vs. AD, CN vs. MCIc, CN vs. MCI and MCInc vs. MCIc, to compare their predictive utility under different levels of separability. For each such experiment, there are two parameters that change the feature extraction (of the mean thickness and the three network features): TNP and the link threshold α. To avoid making an arbitrary choice for these parameter values, we have studied the performance of our method for different combinations of TNP and α, with TNP = 340, 680, 1020, 1360 and 1700, and α was varied from 0.1mm to 1.5mm, in steps of 0.1mm. The AUC for all the combinations are visualized in Figure 2(a).

The best performance (highest AUC) of the ThickNet fusion method for different experiments are summarized in Table 1, with different performance metrics and the optimal ThickNet parameters TNP and α. Corresponding ROCs are visualized in Figure 2(b), which are constructed by averaging the 100 ROCs obtained from the 100 repetitions of the RHsT, using the vertical averaging method as described in [15].

Table 1. Best performance (highest AUC) of the ThickNet fusion method for each experiment, in various classification metrics (with their std. deviation from the 100 repetitions of RHsT) describing the performance. The optimal TNP and threshold (α) is noted for each experiment.

Experiment	AUC (SD)	ACC (SD)	SENS (SD)	SPEC (SD)	TNP	α
CN vs. AD	0.92 (0.06)	0.89 (0.06)	0.80 (0.16)	0.90 (0.06)	340	0.30
CN vs. MCIc	0.83 (0.15)	0.76 (0.04)	0.74 (0.32)	0.76 (0.04)	340	0.30
CN vs. MCI	0.75 (0.10)	0.65 (0.07)	0.64 (0.08)	0.73 (0.17)	1020	1.30
MCIc vs. MCInc	0.68 (0.21)	0.64 (0.06)	0.65 (0.36)	0.64 (0.06)	1700	1.30

The most interesting result in Table 1 is the performance in discriminating MCIc from CN with an AUC of 0.83 (74% sensitivity and 76% specificity). For a *similar* experiment, the mean thickness in each freesurfer label (or ROI, many times larger than our partition), noted as the Thickness-ROI method in [3] resulted in 65% sensitivity and 94% specificity. This is not directly comparable to our result, as we fuse multiple thicknet features whereas the other study uses mean thickness alone. Another study [4] that utilizes mean thickness features for classification between progressive MCI (conversion in 24 months, results for 18 months are not reported) and stable MCI, reports an AUC=0.67, 59% sensitivity and 70% specificity. For a similar experiment on classification between MCInc (stable MCI) and MCIc (conversion in 18 months), we obtain AUC=0.68 with 65% sensitivity and 64% specificity. Our performance is slightly better than [4], although it is to be noted the subsets being studied are different, and the two studies utilize different types of mean thickness.

Another interesting point to note from Table 1 is that when the separability is higher (CN vs. AD and CN vs. MCIc), the best performance was obtained

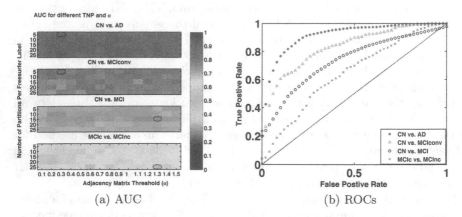

(a) AUC   (b) ROCs

Fig. 2. (a) Comparison of AUC obtained from RHsT method for each combination of NPP and α. The combination with the best performance in each experiment is highlighted with a black oval. The sensitivity and specificity comparisons are included in *supplementary material*. (b) Comparison of ROC curves corresponding to the best performance of thicknet fusion method in each experiment.

with a coarse partitioning ($TNP = 340$, relatively large patches) and a stringent threshold ($\alpha = 0.3mm$ that results in only few links). In contrast, in challenging problems with lower separability (CN vs. MCI and MCIc vs. MCInc), our method needed a very intricate network ($TNP > 1000$ resulting in large number of small areas and a lenient $\alpha = 1.3mm$ resulting in many links). A lenient α results in higher nodal degree (each node is connected to larger number of nodes), and smaller centrality (discourages local clustering) and clustering coefficient. This makes sense clinically and conforms to our understanding of the disease stages.

Individual Significance of Thicknet features: The average weights from the 100 repetitions of RHsT in the CN vs. MCIc experiment for MT=0.37, ND=0.18, BE=0.20 and CL=0.26. Here we notice that all the ThickNet features are contributing to the classifier in a significant way (weights $\gtrsim 20\%$), which asserts their utility. The most discriminative partitions based on their selection frequency from the 100 runs of RHsT (see *supplementary material* for visualizations) are mostly in the medial temporal, occipital and parietal lobes (depending on the feature), which conforms to our understanding of the disease progression.

5   Conclusions and Future Work

We present novel ThickNet features that can be extracted from a single time-point MRI scan and demonstrate their potential for *individual patient diagnosis*. As these features are generic, they can be easily applied to several prognostic problems in neuroimaging. The diagnostic utility of ThickNet features is demonstrated by applying probabilistic multiple kernel learning (preceded by t-statistic feature selection) to the challenging problem of detection of prodromal AD based on baseline MRI scan alone. We report an AUC=0.83 for MCIc/CN classification problem with 74% sensitivity and 76% specificity, which is very promising. Further, we present a useful comparison of the classification performance of ThickNet fusion method in AD/CN, MCIc/MCInc and MCI (MCIc+MCInc)/CN classification experiments. We would like to note that there is likely significant room for improvement e.g. by applying different (or multiple) kernels for each feature as well as tuning the kernel parameters, as opposed to the current results obtained with a fixed kernel (polynomial kernel, degree=3). Moreover we could compute more ThickNet features using additional measures of centrality, segregation and integration, as well as constructing weighted graphs from the regional links in cortical thickness as opposed to current choice of binary and undirected graphs in this study. Although we employed robust techniques for training and evaluation to avoid over-fitting and to obtain unbiased estimates of predictive power, it would be worth investigating the performance of thicknet features on an independent dataset.

Acknowledgments. We gratefully acknowledge funding support from Alzheimer Society Canada for both P. R. Raamana and M. F. Beg. The authors sincerely thank Dr. Michael W. Weiner and the Freesurfer team at University of California, San Francisco for the computation and quality control of Freesurfer processing for ADNI dataset.

References

1. Alzheimer's Association. 2012 Alzheimer's disease facts and figures. Alzheimer's & Dementia: The Journal of the Alzheimer's Association 8(2), 131–168 (2012)
2. Braak, H., et al.: The pathological process underlying Alzheimer's disease in individuals under thirty. Acta Neuropathologica 121(2), 171–181 (2011)
3. Cuingnet, R., et al.: Automatic classification of patients with Alzheimer's disease from structural MRI: a comparison of ten methods using the ADNI database. NeuroImage 56(2), 766–781 (2011)
4. Eskildsen, S.F., et al.: Prediction of Alzheimer's disease in subjects with mild cognitive impairment from the ADNI cohort using patterns of cortical thinning. NeuroImage (October 2012)
5. Wen, W., et al.: Structural brain networks and neuropsychiatric disorders. Current Opinion in Psychiatry 24(3), 219–225 (2011)
6. He, Y., et al.: Structural insights into aberrant topological patterns of large-scale cortical networks in Alzheimer's disease. The Journal of Neuroscience 28(18), 4756–4766 (2008)
7. Bassett, D.S., et al.: Hierarchical Organization of Human Cortical Networks in Health and Schizophrenia. The Journal of Neuroscience 28(37), 9239–9248 (2008)
8. Yao, Z., et al.: Abnormal cortical networks in mild cognitive impairment and Alzheimer's disease. PLoS Computational Biology 6(11), e1001006 (2010)
9. Gibson, E., et al.: Cortical thickness measurement using eulerian pdes and surface-based global topological information. In: 15th Ann. Meeting on Org. Human Brain Mapping (2009)
10. Fischl, B., et al.: Whole brain segmentation: Automated labeling of neuroanatomical structures in the human brain. Neuron 33(3), 341–355 (2002)

11. Lee, J.K., et al.: A novel quantitative cross-validation of different cortical surface reconstruction algorithms using MRI phantom. NeuroImage 31(2), 572–584 (2006)
12. Rubinov, M., et al.: Complex network measures of brain connectivity: uses and interpretations. NeuroImage 52(3), 1059–1069 (2010)
13. Damoulas, T., et al.: Probabilistic multi-class multi-kernel learning: on protein fold recognition and remote homology detection. Bioinformatics 24(10), 1264–1270 (2008)
14. Fitzpatrick, M., et al.: Handbook of medical imaging. Medical image processing & analysis (PM80), vol. 2. SPIE-International Society for Optical Engineering (2000)
15. Fawcett, T.: An introduction to roc analysis. Pattern Recognition Letters 27(8), 861–874 (2006)

Metric Space Structures
for Computational Anatomy

Jianqiao Feng[1,2], Xiaoying Tang[1,2], Minh Tang[1,3],
Carey Priebe[1,3], and Michael Miller[1,4]

[1] Center of Imaging Science, The Johns Hopkins University, United States
[2] Department of Electrical and Computer Engineering,
The Johns Hopkins University, United States
[3] Department of Applied Mathematics and Statistics,
The Johns Hopkins University, United States
[4] Department of Biomedical Engineering,
The Johns Hopkins University, United States

Abstract. This paper describes a method based on metric structures
for anatomical analysis on a large set of brain MR images. A geodesic
distance between each pair was measured using large deformation
diffeomorphic metric mapping (LDDMM). Manifold learning approaches
were applied to seek a low-dimensional embedding in the high-
dimensional shape space, in which inference between healthy control
and disease groups can be done using standard classification algorithms.
In particular, the proposed method was evaluated on ADNI, a dataset
for Alzheimer's disease study. Our work demonstrates that the high-
dimensional anatomical shape space of the amygdala and hippocampi
can be approximated by a relatively low dimension manifold.

Keywords: structural MR image, computational anatomy, Alzheimer's
disease, manifold learning, shape analysis.

1 Introduction

In the past decade, computational anatomy (CA) [1] has emerged as a discipline
to study the neuroanatomical variability via morphometric mapping algorithms.
Quantitative analysis of anatomy has thus become possible. This paper studies the problem of embedding healthy control (HC) and Alzheimer's disease
(AD) subjects into an anatomical shape space by computing a dissimilarity representation between subjects. Manifold learning techniques are applied on the
dissimilarity representation to obtain embeddings for different subjects followed
by classification in the embedded space. A widely-used framework in CA, large
deformation diffeomorphic metric mapping (LDDMM) [2] was used for dissimilarity measurement. The proposed method was evaluated on a dataset of 385 MR
images obtained from the Alzheimer's Disease Neuroimaging Initiative (ADNI)
[3]. Instead of studying the whole brain, here we consider only two anatomical
structures, hippocampus and amygdala, which have been reported to be affected
morphologically by AD.

G. Wu et al. (Eds.): MLMI 2013, LNCS 8184, pp. 123–130, 2013.

There have been several related methods proposed in the literature to apply manifold learning methods to dissimilarities measured on structural images. Most of them quantify inter-subject dissimilarity based on volume image data. For example, a similarity measurement called bending energy is employed in [4]. In [5, 6], random forest has been used to measure dissimilarity on some statistical region-based features extracted from volume images. In [7], dissimilarity was calculated via a small deformation to approximate a large deformation for computational efficiency. Similar approximations can be found in [8, 9, 4]. However, the explosive growth of computing power along with parallel computing resources have made the problem of computation less severe. Thus a full large deformation diffeomorphic metric is adopted in this paper. In this study, we couple the volume imagery to surfaces, and track the variations of shape using surface models. Studying surfaces allows us to capture the variation of neurodevelopment very efficiently [8].

Low-dimensional embedding can be calculated from the dissimilarity information via standard manifold learning approaches, such as multidimensional scaling (MDS) used in [5, 6, 10], Isomap used in [4, 8, 9], Laplacian Eigenmaps (LE) used in [7].

After the embedding in low-dimensional space is calculated, statistical inference is often carried out. One choice is classification between different cohorts. Classification accuracy then becomes an important criteria for evaluating the dimension of the embedding. We note that we only consider the two-class classification problem, i.e., HC and AD. In this paper, a number of standard manifold learning and classification algorithms were employed. Section 3 presents our experiments and result. Compared with related works mentioned above, our investigations are more extensive, i.e., we consider a larger dataset. Our methodology achieves comparable classification accuracy.

2   Methods

In this section, the framework of our method is described step by step. The flowchart is presented in Figure 1.

2.1   Data Acquisition

The dataset used in our experiment contains 385 T1 weighted MR images obtained from ADNI [3]. Although there are more than 800 subjects with 4000 scans in ADNI database, we considered the healthy control and disease groups, with the baseline, i.e. the first scan, for each subject. Some scans (84 out of 840) were excluded if they suffered severe degradation due to motion artifacts or significant clinical abnormalities (e.g., hemispheric infarction). A dataset of 756 subjects was formed after this unbiased selection, including 210 subjects of HC, 175 subjects of AD, and 371 subjects of Mild Cognitive Impairment (MCI). We only considered the HC and AD here. Table 1 presents detailed information of this dataset.

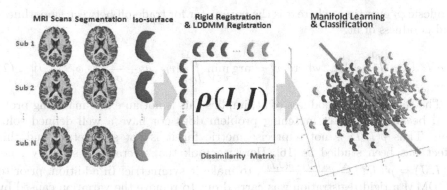

Fig. 1. The flowchart of the framework: data acquisition, segmentation, surface extraction, rigid registration, LDDMM-surface mapping, manifold learning, and classification

Table 1. Demographic characteristics of the dataset used in this paper

Group	HC	AD
number of subjects	210	175
number of male subjects	109	94
Age (year)	76.25 ± 5.01	75.28 ± 7.49

2.2   Preprocessing: Segmentation and Iso-surface Extraction

We followed a similar procedure as used in [11], in which template surfaces are used to initialize the topology of the subcortical structures upon which the inference will be performed, and then target surfaces are inserted into the segmentations from Freesurfer [12, 13] via LDDMM mapping. These transformed template surfaces towards different target surfaces are accurate since the LDDMM mappings used are smooth, and mediate the noise which may be sometimes inherent in segmentations. These surfaces then become the manifolds that our inference proceeds based on.

2.3   Diffeomorphic Metric Mapping

To measure dissimilarity between two subjects, diffeomorphic metric mapping is calculated via LDDMM surface mapping [14, 15]. The diffeomorphisms ϕ_t are constructed as a flow of ordinary differential equation:

$$\dot{\phi}_t = v_t(\phi_t), \phi_0 = Id, t \in [0,1] \ , \tag{1}$$

where v_t is the velocity vector field which determines the corresponding flow ϕ_t. The boundary value of this ODE is the identity map denoted as Id.

The LDDMM surface mapping algorithm seeks the optimal velocity field to minimize a loss function combining smoothness and goodness of fit of the mapping ϕ. Given a pair of surfaces I and J, a dissimilarity $\rho(I,J)$ between them is calculated by integrating the norm of velocity vector field associated with the geodesic ϕ_t over time, where σ is the parameter for trade-off between smoothness and goodness of fit.

$$\rho(I, J) = \int_0^1 \|v_t^*|dt, \quad \text{where } v_t^* = \arg\min_{v \in V} \int_0^1 \|v_t\|_v dt + \frac{1}{\sigma^2}\|I \cdot \phi_1^{-1} - J\|_{L^2} \quad (2)$$

The second term, goodness of fit, implies this is not an exact matching problem, because the exact matching problem does not have a well defined solution. Thus $\rho(I, J)$ is not a precise metric for it is not symmetric, and this effect has been studied in [16]. Here we took the "averaging" strategy , i.e. $\rho'(I, J) = \rho'(J, I) \triangleq \frac{(\rho(I,J)+\rho(J,I))}{2}$, to make it symmetric. In addition, prior to LDDMM a rigid registration was carried out to remove the variation caused by different poses in image acquisition stage.

2.4   Manifold Learning and Classification

Manifold learning is a popular approach of non-linear dimension-reduction. It attempts to find a low-dimensional embedding (i.e., the manifold) in the high-dimensional space. The hypothesis is that the data points are samples from a low-dimensional manifold. There are a number of algorithms in the manifold learning family. Here we consider three of them, i.e., classical MDS, Isomap [17], and Laplacian Eigenmaps (LE) [18].

Four widely used classification algorithms, K-Nearest Neighbor (KNN) and Fisher's linear discriminant analysis (LDA), Support Vector Machine (SVM), and Random Forest (RF) were employed to discriminate HC and AD cohorts.

For SVM, LIBSVM was used [19]. Beside the original linear SVM, another nonlinear kernel function, Radial Basis, was tried. Random forest [20] is an extension of traditional decision tree, which makes an overall prediction based on decisions of all individual trees.

3   Experiments and Results

We tested the proposed method on two anatomical structures, the hippocampus and amygdala. For each subject, four surfaces including both left and right sides are studied. On any of these surfaces, an inter-subject dissimilarity was calculated via LDDMM following a rigid registration as described in 2.3.

After surface mapping finished, one of three manifold learning methods, MDS, Isomap, and Laplacian Eigenmaps, was employed to calculate embedding, on which several classifiers were trained and tested. A 6-fold cross-validation was carried out to evaluate the performance on 385 subjects (210 HC and 175 AD). The performance was measured using misclassification rate.

In order to understand whether the dimension of representation for the anatomical shape space is large or small, misclassification rate was calculated by varying the dimensions of the embedding. In particular, we considered the first d dimensions corresponding to the largest d eigen-values for $d = 1, ...90$.

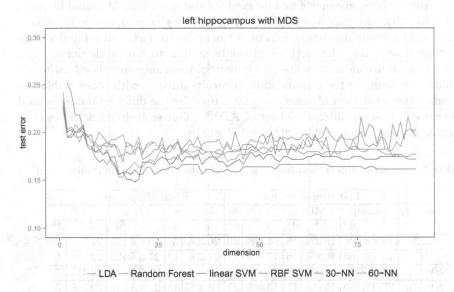

Fig. 2. Misclassification rate as a measure of the embedding dimensions from the left hippocampus via MDS

As a result, a curve of misclassification rates over different dimensions was obtained for each classification algorithm. Figure 2 presents misclassification rates, using MDS followed by a certain classification algorithm, as a function of the number of embedding dimensions calculated from the left hippocampus. From the misclassification curves, one can observe that the misclassification rate first decreases rapidly then increases slowly, as the embedding dimensions increases. Thus, a low dimension embedding is sufficient to achieve a low misclassification rate. However, increasing the dimensionality can lead to noises and over-fitting. The dimensions with lowest misclassification rate under our setup, is 15 to 20 for most classification algorithms approximately. This suggests that anatomical shape lies in a space of relatively low dimensionality. Other combinations of {MDS, Isomap, Laplacian Eigenmaps} and {left/right hippocampus, left/right amygdala} give similar results and are not reported here due to space constraints.

Table 2 is a full comparison of minimum misclassification rates and the corresponding number of dimensions from different embedding algorithms and classification algorithms (on left/right hippocampus). In that table, SVM_L indicates SVM using linear kernel (original version). SVM_R represents the radial basis kernel. RF represents random forest. The number of dimension corresponding to minimum misclassification rates, are highlighted in each column. The standard error for each of entry of Table 2 is approximately one percent. The minimum misclassification rate is around 14% which is achieved via Laplacian Eigenmaps on the left hippocampus. Lower misclassification rates are achieved on the left hippocampus than on right hippocampus regardless of which manifold learning algorithm is used. Similar phenomena can be observed for the amygdala. Manifold learning algorithms, MDS, Isomap, and Laplacian Eigenmaps give comparable results.

Table 3 is a summary comparison of performance reported in related works. Note that it only lists the methods strongly similar to our methodology, i.e., computation of dissimilarity followed by manifold learning and classification. It is difficult to compare the classification accuracy directly with other published methods, given that the difference may be caused by the different datasets used (different database or different subset of ADNI). Our embedding achieves classification accuracy comparable with related works.

Table 2. Smallest Misclassification rate L* and the corresponding dimension d*

Classifier	Left Hippocampus						Right Hippocampus					
	Isomap		MDS		LE		Isomap		MDS		LE	
	L*	d*	L*	d*	L*	d*	L*	d*	L*	d*	L*	d*
LDA	18.7%	9	15.3%	15	**14.0%**	**26**	20.2%	7	19.5%	25	21.3%	20
RF	19.2%	65	16.9%	16	17.9%	27	21.3%	13	21.3%	33	22.6%	6
SVM_L	18.2%	53	**14.8%**	**19**	14.8%	42	19.2%	17	**19.2%**	**27**	22.1%	3
SVM_R	**17.4%**	**53**	15.6%	15	15.6%	25	**18.9%**	**38**	20.8%	16	22.3%	3
30-NN	19.2%	24	17.1%	88	18.9%	13	21.6%	20	21.3%	55	22.3%	3
60-NN	17.7%	43	17.1%	39	18.4%	7	19.5%	26	22.1%	18	**21.0%**	**9**

Table 3. Summary of representative methods in the literature[1]

Method	[4]	[5]	[6]	[7]	[10]	Our method
{#subjects of HC}/{#subject of AD}	25/25	69/71	37/35	116/103	57/44	210/175
Accuracy	76-84%	87%	83%	86%	77%	85%

3.1   Comparison to Template Based Classifiers

In the framework of LDDMM, we calculated a geodesic from the template coordinate space to the target coordinates. The method proposed in this paper is template-free, since there does not exist a fixed template. For template-based methods, given a fixed template, the anatomical variability within a group of subjects is encoded via the geodesic. In [21], computational tools are provided for comparing these geodesic transformations and derived a fundamental "conservation of momentum" property of these geodesics: the initial momentum encodes the geodesic connecting the template to the subject. Anatomical differences among different target groups can, therefore, be studied by analyzing the initial momentum associated with different subjects. In [22], the initial momentum space is demonstrated to be linear, and thus linear statistical analysis such as the principal component analysis (PCA) can be applied to that space. Another paper [23] successfully utilized the initial momentum space associated with volume to discriminate disease groups. In our experiment, we combined

---

[1] The accuracy listed here is only that based on MR images (one scan for each subject).

PCA and LDA to differentiate HC and AD. According to the cross-validation results, we observed, in terms of misclassification rate, 15%, 19%, 20%, and 21% respectively from the PCA+LDA procedure applied on the initial momentum space of left hippocampus, right hippocampus, left amygdala, and right amygdala. This implies the performance of our template-free method proposed in this paper is comparable to the template-based classification method.

4 Conclusion

In this paper, we present a framework of embedding anatomical shape information into a low-dimensional space and discriminating subjects with AD from healthy controls using various classification algorithms. The LDDMM algorithm was used for measuring dissimilarity between every pair of anatomical shapes. This is in some sense a special way to extract biomarkers from MR image data. This framework achieves the comparable performance with similar application of manifold learning in discriminating subjects with cognitive dementia from healthy controls. A potential application or extension of our work is to combine the shape information extracted using this method and other imaging features extracted from different imaging modalities with their fusion improving classification accuracy [5–7].

Our result suggests that a suitable representation of anatomical shape space is inherently of low dimension. Another conclusion can be drawn from the result is that the key step in this manifold learning framework is the dissimilarity measurement because as shown in Section 3 similar results can be achieved when different manifold learning or classification algorithms were used.

References

1. Grenander, U., Miller, M.: Computational anatomy: An emerging discipline. Quarterly of Applied Mathematics 56(4), 617–694 (1998)
2. Beg, M., Miller, M., Trouvé, A., Younes, L.: Computing large deformation metric mappings via geodesic flows of diffeomorphisms. International Journal of Computer Vision 61(2), 139–157 (2005)
3. Mueller, S., Weiner, M., Thal, L., Petersen, R., Jack, C., Jagust, W., Trojanowski, J., Toga, A., Beckett, L.: The Alzheimers disease neuroimaging initiative. Neuroimaging Clinics of North America 15(4), 869 (2005)
4. Park, H.: Isomap induced manifold embedding and its application to Alzheimer's disease and mild cognitive impairment. Neuroscience Letters (2012)
5. Gray, K.R., Aljabar, P., Heckemann, R.A., Hammers, A., Rueckert, D.: Random forest-based manifold learning for classification of imaging data in dementia. In: Suzuki, K., Wang, F., Shen, D., Yan, P. (eds.) MLMI 2011. LNCS, vol. 7009, pp. 159–166. Springer, Heidelberg (2011)
6. Gray, K., Aljabar, P., Heckemann, R., Hammers, A., Rueckert, D.: Random forest-based similarity measures for multi-modal classification of Alzheimer's disease. NeuroImage (2012)
7. Wolz, R., Aljabar, P., Hajnal, J., Lötjönen, J., Rueckert, D.: Nonlinear dimensionality reduction combining mr imaging with non-imaging information. Medical Image Analysis (2011)

8. Yang, X., Goh, A., Qiu, A.: Approximations of the diffeomorphic metric and their applications in shape learning. In: Székely, G., Hahn, H.K. (eds.) IPMI 2011. LNCS, vol. 6801, pp. 257–270. Springer, Heidelberg (2011)
9. Gerber, S., Tasdizen, T., Fletcher, P., Joshi, S., Whitaker, R.: Manifold modeling for brain population analysis. Medical Image Analysis 14(5), 643 (2010)
10. Miller, M., Priebe, C., Qiu, A., Fischl, B., Kolasny, A., Brown, T., Park, Y., Ratnanather, J., Busa, E., Jovicich, J., et al.: Collaborative computational anatomy: an mri morphometry study of the human brain via diffeomorphic metric mapping. Human Brain Mapping 30(7), 2132–2141 (2008)
11. Qiu, A., Miller, M.I., et al.: Multi-structure network shape analysis via normal surface momentum maps. NeuroImage 42(4), 1430 (2008)
12. Fischl, B., Salat, D., Busa, E., Albert, M., Dieterich, M., Haselgrove, C., van der Kouwe, A., Killiany, R., Kennedy, D., Klaveness, S., et al.: Whole brain segmentation: automated labeling of neuroanatomical structures in the human brain. Neuron 33(3), 341–355 (2002)
13. Khan, A.R., Wang, L., Beg, M.F.: Freesurfer-initiated fully-automated subcortical brain segmentation in mri using large deformation diffeomorphic metric mapping. NeuroImage 41(3), 735 (2008)
14. Vaillant, M., Qiu, A., Glaunès, J., Miller, M.: Diffeomorphic metric surface mapping in subregion of the superior temporal gyrus. NeuroImage 34(3), 1149–1159 (2007)
15. Vaillant, M., Glaunès, J.: Surface matching via currents. In: Christensen, G.E., Sonka, M. (eds.) IPMI 2005. LNCS, vol. 3565, pp. 381–392. Springer, Heidelberg (2005)
16. Trosset, M.W., Priebe, C.E., Park, Y., Miller, M.I.: Semisupervised learning from dissimilarity data. Computational Statistics & Data Analysis 52(10), 4643–4657 (2008)
17. Tenenbaum, J., De Silva, V., Langford, J.: A global geometric framework for nonlinear dimensionality reduction. Science 290(5500), 2319–2323 (2000)
18. Belkin, M., Niyogi, P.: Laplacian eigenmaps and spectral techniques for embedding and clustering. In: Advances in Neural Information Processing Systems, vol. 14, pp. 585–591 (2001)
19. Chang, C.C., Lin, C.J.: LIBSVM: A library for support vector machines. ACM Transactions on Intelligent Systems and Technology 2, 27:1–27:27 (2011), Software available at http://www.csie.ntu.edu.tw/~cjlin/libsvm
20. Liaw, A., Wiener, M.: Classification and regression by randomforest. R News 2(3), 18–22 (2002)
21. Miller, M., Trouvé, A., Younes, L.: Geodesic shooting for computational anatomy. Journal of Mathematical Imaging and Vision 24(2), 209–228 (2006)
22. Vaillant, M., Miller, M.I., Younes, L., Trouvé, A., et al.: Statistics on diffeomorphisms via tangent space representations. NeuroImage 23(1), 161 (2004)
23. Wang, L., Beg, F., Ratnanather, T., Ceritoglu, C., Younes, L., Morris, J.C., Csernansky, J.G., Miller, M.I.: Large deformation diffeomorphism and momentum based hippocampal shape discrimination in dementia of the Alzheimer type. IEEE Transactions on Medical Imaging 26(4), 462–470 (2007)

Discriminative Group Sparse Representation for Mild Cognitive Impairment Classification

Heung-Il Suk, Chong-Yaw Wee, and Dinggang Shen

Department of Radiology and Biomedical Research Imaging Center (BRIC),
University of North Carolina, Chapel Hill, USA

Abstract. Witnessed by recent studies, functional connectivity is a useful tool in extracting brain network features and finding biomarkers for brain disease diagnosis. It still remains, however, challenging for the estimation of a functional connectivity from fMRI due to the high dimensional nature. In order to tackle this problem, we utilize a group sparse representation along with a structural equation model. Unlike the conventional group sparse representation, we devise a novel supervised discriminative group sparse representation by penalizing a large within-class variance and a small between-class variance of features. Thanks to the devised penalization term, we can learn connectivity coefficients that are similar within the same class and distinct between classes, thus helping enhance the diagnostic accuracy. In our experiments on the resting-state fMRI data of 37 subjects (12 mild cognitive impairment patients; 25 healthy normal controls) with a cross-validation technique, we demonstrated the validity and effectiveness of the proposed method, showing the best diagnostic accuracy of 89.19% and the sensitivity of 0.9167.

1 Introduction

Although it's still unclear why some people with Mild Cognitive Impairment (MCI) progress to Alzheimer's Disease (AD) and some do not, MCI is considered as an early stage of dementia and it's estimated that approximately 10% to 15% of individuals with MCI progress to AD in one year [6]. While there is no medical treatment to stop or reverse it, recent dementia specific pharmacological advances can slow its progression. Therefore, it has been of great importance for early detection of MCI and a proper treatment.

A lot of studies have witnessed that the functional connectivity, defined as the temporal correlations between spatially distinct brain regions [1], can be a useful tool in finding biomarkers for brain disease diagnosis. Although a large part of the literature has considered the correlation approach to model the functional connectivity, it is hard to interpret the resulting connectivity due to its pairwise computation and full connectedness, while which can be addressed by simple thresholding.

Based on the assumption of the small-world network characteristics in human brain functions, many groups have focused their research on the sparse connectivity [7,15]. A sparse connectivity can be constructed via the least absolute shrinkage and selection operator (lasso), which penalizes a linear regression

G. Wu et al. (Eds.): MLMI 2013, LNCS 8184, pp. 131–138, 2013.
© Springer International Publishing Switzerland 2013

model with l_1-norm. While lasso induces sparsity in the regression coefficients, it selects variables in a subject- or task-dependent manner and therefore has a limitation in inducing the group-wise information. Group analysis of brain connectivity has long been a challenging topic, since biomedical research is usually conducted at a group level to extract the population features, especially for disease diagnosis. Efficient group analysis requires appropriate handling of expected inter-subject variability without destroying inter-group differences. To this end, Wee *et al.* proposed a constrained sparse functional connectivity network [15] via a group sparse representation [16].

Interestingly, while discrimination is the main goal of the computer-aided brain disease diagnosis, the optimization of the sparse representation is based on regression with a criterion that does not explicitly include a discrimination task. To our best knowledge, there has been no work on brain disease diagnosis and/or medical image analysis with the application of the supervised sparse modeling that explicitly combines the regression and discriminative methods in a unified framework. In this work, we present a novel method of classifying MCI and Normal Control (NC) with sparse modeling in a supervised and discriminative manner. Specifically, we combine a group analysis with a class-discriminative feature extraction by extending the group lasso [16] with the introduction of a label-informed regularization term, which penalizes a large within-class variance and a small between-class variance of connectivity coefficients.

2   Materials and Methods

2.1   Materials

We use resting state fMRI (rs-fMRI) images acquired from 37 subjects (12 MCI, 25 NC). For each subject, 150 rs-fMRI volumes were acquired per scan. During scanning, all the subjects were asked to keep their eyes open and to fixate on a crosshair in the middle of the screen. The T1-weighted anatomical MRI images were also acquired from the same machine.

We discarded the first 10 fMRI image volumes of each subject for magnetization equilibrium. The remaining 140 fMRI images were preprocessed by applying the typical procedures of slice timing, motion correction, and spatial normalization using SPM8[1]. In this study, we realigned images with TR/2 as a reference time point to minimize the relative errors across TRs. In the head motion correction step, we realigned images to the first volume across the subjects. In order to reduce the effects of CerebroSpinal Fluid (CSF), ventricles, and White Matter (WM), and to focus on the signals of Gray Matter (GM), we regressed out the nuisance signals caused from those regions along with the six head-motion profiles. Then we considered only the signals in GM for further processing by minimizing the physiological noises caused by cardiac and respiratory cycles from WM and/or CSF [13].

---

[1] Available at http://www.fil.ion.ucl.ac.uk/spm/software/spm8/

In the spatial normalization, the fMRI images of each subject were coregistered to their respective T1-weighted structure images. The fMRI brain space was then parcellated into 116 ROIs based on the Automated Anatomical Labeling (AAL) template [12]. A mean time series of each ROI was computed from the intensity of all voxels in the ROI. Therefore, we had a set of time series $\mathbf{X} \in \{X^{(n)} \in \mathbb{R}^{V \times R}\}_{n=1}^{N}$, where N is the number of subjects, R and V denote, respectively, the number of ROIs (=116) and the number of volumes (=140).

Following research in the literature, we utilize the low frequency fluctuation features in rs-fMRI with a frequency interval of $0.025 \leq f \leq 0.100$ Hz on $\mathbf{X}$. Based on Wee *et al.*'s work [15], we further decomposed this frequency interval into five equally spaced non-overlapping frequency bands (0.025-0.039 Hz, 0.039-0.054 Hz, 0.054-0.068 Hz, 0.068-0.082 Hz, 0.082-0.100 Hz).

2.2 Methods

In this section, we describe a novel method of jointly learning common functional brain networks across subjects via group sparse representation and class-discriminative connectivity coefficients with a label-informed regularization term. We exploit a Structural Equation Model (SEM) [5], assuming that the brain activity of a ROI can be represented by a linear combination of the activity of the other ROIs. Given a set of time series of R ROIs for N subjects, $\{X^{(n)} = [\mathbf{y}_1^{(n)}, \cdots, \mathbf{y}_r^{(n)}, \cdots, \mathbf{y}_R^{(n)}]\}_{n=1}^{N}$, where $\mathbf{y}_r^{(n)} = [y_r^{(n)}(1), y_r^{(n)}(2), \cdots, y_r^{(n)}(V)]^T$ is a V-length time series of r-th ROI for n-th subject, let us consider the SEM for r-th ROI formulated as follows:

$$L(\mathbf{W}_r) = \frac{1}{2} \sum_{n}^{N} \left\| \mathbf{y}_r^{(n)} - \mathbf{A}_r^{(n)} \mathbf{w}_r^{(n)} \right\|_2^2 \tag{1}$$

where $\mathbf{A}_r^{(n)} = \left[\mathbf{y}_1^{(n)} \cdots \mathbf{y}_{r-1}^{(n)}, \mathbf{y}_{r+1}^{(n)} \cdots \mathbf{y}_R^{(n)} \right] \in \mathbb{R}^{V \times (R-1)}$ is a data matrix composed of time series of all ROIs except for r-th ROI, $\mathbf{w}_r^{(n)} = [w_r^{(n)}(1), \cdots, w_r^{(n)}(r-1), w_r^{(n)}(r+1), \cdots, w_r^{(n)}(R)]^T \in \mathbb{R}^{(R-1) \times 1}$ is a regression coefficient vector, and $\mathbf{W}_r = \left[\mathbf{w}_r^{(1)} \cdots \mathbf{w}_r^{(n)} \cdots \mathbf{w}_r^{(N)} \right] \in \mathbb{R}^{(R-1) \times N}$ is a coefficient matrix of r-th ROI over N subjects. Note that an element of the coefficient vector $\mathbf{w}_r^{(n)}$ represents the respective ROI's relationship to r-th ROI for n-th subject. Therefore, we can consider the coefficients as the connectional strengths between ROIs. Hereafter, we use the regression coefficients and the connectivity coefficients interchangeably.

Let $\mathbf{W}_r[g] = [w_r^{(1)}(g), \cdots, w_r^{(n)}(g), \cdots, w_r^{(N)}(g)]$ denote the g-th row of the coefficient matrix $\mathbf{W}_r$. In order to incorporate the class-label information, we utilize the metric of within-class-variance (WCV) $f_W(\mathbf{W}_r[g])$ and between-class-variance (BCV) $f_B(\mathbf{W}_r[g])$ defined as follows:

$$f_W(\mathbf{W}_r[g]) = \frac{1}{|\mathrm{N}^+|} \sum_{n \in \mathrm{N}^+} \left(w_r^{(n)}(g) - \hat{w}_r^+[g] \right)^2 + \frac{1}{|\mathrm{N}^-|} \sum_{n \in \mathrm{N}^-} \left(w_r^{(n)}(g) - \hat{w}_r^-[g] \right)^2 \tag{2}$$

$$f_B(\mathbf{W}_r[g]) = \left(\hat{w}_r^+[g] - \hat{w}_r^-[g]\right)^2 \tag{3}$$

where $\mathbb{N}^+$ and $\mathbb{N}^-$ denote, respectively, the set of subjects belonging to the class '+' and '−', $|\mathbb{N}^+|$ and $|\mathbb{N}^-|$ denote, respectively, the cardinality of the sets $\mathbb{N}^+$ and $\mathbb{N}^-$, $\hat{w}_r^+[g] = \frac{1}{|\mathbb{N}^+|}\sum_{n\in\mathbb{N}^+} w_r^{(n)}(g)$, and $\hat{w}_r^-[g] = \frac{1}{|\mathbb{N}^-|}\sum_{n\in\mathbb{N}^-} w_r^{(n)}(g)$.

The idea of exploiting WCV and BCV to extract class-discriminative features is similar to the Linear Discriminant Analysis (LDA) [2]. Unlike LDA, in this paper, we take the difference of WCV and BCV for computational efficiency. Incorporating the functions of $f_W(\mathbf{W}_r[g])$ and $f_B(\mathbf{W}_r[g])$ into the conventional group sparse representation, we devise a new objective function formulated as follows:

$$J(\mathbf{W}_r) = \min_{\mathbf{W}_r} L(\mathbf{W}_r) + \lambda_1 \|\mathbf{W}_r\|_{2,1} + \lambda_2 \left(\sum_g \|f_W(\mathbf{W}_r[g])\|_2 - \sum_g \|f_B(\mathbf{W}_r[g])\|_2 \right). \tag{4}$$

In this objective function, we penalize the high WCV and the low BCV. With the introduction of the newly devised penalty terms, the connectivity for the subjects within a class are imposed to be similar to each other, while those between classes to be distinct. We call this novel label-informed sparse model as 'Supervised Discriminative Group Lasso' (SDGL).

With appropriate algebraic operations, we can simplify the variance related terms in Eq. (4) as follows

$$\sum_g \|f_W(\mathbf{W}_r[g])\|_2 = \|\mathbf{W}_r D_1\|_{2,1}^2 \tag{5}$$

$$\sum_g \|f_B(\mathbf{W}_r[g])\|_2 = \|\mathbf{W}_r D_2\|_{2,1}^2 \tag{6}$$

where $D_1 \in \mathbb{R}^{N\times N}$ and $D_2 \in \mathbb{R}^{N\times N}$ denote, respectively, definitive matrices to compute WCV and BCV of the connectivity coefficients in $\mathbf{W}_r$. Specifically, D_1 is a composite matrix that computes the sum of the differences between the connectivity coefficients and their mean in each class, and D_2 is a matrix that computes the difference between the mean of the connectivity coefficients of two different classes. In our experiments, we used a SLEP toolbox[2] [4] to optimize the objective function.

2.3   Functional Connectivity and Feature Selection

In this work, we benefit from the brain functional information of the test samples in finding functional connectivity. That is, in order to obtain a robust network structure from a larger number of samples, we use both the training and test samples in optimization of the proposed SDGL. However, since we do not have the label information for the test samples, the composite matrices of D_1 and

---

[2] Available at 'http://www.public.asu.edu/~jye02/Software/SLEP/index.htm'

D_2 cannot be defined, and thus the optimization problem in Eq. (4) cannot be solved in its current form. To this end, we define composite matrices $\hat{D}_1$ and $\hat{D}_2$ by concatenating zero-vectors to D_1 and D_2 in Eq. (5) and Eq. (6) as follows:

$$\hat{D}_i = \begin{bmatrix} D_i & \mathbf{0} \\ \mathbf{0} & \mathbf{0} \end{bmatrix} \in \mathbb{R}^{(K+L)\times(K+L)} \tag{7}$$

where $i \in \{1,2\}$, and K and L denote, respectively, the number of training and test samples. By setting the row and column vectors corresponding to the test samples zero[3], and solving the optimization problem of Eq. (4) with the replacement of D_1 and D_2 with $\hat{D}_1$ and $\hat{D}_2$, we can find the network structures consistent across the training and test samples, and the connectivity coefficients to be similar within a class and distinct between classes. Note that during the optimization, we use the label information of only the training samples, and optimize Eq. (4) for each ROI and then concatenate the optimized coefficient vectors across ROIs to construct a connectivity matrix for each subject.

The connectivity matrix $\mathbf{Q}^{(n)}$ that represents inter-regional correlations in neuronal variability for n-th subject can then be estimated from the trained sparse regression coefficients over R ROIs, i.e., $\mathbf{Q}^{(n)} = \left[\mathbf{q}_1^{(n)}, \cdots, \mathbf{q}_r^{(n)}, \cdots, \mathbf{q}_R^{(n)}\right]$, where $\mathbf{q}_r^{(n)} = \left[w_r^{(n)}(1), \cdots, w_r^{(n)}(r-1), 0, w_r^{(n)}(r+1), \cdots, w_r^{(n)}(R)\right]^T$. In order to obtain a symmetric functional connectivity representation, we take the average of the connectivity matrix and its transposed one, $\mathbf{C} = \left(\mathbf{Q} + \mathbf{Q}^T\right)/2$. Fisher's z-transformation, $\mathbf{Z}_{ij} = \left[ln(1 + \mathbf{C}_{ij}) - ln(1 - \mathbf{C}_{ij})\right]/2$, where $\mathbf{C}_{ij}$ denotes the (i,j)-th entry in $\mathbf{C}$, is then performed to improve the normality of correlation coefficients. The functional connectivity is finally represented by a z-map. In this work, we utilize the weighted local clustering coefficients computed from $\mathbf{Z}$ as features.

Given training samples from N subjects[4], we first leave one subject out for test, and consider the samples from the remaining $N - 1$ subjects for feature selection and parameter setting for the optimal classifier learning. We select features by applying three methods sequentially: t-test, minimum redundancy and maximum relevance [8], and recursive feature elimination with a linear Support Vector Machine (SVM) [9], and find an optimal parameter for SVM with a grid search algorithm.

3 Experimental Results and Discussions

The most direct comparison between two methods can be the accuracy, which counts the number of correctly classified samples in a test set. Table 1 presents that the proposed method outperforms the conventional group lasso in both single- and multi-spectrum approaches, showing the diagnostic accuracies of 86.49% and 89.19% in single- and multi-spectrum, respectively. Here, we should

---

[3] In Eq. (7), it's assumed that the last L samples are for the test.

[4] In our case, we have one sample from each subject.

Table 1. A summary of the performances of the competing methods

Methods		Accuracy (%)	AUC	Sensitivity	Specificity
Single-spectrum	Group lasso (λ=0.15)	75.68	0.67	0.3333	0.96
	Proposed SDGL (λ_1=0.15, λ_2=0.15)	**86.49**	0.81	0.5833	**1.0**
Multi-spectrum	Group lasso (λ=0.15)	78.38	0.8	0.5	0.88
	Proposed SDGL (λ_1=0.05, λ_2=0.5)	**89.19**	**0.9567**	**0.9167**	0.88

note that the accuracy of the group lasso in multi-spectrum is lower than the one reported in [15]. The main reason for that comes from the difference in pre-processing. In this work, we regressed out the nuisance signals from the regions of CSF, WM, GM along with the six head-motion profiles, which were not per-formed in Wee *et al.*'s work. From a signal processing point of view, the regression step allows us to acquire more noise-free signals to be analyzed. Henceforth, we believe that the results from our experiment are more faithful.

Regarding the sensitivity and specificity, the higher the sensitivity, the lower the chance of mis-diagnosing MCI patients, and the higher the specificity, the lower the chance of mis-diagnosing normal to MCI. Although the specificity of the proposed method is similar or slightly better than the other methods, the proposed SDGL in multi-spectrum overwhelms the competing methods, report-ing a sensitivity of 0.9167. Clinically, it's much more beneficial to have a high sensitivity, *i.e.*, correct identification of MCI patients, which can result in taking proper treatments and, to the end, slowing the risk of progressing to AD.

One of the most effective methods of evaluating the performance of diagnostic tests in brain disease as well as other medical areas is the Area Under the receiver operating characteristic Curve (AUC), a combined measure of sensitivity and specificity. The AUC can be thought as a measure of the overall performance of a diagnostic test. The larger the AUC, the better the overall performance of the diagnostic test. The AUC of the multi-spectrum SDGL is 0.9567, which also outperforms the other methods.

In order to see which ROIs are discriminative for MCI identification, we define the Most Discriminant ROIs (MDRs) based on the following rules:

$$\text{MDRs} = \{r : F_i(r) > \mu_i + 2\sigma_i, \forall i\}$$

where $F_i(r)$ is the frequency of the r-th ROI being selected in the i-th frequency band, $\mu_i = 1/R \sum_{r=1}^{R} F_i(r)$ and $\sigma = \left[1/R \sum_{r=1}^{R} (F_i(r) - \mu_i)^2\right]^{1/2}$ denote, re-spectively, the mean and the standard deviation of the frequencies. The selected MDRs are Left Posterior Cingulate Gyrus [10], Left Postcentral Gyrus [14], Left Putamen [3], Left Lobule IV, V of Cerebellar Hemisphere, Left Lobule VI of Cerebellar Hemisphere, and Lobule VI of Vermis [11].

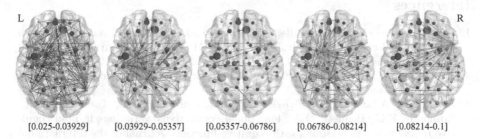

L   R

[0.025-0.03929]   [0.03929-0.05357]   [0.05357-0.06786]   [0.06786-0.08214]   [0.08214-0.1]

Fig. 1. Functional connectivities in the five decomposed frequency bands

We also illustrated the functional connectivity estimated by the proposed method with a multi-spectrum approach in Fig. 1. From the figure, we can see that the connectivity varies across decomposed frequency bands. Interestingly, the connections are the densest in the frequency band of [0.025-0.03929], which means that a huge amount of the functional connectivities occur in the low frequency range. There is a tendency for the connections to concentrate on a small number of ROIs in the higher frequency ranges.

4   Conclusion

We propose a novel method of identifying MCI with group sparse representation in a supervised and discriminative manner. Specifically, in order to reflect the class-label information in the model, we utilize a well-known discriminative information of the within-class-variance and the between-class-variance [2] for penalization. We should note that the proposed method jointly learns the coherent brain network structures across subjects regardless of the classes, while imposing similar connectional coefficients within a class and distinct coefficients between classes, but still maintaining individual network characteristics. Our experimental results on rs-fMRI data validated the effectiveness of the proposed method showing the classification accuracy of 89.19% and the sensitivity of 0.9167 in a multi-spectrum approach. The class discriminative ROIs selected in our framework coincide with those reported in the studies on MCI and AD in the literature. It is also observed that the functional connectivities vary across the frequency ranges, showing the densest connectivities in the low frequency range of [0.025-0.03929].

While we did not consider the joint graphical lasso [7] due to the limited space, it's another widely used method to estimate a sparse functional connectivity at a group level as the group lasso does. We believe that the proposed regularization term can be also applied to this method, possibly enhancing its performance in brain disease diagnosis.

References

1. Friston, K.J., Frith, C.D., Liddle, P.F., Frackowiak, R.S.: Functional connectivity: The principal-component analysis of large (PET) data sets. Journal of Cerebral Blood Flow and Metabolism 13, 5–14 (1993)
2. Fukunaga, K.: Introduction to Statistical Pattern Recognition, 2nd edn. Academic Press Professional (1990)
3. Han, S.D., Arfanakis, K., Fleischman, D.A., Leurgans, S.E., Tuminello, E.R., Edmonds, E.C., Bennett, D.A.: Functional connectivity variations in mild cognitive impairment: associations with cognitive function. Journal of the International Neuropsychological Society 18, 39–48 (2012)
4. Liu, J., Ji, S., Ye, J.: SLEP: Sparse Learning with Efficient Projections. Arizona State University (2009)
5. Mcintosh, A.R., Grady, C.L., Ungerleider, L.G., Haxby, J.V., Rapoport, S.I., Horwitzl, B.: Network analysis of cortical visual pathways mapped with PET. Journal of Neuroscience 14, 655–666 (1994)
6. Misra, C., Fan, Y., Davatzikos, C.: Baseline and longitudinal patterns of brain atrophy in MCI patients, and their use in prediction of short-term conversion to AD: results from ADNI. NeuroImage 44, 1414–1422 (2009)
7. Ng, B., Varoquaux, G., Poline, J.-B., Thirion, B.: A novel sparse graphical approach for multimodal brain connectivity inference. In: Ayache, N., Delingette, H., Golland, P., Mori, K. (eds.) MICCAI 2012, Part I. LNCS, vol. 7510, pp. 707–714. Springer, Heidelberg (2012)
8. Peng, H., Long, F., Ding, C.: Feature selection based on mutual information: criteria of max-dependency, max-relevance, and min-redundancy. IEEE Transactions on Pattern Analysis and Machine Intelligence 27(8), 1226–1285 (2005)
9. Rakotomamonjy, A.: Variable selection using SVM based criteria. Journal of Machine Learning Research 3, 1357–1370 (2003)
10. Supekar, K., Menon, V., Rubin, D., Musen, M., Greicius, M.D.: Network analysis of intrinsic functional brain connectivity in Alzheimer's disease. PLoS Computational Biology 4, e1000100 (2008)
11. Thomann, P.A., Schläfer, C., Seidl, U., Santos, V.D., Essig, M., Schröder, J.: The cerebellum in mild cognitive impairment and Alzheimer's disease - a structural MRI study. Journal of Psychiatric Research 42(14), 1198–1202 (2008)
12. Tzourio-Mazoyer, N., Landeau, B., Papathanassiou, D., Crivello, F., Etard, O., Delcroix, N., Mazoyer, B., Joliot, M.: Automated anatomical labeling of activations in SPM using a macroscopic anatomical parcellation of the MNI MRI single-subject brain. NeuroImage 15(1), 273–289 (2002)
13. Van Dijk, K.R.A., Hedden, T., Venkataraman, A., Evans, K.C., Lazar, S.W., Buckner, R.L.: Intrinsic functional connectivity as a tool for human connectomics: Theory, properties and optimization. Journal of Neurophysiology 103, 297–321 (2010)
14. Wang, Z., Nie, B., Li, D., Zhao, Z., Han, Y.: Effect of acupuncture in mild cognitive impairment and Alzheimer Disease: a functional MRI study. PLoS ONE 7(8), e42730 (2012)
15. Wee, C.-Y., Yap, P.-T., Zhang, D., Wang, L., Shen, D.: Constrained sparse functional connectivity networks for MCI classification. In: Ayache, N., Delingette, H., Golland, P., Mori, K. (eds.) MICCAI 2012, Part II. LNCS, vol. 7511, pp. 212–219. Springer, Heidelberg (2012)
16. Yuan, M., Lin, Y.: Model selection and estimation in regression with grouped variables. Journal of the Royal Statistical Society Series B 68(1), 49–67 (2006)

Temporally Dynamic Resting-State Functional Connectivity Networks for Early MCI Identification

Chong-Yaw Wee[1], Sen Yang[2], Pew-Thian Yap[1], and Dinggang Shen[1]

[1] Department of Radiology and BRIC,
University of North Carolina at Chapel Hill, NC, USA
[2] Department of Computer Science and Engineering,
Arizona State University, Tempe, AZ, USA
dgshen@med.unc.edu

Abstract. Resting-state functional Magnetic Resonance Imaging (R-fMRI) scan provides a rich characterization of the dynamic changes or temporal variabilities caused by neural interactions that may happen within the scan duration. Multiple functional connectivity networks can be estimated from R-fMRI time series to effectively capture subtle yet short neural connectivity changes induced by disease pathologies. To effectively extract the temporally dynamic information, we utilize a sliding window approach to generate multiple shorter, yet overlapping sub-series from a full R-fMRI time series. Whole-brain sliding window correlations are computed based on these sub-series to generate a series of temporal networks, characterize the neural interactions between brain regions at different time scales. Individual estimation of these temporal networks overlooks the intrinsic temporal smoothness between successive overlapping R-fMRI sub-series. To handle this problem, we suggest to jointly estimate temporal networks by maximizing a penalized log likelihood via a fused lasso regularization: 1) l_1-norm penalty ensures a sparse solution; 2) fused regularization preserves the temporal smoothness while allows correlation variability. The estimated temporal networks were applied for early Mild Cognitive Impairment (eMCI) identification, and our results demonstrate the importance of including temporally dynamic R-fMRI scan information for accurate diagnosis of eMCI.

1 Introduction

There is ample of literature suggests that pathological manifestation of Alzheimer's disease (AD) begins many years before any clinical symptom occurs [8, 14]. When AD symptoms are observed, significant neurodegeneration has already occurred in the brain, either anatomically or functionally. Early detection of MCI is crucial for providing possible treatments at the early stage, delaying its progression to more severe stages, mainly AD. Recently, resting-state functional magnetic resonance imaging (R-fMRI) has been dramatically used in AD/MCI analysis [10–12] due to its capability to detect AD/MCI many years before any clinical symptom through the functional connectivity abnormalities [8], demonstrating its potential use in early MCI (eMCI) diagnosis.

In conventional connectivity network-based analysis, it is assumed that correlations between different brain regions in a typical R-fMRI scanning session are not changing

G. Wu et al. (Eds.): MLMI 2013, LNCS 8184, pp. 139–146, 2013.

over time (i.e., *temporally stationary*). Because of this assumption, brain region correlations are computed over the entire duration of R-fMRI scan to characterize network connection strengths [1, 6]. However, in recent studies [2, 7, 9] functional connectivity between different brain regions may not be temporally stationary over the duration of the R-fMRI scan. Therefore, these time varying dynamic properties in R-fMRI scans may have been overlooked by conventional approaches. One effective way to extract these dynamic properties, correlation between two groups can be estimated from multiple overlapping R-fMRI sub-series that are generated using a sliding window approach. Based on the estimated sliding window connectivity networks (or temporal networks), we develop a novel framework that utilizes temporally dynamic brain activation patterns during R-fMRI scan for disease identification. We evaluate the performance of our proposed framework using eMCI individuals obtained from the Alzheimer's Disease Neuroimaging Initiative (ADNI) database.

2   Materials and Methods

2.1   Materials and Preprocessing

Data used in this study were obtained from the ADNI 2 dataset[1]. In total, we use 29 eMCI subjects (13F/16M) and 30 normal controls (NC) (17F/13M). Subjects from both groups are age-matched ($p = 0.6174$), with mean age in terms of year for eMCI and NC groups are 73.6 ± 4.8 and 74.3 ± 5.7, respectively. All subjects were scanned with the same scanning protocol at different centers using 3.0 T Philips Achieva scanners with the following parameters: TR/TE = $3000/30$ ms, flip angle = $80°$, imaging matrix = 64×64, 48 slices, 140 volumes, and voxel thickness = 3.3 mm. The first 10 R-fMRI volumes of each subject were discarded to achieve magnetization equilibrium. The remaining 130 images were processed with standard preprocessing procedure using the SPM8 package[2]. These R-fMRI images were corrected for the acquisition time delay before they were realigned to the first volume of the remaining images to primarily remove movement artifact in R-fMRI time series. Functional images were normalized to the MNI space with resolution $3 \times 3 \times 3$ mm^3. Regression of nuisance signals including ventricle, white matter signals, and six head-motion profiles was performed. The preprocessed R-fMRI images were parcellated into 116 regions-of-interest (ROIs) according to the automated anatomical labeling atlas. Prior to functional connectivity estimation, mean R-fMRI time series of each ROI was band-pass filtered ($0.01 \leq f \leq 0.08$Hz).

2.2   Motivation

Since the human brain is constantly active, functional connectivity between brain regions varies over time during R-fMRI scan [2]. The temporally correlation variations potentially reflect neural interactions between brain regions that occur at shorter time scales than a typical R-fMRI scanning session of $6 \sim 12$ minutes. These temporally correlation changes can be extracted by estimating a series of connectivity networks from

---

[1] http://www.loni.ucla.edu/ADNI
[2] http://www.fil.ion.ucl.ac.uk/spm/software/spm8/

an R-fMRI time series [7, 9]. These functional connectivity networks, which are referred as temporal networks, are estimated from multiple overlapping sub-series, which are generated using a sliding window with window length shorter than a full R-fMRI time series. Temporal networks can potentially be used to capture subtle temporal pattern changes induced by disease pathology. These temporal networks should share some similarities due to the overlapped temporal volumes, but should not be exactly identical due to the variability conveyed by the non-overlapped distinct temporal volumes [9].

Estimating temporal networks individually using l_1-norm fail to capture temporal smoothness of the overlapped R-fMRI sub-series, introducing spurious sliding window correlation variabilities between adjacent networks. Joint estimation of temporal networks using l_2-norm, however, forces identical network topology, suppressing the actual correlation variabilities. To remedy these two problems, a sparse learning algorithm, referred as Fused Multiple Graphical Lasso (FMGL) algorithm [15], is used to simultaneously preserve the temporal smoothness and temporal dynamics of the estimated functional networks.

2.3   Problem Formulation

Generation of multiple R-fMRI sub-series using the sliding window approach is graphically illustrated in Figure 1. In particular, given an R-fMRI time series with M temporal image volumes, $K = \lfloor (M - N)/s \rfloor + 1$ is the number of sub-series that can be generated, where N denotes the length of sliding window and s denotes the trans-

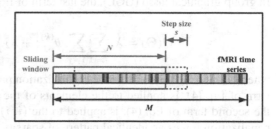

Fig. 1. Generation of multiple R-fMRI sub-series

lation step size. The k-th sub-series is represented in the form of a matrix $\mathbf{X}^{(k)} = \{\mathbf{x}_1^{(k)}, \mathbf{x}_2^{(k)}, \ldots, \mathbf{x}_P^{(k)}\} \in \mathbb{R}^{N \times P}, k = 1, \ldots, K$, where $P = 116$ is the total number of regions-of-interest (ROIs), and $\mathbf{x}^{(k)} = [x^{(k)}(1), x^{(k)}(2), \ldots, x^{(k)}(N)]^T$ is the k-th sub-series of N image volumes for a particular ROI. A symmetric connectivity matrix $\mathbf{C}^{(k)} = [C_{ij}^{(k)}] \in \mathbb{R}^{P \times P}$ can be constructed using $\mathbf{X}^{(k)}$, where each element in the connectivity matrix defines the correlation strength between two different ROIs. Specifically, the correlation strength is defined as

$$C_{ij}^{(k)} = corr(\mathbf{x}_i^{(k)}, \mathbf{x}_j^{(k)}), \tag{1}$$

where i and j are two different brain regions, and $corr(\cdot)$ computes the correlation between region i and region j. For instance, if $i = 1$ and $j = 2$ Eq. (1) would compute the correlation strength between regions 1 and 2 for sub-series k. In this study, the total number of image volumes in R-fMRI time series, M, is 130, while the length of sliding window N, is set to 90. Similar sliding window length $((90 \times 3)/60 = 4.5$ minutes) has been used in previous study [2].

Assuming that the image volumes within each R-fMRI sub-series are identically distributed with P-variate Gaussian distribution with zero mean and positive definite covariance matrix $\Sigma^{(k)}$. Due to sparse nature of brain network, there are many conditionally independent connection pairs. These null connections are denoted as zero elements in the precision matrix, i.e., network matrix $\Theta^{(k)} = (\Sigma^{(k)})^{-1}$. If the covariance matrix of each $\mathbf{X}^{(k)}$ is $\mathbf{S}^{(k)} = (1/N)(\mathbf{X}^{(k)})^T \mathbf{X}^{(k)}$, then the negative log likelihood of $\Theta^{(k)}$ is given as

$$\mathcal{L}(\Theta) = \sum_{k=1}^{K} \left(-\log det(\Theta^{(k)}) + tr(\mathbf{S}^{(k)}\Theta^{(k)}) \right), \tag{2}$$

where $\Theta = \{\Theta^{(1)}, \ldots, \Theta^{(K)}\}$. Minimizing Eq. (2) leads to the maximum likelihood estimate (MLE) of $\hat{\Theta}^{(k)} = (\mathbf{S}^{(k)})^{-1}$, which is unlikely to be sparse. Eq. (2) can then be solved by minimizing the penalized negative log likelihood as

$$\min_{\Theta^{(k)} \succ 0, k=1,\ldots,K} \mathcal{L}(\Theta) + Q(\Theta), \tag{3}$$

where $Q(\Theta)$ will be defined in following subsections.

2.4 Group Graphical Lasso

In group graphical lasso (GGL), the last term of Eq. (3) is defined as [3]

$$Q(\Theta) = \lambda_1 \sum_{k=1}^{K} \sum_{i \neq j} \left| \theta_{i,j}^{(k)} \right| + \lambda_2 \sum_{i \neq j} \sqrt{\sum_{k=1}^{K} (\theta_{i,j}^{(k)})^2}, \tag{4}$$

where λ_1 and λ_2 are nonnegative regularization parameters. The l_1-norm, i.e., the first term of Eq. (4), is applied to the elements of the networks, while the $l_{2,1}$-norm, i.e., the second term of Eq. (4), is applied to the (i,j) elements across all networks. This penalization forces an identical pattern of sparsity across all networks, i.e., same nonzero locations in the estimated temporal networks, thus is mediocre in preserving the temporal smoothness and temporal dynamics.

2.5 Fused Multiple Graphical Lasso

To better preserve the temporal smoothness and temporal dynamics between adjacent networks, the last term in Eq. (3) is redefined using the recently proposed fused multiple graphical lasso (FMGL) algorithm [15]

$$Q(\Theta) = \lambda_1 \sum_{k=1}^{K} \sum_{i \neq j} \left| \theta_{i,j}^{(k)} \right| + \lambda_2 \sum_{k=1}^{K-1} \sum_{i \neq j} \left| \theta_{i,j}^{(k)} - \theta_{i,j}^{(k+1)} \right|. \tag{5}$$

This algorithm employs l_1-norm penalization and fused regularization simultaneously to estimate temporal networks with explicit consideration of their temporal smoothness and correlation variabilities. Specifically, an l_1-norm penalization is imposed to induce sparsity [5], and the fused regularization is imposed to preserve the temporal smoothness and temporal dynamics by encouraging $\Theta^{(k)}$ to have similar topology to their neighboring networks while allows discontinuous jump of brain state transitions [13] to preserve correlation variabilities, thus solving two problems, i.e., temporal smoothness and temporal dynamics of sliding window connectivity networks, simultaneously. In this study, the optimal λ values in Eq. (5) were determined using grid search approach.

2.6 Feature Extraction and Classification

Local weighted clustering coefficient of each ROI is computed to generate a feature vector of 116 elements for every network. Feature vectors of all temporal networks are concatenated into a long feature vector, and a subset of the most discriminative features that maximizes the eMCI identification performance was selected using t-tests and the support vector machine (SVM) recursive feature elimination algorithm. The most discriminative features were selected solely based on the training subjects. Performance of eMCI identification was evaluated using linear SVM with leave-one-out cross-validation.

3 Experimental Results

Before performing eMCI identification, we explored the dynamic changes of temporal networks for two clinical groups. Across subjects average temporal networks for eMCI and NC groups with $N = 90$ and $s = 2$ are shown in Figure 2. It is clearly observed that the topologies of within group temporal networks are similar, indicating their temporal smoothness. Although with similar topologies, we can observe certain degrees of correlation variations between adjacent temporal networks, indicating their temporal dynamics. In contrast, significant topology and correlation differences are observed between eMCI and NC groups.

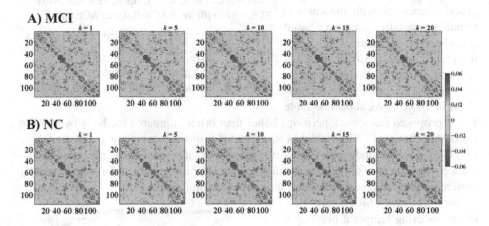

Fig. 2. Across subjects average temporal networks with $N = 90$ and $s = 2$. The upper and bottom rows are the temporal networks for eMCI and NC groups, respectively.

To quantitatively illustrate the temporally dynamic changes, we computed the clustering coefficients of different temporal networks for each group. Clustering coefficients of each temporal network with $N = 90$ and $s = 2$ are plotted in Figure 3. The temporally dynamic pattern across temporal networks is significantly different between eMCI and NC groups. This observation further supports that, at least partially, the variations of sliding window correlation of an R-fMRI scan are obvious, implying their potential application in disease diagnosis.

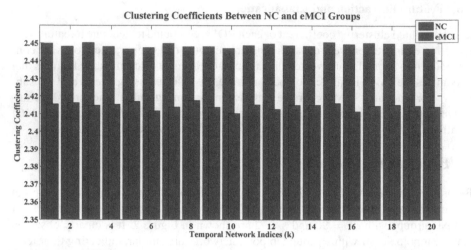

Fig. 3. Temporally dynamic patterns in terms of clustering coefficients for temporal networks with $N = 90$ and $s = 2$

We compared the eMCI identification performance of the proposed framework with the conventional temporally stationary-based (i.e., Pearson correlation (PC)), and the graph graphical LASSO (GGL)-based frameworks. Performances of all compared methods are summarized in Table 1. As shown in Table 1, the proposed framework performs better than other compared methods by yielding the best accuracy of 79.7%, which is at least 6.5% improvement compared to the second best GGL-based framework. A cross-validation estimation of the generalization performance shows an area of 0.792 under the receiver operating characteristic curve (AUC), indicating good diagnostic power of the proposed framework.

Table 1. Classification performance of all compared frameworks. (ACC = ACCuracy; SEN = SENsitivity; SPE = SPEcificity; BAC = Balance ACcuracy).

Method	ACC	AUC	SEN	SPE	BAC
PC	0.6610	0.6138	0.5517	0.7667	0.6592
GGL	0.7288	0.7315	0.7586	0.7000	0.7293
FMGL	**0.7966**	**0.7920**	**0.7586**	**0.8333**	**0.7920**

We performed eMCI identification using temporal networks with different step sizes ($s = 1, 2, 4, 8, 10$) to evaluate effects of step size in the proposed framework. eMCI identification performance is summarized in Figure 4. The proposed framework performed relatively better when the step size is small ($s = 1, 2, 4$). Significantly higher sensitivity and AUC values at small

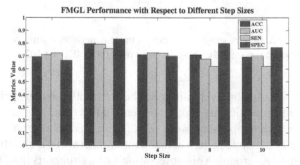

Fig. 4. eMCI identification performance at different step sizes (s) using temporal networks with $N = 90$

step size implies successful extraction of disease associated temporally dynamic disruptions. When the step size is relatively large ($s = 8, 10$), intrinsic temporally dynamic disruptions are largely overlooked. Furthermore, we also found that the proposed framework with smaller window length performed relatively better when compared with larger window length. The possible reason of these observations is that the disease induced neural activity disruptions may occur at time scales which are shorter than the step size.

Most of the selected discriminant regions are components of the default mode network, the frontal lobe (superior frontal gyrus (dorsal) and inferior orbitofrontal cortex), the temporal lobe (superior temporal pole and inferior temporal), the occipital lobe (inferior occipital gyrus, cuneus and bilateral fusiform gyrus), the parietal lobe (postcentral gyrus), the subcortical regions (caudate and amygdala), and the cerebellum regions, which have been reported in previous studies to be associated with the MCI and AD pathologies. Due to widespread functional connectivity disruptions in MCI brain even at its prodromal phase [4], many ROIs are required for more accurate diagnosis. Since there are very few studies focused in eMCI individuals, the selected most discriminative regions can only be compared with the AD/MCI findings which uses the conventional stationary approach. Hence, careful interpretations of the results are required, and more works shall be performed to enhance our understanding on the biological underpinnings of eMCI. The selected regions are graphically shown in Figure 5.

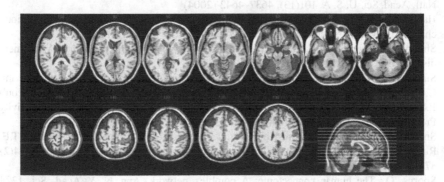

Fig. 5. Most discriminative regions that were selected for eMCI identification. The colors indicate different ROIs.

4   Conclusion

In this paper, we propose to utilize the temporally dynamic information of an R-fMRI scan for eMCI identification. This work is inspired by the variability of sliding window correlation induced by neural interactions that happen within the time scales of seconds to minutes. We believe that the temporally dynamic patterns of eMCI subjects might be disrupted by disease pathology. We thus estimate temporal networks from a set of sub-series generated from an R-fMRI scan to better reflect the between-region neural interactions across time. We employ a fused lasso regularization based sparse learning algorithm to simultaneously estimate temporal networks. These temporal networks share similar network topology, while allow discontinuous jump of brain state transitions. The promising results obtained in this work support the soundness of utilizing the temporally dynamic information of an R-fMRI scan for accurate diagnosis of neurological disorders.

References

1. Achard, S., Salvador, R., Whitcher, B., Suckling, J., Bullmore, E.T.: A resilient, low-frequency, small-world human brain functional network with highly connected association cortical hubs. J. Neurosci. 26(1), 63–72 (2006)
2. Chang, C., Glover, G.H.: Time-frequency dynamics of resting-state brain connectivity measured with fMRI. Neuroimage 50(1), 81–98 (2010)
3. Danaher, P., Wang, P., Witten, D.M.: The joint graphical lasso for inverse covariance estimation across multiple classes. Arxiv preprint arXiv:1111.0324 (2012)
4. Fennema-Notestine, C., Hagler Jr., D.J., McEvoy, L.K., Fleisher, A.S., Wu, E.H., Karow, D.S., Dale, A.M., Alzheimer's Disease Neuroimaging Initiative: Structural MRI biomarkers for preclinical and mild Alzheimer's disease. Hum. Brain Mapp. 30(10), 3238–3253 (2009)
5. Friedman, J., Hastie, T., Tibshirani, R.: Sparse inverse covariance estimation with the graphical lasso. Biostatistics 9(3), 432–441 (2008)
6. Greicius, M.D., Srivastava, G., Reiss, A.L., Menon, V.: Default-mode network activity distinguishes Alzheimer's disease from healthy aging: Evidence from functional MRI. Proc. Natl. Acad. Sci. U. S. A. 101(13), 4637–4642 (2004)
7. Handwerker, D.A., Roopchansingh, V., Gonzalez-Castillo, J., Bandettini, P.A.: Periodic changes in fMRI connectivity. Neuroimage 63(3), 1712–1719 (2012)
8. Sheline, Y.I., Raichle, M.E.: Resting state functional connectivity in preclinical Alzheimer's disease. Biol. Psychiatry (in press, 2013)
9. Smith, S.M., Miller, K.L., Moeller, S., Xu, J., Auerbach, E.J., Woolrich, M.W., Beckmann, C.F., Jenkinson, M., Andersson, J., Glasser, M.F., Van Essen, D.C., Feinberg, D.A., Yacoub, E.S., Ugurbil, K.: Temporally-independent functional modes of spontaneous brain activity. Proc. Natl. Acad. Sci. U. S. A. 109(8), 3131 (2012)
10. Smith, S.M., Miller, K.L., Salimi-Khorshidi, G., Webster, M., Beckmann, C.F., Nichols, T.E., Ramsey, J.D., Woolrich, M.W.: Network modelling methods for fMRI. Neuroimage 54(2), 875–891 (2011)
11. Sporns, O.: The human connectome: A complex network. Ann. N. Y. Acad. Sci. 1224, 109–125 (2011)
12. Supekar, K., Menon, V., Rubin, D., Musen, M., Greicius, M.D.: Network analysis of intrinsic functional brain connectivity in Alzheimer's disease. PLoS Comput. Biol. 4, e1000100 (2008)
13. Tibshirani, R., Sauders, M., Zhu, J., Knight, K.: Sparsity and smoothness via the fused lasso. J. R. Statist. Soc. B 67(1), 91–108 (2005)
14. Whitwell, J.L., Przybelski, S.A., Weigand, S.D., Knopman, D.S., Boeve, B.F., Petersen, R.C., Jack Jr., C.R.: 3D maps from multiple mri illustrate changing atrophy patterns as subjects progress from mild cognitive impairment to Alzheimer's disease. Brain 130(7), 1777–1786 (2007)
15. Yang, S., Pan, Z., Shen, X., Wonka, P., Ye, J.: Fused multiple graphical lasso. Arxiv preprint arXiv:1209.2139 (2012)

An Improved Optimization Method
for the Relevance Voxel Machine

Melanie Ganz[1,2], Mert R. Sabuncu[1], and Koen Van Leemput[1,3,4]

[1] Martinos Center for Biomedical Imaging, MGH, Harvard Medical School, USA
ganz@nmr.mgh.harvard.edu
[2] Department for Computer Science, University of Copenhagen, Denmark
[3] Department of Applied Mathematics and Computer Science, DTU, Denmark
[4] Departments of Information and Computer Science and of Biomedical Engineering
and Computational Science, Aalto University, Finland

Abstract. In this paper, we will re-visit the Relevance Voxel Machine (RVoxM), a recently developed sparse Bayesian framework used for predicting biological markers, e.g., presence of disease, from high-dimensional image data, e.g., brain MRI volumes. The proposed improvement, called IRVoxM, mitigates the short-comings of the greedy optimization scheme of the original RVoxM algorithm by exploiting the form of the marginal likelihood function. In addition, it allows voxels to be added and deleted from the model during the optimization. In our experiments we show that IRVoxM outperforms RVoxM on synthetic data, achieving a better training cost and test root mean square error while yielding sparser models. We further evaluated IRVoxM's performance on real brain MRI scans from the OASIS data set, and observed the same behavior - IRVoxM retains good prediction performance while yielding much sparser models than RVoxM.

1   Introduction

Multivariate pattern analysis (MVPA) methods provide an alternative approach to examining subtle and complex relationships between biomedical images, e.g., structural [1] or functional [2] neuroimage data, and clinical variables of interest. They further offer the ability to make accurate individual-level predictions of clinical outcome, paving the way to personalized medicine. One specific class of MVPA algorithms employs sparse Bayesian learning; a well-known algorithm of that class is the Relevance Vector Machine (RVM) [3] which is similar to a support vector machine (SVM) [4]. In contrast to SVM, it provides probabilistic outcomes and has no free parameters to tune. Problems with RVM are the computational time, which is approximately cubic in the number of inputs, as well as the greedy optimization. Thus different approaches have been developed to overcome these shortcomings, e.g. FastRVM [5].

Recently, Sabuncu and Van Leemput [6] extended the relevance vector machine by incorporating an additional spatial regularization term in the Gaussian prior on the regression weights or classification features (RVoxM). RVoxM encourages spatial clustering of the features used for regression or classification, and computes predictions as linear combinations of their content. While the model of RVoxM produced nice results on age regression data [6], the algorithm used a simple fixed point optimization scheme,

G. Wu et al. (Eds.): MLMI 2013, LNCS 8184, pp. 147–154, 2013.
© Springer International Publishing Switzerland 2013

which is not guaranteed to decrease the cost function at every step and is computationally expensive. In addition, RVoxM prunes voxels from the linear model by applying an artificial numerical threshold to the weight hyperparameters, which creates a free parameter that affects model sparsity. Lastly, RVoxM can only remove voxels from the model, but not re-introduce them later on. Thus in its current form, it is reminiscent of a greedy forward feature selection algorithm.

In this paper, we aim to solve the problems of the original RVoxM algorithm in the spirit of FastRVM [5]. We call the new algorithm Improved Relevance Voxel Machine (IRVoxM). Our contributions improve the greedy optimization algorithm of RVoxM by deriving an analytic expression for the optimal hyperparameter of each voxel, given the current hyperparameter of all other voxels. This enables us to maximize the marginal likelihood function in a principled and efficient manner. As a result, IRVoxM optimizes the objective function better during training, and the resulting models predict better on unseen cases. Lastly, IRVoxM enables us to easily add and/or remove voxels during the optimization procedure, allowing us to start from an empty model which has the potential for large computational advantages.

2 Regression with the Relevance Voxel Machine - RVoxM

We base IRVoxM on the same theoretical model as RVoxM [6]. In the regression problem, the target variable t, e.g., age or clinical test score, is assumed to be Gaussian distributed:

$$p(t|\mathbf{x}, \mathbf{w}, \beta) = \mathcal{N}(t|y(\mathbf{x}, \mathbf{w}), \beta^{-1}), \tag{1}$$

with variance β^{-1} and mean $y(\mathbf{x}, \mathbf{w}) = \sum_{i=1}^{M-1} x_i w_i + w_M = \mathbf{w}^\mathrm{T}\mathbf{x}$, where $\mathbf{x} \in \mathbb{R}^M$ is a vector that represents the input data, e.g., an image, plus a constant element of one ($x_M = 1$), and $\mathbf{w} \in \mathbb{R}^M$ are weights.

We further assume a Gaussian prior on $\mathbf{w}$ with hyperparamters $\boldsymbol{\alpha}$ and λ of the form

$$p(\mathbf{w}|\boldsymbol{\alpha}, \lambda) = \mathcal{N}(\mathbf{w}|0, \mathbf{P}^{-1}), \tag{2}$$

where $\mathbf{P} = \mathrm{diag}(\boldsymbol{\alpha}) + \lambda\mathbf{K}$. $\mathbf{K} = \boldsymbol{\Gamma}^\mathrm{T}\boldsymbol{\Gamma}$ is the graph Laplacian matrix which is a sparse, symmetric matrix and can be defined as the inner product of the incidence matrix $\boldsymbol{\Gamma}$. $\boldsymbol{\Gamma}$ is a sparse matrix of dimension $N_{\mathrm{Edg}} \times M$, where N_{Edg} denotes the number of edges in the graph spanned by $\mathbf{K}$. Each row of $\boldsymbol{\Gamma}$ has only two entries that denote the outgoing ($+1$) and incoming (-1) nodes of an edge in the graph. In our case, edges connect physically neighboring locations, e.g., all voxels in the 6-neighborhood are connected to a central voxel in a volumetric image, but other configurations can also be considered. $\boldsymbol{\alpha} = (\alpha_1, \ldots, \alpha_M)^\mathrm{T}$ and λ are hyperparameters; the α_i are inverse covariances of the weight prior and hence control the sparsity of the weights. A large α_i means the weight w_i of the associated voxel is tending to zero, while a small α_i implies that the value w_i is largely determined by its neighbors. The parameter λ encourages spatial smoothness and the larger it is the smoother the resulting weight maps are.

Training. With the above prior, the hyperparameters can be estimated by maximizing the following type-II likelihood given a collection of training target values $\mathbf{t} = (t_1, \ldots, t_N)^\mathrm{T}$ and a set of N training images $\mathbf{X} = [\mathbf{x}_1, \ldots, \mathbf{x}_N]^\mathrm{T}$:

$$p(\mathbf{t}|\mathbf{X}, \alpha, \beta, \lambda) = \int_{\mathbf{w}} p(\mathbf{t}|\mathbf{X}, \mathbf{w}, \beta)p(\mathbf{w}|\alpha, \lambda)d\mathbf{w} \tag{3}$$

$$= \int_{\mathbf{w}} \left(\prod_{n=1}^{N} p(t_n|\mathbf{x}_n, \mathbf{w}, \beta) \right) p(\mathbf{w}|\alpha, \lambda)d\mathbf{w} = \mathcal{N}(\mathbf{t}|\mathbf{0}, \mathbf{C}),$$

where we define $\mathbf{C} = \beta^{-1}\mathbf{I} + \mathbf{X}\mathbf{P}^{-1}\mathbf{X}^{\mathrm{T}}$. We can estimate the hyperparameters α, β, λ, which is equivalent to maximizing Eq. 4:

$$\hat{\alpha}, \hat{\beta}, \hat{\lambda} = \underset{\alpha, \beta, \lambda}{\mathrm{argmax}}\, \mathcal{L}(\alpha, \beta, \lambda) = \underset{\alpha, \beta, \lambda}{\mathrm{argmax}} \left(-\frac{1}{2}(N \ln(2\pi) + \ln|\mathbf{C}| + \mathbf{t}^{\mathrm{T}}\mathbf{C}^{-1}\mathbf{t}) \right).$$
$$\tag{4}$$

Here, $\mathcal{L}(\alpha, \beta, \lambda)$ denotes the logarithm of the marginal likelihood function, which is obtained by integrating out the weight parameters as shown in Eq. 3. In RVoxM [6], this optimization was solved by a coordinate ascent over β and λ, while optimizing over all α simultaneously using a fixed point equation and a greedy approach, where single α_i's exceeding a numerical threshold are pruned from the model. This optimization of α has no theoretical guarantees of convergence and is computationally expensive. Hence, in this paper we focus on deriving a better optimization algorithm for α.

Prediction. After obtaining $\hat{\alpha}, \hat{\beta}, \hat{\lambda}$ from training data, we can make predictions for a new $\mathbf{x}^*$ according to

$$p(t^*|\mathbf{x}^*, \mathbf{X}, \mathbf{t}, \hat{\alpha}, \hat{\beta}, \hat{\lambda}) = \int p(t^*|\mathbf{x}^*, \mathbf{w}, \hat{\beta})p(\mathbf{w}|\mathbf{X}, \mathbf{t}, \hat{\alpha}, \hat{\lambda})d\mathbf{w} = \mathcal{N}(\mu^*, \Sigma^*), \tag{5}$$

where $p(t^*|\mathbf{x}^*, \mathbf{w}, \hat{\beta})$ is given by the regression model in Eq. 1 and $\mu^* = \mu^T\mathbf{x}$ and $\Sigma^* = \frac{1}{\beta} | \mathbf{x}^T\Sigma\mathbf{x}$, in which $\Sigma = (\mathbf{P} + \beta\mathbf{X}^T\mathbf{X})^{-1}$ and $\mu = \Sigma\mathbf{X}^T\mathbf{t}$.

3 The Improved Relevance Voxel Machine - IRVoxM

The greedy optimization method employed by RVoxM suffers from several weaknesses. First of all, the fixed point updates used for α in [6] are not guaranteed in each update step to increase the logarithm of the marginal likelihood $\mathcal{L}(\alpha, \beta, \lambda)$ given in Eq. 4. Thus the optimization can become unstable, if it is not well initialized. Another difficulty is the use of an artificial numerical threshold that controls the sparsity of the solution by deciding at which point an α_i is considered to be large enough to yield a weight w_i close enough to zero to be effectively pruned from the model. Finally, RVoxM works by pruning voxels from a larger set until only relevant voxels are left. But once voxels are removed from the model there is no way to re-introduce them; the set of voxels included in the sparse model can only decline.

In this paper, we present a way of tackling all of the above issues. First, we ensure that single updates are guaranteed to increase the logarithm of the marginal likelihood. Then we introduce a conceptual change that allows us to analytically judge if a voxel should be included in the model or not. This change also enables us to re-visit and re-introduce voxels into our sparse model during the optimization, which addresses the third problem. To derive the improved Relevance Voxel Machine (IRVoxM) we study $\mathcal{L}(\boldsymbol{\alpha}, \beta, \lambda)$ for fixed β and λ; thus $\mathcal{L}(\boldsymbol{\alpha}, \beta, \lambda)$ is only dependent on $\boldsymbol{\alpha}$. We can rewrite the logarithm of the marginal likelihood function $\mathcal{L}(\boldsymbol{\alpha})$ (Eq. 4) to expose the marginal contribution of α_i.

But first, let us introduce some notation:

$$\tilde{\mathbf{X}} = \begin{pmatrix} \mathbf{X} \\ \boldsymbol{\Gamma} \end{pmatrix}, \quad \tilde{\mathbf{t}} = \begin{pmatrix} \mathbf{t} \\ 0 \end{pmatrix}, \quad \tilde{\mathbf{B}} = \begin{pmatrix} \beta \mathbf{I}_N & 0 \\ 0 & \lambda \mathbf{I}_M \end{pmatrix}. \tag{6}$$

Now we can define $\tilde{\mathbf{C}} = \tilde{\mathbf{B}}^{-1} + \tilde{\mathbf{X}}\text{diag}(\boldsymbol{\alpha}^{-1})\tilde{\mathbf{X}}^{\mathrm{T}}$ and therefore $|\tilde{\mathbf{C}}| = \beta^{-N}\lambda^{-N_{\text{Edg}}}\frac{|\boldsymbol{\Sigma}|}{|\text{diag}(\boldsymbol{\alpha})|}$. In addition, we write $\tilde{\mathbf{C}}^{-1} = \tilde{\mathbf{B}} - \tilde{\mathbf{B}}\tilde{\mathbf{X}}\tilde{\boldsymbol{\Sigma}}\tilde{\mathbf{X}}^{\mathrm{T}}\tilde{\mathbf{B}}$ and express the logarithm of the marginal likelihood (Eq. 4) as:

$$
\begin{aligned}
\mathcal{L}(\boldsymbol{\alpha}) &= -\frac{1}{2}\left(N\ln(2\pi) + \ln(\beta^{-N}\frac{|\boldsymbol{\Sigma}|}{|\mathbf{P}|}) + \mathbf{t}^{\mathrm{T}}\mathbf{C}^{-1}\mathbf{t} \right) \\
&= -\frac{1}{2}\left(N\ln(2\pi) + \ln|\tilde{\mathbf{C}}| + \tilde{\mathbf{t}}^{\mathrm{T}}\tilde{\mathbf{C}}^{-1}\tilde{\mathbf{t}} \right) - \frac{1}{2}\left(N_{\text{Edg}}\ln(\lambda) - \ln|\mathbf{P}| + \ln|\text{diag}(\boldsymbol{\alpha})| \right) \\
&= \underbrace{-\frac{1}{2}\left(N\ln(2\pi) + \ln|\tilde{\mathbf{C}}_{-i}| + \tilde{\mathbf{t}}^{\mathrm{T}}\tilde{\mathbf{C}}_{-i}^{-1}\tilde{\mathbf{t}} + N_{\text{Edg}}\ln(\lambda) - \ln(|\boldsymbol{\Psi}_{-i}|) \right)}_{\mathcal{L}(\boldsymbol{\alpha}_{-i})} \\
&\quad + \underbrace{\frac{1}{2}\left(-\ln(\alpha_i + \tilde{s}_i) + \frac{\tilde{q}^2}{\alpha_i + \tilde{s}_i} + \ln(\alpha_i + a_i) \right)}_{l(\alpha_i)}.
\end{aligned}
\tag{7}
$$

As in [5], we first use the definitions of $|\mathbf{C}|$, $|\tilde{\mathbf{C}}|$ and $\tilde{\mathbf{C}}^{-1}$ to rewrite Eq. 4 and then employ established matrix determinant and inverse identities to separate the contribution of α_i from $\tilde{\mathbf{C}}$ and its inverse. This yields $\tilde{\mathbf{C}}_{-i}$ and $\tilde{\mathbf{C}}_{-i}^{-1}$ which are $\tilde{\mathbf{C}}$ and its inverse with the contribution of the i-th voxel removed. Lastly, we define

$$\tilde{s}_i = \tilde{\mathbf{X}}_i^{\mathrm{T}}\tilde{\mathbf{C}}_{-i}^{-1}\tilde{\mathbf{X}}_i, \tilde{q}_i = \tilde{\mathbf{X}}_i^{\mathrm{T}}\tilde{\mathbf{C}}_{-i}^{-1}\tilde{\mathbf{t}}, \boldsymbol{\Psi}_{-i} = \mathbf{I} + \sum_{j\neq i}\frac{\lambda}{\alpha_j}\boldsymbol{\Gamma}_j\boldsymbol{\Gamma}_j^{\mathrm{T}}, a_i = \frac{\lambda\boldsymbol{\Gamma}_i\boldsymbol{\Psi}_{-i}^{-1}\boldsymbol{\Gamma}_i^{\mathrm{T}}}{\alpha_i}, \tag{8}$$

in which $\tilde{\mathbf{X}}_i$ and $\boldsymbol{\Gamma}_i$ denote the i-th column of $\tilde{\mathbf{X}}$ and $\boldsymbol{\Gamma}$, respectively.

In Eq. 7 we have replaced $\mathcal{L}(\boldsymbol{\alpha})$ by $\mathcal{L}(\boldsymbol{\alpha}_{-i})$ and $l(\alpha_i)$. $\mathcal{L}(\boldsymbol{\alpha}_{-i})$ includes the contributions of all $\boldsymbol{\alpha}$ except for the i-th α to the marginal likelihood, whereas $l(\alpha_i)$ comprises only the contribution of α_i. Equation 7 can now be optimized with respect to α_i in closed form (while keeping all other α's fixed to their current values):

1. If $a_i \geq \tilde{s}_i$, the optimal solution is $\hat{\alpha}_i = 0$, since we do not allow negative alphas as in [6].
2. If $a_i < \tilde{s}_i$ and $\tilde{s}_i - a_i < \tilde{q}_i^2$, the optimal solution is $\hat{\alpha}_i = \frac{a_i(\tilde{s}_i + \tilde{q}_i^2) - \tilde{s}_i^2}{\tilde{s}_i - a_i - \tilde{q}_i^2}$. If this solution is negative, the optimal solution is $\hat{\alpha}_i = 0$.
3. If $a_i < \tilde{s}_i$ and $\tilde{s}_i - a_i \geq \tilde{q}_i^2$, the optimal solution is $\hat{\alpha}_i = \infty$, which corresponds to removing the i'th voxel from the model (see [3,6]).

The above rules enable us to loop over all voxels and update a single α_i at a time. An overview of the IRVoxM algorithm is given in Algorithm 1. Details regarding the derivation of $l(\alpha_i)$ as well as a functional analysis of the marginal likelihood function are excluded due to space constraints, but can be found in a technical report [7].

Algorithm 1. IRVoxM algorithm

1: Initialize λ, β and all α as in RVoxM [6].
2: **loop**
3:    **loop**
4:       Randomly pick a voxel i.
5:       Compute $\tilde{s}_i, \tilde{q}_i$ and a_i according to Eqs. 8.
6:       **if** $a_i \geq \tilde{s}_i$ **then**
7:          $\alpha_i = 0$
8:       **else if** $a_i < \tilde{s}_i$ **then**
9:          **if** $\tilde{s}_i - a_i < \tilde{q}_i^2$ **then**
10:             $\alpha_i = \frac{a_i(\tilde{s}_i + \tilde{q}_i^2) - \tilde{s}_i^2}{\tilde{s}_i - a_i - \tilde{q}_i^2}$
11:             **if** $\alpha_i < 0$ **then**
12:                $\alpha_i = 0.$
13:             **end if**
14:          **else if** $\tilde{s}_i - a_i \geq \tilde{q}_i^2$ **then**
15:             $\alpha_i = \infty$
16:          **end if**
17:       **end if**
18:       Update all quantities in an efficient manner as derived in [7].
19:    **end loop**
20:    Update β and λ by a simple search of the two-dimensional cost function.
21: **end loop**

---

4 Experiments and Results

In order to demonstrate that our proposed optimizer outperforms RVoxM's, we will evaluate the performance of IRVoxM and RVoxM on a synthetic and a real data set. To make the comparison fair, we initialize the two algorithms identically with $\alpha = 1$, $\beta = 1$ and $\lambda = 1$.

4.1 Experiments on Synthetic Data

First, we ran experiments on synthetic data. To model a single target value t, we generated a random vectorized image $\mathbf{x}$ by drawing random samples from a Gaussian distribution with mean 0 and standard deviation 1 of size $M \times 1$. Using pre-determined constants $\alpha_{\text{true}} = (10^{12}\mathbf{v}, 0.5\mathbf{v}, 10^{12}\mathbf{v})^{\mathsf{T}}$, where $\mathbf{v}$ is a vector of ones and of dimension $\frac{M}{3} \times 1$, and $\lambda_{\text{true}} = 10$, we constructed $\mathbf{P}_{\text{true}} = \text{diag}(\alpha_{\text{true}}) + \lambda_{\text{true}}\Gamma^{\mathsf{T}}\Gamma$. Here, Γ is the incidence matrix for a 4-neighborhood. From $\mathbf{P}_{\text{true}}$ we sampled weights $\mathbf{w}_{\text{true}}$ and computed targets as $t = \mathbf{w}_{\text{true}}^{\mathsf{T}}\mathbf{x} + \epsilon$, where the noise ϵ was sampled from a normal distribution with mean zero and inverse variance $\beta_{\text{true}} = 10$. We constructed data this way for a varying number of training images N, yielding collections of image vectors $\mathbf{X}$ of size $N \times M$ as well as vectors of target values $\mathbf{t}$ of size $N \times 1$. We used an image size $M = 10 \times 10$. Lastly, we varied N from 10 to 100 and generated 100 independent pairs of $\mathbf{X}$ and $\mathbf{t}$ with the same weight vector $\mathbf{w}_{\text{true}}$ for each value of N. For the test data, we generated another 100 independent pairs of $\mathbf{X}$ and $\mathbf{t}$ using $N = 100$, and applied the same weight vector $\mathbf{w}_{\text{true}}$ as for the training data. Examples of two random

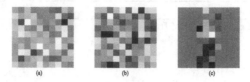

Fig. 1. Examples of two random images (a) and (b) as well as the weight vector (c) we used in our synthetic data experiment

images and the weight vector we used can be seen in Fig. 1. Fig. 2 shows the sparsity of the trained models, the training cost, which is the negative logarithm of the marginal likelihood given in Eq. 4, and the root mean square error (RMSE) between the true and the predicted target values computed on the test data sets. It also shows a comparison of the predicted and true weights by showing the l_2-norm of the difference between the true and the predicted weights of the two algorithms.

The results reveal several weaknesses of the original RVoxM. First, while the true sparsity of our synthetic data is always 33% (since we set 1/3 of the 100 weights to be different from zero), RVoxM grossly overestimates the number of weights that are included in the model (see Figure 1 a). IRVoxM on the other hand produces sparser models, while still achieving a better training cost on the training data (see Figure 1 b). Hence IRVoxM is not over fitting to the training data, but finding sparse models that represent the data well. Furthermore, RVoxM and IRVoxM yield comparable RMSE on the test data with IRVoxM considerably outperforming RVoxM for larger N (see Figure 1 c). Finally, IRVoxM produces weights that are much closer to the true weights for all values of N (see Figure 1d).

4.2 Experiments on OASIS

Next, we ran experiments on the publicly available cross-sectional Open Access Series of Imaging Studies (OASIS) [8]. We used structural brain MRI scans (T1-weighted) from 336 healthy subjects and processed them with SPM8[1] to obtain spatially aligned gray matter maps. The gray matter density values were used as voxel-level input data x_i. To lighten the computational burden for our experiments, we generated masks with $N = 1000, 5000, 10000$ voxels for subsequent analysis. To acquire these masks, we calculated a univariate correlation of each voxel with age (only on the training data set) and sorted the voxels based on their correlation value, as was done in [9]. Then we used only the top N voxels in the analysis. We randomly chose half of the subjects and trained a model for age regression on this training dataset. Then we used the trained model to predict the age on the other half of the OASIS data set and calculated the correlation and the root mean square error (RMSE) between the predicted and the real age. The correlations and RMSE are shown in table 4.2. Again, we can observe that IRVoxM yields much sparser models than RVoxM, while achieving a high age correlation and low RMSE.

---

[1] http://www.fil.ion.ucl.ac.uk/spm/software/spm8/

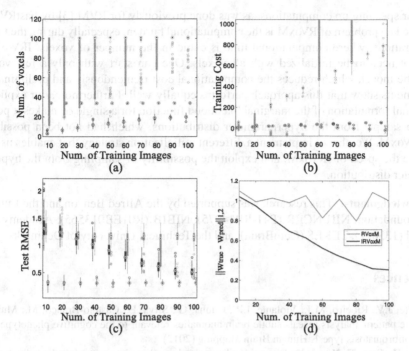

Fig. 2. Results for the synthetic data showing the resulting training sparsity (a), the training cost (b) and the root mean square error (RMSE) on the test data (c) for 100 independent repetitions. The box plots in (a), (b) and (c) show the ground truth (red), RVoxM (green) and IRVoxM (blue). In (d) we show the l_2-norm of the differences between the true weights and the weights RVoxM produces (green) and the true weights and the weights IRVoxM produces (blue).

Table 1. Model sparsity, test correlation and root mean square error (RMSE) for the OASIS data set including a different number of voxels in the mask

OASIS test set	RVoxM			IRVoxM		
168 images	1000	5000	10000	1000	5000	10000
Num. voxels in the model	173	176	151	42	44	17
Correlation	0.90	0.89	0.89	0.91	0.92	0.89
RMSE	10.47	10.85	10.82	10.17	9.97	11.02

5 Discussion and Conclusion

We have re-visited the relevance voxel machine and introduced a better optimization scheme. Our algorithm IRVoxM outperforms RVoxM on synthetic data; it yields sparser models with good prediction performance and retains weight maps that are closer to the true synthetic weights than RVoxM's. On the OASIS data we observe that while retaining good prediction performance, IRVoxM yields much sparser models than RVoxM.

Our aim in this paper was to show that our proposed algorithm IRVoxM improves over RVoxM's optimization scheme; thus we compared the two algorithms side by side. Our new optimization strategy performs as anticipated, and opens up a whole new avenue for speeding up computations, as was done previously for RVM [3] by FastRVM [5]. One key problem of RVoxM is the computational burden, especially during the first few iterations, where computational time is cubic in the number of voxels. IRVoxM does not need to be initialized with all voxels. One can start with only a few voxels in the model, which reduces the computational cost tremendously and preliminary experiments show that this approach performs equally well. Furthermore, our explicit functional formulation of the marginal likelihood function for a single α_i makes it possible to sample from the hyperparameter distributions, which had not been possible with RVoxM. We plan to implement a different initialization strategy that enables us to increase the speed of IRVoxM, and exploit the possibility of sampling from the hyperparameter distribution.

Acknowledgments. This research was supported by the Alfred Benzon and the Lundbeck Foundation, NIH NCRR (P41-RR14075), NIBIB (R01EB013565), Academy of Finland (133611), TEKES (ComBrain), and the Technical University of Denmark.

References

1. Duarte, J.V., Ribeiro, M.J., Violante, I.R., Cunha, G., Silva, E., Castelo-Branco, M.: Multivariate pattern analysis reveals subtle brain anomalies relevant to the cognitive phenotype in neurofibromatosis type 1. Human Brain Mapping (2012)
2. Yang, Z., Fang, F., Weng, X.: Recent developments in multivariate pattern analysis for functional mri. Neuroscience Bulletin 28(4), 399–408 (2012)
3. Tipping, M.: Sparse bayesian learning and the relevance vector machine. The Journal of Machine Learning Research 1, 211–244 (2001)
4. Cortes, C., Vapnik, V.: Support-vector networks. Machine Learning 20(3), 273–297 (1995)
5. Tipping, M.E., Faul, A.: Fast marginal likelihood maximisation for sparse bayesian models. In: Proceedings of the Ninth International Workshop on Artificial Intelligence and Statistics, pp. 3–6 (2003)
6. Sabuncu, M., Van Leemput, K.: The relevance voxel machine (rvoxm): A self-tuning bayesian model for informative image-based prediction. IEEE Transactions on Medical Imaging 31(12), 2290–2306 (2012)
7. Ganz, M., Sabuncu, M.R., van Leemput, K.: The improved relevance voxel machine. Technical Report DTU Compute-2013-10, Institute for Mathematical Modeling, DTU (2013)
8. Marcus, D., Wang, T., Parker, J., Csernansky, J., Morris, J., Buckner, R.: Open access series of imaging studies (oasis): cross-sectional mri data in young, middle aged, nondemented, and demented older adults. Journal of Cognitive Neuroscience 19(9), 1498–1507 (2007)
9. Michel, V., Eger, E., Keribin, C., Thirion, B.: Multiclass sparse bayesian regression for fmri-based prediction. Journal of Biomedical Imaging 2011, 2 (2011)

Disentanglement of Session and Plasticity Effects in Longitudinal fMRI Studies

Vittorio Iacovella[1,2], Paolo Avesani[1,2], and Gabriele Miceli[1,3]

[1] NeuroInformatics Laboratory (NILab), Fondazione Bruno Kessler, Trento, Italy
[2] Centro Interdipartimentale Mente e Cervello (CIMeC), Università di Trento, Italy
[3] Center for Neurocognitive Rehabilitation (CeRiN), Università di Trento, Italy
{iacovella,avesani}@fbk.eu, gabriele.miceli@unitn.it

Abstract. In longitudinal studies, such as those about neurocognitive rehabilitation or brain plasticity, functional MRI sessions are subsequently
recorded to detect how the patterns of activation differs through time.
Usually, consecutive recordings are interleaved by a period of treatment
or training. The general purpose of fMRI data analysis is to compute a
brain map accounting for plasticity effects on BOLD response. Specifically, the challenge of longitudinal studies analysis is to disentangle plain
session effect from the plasticity one. To date, a commonly used practice is
to separately compute these two effects and then combine results through
a comparison. The brain map for session effect is obtained with a univariate analysis of the contrast between two subsequent recordings. We argue
that such a brain map includes also the bias of the coregistration error related to the alignment of two sessions. Here we do not propose a method
to reduce the coregistration error but a method to reduce the effect of this
bias when estimating the session effect. We show how, combining functional hyperalignment and multivariate pattern analysis, it is possible to
summarize a single brain map that accounts for plasticity effect without
the session effect.

1 Introduction

Functional magnetic resonance imaging (fMRI) longitudinal studies are collection of datasets where participants are scanned repeatedly over time. These
studies build on the strength of functional MRI in finding out patterns of brain
responses in time. Specifically, this feature is exploited to observe induced
(through training or treatment) or natural modifications in plasticity and potential spatial rearrangement of patterns which may occur between sessions. Results
from these studies turn out to be interesting especially when dealing with patients: for example Meinzer and colleagues [4] discuss the fact that several issues
in studying the aphasia disease, like the heterogeneity of patient samples, were
sorted out only by combining behavioral techniques with longitudinal (pre and
post treatment) neuroimaging studies.

Extracting a neat effect (e.g. the one related to plasticity) solely referring to
the actual goal of the study turns out to be critical. Potential unrelated outcomes

G. Wu et al. (Eds.): MLMI 2013, LNCS 8184, pp. 155–162, 2013.
© Springer International Publishing Switzerland 2013

(session effects), plainly due to the fact that datasets come from experimental sessions distant in time, are difficult to characterize and disentangle from the relevant ones. For fMRI longitudinal studies, one strategy [5] is to present the participants with a variety of cognitive tasks: some thought to be influenced by the actual progress of relevant longitudinal variables, some others thought to remain stable. Then the concurrent reading of brain maps coming from different sessions should allow the disentaglement of session and plasticity effects.

The working assumption here is that the extraction of a summarizing indicant from two different session is straightforward. This strategy, however, includes two steps leading to potential flaws. First, joint analysis of two fMRI sessions introduces coregistration biases influencing final result: for fMRI longitudinal studies, where the spatial information plays a fundamental role, this could turn out to be crucial. Secondly, the estimation of actual effect of plasticity on the relevant sessions, is performed using a mass-univariate analysis, avoiding several interesting issues (like spatially distributed contributions) making the overall effort in constructing the patient sample and in building the longitudinal dataset fruitless.

Here we propose a novel method to evaluate the nature of an effect on brain maps coming from longitudinal studies. This method is based on two main ideas, reflecting the two main steps previously mentioned: functional hyperalignment of two subsequent fMRI sessions and multivariate pattern analysis for the detection of plasticity effect.

First, we thought about the source of differences between time-series coming from the same participant, undergoing the same task in two different sessions, interleaved by a treatment. On one hand, differences might reflect a plain session effect, due to different environmental conditions. On the other hand they might be the index of something more interesting, related to plasticity. To deal with this we construct a common representation space between two subsequent sessions using functional hyperalignment [3]. This method builds on the characterization of shared patterns of fMRI fluctuations between different datasets. In this way we claim on one hand to avoid the production of the result through a plain superimposition of maps coming from different sessions, running into coregistration biases. On the other hand, we preserve the longitudinal functional information considering time-series coming from the two sessions as shapes and evaluating their functional alignment. We hypothesize that hyperalignment could work in adjusting session effects, but it could fail in recovering deeper functional modulations related to plasticity.

Second, we take into account distributed spatial patterns of brain fluctuations all at once. This multivariate approach[6] is adopted for the evaluation of session and plasticity effects. We insert functionally realigned shapes into a classification procedure indicating which is the estimated nature of the functional effect. In this way the production of the result is not directly influenced by coregistration strategies, arising only from a discrimination task on functionally hyperaligned time-series.

Here we provide a description of the method and an empirical analysis on a case study of naming learning on healthy participants.

2   Method

We focus the formulation of the disentanglement method to the scenario of a group study where for each participant two fMRI recording sessions are available, both sessions acquired with the same stimulation protocol. We don't do any specific assumption on the interleaving period, e.g. treatment or training.

The premise is that data analysis is accomplished in advance on the second session according to the common univariate methods. The analysis may address contrasts with respect to a control stimulusand a target stimulus which is expected to be affected by what occurred in the interleaving period between the two sessions. We assume that brain maps computed for each single participant have been summarized in a brain map at the group level. The resulting brain map will report one or more areas of activation. The open question is whether to qualify each of them as session effect or plasticity effect.

We define a procedure based on 6 steps. In the following we denote S_1 and S_2 the two subsequent sessions of fMRI recordings.

Step 1: Cluster Partitioning. This step takes as input a brain map where are reported the relevant voxels related to a predefined contrast. This set of voxels is partitioned into clusters taking into account spatial constraints. The output is a set of clusters $C = (c_1, \ldots, c_n)$ and each cluster might collect a different number of voxels according to the clustering criteria. The assumption is that this operation takes place in a common space where each participant has been coregistered. Each cluster will be considered a distinct pattern of activation that we are interested to classify as session effect or plasticity effect.

Step 2: Cluster Projection. Clusters defined at the group level are projected to single participant's space. For each cluster the single voxel time-series are collected and shaped into a matrix V of size $N_v \times N_t$ where N_v is the number of voxels and N_t is the number of volumes. This operation is performed twice: a first time for session 1 and a second time for session 2. The operation is iterated for each participant. The output is a set of matrices V_{ij}^1 and V_{ij}^2 for each cluster i and participant j.

Step 3: Cluster Alignment. Given a participant j, for each cluster i we have a shared data representation between sessions according to the registration to a common space. This step introduces a new shared representation based on the notion of functional hyperalignment[3]. With this alignment method a set of time-series, like those within a single cluster, can be considered as high-dimensional Euclidean vectors where each one represents one dimension. Alignment between two of these objects is performed using Procrustean transformation, a procedure considering first scale and position of the single objects and then a geometrical rotation between the two. The voxels of V_{ij}^1

and V_{ij}^2 are aligned with respect to their time - courses without taking into account spatial constraints. The output is a new matrix $\overline{V}_{ij}^1$ where the voxels of a cluster of S_1 are aligned to the voxel of the same cluster on S_2.

Step 4: Trial Encoding. The input to this step for each cluster is a pair of matrices, $\overline{V}_{ij}^1$ and V_{ij}^2, respectively for S_1 and S_2. Here we shape a multivariate analysis of a cluster. The time - courses of voxels are segmented according to the stimuli chosen at the beginning as contrast design. For each stimuli is defined a trial interval that includes only a few relevant fMRI volumes. A multivariate encoding of each trial is obtained by a vector representation of the values of all voxels of the cluster along the trial interval. Each vector is finally labelled as S_1 or S_2. The output is a set $X = (x_1, \ldots, x_S)$ where $x_s \in \mathcal{R}^d$ is a sample of trial that encodes the multivariate BOLD response of the cluster. This step is iterated for each cluster and for each participant.

Step 5: Trial Classification. This step takes as input the multivariate encoding of the clusters of all participants. For each cluster it is defined a discrimination task: to recognize whether a trial belongs to session S_1 or session S_2. Using a cross-validation approach a learning model is trained to classify the trials as S_1 or S_2. The final estimate of misclassification error is evaluated according to a statistical test, namely a binomial test, to assess if the trials can't be discriminated.

Step 6: Cluster Labelling. The output of the previous step provides the information for each cluster and for each participant whether after a functional hyperalignment it is still possible to discriminate the trials between session. Clusters where trials can be discriminated are labeled *plasticity effect* while cluster whose trials can not be discriminated are labelled *session effect*.

3   Material

As case study to perform an empirical evaluation of the disentanglement method we refer to an fMRI dataset designed to assess the training effect on a task of language rehabilitation. The stimulation protocol was validated in advance with a population of healthy participants. In the following we consider this version of the pilot study.

10 healthy participants, native Italian speakers, strongly right-handed, free from neurological or psychiatric disease participated in this fMRI study. The study was in compliance with the Declaration of Helsinki, and was approved by the Ethical Committee of the University of Trento. All participants signed informed consent forms.

Participants completed two fMRI sessions (session 1, before training, and session 2, after training) with an identical overt naming task, interleaved by a training procedure on some terms. Each fMRI session included 80 trials (60 black-and-white line drawings and 20 squiggles) presented in the same order, with the same timing, in a single-event design (each trial lasted 11.5 seconds starting with 2 secs of picture presentation). Each fMRI session lasted for 508 scans $\times$ 2.2 $T_R = 1117.6$ s. Participants were asked to whisper the name of the picture. The 60 drawings were made of three subsets (20 each), based on their frequency of usage: *high-frequency* (HF); *low-frequency target* (LFT) made of stimuli that were going to be trained; and *low-frequency non-target* (LFnT) made of stimuli that were not going to be trained and fully matched to LFT stimuli for the main psycholinguistic variables.

Brain images were collected with a 4-Tesla Bruker MedSpec scanner using an 8-channel head coil. Functional images were acquired using a T2*-weighted gradient-echo echoplanar sequence (repetition time (TR)=2200 ms, echo time (TE)=33 ms, flip angle=75°, 64x64 acquisition matrix, 3-mm slice thickness, 0.45-mm inter-slice gap, FOV=192x192 mm, number of slices=37).

4   Results

We report results from two different empirical analyses. First analysis aims to provide an evidence of how the choice of coregistration technique may have an impact on the estimate of the session effects. Second analysis illustrates how the disentanglement method works and how, including functional hyperalignment, it differs from the common practice. All the analysis are performed using AFNI [2] and in-house Python code.

In the first analysis, we consider the task of naming high frequency word, i.e. HF (see Section 3), because by design it shouldn't be affected by the training interleaving the fMRI recording of the two sessions. We illustrate how the choice of different coregistering algorithms might influence in a significant way the subsequent univariate analysis of voxels. Each participant's HF - related brain map is coregistered to a reference space (Talairach): this operation is performed twice, using two different coregistration algorithms. Maps in Figure 1 show binary masks of thresholded ($T(10) = 1.81$, $p < 0.05$ unc.) group results using (Figure 1A) nearest neighbours algorithm and a linear interpolation algorithm (Figure 1B) as coregistration algorithms.

From the maps, the presence of several spots, including the right posterior cingulate cortex (rPCC) turns out to be dramatically dependent on the algorithm implemented. A significant (t(100)=2.05, p=0.04) difference between these two maps is also shown in another way by comparing the distributions (Figure 1C) of group - level beta values.

Table 1. Nature of the functional effects. Clusters are sorted according to their extension, in a descending order.

ID	L/R	Atlas	BA	Size	Effect	Align	¬Align
1	R	Inferior Temporal Gyrus	BA21	417	Training	Y	Y
2	L	Inferior Temporal Gyrus	BA21	363	Training	Y	Y
3	R	Posterior Cingulate	BA31	237	Session	N	Y
4	L	Angular Gyrus	BA39	209	Training	Y	Y
5	R	Superior Temporal Gyrus	BA22	137	Session	N	Y
6	L	Precuneus	BA30	50	Session	N	Y
7	R	Angula Gyrus	BA39	49	Session	N	Y

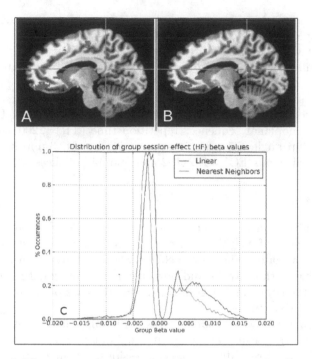

Fig. 1. Effect of different coregistration algorithm on a group level map. (A) Binary mask of a group - level activation map using Nearest - Neighbour coregistration algorithm, shown on a standard Talairach template (X = 10mm); (B) Same as panel (A), but using Linear interpolation algorithm. Focus of the crosshair is in the Posterior Cingulate region. Different coregistering algorithms return different maps, influencing the evaluation of the nature of the functional effects. (C) Distribution of group - level coefficients within the maps shown in the A (green) and B (blue) panels.

The second analysis is performed using the disentanglement method illustrated in Section 2. The fMRI dataset was first preprocessed using a conventional pipeline: correction for movement artifacts, isotropic (FWHM = 6mm) spatial smoothing and scaling of the time series with respect to the temporal mean. We then computed task-related effects for the session S_2 and produced the contrast of interest: first we extracted task-related brain maps using a voxelwise, mass-univariate linear regression of the fMRI time - series against a model representing the task. Contrast was evaluated between effects related to a task supposed to be affected by training (less frequent word, trained: LFT) and control ones (less frequent word, not trained: LFnT). We then projected single-participant contrast maps to a standard (Talairach) space and computed, within S_2, LFT vs LFnT group-level contrasts. We then applied the disentanglement method. Following the pipeline, we first clustered the group map according to the statistical significance test ($T(10) = 4.14$, $p < 0.001$ unc.), obtaining 7 distinct regions. The list of clusters is reported in Table 1, sorted by their extension in a descending order. There, we also include their description according to the

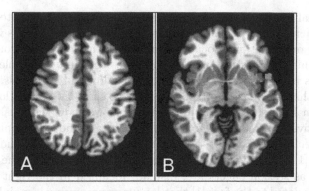

Fig. 2. Spatial characterization of the nature of functional effects. Information from Table 1 is combined with the spatial one. Clusters are mounted over a standard Talairach template (Right=Left; A: Z = 34mm; B: Z = -2mm). Clusters shown in orange are those labelled as *training*. Clusters shown in red are, on the other hand, those relative to the *session* effects.

Talairach and Brodmann atlases. For the Cluster Projection, the 7 cluster were back-projected to both sessions, S_1 and S_2, of each participant. We obtained for each participant $7 + 7$ matrices of 508 (number of volumes) columns, and rows referring to the number of voxels (see Table 1). We then computed, for each matrix in session S_1, functional hyperalignment with respect to session S_2 ones. This operation was iterated for each participant. For the trial encoding step, we considered as relevant only a portion of the voxel timecourses: we focused only on the subintervals (20) when participants were presented with LFT trials. Each subinterval was encoded as a trial considering 5 volumes after the beginning of task presentation. A trial was defined as a vector of size $5 \cdot N_c$, where N_c is the number of voxels for cluster c. The trial encoding was performed considering the session S_2 and the session S_1 after the hyper - alignment, and iterated for each cluster and for each participant. In the fifth step, Trial Classification, we shaped several binary discrimination problems considering the trials which encoded LFT task in the same cluster projected on both session S_1 and S_2. A classifier was trained and tested for each cluster and for each participant. The performance of every classifier was measured using a cross-validation based on leave-two-out folding strategy. An accuracy for each classification of the cross-validation replication was evaluated and then averaged over all the $N_s - 2$ folds, where $N_s = 40$ was the number of trials encoding the LFT task on both session S_1 and S_2. The significance of the mean accuracy was tested using a binomial test (n=40, p=0.5) and judged successful if its probability fell below 0.05. At the end of fifth step, for each of the 7 cluster, we ended up with 10 estimates of the capability, for a classifier, to discriminate the trials before or after the training. In sixth step, Cluster Labeling, we aggregated the results of previous step: we denoted as *training effect* cases where the classifier succeeded to discriminate the trials even after the functional hyperalignment, and *session effect* when the classifier failed. Each cluster was labelled according to the majority of the labels we obtained at single participant level.

Conventional strategy resorts to a comparison of the effects elicited by two different tasks. Here, on the other hand, labelling of functional effects was obtained involving only one functional localization, within the second session.

Out of the initial 7 clusters, as we show in the 6th column of Table 1, 3 of them are labelled as *training*, with the remaining 4 falling into the *session* category. We arranged this information on a brain map, to show the spatial localization of the clusters, in Figure 2A and Figure 2B, where we show them using two axial slices (respectively: Z= 34mm, Z= -2mm) from a standard template. The set of training effect areas includes the left inferior temporal gyrus and the angular gyrus, known [1] to be involved in language processing. Most of the areas (3 out of 4) labelled as session effects are, instead, localized in the right hemisphere. This could be related to the fact [1] that language processing is mainly lateralized on the left hemisphere.

We finally report (Table 1, columns 7-8) how the hyperalignment procedure improved the overall description of the effects. Before it, all the classifiers discriminated (Y) between the two sessions, attributing all the clusters to the training category. After hyperaligning, 4 out 7 clusters fell into the session effect case. These results suggest this method to be helpful in avoiding false positives when judging the nature of functional effects.

References

1. Binder, J.R., Frost, J.A., Hammeke, T.A., Cox, R.W., Rao, S.M., Prieto, T.: Human brain language areas identified by functional magnetic resonance imaging. The Journal of Neuroscience: the Official Journal of the Society for Neuroscience 17(1), 353–362 (1997)
2. Cox, R.W.: AFNI: software for analysis and visualization of functional magnetic resonance neuroimages. Computers and Biomedical Research, an International Journal 29(3), 162–173 (1996)
3. Haxby, J.V., Guntupalli, S.S., Connolly, A.C., Halchenko, Y.O., Conroy, B.R., Gobbini, I.I., Hanke, M., Ramadge, P.J.: A common, high-dimensional model of the representational space in human ventral temporal cortex. Neuron 72(2), 404–416 (2011)
4. Meinzer, M., Flaisch, T., Breitenstein, C., Wienbruch, C., Elbert, T., Rockstroh, B.: Functional re-recruitment of dysfunctional brain areas predicts language recovery in chronic aphasia. NeuroImage 39(4), 2038–2046 (2008)
5. Meltzer, J.A., Postman-Cauchateux, W.A., McArdle, J.J., Braun, A.R.: Strategies for longitudinal neuroimaging studies of overt language production. NeuroImage 47(2), 745–755 (2009)
6. Pereira, F., Mitchell, T., Botvinick, M.: Machine learning classifiers and fMRI: a tutorial overview. NeuroImage 45(1 suppl.), S199–S209 (2009)

Identification of Alzheimer's Disease Using Incomplete Multimodal Dataset via Matrix Shrinkage and Completion

Kim-Han Thung, Chong-Yaw Wee, Pew-Thian Yap, and Dinggang Shen

Department of Radiology and BRIC,
University of North Carolina at Chapel Hill, USA
dgshen@med.unc.edu

Abstract. Incomplete dataset due to missing values is ubiquitous in multimodal neuroimaging data. Denoting an incomplete dataset as a feature matrix, where each row contains feature values of the multi-modality data of a sample, we propose a framework to predict the corresponding interrelated multiple target outputs (e.g., diagnosis label and clinical scores) from this feature matrix. This is achieved by applying a *matrix completion algorithm* on a *shrunk version of the feature matrix that is augmented with the corresponding target output matrix*, to simultaneously predict the missing feature values and the unknown target outputs. We shrink the matrix by *first partition the large incomplete feature matrix into smaller submatrices that contain complete feature data*. Treating each target output prediction from the submatrix as a task, we perform *multi-task learning based feature and sample selections* to select the most discriminative features and samples from each submatrix. Features and samples which are not selected from any of the submatrices are removed, resulting in a shrunk feature matrix, which is still incomplete. This shrunk matrix together with its corresponding target matrix (of possibly unknown values) are finally simultaneously completed using a low rank matrix completion algorithm. Experimental results using the ADNI dataset indicate that our proposed framework yields better identification accuracy at higher speed compared with conventional imputation-based identification methods.

Keywords: Matrix completion, classification, incomplete data, ADNI, Alzheimer's disease.

1 Introduction

Alzheimers Disease (AD) is the most common type of dementia. In AD, neurons are degenerated progressively, causing patients to gradually lose memory, cognitive and motor functions, and eventually life. Therefore, it is vital to diagnose AD accurately so that treatment can be provided to slow down or stop the progression of the disease. A lot of AD biomarkers have been developed, including measurements derived from neuroimaging data (i.e., magnetic resonance imaging (MRI) and flurodeoxglucose positron emission tomography (FDG-PET)),

G. Wu et al. (Eds.): MLMI 2013, LNCS 8184, pp. 163–170, 2013.

and from biological data like the cerebruspinal fluid (CSF). The information obtained from different data modality is complementary to each other and recent studies show that identification accuracy can be improved by building a predictive model based on multi-modality data [9]. Unfortunately, samples with complete multi-modality data are limited. In the Alzheimer's Disease Neuroimaging Initiative (ADNI) dataset, for example, only about 1/3 of its total samples contains complete MRI, PET and CSF data at baseline. Most of the current multi-modality analysis are based on the samples with complete data, discarding samples with at least one missing modality.

With the help of data imputation algorithm, the missing values in the dataset can be imputed, so that the incomplete samples, instead of being discarded, can now be included for analysis. However, most of the existing imputation methods [5,7] do not work well when a large amount of data is missing. Low rank matrix completion [1], on the other hand, can recover a large amount of missing values in a matrix using trace norm minimization. However, its formulation is based on the assumption that the missing data is distributed randomly and uniformly [1], which unfortunately does not hold in our case, as the data is missing in blocks, i.e., the entire data from a single modality might be missing.

In this paper, we attempt to identify AD patients from normal controls (NCs) using the ADNI dataset, which is composed of MRI, PET, and CSF data. Denoting the incomplete dataset as a matrix with each row being a feature vector derived from the multi-modality data of a sample, conventional approach for solving this problem is to impute the missing data and build a classifier based on the completed matrix. However, it is too time consuming (as matrix size is large) and inaccurate (as there are too many missing values) to apply existing imputation methods directly. In addition, the errors introduced during the imputation process may affect the performance of the classifier. In this paper, we mitigate the problems of the conventional approach by proposing a framework that 1) shrinks the large incomplete matrix through feature and sample selection, and 2) predicts the output labels directly by applying matrix completion on the shrunk matrix (i.e., without building another classifier on the completed matrix).

Specifically, we first partition the incomplete dataset into two portions - training set and testing set. Each set is represented by an incomplete data matrix (which contains feature vector of a sample in each row), and a corresponding multiple interrelated target output matrix (i.e., diagnosis label and clinical scores). Our goal is to remove redundant/noisy features and samples from the data matrix so that the imputation problem can be simplified. However, due to the missing values in the data matrix, feature and sample selections can not be performed directly. We thus group the incomplete data matrix into submatrices that contain only complete data, so that a 2-step multi-task learning algorithm can be applied on these submatrices, along with the corresponding target outputs, for selection of features and samples that are discriminative. The selected features and samples form a shrunk incomplete matrix which is more "friendly" to imputation algorithms, as redundant/noisy features and samples have been

Table 1. Information about ADNI dataset used in this study. (Edu.: Education, std: standard deviation)

	Gender		Age (years)	Edu. (years)	Modalities		
	male	female	mean ± std	mean ± std	MRI	PET	CSF
AD subjects	95	84	75.5 ± 7.6	15.1 ± 2.9	179	91	100
NC subjects	113	108	75.8 ± 5.0	15.7 ± 3.1	221	98	110
	Total number of subjects				400	189	210
	Number of features				93	93	5

removed and there are lesser missing values that require imputation. Finally, the output targets of the testing set and the missing data features of the shrunk matrix are predicted concurrently by using a low rank matrix completion algorithm. Experimental results show that our framework yields faster imputation and more accurate identification than the conventional imputation-based classification approach.

2 Data

In this study, we used 179 AD and 221 NC subjects with MRI, PET or/and CSF data from ADNI baseline dataset (http://adni.loni.ucla.edu). Processing steps of MRI images include AC-PC correction using the MIPAV software package (http://mipav.cit.nih.gov), intensity inhomogeneity correction using N3 algorithm, skull stripping [8], manual editing and cerebelum removal. We then used FAST [10] for segmentation and HAMMER [6] for registration to extract grey matter (GM) volumes from 93 region of interests (ROIs) based on the template defined in [3]. For PET images, we used the average image intensities of the same 93 ROIs. Five CSF biomarkers were used, i.e., amyloid β ($A\beta_{42}$), CSF total tau (t-tau), tau hyperphosphorylated at threonine 181 (p-tau) and two tau ratios with respective to $A\beta_{42}$ (i.e., t-tau/$A\beta_{42}$ and p-tau/$A\beta_{42}$). In addition, 3 clinical scores were included (i.e., CDR global, CDR average, and MMSE) as output targets as they might convey information complementary to the diagnosis label. Demographic information together with the number of samples and features used in this study are summarized in Table 1.

3 Classification through Matrix Shrinkage and Completion

Figure 1 illustrates our framework, which consisted of three components: 1) feature selection, 2) sample selection, and 3) matrix completion. Let $\mathbf{X} \in \mathbb{R}^{n \times d}$ (n samples, d features) and $\mathbf{Y} \in \mathbb{R}^{n \times t}$ (n samples, t targets) denote the data matrix (which contains features derived from MRI, PET and CSF data) and target matrix (which contains label [-1 1] and clinical scores), respectively. As shown in the leftmost diagram in Figure 1, $\mathbf{X}$ is incomplete, and about half of the

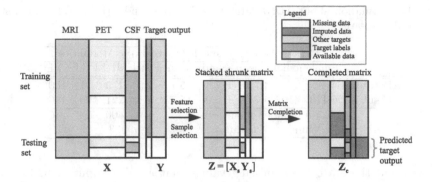

Fig. 1. Classification via matrix shrinkage and completion. There are three main parts in this framework: feature selection, sample selection, and matrix completion. Note that feature selection step only involves training set. ($\mathbf{X_s}$, $\mathbf{Y_s}$: Shrunk versions of $\mathbf{X}$ and $\mathbf{Y}$; $\mathbf{Z_c}$: Completed version of $\mathbf{Z}$.)

subjects do not have PET and CSF data. Matrix $\mathbf{X}$ is divided into two parts, one for training and one for testing. The target outputs for all the training samples are known, but the target outputs for the testing samples are set to unknown for testing purposes. The feature values in $\mathbf{X}$ and clinical scores in $\mathbf{Y}$ are first z-normalized across all the training samples, ignoring the missing data in the normalization process. Then, two stages of sparse regression are used to remove indiscriminant features and samples in the training set, resulting in a shrunk matrix containing the most discriminative features and samples from the training set. The same set of selected features are extracted from the testing set. A matrix completion algorithm [2,4,5] is finally applied on the shrunk matrix and the signs of the imputed target labels are used as the classification outputs for the testing samples. The following subsections describe the three main components of the framework in more detail.

3.1 Feature Selection

The training set in $\mathbf{X}$ is first partitioned based on the largest possible availability of the samples and features. For the ADNI dataset with MRI, PET and CSF data, four data groups (i.e., submatrices) can be obtained as shown by the red blocks in Figure 2. Each submatrix has four corresponding target outputs (i.e. 1 label and 3 clinical scores), which can be jointly predicted through multi-task learning. Let $\mathbf{X}_i \in \mathbb{R}^{n_i \times d_i}$ and $\mathbf{Y}_i \in \mathbb{R}^{n_i \times t_i}$ denote the input matrix and output matrix for the i-th multi-task learning problem, respectively. Then the multi-task sparse regression associated with each submatrix is given as

$$\min_{\boldsymbol{\alpha}_i} 1/2 \left\| \mathbf{X}_i \boldsymbol{\alpha}_i - \mathbf{Y}_i \right\|_2^2 + \lambda \left\| \boldsymbol{\alpha}_i \right\|_{2,1} , \tag{1}$$

where n_i, d_i, t_i and $\boldsymbol{\alpha}_i \in \mathbb{R}^{d_i \times t_i}$ denote the number of samples, the number of features, the number of output targets, and the weight matrix for the i-th

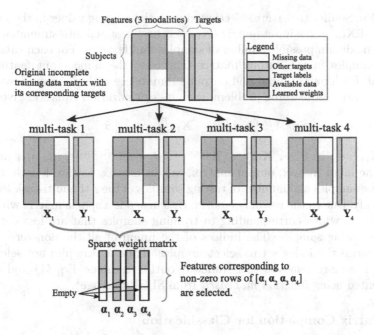

Fig. 2. Feature selection for incomplete multi-modal data matrix with multiple related output targets by using multi-task learning. The red boxes marks the portion of the data with the largest possible number of samples for each modality combination.

multi-task learning, respectively. $\|\boldsymbol{\alpha}_i\|_{2,1}$ is the $l_{2,1}$-norm of $\boldsymbol{\alpha}_i$ which is defined as $\sum_{k=1}^{d_i} \|\boldsymbol{\alpha}_i^k\|_2$, where $\boldsymbol{\alpha}_i^k$ denotes k-th row of $\boldsymbol{\alpha}_i$. The use of l_2-norm for $\boldsymbol{\alpha}_i^k$ forces the weights corresponding to the k-th feature (of $\mathbf{X}_i$) across multiple tasks to be grouped together and (1) tends to select the common features for all the prediction tasks. Thus, $\boldsymbol{\alpha}_i$ is a sparse matrix with a significant number of zero-valued rows which correspond to redundant features in each submatrix. The features that are selected for at least one of the submatrices (i.e., union of non-zero rows of $\{\boldsymbol{\alpha}_i\}$) are used for the training and the testing sets. The training and the testing sets with the selected features are used in sample selection as described in the following subsection.

3.2 Sample Selection

In this step, multi-task learning is applied one more time to select representative samples from the training set that are closely related to the samples in the testing set. The steps involved in sample selection is similar to those of feature selection described previously, with some modifications to the input and output matrices of the multi-task learning algorithm.

Let $\mathbf{X}_{tr}$ and $\mathbf{X}_{te}$ denote the shrunk training and testing data matrices that contain only the selected features, respectively. $\mathbf{X}_{tr}$ and $\mathbf{X}_{te}$ are first transposed so that the rows now correspond to the features and the columns now correspond to samples. Similar to feature selection, due to the missing values in the matrices ($\mathbf{X_{tr}}^T$ and $\mathbf{X_{te}}^T$), the input matrix ($\mathbf{X_{tr}}^T$) is first grouped into submatrices that contain maximum possible number of samples and features. For each submatrix, all the samples in the output matrix that have the same input features are identified. Each pair of input and output submatrices with the same features set forms a multi-task learning problem, with its optimization equation given as

$$\min_{\beta_i} 1/2 \left\| \mathbf{X_{tr}}_i^T \boldsymbol{\beta}_i - \mathbf{X_{te}}_i^T \right\|_2^2 + \lambda \left\| \boldsymbol{\beta}_i \right\|_{2,1} , \tag{2}$$

where $\mathbf{X_{tr}}_i^T \in \mathbb{R}^{d_i \times n_{tri}}$, $\mathbf{X_{te}}_i^T \in \mathbb{R}^{d_i \times n_{tei}}$, $\boldsymbol{\beta}_i \in \mathbb{R}^{n_{tri} \times n_{tei}}$, d_i, n_{tri} and n_{tei} denote the input matrix, output matrix, weight matrix, feature length, number of training samples and number of testing samples of the i-th multi-task learning, respectively. Due to the use of $l_{2,1}$-norm, $\boldsymbol{\beta}_i$ learned is a sparse matrix with some all-zero rows, which corresponding to training samples that are less correlated with the testing samples. The indices of the union of all the non-zero rows of each $\boldsymbol{\beta}_i$ forms the index set to select samples. Training samples not selected in this union set are removed as redundant/outlier samples. Eq. (1) and (2) are implemented using function $mcLeastR$ from SLEP package[1].

3.3 Matrix Completion for Classification

The original incomplete matrix is shrunk significantly after the feature and sample selection steps. Let $\mathbf{X_s}$ and $\mathbf{Y_s}$ denote the shrunk version of matrix $\mathbf{X}$ and $\mathbf{Y}$, respectively, while n_s and d_s denote the number of remaining samples and data features, respectively. The stacked matrix $\mathbf{Z} = [\mathbf{X_s} \ \mathbf{Y_s}] \in \mathbb{R}^{n_s \times (d_s + t)}$ still contains some missing values, including the output targets of the test set which are to be estimated. The objective of this step is to impute the missing input features, missing target labels, and missing clinical scores simultaneously. Two imputation methods are tested for this step. First, we assume $\mathbf{Z}$ is low rank (e.g., each row of $\mathbf{Z}$ that corresponding to a testing sample can be linearly represented by other rows of $\mathbf{Z}$ that corresponding to training samples) and use modified Fixed-point Continuation (mFPC) algorithm in [2] to solve the following optimization problem:

$$\arg\min_{\mathbf{Z}} \mu \left\| \mathbf{Z} \right\|_* + \frac{\lambda}{|\Omega_{\mathbf{P}}|} \sum_{(i,j) \in \Omega_{\mathbf{P}}} L_p(z_{ij}, p_{ij}) + \frac{1}{|\Omega_{\mathbf{Q}}|} \sum_{(i,j) \in \Omega_{\mathbf{Q}}} L_q(z_{ij}, q_{ij}) , \tag{3}$$

where $\Omega_{\mathbf{P}}$ and $\Omega_{\mathbf{Q}}$ denote the set of observed (i.e., non-missing) labels in $\mathbf{Y_s}$ and the set of observed values for the rest of the data, respectively; z_{ij}, p_{ij}, q_{ij}, L_p, L_q and $\|.\|_*$ denote the predicted observed values, the observed target labels, the observed data other than target labels, the logistic loss function, the square loss function and the trace norm operator (for low rank assumption of the data), respectively; while λ and μ are the positive regularization parameters to control the weight for L_p and the trace norm minimization, respectively. In addition, regularized Expectation Maximization (rEM) [5] is also tested for this step.

---

[1] http://www.public.asu.edu/~jye02/Software/SLEP/index.htm

4   Result and Discussion

Four imputation methods (i.e., zero imputation, k-nearest neighbour (KNN), rEM [5], and Fixed-Point Continuation (FPC) [4]) were used for comparison using two baseline methods. The first baseline method imputes the original incomplete matrix directly, while the second baseline method uses our proposed feature and sample selection methods before the imputation. Both the baseline method 1 and baseline method 2 impute only the input data matrix $\mathbf{X}$ and use the completed training set to train a sparse regression model (as in Eq. (1)) as classifier for the test set. Classification performances of all compared methods were evaluated using a 10-fold cross-validation (CV) scheme. For each fold, another 5-fold CV scheme was used to select the best parameters for feature selection and the sparse regression classifier. The performance measures used in this study are accuracy (# correctly classified/total samples), sensitivity (# correctly classified AD/# AD), specificity (# correctly classified NC/# NC) and area under ROC curve (AUC), where # denotes "number of".

Table 2 shows the classification performances for all compared methods. All the results reported are the average measurements of the 10 repeatations of 10-fold CV. As shown in the Table 2, all the imputation methods perform similarly for the baseline methods 1 and 2, irrespective of the complexity of the imputation methods. For example, the classification accuracies for the baseline method 1 are around 0.82-0.84 for all the imputation methods. However, after using the proposed feature and sample selection methods, the classification performance of the baseline method 2 is significantly improved to around 0.88. In addition, the average imputation time is significantly reduced, as shown in the last column of Table 2. For instance, FPC and rEM respectively complete the imputation about 9 times and 4 times faster in the baseline method 2, if compared with the baseline method 1. We thus have shown the efficacy of the proposed feature and sample selection methods in removing the redundant features and samples, which is beneficial to the imputation process, both in terms of accuracy and speed. In addition,

Table 2. Classification result. The best value for each performance measure is highlighted in bold. (AUC: area under ROC curve, time: the average imputation time for each fold, mFPC: modified FPC as in (3)).

	Imputation	Accuracy	Sensitivity	Specificity	AUC	time(s)
Baseline 1	Zero	0.825	0.854	0.801	0.912	**0.00**
	KNN	0.832	0.848	0.818	0.912	1.38
	rEM	0.844	0.854	0.835	0.910	79.43
	FPC	0.843	0.857	0.831	0.905	128.62
Baseline 2	Zero	0.877	0.877	0.877	0.936	**0.00**
	KNN	0.879	0.881	0.877	0.939	0.31
	rEM	0.881	0.874	0.887	0.944	22.47
	FPC	0.883	**0.884**	0.881	0.942	14.20
Proposed	EM	**0.912**	0.856	**0.957**	0.959	21.72
	mFPC	0.904	0.871	0.932	**0.960**	0.67

the identification performance is further improved to 0.90-0.91 if the target labels are imputed simultaneously with the incomplete shrunk matrix using the modified FPC (mFPC) and rEM methods, as proposed in our framework. Although the identification performances of both mFPC and rEM are similar, mFPC performs significantly better than rEM in terms of imputation speed.

5   Conclusion

In this work, we propose a novel framework to deal with large datasets with a lot of data missing in blocks. Our framework largely averts the problems of conventional imputation-based classification approach, which is slow and inaccurate for this type of dataset. We achieve this by predicting the target labels directly through matrix completion on the shrunk version of the incomplete matrix. The experimental results show that the feature selection and sample selection of our framework significantly improve the classification performance of the conventional imputation-based classification methods. This study also shows that our proposed framework (using both the mFPC and rEM) yields faster imputation and more accurate identification than all the baseline methods.

References

1. Candès, E.J., Recht, B.: Exact matrix completion via convex optimization. Foundations of Computational Mathematics 9(6), 717–772 (2009)
2. Goldberg, A., Zhu, X., Recht, B., Xu, J., Nowak, R.: Transduction with matrix completion: three birds with one stone. In: Advances in Neural Information Processing Systems, vol. 23, pp. 757–765 (2010)
3. Kabani, N.J.: A 3D atlas of the human brain. Neuroimage 7, S717 (1998)
4. Ma, S., Goldfarb, D., Chen, L.: Fixed point and Bregman iterative methods for matrix rank minimization. Mathematical Programming 128(1), 321–353 (2011)
5. Schneider, T.: Analysis of incomplete climate data: Estimation of mean values and covariance matrices and imputation of missing values. Journal of Climate 14(5), 853–871 (2001)
6. Shen, D., Davatzikos, C.: Hammer: hierarchical attribute matching mechanism for elastic registration. IEEE Trans. on Medical Imaging 21(11), 1421–1439 (2002)
7. Troyanskaya, O., Cantor, M., Sherlock, G., Brown, P., Hastie, T., Tibshirani, R., Botstein, D., Altman, R.B.: Missing value estimation methods for dna microarrays. Bioinformatics 17(6), 520–525 (2001)
8. Wang, Y., Nie, J., Yap, P.-T., Shi, F., Guo, L., Shen, D.: Robust deformable-surface-based skull-stripping for large-scale studies. In: Fichtinger, G., Martel, A., Peters, T. (eds.) MICCAI 2011, Part III. LNCS, vol. 6893, pp. 635–642. Springer, Heidelberg (2011)
9. Zhang, D., Shen, D.: Multi-modal multi-task learning for joint prediction of multiple regression and classification variables in Alzheimer's disease. Neuroimage 59(2), 895–907 (2012)
10. Zhang, Y., Brady, M., Smith, S.: Segmentation of brain MR images through a hidden markov random field model and the expectation-maximization algorithm. IEEE Trans. on Medical Imaging 20(1), 45–57 (2001)

On Feature Relevance in Image-Based Prediction Models: An Empirical Study

Ender Konukoglu[1,*], Melanie Ganz[1,*],
Koen Van Leemput[2,1,3], and Mert R. Sabuncu[1] for the Alzheimers Disease
Neuroimaging Initiative[**]

[1] Martinos Center for Biomedical Imaging, MGH, Harvard Medical School, USA
[2] Department of Applied Mathematics and Computer Science, DTU, Denmark
[3] Departments of Information and Computer Science and of Biomedical
Engineering and Computational Science, Aalto University, Finland

Abstract. Determining disease-related variations of the anatomy and
function is an important step in better understanding diseases and developing early diagnostic systems. In particular, image-based multivariate
prediction models and the "relevant features" they produce are attract-
ing attention from the community. In this article, we present an empirical study on the relevant features produced by two recently developed
discriminative learning algorithms: neighborhood approximation forests
(NAF) and the relevance voxel machine (RVoxM). Specifically, we examine whether the sets of features these methods produce are exhaustive; that is whether the features that are **not** marked as relevant carry
disease-related information. We perform experiments on three different
problems: image-based regression on a synthetic dataset for which the set
of relevant features is known, regression of subject age as well as binary
classification of Alzheimer's Disease (AD) from brain Magnetic Resonance Imaging (MRI) data. Our experiments demonstrate that aging-
related and AD-related variations are widespread and the initial sets of
relevant features discovered by the methods are not exhaustive. Our findings show that by knocking-out features and re-training models, a much
larger set of disease-related features can be identified.

1 Introduction

Image-based prediction models hold great promise for improving clinical practice. The ability to predict the state of a disease based on its anatomical and
functional signatures opens up new avenues for early diagnostic systems. To this
end, great progress has been made in developing accurate prediction tools. In
particular, multivariate discriminative learning models have been successfully
employed both for image-based classification and regression.

Furthermore, medical images provide in-vivo observations that reveal the
disease-related variations of the anatomy and function. Comparing images of

---

* E. Konukoglu and M. Ganz contributed equally to this work.
** Data used in preparation of this article was obtained from the Alzheimers Disease
Neuroimaging Initiative (ADNI) database (http://www.adni-info.org/). The investigators within the ADNI contributed to the design and implementation of ADNI
and/or provided data, but did not participate in analysis or writing of this report.

healthy controls and patients can highlight such variations on a macro-scale that would be difficult to identify using histopathology. This is essential for improving our understanding of disease and refining the predictive power of learning methods.

Supervised image-based prediction models have started to play an important role in determining regions that exhibit disease-related variations. These models determine a set of regions, also referred to as "relevant features", on which measurements are pertinent to achieve good prediction accuracy. The statistical significance of the predictions, i.e. that they are different than a random guess, suggests that such sets of relevant features indeed carry information about disease-specific changes. Although this is a good starting point, an important question remains: Do the methods produce exhaustive sets? That is, does the set of relevant features reflect most of the variation associated with the disease-specific effects? Recent work has focused on constructing prediction models aiming to determine relevant sets [1] and developing efficient statistical tests for creating maps of relevant regions [2]. To the best of our knowledge, no previous work has analyzed the question whether the set of regions **not** chosen as "relevant" by prediction models exhibit any disease-specific changes. Here, we empirically study this issue.

This article presents a set of experiments with two different image-based prediction models: neighbourhood approximation forests (NAF) [3] and the relevance voxel machine (RVoxM) [1]. Both of these methods have been used to perform image-based classification and regression; both methods offer a way to quantify feature relevance for prediction. We designed an experimental setup that aims to answer whether the relevant features provided by these models form an exhaustive set. Using this setup we performed experiments on three different datasets: synthetic, OASIS [4] and ADNI. The first two are image-based regression tasks, while the last one is a classification task. We present the experimental setup, briefly describe the methods and present experimental findings.

2   Experimental Design

Our experimental design relies on the following observation: if the set of relevant features is exhaustive, then removing it from the pool of measurements should result in a set of features that contains no information about the disease. Consequently, an image-based prediction model trained on this non-informative set, should be as predictive as a random prediction model, i.e. prediction should not be statistically significant. Based on this consideration, we designed an iterative setup. At the first iteration, we learn a prediction model using a training dataset and the entire set of measurements available. We first record the relevant features suggested by the method and then compute the model's accuracy on a separate test dataset. We then perform random permutation tests as suggested in [5]; we randomly permute the labels in the test set and recompute the prediction accuracies using the trained model. Based on the random permutation tests,

Feature Set = Entire feature set of measurements;
iteration = 1;
while *iteration < Total Number of Iterations && #(Feature Set) != 0* **do**
  Train on the training set using Feature Set;
  Compute accuracy on the test set;
  Perform random permutation tests on the trained prediction model;
  Compute the most relevant features;
  Knockout - remove the most relevant features from Feature Set;
  iteration++;
end

Algorithm 1: Pseudocode for the experimental design

we compute the statistical significance of the prediction model at that iteration, i.e. percentage of random permutations achieving better accuracy than the trained model. For the second iteration we "knock-out" the relevant features, i.e. remove them from the feature set, and **retrain** the model on the remaining set of measurements. Then we repeat the same procedure multiple times. Algorithm 1 presents the pseudocode for this procedure.

3 Materials

3.1 Algorithms

We represent images as feature vectors $\mathbf{x}$, where each $\mathbf{x}$ is a concatenation of measurements taken from different locations within the image, e.g. intensities. The quantities to predict are denoted as y for the regression tasks and as c for the binary classification tasks. Both methods we consider are supervised; they use a training database $\{\mathbf{x}_n, (y, c)_n\}_1^N$ to learn the prediction model. Below, we briefly describe each method.

Neighbourhood Approximation Forests (NAF). Neighbourhood approximation forests [3], a variant of random decision forests [6], is a supervised discriminative learning method that uses tree-based approximate nearest neighbour search. During the training phase NAF learns sequences of axis aligned binary tests on the feature space that approximate the neighbourhood structure induced by a user-defined distance on the labels. Once learning is complete, for a test image $\mathbf{x}$, NAF computes its predicted label by identifying the "closest" M training images and using their labels. The prediction model combines these labels by weighting them based on the approximate affinities of the training images to the test image as computed by NAF. As a decision forest based system, various feature relevancy measures can be used with NAF [7]. Here, we adopt "selection frequency", $\text{freq}(\mathbf{x}_i)$, which basically counts the number of times each element $\mathbf{x}_i$ is used within the learned forest. Ordering $\text{freq}(\mathbf{x}_i)$ provides a relative "importance" measure to each element in $\mathbf{x}$. For further details on NAF, its parameters and the selection frequency we refer the reader to [3] and [7].

Relevance Voxel Machine (RVoxM). The Relevance voxel machine [1], a variant of the relevance vector machine (RVM), is a sparse learning algorithm.

The prediction model is linear: $y(\mathbf{x}, \mathbf{w}) = \sum_{i=1}^{M} w_i x_i = \mathbf{w}^T \mathbf{x}$, were $\mathbf{w}$ is a weight vector that is optimally sparse. In RVoxM, the algorithm learns $\mathbf{w}$ for a training dataset by optimizing a cost function that is a combination of the data likelihood and a prior model that encourages sparsity and spatial clustering of features. RVoxM is applied to regression tasks as $\hat{y} = \mathbf{w}^T \mathbf{x}$ and to binary classification tasks as $p(c = 1) = \sigma(\mathbf{w}^T \mathbf{x})$, where $\sigma(\cdot)$ is a sigmoid function mapping scalars to class probabilities. In the training phase, RVoxM computes the optimal sparse $\mathbf{w}$ vector. During prediction, only the corresponding elements in the feature vector $\mathbf{x}$ contribute and therefore, these elements are the "relevant" features of the model. For further details on RVoxM we refer the reader to [1].

3.2   Data

Synthetic Data - Image-Based Regression. In the first experiment, we used NAF and RVoxM on a synthetic dataset for an image-based regression problem, where the ground truth set of relevant pixels is known. Our aim with this dataset is to test the validity of the experimental design described in Section 2. The dataset contains images synthetically generated from an underlying natural image. Each image is composed of 121 7×7 non-overlapping patches, where the intensities of each patch are computed by multiplying a 2D Gaussian kernel centered at the patch center with the intensities of the underlying image. The magnitude of each kernel is drawn uniformly from the interval $[-1, 1]$. We further add normally distributed iid white noise to the images to achieve an SNR of 20dB. For each image we assign the kernel magnitude of the 50th patch as the variable of interest. Figure 1 shows the relevant pixels, some example images and the corresponding scalar values. The feature vector $\mathbf{x}$ for each image contains the intensity values of all pixels, i.e. 5929 values. In this fashion, we constructed 10 different datasets each containing 400 training and 40 test images.

OASIS - Image-Based Regression. In the second experiment, we used the methods for image-based regression of subject age on the publicly available cross-sectional Open Access Series of Imaging Studies (OASIS) [4]. We used structural brain MRI (T1-weighted) scans of 414 healthy subjects that were processed with the FreeSurfer software suite [8,9] and transferred to a common coordinate system via affine registration. From the skull-stripped and normalized brains at resolution $2 \times 2 \times 2$ mm^3, we randomly sampled 15,613 intensity values for computational efficiency and used those as our features. We randomly chose 100 of the 414 subjects as a test set and used the remaining 314 for training; we repeated this procedure ten times.

ADNI - Image-Based Classification. In the last experiment we used NAF and RVoxM for image-based classification of Alzheimer's Disease (AD)of the publicly available Alzheimer's Disease Neuroimaging Initiative (ADNI) dataset. Our analysis used MRI scans from 180 AD patients and an age and sex-matched group of 180 controls. We processed all MRI scans with the FreeSurfer software suite and computed subject-specific models of the cortical surface as well as thickness measurements across the entire cortical mantle [10]. Subject-level thickness measurements were then transferred to a common coordinate system, via a surface-based

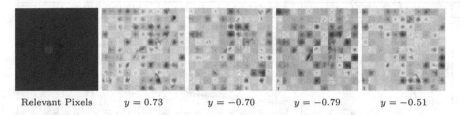

Relevant Pixels $y = 0.73$ $y = -0.70$ $y = -0.79$ $y = -0.51$

Fig. 1. Images from the synthetic dataset. Left-most: ground truth relevant pixels. Right: four example images with their corresponding scalar variables.

nonlinear registration procedure [11]. For computational efficiency, we utilized the left-hemisphere of the *fsaverage5* representation, consisting of 10,242 vertices. We smoothed the cortical thickness maps with a Gaussian kernel with a full-width-half-maximum of 5 mm. To evaluate our algorithms, we conducted a ten-fold cross-validation. First we divided the data into 10 subgroups (of 18 patients and 18 controls); then during each fold, one patient and one control subgroup were set aside as the test set, while the rest of the data were used for training.

4 Results and Discussions

On the datasets described above we performed the iterative experiment as explained in Section 2. For RVoxM, we let the algorithm converge during the training phase, which produced a set of relevant features. At each iteration of the experiment these relevant features were knocked-out. For NAF, the selection frequency provided an ordering for all features. At each iteration of the experiment, we knocked out the top 3% (1% for the synthetic dataset) of the features with respect to the selection frequency ordering. For each experiment, at each iteration we computed: i) prediction accuracies, ii) 1000 random permutation tests (100 permutations for each fold) and iii) p-values of the prediction accuracies with respect to the permutation tests. As prediction accuracies, we used root-mean-square error (RMSE) for the regression and misclassification rate for the classification task. The p-values were computed with respect to the average accuracy obtained over different folds of the same experiment.

Figure 2 summarizes the results. For each experiment we provide two graphs. The first one plots the prediction accuracy with respect to % of features that were knocked-out. The solid lines are the average accuracies obtained in our 10 fold experiments and the error bars correspond to standard deviations and standard errors. The same plot also presents the average statistics on the accuracies obtained during the random permutation tests. The second graph plots the % of features knocked-out vs. the p-values with respect to random permutation tests.

The results for the experiments on the synthetic dataset (first column in Figure 2) demonstrate the validity of our experimental design. After the first few iterations, the trained prediction models for both algorithms behave the same way as random permutation tests. This means both algorithms identified all the relevant pixels in the first few iterations and in the latter iterations the models are trained on non-informative pixels only. To validate this, we computed

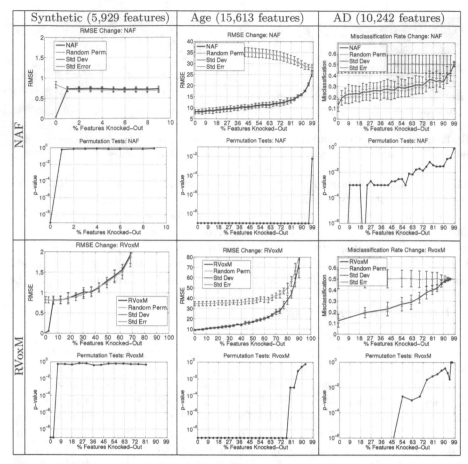

Fig. 2. How prediction models change with feature knock-out. For each experiment we plot i) accuracy change and ii) p-values with respect to random permutation tests. In synthetic experiments both models identify the ground truth relevant features quickly and thereafter the prediction model becomes similar to random prediction ($p > 0.5$). Results for age regression and AD classification demonstrate that only after knocking out more than 70% of the features p-values for the prediction models become $p > 0.05$.

the least common set of relevant pixels at each iteration by intersecting the sets of knocked-out pixels over the different folds. Figure 3(a) plots the % of ground truth (GT) relevant pixels identified by the least common feature sets. Indeed we see that both algorithms discover all the relevant pixels and after that point both prediction models lose their significance.

The experimental results for the age regression problem on the OASIS dataset display a different behavior. The prediction model remains significant ($p < 0.01$) until we knocked-out 96% of the total number of features for NAF and 83% of the features for RVoxM. This indicates that over 80% of the features might carry information for predicting subject age, which is not surprising since the effect of age is expected to be widespread. Furthermore, the accuracies of the prediction

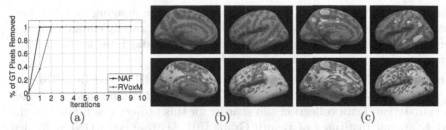

Fig. 3. (a) % of ground truth relevant pixels identified by the methods in the synthetic experiments. (b) Knocked-out features in NAF - in the first iteration (top) and until the point NAF prediction became non-significant (bottom). (c) Same maps for RVoxM.

models decrease with each knock-out suggesting that the algorithms can make better use of some regions in the brain to perform predictions than others.

The results for the AD classification problem on the ADNI dataset show a yet different type of behavior. The prediction models remain significant until 66% of the features are knocked-out for NAF and 75% for the RVoxM. This suggests that the effect of AD is also widespread across the cortex. But in contrast to the age regression problem, the accuracy changes faster in the first iterations of the experiment. This suggests that there is a small set of features, which the algorithms can exploit substantially better for prediction. The difference is striking between the first and the second iteration of the experiments using NAF.

The plots given in Figure 2 demonstrate that the set of relevant features suggested by image-based prediction algorithms, such as RVoxM, might not be exhaustive. For NAF and other forest-based methods, there is no obvious way to determine a set of relevant features without using an ad-hoc threshold like the 3% value we used. Nevertheless, observing the plots we can say that the set of most frequently used features in NAF might not capture the entire set of relevant ones. In Figures 3(b) and (c) we visualize this behavior for NAF and the RVoxM, respectively. The top rows display the regions which were suggested as relevant by the algorithms at the first iteration of the experiment. The bottom rows display the regions which were knocked-out to achieve prediction models that are not significant anymore.

One important aspect our experiments have shown is the importance of knocking-out features and retraining. Image-based prediction models aim to achieve good accuracies; and not necessarily to capture the entire set of relevant features. As a result, it is not trivial to interpret the features suggested as relevant by these methods. Thus, we believe the knock-out/retrain strategy is crucial in understanding feature relevance for image-based prediction models.

5   Conclusions

In this article, we presented an empirical study of feature relevance for image-based prediction models. Our main question was whether sets of relevant features suggested by image-based prediction models form an exhaustive set of all features that carry information on disease-specific changes. Our experimental findings demonstrate that this is not necessarily the case in aging and AD. Furthermore, our results show that the knock-out/retrain strategy employed in our experimental design can be critical in understanding and interpreting feature relevance for image-based prediction models.

Acknowledgments. This research was supported by NIH (P41-EB015896,P41-RR14075), NIBIB (R01EB013565), as well as the Alfred Benzon and the Lundbeck Foundation. Data collection and sharing for this project was funded by the ADNI (National Institutes of Health Grant U01 AG024904). ADNI is funded by the National Institute on Aging, the National Institute of Biomedical Imaging and Bioengineering, and through generous contributions from private sector institutions. The Canadian Institutes of Health Research is providing funds to support ADNI clinical sites in Canada. Private sector contributions are facilitated by the Foundation for the National Institutes of Health (www.fnih.org). The grantee organization is the Northern California Institute for Research and Education, and the study is coordinated by the Alzheimer's Disease Cooperative Study at the University of California, San Diego. ADNI data are disseminated by the Laboratory for Neuro Imaging at the University of California, Los Angeles.

References

1. Sabuncu, M., Van Leemput, K.: The relevance voxel machine (rvoxm): A self-tuning bayesian model for informative image-based prediction. IEEE Transactions on Medical Imaging 31(12), 2290–2306 (2012)
2. Gaonkar, B., Davatzikos, C.: Deriving statistical significance maps for svm based image classification and group comparisons. In: Ayache, N., Delingette, H., Golland, P., Mori, K. (eds.) MICCAI 2012, Part I. LNCS, vol. 7510, pp. 723–730. Springer, Heidelberg (2012)
3. Konukoglu, E., Glocker, B., Zikic, D., Criminisi, A.: Neighbourhood approximation using randomized forests. Medical Image Analysis (2013)
4. Marcus, D., Wang, T., Parker, J., Csernansky, J., Morris, J., Buckner, R.: Open access series of imaging studies (oasis): cross-sectional mri data in young, middle aged, nondemented, and demented older adults. Journal of Cognitive Neuroscience 19(9), 1498–1507 (2007)
5. Good, P.I.: Permutation, parametric and bootstrap tests of hypotheses. Springer Science+Business Media (2005)
6. Amit, Y., Geman, D.: Shape quantization and recognition with randomized trees. Neural Computation 9(7), 1545–1588 (1997)
7. Strobl, C., Boulesteix, A.L., Zeileis, A., Hothorn, T.: Bias in random forest variable importance measures: Illustrations, sources and a solution. BMC Bioinformatics 8(1) 25 (2007)
8. Dale, A.M., Fischl, B., Sereno, M.I.: Cortical surface-based analysis: I. Segmentation and surface reconstruction. Neuroimage 9(2), 179–194 (1999)
9. Fischl, B., Sereno, M.I., Dale, A.M.: Cortical surface-based analysis ii: Inflation, flattening, and a surface-based coordinate system. Neuroimage 9(2), 195–207 (1999)
10. Fischl, B., Dale, A.M.: Measuring the thickness of the human cerebral cortex from magnetic resonance images. Proceedings of the National Academy of Sciences 97(20), 11050–11055 (2000)
11. Fischl, B., Sereno, M.I., Tootell, R.B., Dale, A.M., et al.: High-resolution inter-subject averaging and a coordinate system for the cortical surface. Human Brain Mapping 8(4), 272–284 (1999)

Decision Forests with Spatio-Temporal Features for Graph-Based Tumor Segmentation in 4D Lung CT

Hamidreza Mirzaei[1], Lisa Tang[2], Rene Werner[3], and Ghassan Hamarneh[2]

[1] Computational Vision Lab., Simon Fraser University, Canada
[2] Medical Image Analysis Lab., Simon Fraser University, Canada
[3] Department of Computational Neuroscience,
University Medical Center Hamburg-Eppendorf, Germany

Abstract. We propose an automatic lung tumor segmentation in dynamic CT images that incorporates the novel use of tumor tissue deformations. In contrast to elastography imaging techniques for measuring tumor tissue properties, which require mechanical compression and thereby interrupt normal breathing, we completely avoid the use of any external physical forces. Instead, we calculate the tissue deformations during normal respiration using deformable registration. We investigate machine learning methods in order to discover the spatio-temporal dynamics that would help distinguish tumor from normal tissue deformation patterns and integrate this information into the segmentation process. Our method adapts an ensemble of decision trees combined with a 3D graph-based optimization that takes into account spatio-temporal consistency. The experimental results on patients with large tumors achieved an average F-measure accuracy of 0.79.

Keywords: Lung tumor, image segmentation, registration, CT images, imbalance data, machine learning, graph-based optimization.

1 Introduction

Methods for lung tumor segmentation in non-small-cell lung cancer (NSCLC) computed tomographic (CT) images have gained much attention in the past few years due to their importance in tumor visualization and quantification for diagnosis, radiation and surgical therapy planning, as well as in tracking of treatment outcome [1],19,20]. The workload associated with manual contouring of target volumes on 4-dimensional CT scans for clinical treatments is considerably confounded by intra- and inter-clinician variations. One approach would be to employ automatic tumor segmentation based on image intensity values, e.g. Hounsfield units, and other regularization or shape priors, but this remains a challenging problem due to the large variations and complexity of the appearance of both the human anatomy and the pathological lesions. It is generally agreed that, at the macro level, tissue changes with physiologic and pathologic processes can be best captured through elasticity measures [2]. It has been shown that changes in soft tissue elasticity are strongly related to abnormal pathological processes [19,20]. In other words, difference in the elasticity

G. Wu et al. (Eds.): MLMI 2013, LNCS 8184, pp. 179–186, 2013.
© Springer International Publishing Switzerland 2013

property of normal and abnormal parts presents an alternative, yet effective strategy for detecting tumor. Accordingly, elastography imaging, which is a set of techniques for noninvasive assessment of the mechanical properties of tissues, often plays a crucial role. Elastographic techniques have proved to be a useful for medical diagnosis purposes and tumor segmentation. For example, in [3], elastography has been used to characterize solid liver, while [4] has investigated normal and abnormal breast tissues in ultrasound images based on differences in their elasticity values under absence or presence of external stress. However, in the aforementioned works and others, e.g. MR elastography (MRE) [5], elastography was only used to measure internal displacement or strain in tissue that results from the application of external stress to that tissue, but never been employed for tumor segmentation.

In this paper, we propose a framework for lung tumor segmentation, one of the most common and lethal cancers in both men and women worldwide. On one hand, our work is motivated by the successful application of elastography imaging to the evaluation of abnormal tissues, such as brain tumors. On another hand, we seek to avoid the application of external deformation simulation forces as commonly done in elastography, i.e. we seek to deduce elasticity related properties without imposing any external stress. To this end, we base our work on the fact that lung tumor follows characteristically small deformations in response to respiration (while normal lung tissue deforms considerably during breathing) [6] and test the hypothesis that such tumor deformation characteristic can be used to aid the segmentation of lung tumors in images acquired during normal respiration conditions.

Specifically, we propose a method for lung tumor segmentation from dynamic CT (4D) exams of the lung at different phases of one breathing cycle during normal respiration. Although the apparent intensity changes in the dynamic images cannot always be unambiguously related to elasticity [6], we will first estimate tissue displacements with deformable image registration and *leverage pattern recognition and machine learning techniques to discover deformation (spatio-temporal) features that best discriminate tumor from normal tissue*. To the best of our knowledge, this is the first work to propose such a novel learning-based approach for lung tumor segmentation that is *applicable for images acquired under normal circumstances* (does not require breadth-hold imaging). It also does not require the application of external stress that patients had to endure as required in previous studies [1,9].

One important issue in machine learning is having a proper class distribution in the training set [7]. It has been generally agreed in the literature that the training set sampled from the natural distribution of training samples is best for learning. However, studies have shown that this claim is not true in cases where highly imbalanced class distributions are observed. In these cases, the classifier usually has a poor performance on the minority class. For our problem, where the malicious voxels constitute the minority class, we *address this class imbalance problem by examining various well-established cost-sensitive re-sampling methods*.

Another important obstacle towards distinguishing the tumor tissue based on its elasticity is that the magnitude and direction of tumor motion may differ between different patients due to various factors. In [8], it was shown that direct relationships exist between tumor motion patterns, tumor location, and patients' breathing patterns. However, these observations were based on a limited number of patients and have yet to be verified using more 4D data sets. The elasticity properties can aid in discriminating the tumor tissue, however, a global (over all voxels) threshold is not a viable option given the complex movements of different tissues. Instead, we combine our classifier with a 3D graph-based optimization (Markov random field energy minimization) to ensure spatio-temporal consistency.

2   Methods

At a high level, our method consists of a training (or learning) stage and an application (or tumor segmentation) stage. The training stage uses a set of dynamic 4D CT images capturing the lung motion in cancer patients during normal respiration, along with a set of ground truth expert segmentations of the tumor. For each sequence, the image frames captured at two time points that correspond to the peak-exhale and peak-inhale breathing phases (phases in which the most varied lung positions are captured) are non-rigidly registered and the displacement fields are extracted. Features from the displacement vectors at tumorous and normal tissues from all training data are used to train a classifier. In the application stage, a novel 4D data is processed similarly (registration and feature extraction). Next, using the trained classifier and Markov random field (MRF) energy minimization, each voxel in the image is then labeled as either normal or tumor, thus giving the desired tumor segmentation.

2.1   Image Registration

To extract lung and lung tumor tissue motion patterns between two 3D frames of the considered 4D CT image sequences, we used a diffeomorphic non-rigid intensity-based registration scheme similar to [9], which has been reported to result in registration accuracy in the order of and below voxel size [10]. The registration searches for a deformation that minimizes an energy functional consisted of a dissimilarity cost that measures intensity difference between the registered images and a regularization cost that ensures regularity of the deformation fields. As in [9], we used a normalized version of the sum of squared intensity differences (SSD) and a diffusion regularization term. The evaluation of the dissimilarity measure was further restricted to the lungs by using expert-segmented binary lung masks. Automatic lung segmentation is not related to our core contribution, although several approaches may be applied for that purpose [11]. The spatial transformation space considered during optimization has been restricted to diffeomorphisms by employing diffeomorphic demons (i.e. parameterization of the transformation by stationary velocity fields; cf. [12]) in order to avoid physically implausible motion patterns like singularities in the estimated deformation fields.

2.2   Feature Extraction

With the deformation field obtained from Sec. 2.1, we then extract at each location a set of features. In this paper, we employed features that are related to local volume changes. Generally, the evolution of a small volume in time between the source and target frames is captured by the Jacobian determinant of the deformation field, $|J|$. Although $|J|$ provides insight about the amount of compression and expansion experienced by tissues, it was found insufficient for distinguishing normal tissues from tumorous tissues. Thus, in addition to $|J|$, our dynamic features include the x, y, and z components of the displacement vectors (denoted as dx, dy, dz), as well as the divergence and the curl of the deformation field. This results in a 6-element feature vector at every voxel.

As effective static features, we also examine intensity-based features like geometric features (Hessian eigenvalues, 1st and 2nd principal curvatures, which define shape indices) and Haar-like filters. For the Haar-like features, we employed different sizes and types of Haar filters and extracted these features within 10x10x10 neighbourhoods at a subset of locations residing in the lung volumes.

2.3   Addressing the Class Imbalance Problem

Since the number samples corresponding to tumorous voxels is small relative to the number of samples corresponding to normal voxels, we face what is referred to as the class imbalance problem. Therefore a proper class distribution sampling of the training set must be used. We investigated three different sampling methods for training cost-sensitive learning: (1) under-sampling, which changes the distribution by removing lower-cost training examples until the number of different training examples is proportional to their costs [7]; (2) over-sampling, which changes the training data distribution by duplicating higher-cost training examples until the number of different training examples is proportional to their costs [7]; and (3) synthetic minority over-sampling, which resamples the small class through taking each small class example and introducing synthetic examples along the line segments joining its nearest neighbors from the same class [7]. Based on empirical experiments (which we have omitted due to space constraints), we chose cost-sensitive under-sampling, which gave the best segmentation performance.

2.4   Decision forests for Graph-Based Segmentation

The balanced data set can now be used to for training our classifier. In this work, we chose decision forests (DF), an ensemble of 50 decision trees, as a strong classifier. We made this choice because they 1) additionally infer the importance of features, 2) remove outliers with high accuracy, 3) resistant to over-fitting, 4) train rapidly, even for a large set of input features, and 5) require minimal feature normalization.

While one could employ DF to perform per-voxel classification, we instead employ the DF predictions in an adapted form of a MRF-based segmentation framework [13]. In particular, we model the image as a graph $G(V,E,W)$ whose nodes correspond to voxel coordinates. The set of edges E encode voxel-connectivity (we use 26-connectivity) while the set of weights W ensure that neighboring pixels with similar deformation-based and intensity-based features will likely be classified with the same class label, thereby ensuring that the overall binary tumor segmentation is spatially regular and homogenous. In this work, we compute W as follows:

$$W(i,j) = \exp^{-\|X_i - X_j\|/\delta_x - \sum_k \|Feature^k(i) - Feature^k(j)\|/\delta_k} \tag{1}$$

where i and j are the indices of two neighboring voxels, X is the spatial location of the voxel, $Feature^k$ is the kth feature (static or dynamic) of the voxel, and the δ parameters are the penalty weights for each of the terms, which are set based on the feature importance value output from DF training. Finally, the unary data cost at each node, i.e., the cost of assigning class L to the ith voxel, is defined as:

$$Cost(i,L) = e^{-\sum_k \|Feature^k(i) - G^k(L)\|} \tag{2}$$

where $G^k(L)$ is the expected value for the kth feature for the class L.

3   Results and Discussion

Materials. While there exist various public databases for 4D CT images (e.g. COPDgene, DIR), these sources do not include NSCL images. Consequently, the collection of **4D CT studies involving cancer patients acquired with normal breathing condition** has been extremely difficult. To this end, nine 4D CT studies with a wide range of tumor sizes, locations, radiological appearances and extents of respiratory motion, were collected from [8]. The images were acquired from a 16-slice CT scanner. The patients were instructed to breathe naturally. Volumes 1-5 were acquired from patients with large lung tumors (diameter>3cm; categorization according to [14]) while volumes 6-9 were acquired from patients with small lung tumors. Manual delineations of the gross tumor volumes were completed by expert clinicians. Note that large variability in the structure and size of the tumors yielded large variations in the observed tumor motion patterns [8], which is consistent with observations of Plathow et al. [14]. Due to this large variability, our evaluation has been separately performed on 2 groups: studies involving tumors whose diameter exceeded 3cm and those in the remaining set.

Evaluation. We first evaluated our proposed method using BOTH intensity and six spatio-temporal features. Figure 1 illustrates an example slice from patient 1, the obtained deformation fields in x, y, and z directions, the Jacobian determinant, and the final segmentation result. The precision, recall, and F-Measure of the segmentation obtained for each case are reported in Table 1 and Table 2 for group 1 and 2, respectively. Results were obtained using a leave-one-out cross-validation (LOOCV) experiment.

Fig. 1. Sample slices from patient 4 with a tumor delineated by red contours, the deformation fields in x, y, and z directions, Jacobian determinant, and segmentation result, respectively

Table 1. LOOCV results for studies in group 1

Patients with Large Tumor	P1	P2	P3	P4	P5	Median	Mean
Precision	0.56	0.76	0.78	0.93	0.84	**0.78**	**0.77**
Recall	0.88	0.76	0.83	0.83	0.85	**0.83**	**0.83**
F-Measure	0.69	0.76	0.81	0.88	0.84	**0.81**	**0.79**

Table 2. LOOCV results studies in group 2

Patients with Small Tumor	P6	P7	P8	P9	Median	Mean
Precision	0.24	0.08	0.11	0.09	**0.1**	**0.13**
Recall	0.76	0.82	0.7	0.45	**0.73**	**0.68**
F-Measure	0.37	0.16	0.2	0.15	**0.18**	**0.22**

We notice that the method is very effective for detecting tumors in group 1. The average *F-Score of about 0.79 is remarkable for such a method that neither requires any external force nor any prior information*. The overall tumor tissue classification also has both high recall (0.83) and good precision (0.78) and our segmentation results did not contain spatial irregularities, as were found in [15]. However, the performance of the proposed method was inferior for images in group 2 (0.18 median). Upon inspection, we identified various explanations for the inferior performance. Firstly, the tumor volumes in these images were smaller than those in group 1. Secondly, unusual patient conditions played another role. For instance, abnormal breathing pattern was imaged for patient 8 who suffers from Emphysema (a long-term lung disease that damages some of the tissues supporting the physical shape and functionality of the lungs. As another example, the tumor in patient 9 is attached to the chest wall, which hindered movement of the tumor, thus rendering its segmentation problematic.

Note that the results reported in Table 1 were derived using the cost-sensitivity under-sampling method. When we did not use the cost-sensitivity under-sampling, the F-measure significantly dropped on average to 0.20. As a side note, an interesting property that we of the cost-sensitive-sampling method is that we were able to obtain results with different sensitivities by varying the cost associated to the tumorous class. Lastly, we examined the *effect of using only the static features on overall segmentation accuracy*. Results are shown in Tables 3 and 4. Comparing them with Tables 1 and 2, we can see that employing hundreds of static features, even at the expense of much higher computation time, did not improve segmentation performance. This confirms the value of incorporating spatio-temporal features into the proposed tumor segmentation algorithm.

Table 3. LOOCV results for studies in images in group 1, when *only static features* were used

Patients With Large Tumor	P1	P2	P3	P4	P5	Median	Mean
Precision	0.63	0.33	0.18	0.63	0.11	**0.33**	**0.37**
Recall	0.56	0.73	0.76	0.77	0.84	**0.76**	**0.73**
F-Measure	0.59	0.45	0.3	0.69	0.2	**0.45**	**0.44**

Table 4. LOOCV results for studies in images in group 2, when *only static features* were used

Patients With Small Tumor	P6	P7	P8	P9	Median	Mean
Precision	0.51	0.09	0.34	0.24	**0.29**	**0.29**
Recall	0.37	0.45	0.73	0.76	**0.59**	**0.57**
F-Measure	0.42	0.15	0.46	0.37	**0.39**	**0.35**

Note that comparing our automatic method to previous methods, such as [1] or the very recent work reported in [17], is unfair because they either require the application of external stress forces on patients or interruption of the normal breathing cycle. Furthermore, some also require user interaction, such as identification of segmentation seed points. All of these were not required by our method.

4   Conclusion

Motivated by the successful application of MRE to the evaluation of brain tumors, and promising results observed in previous studies relating to analysis of lung tissue deformations, we sought to evaluate the utility of the stiffness property of the tissues in characterizing lung tumors. The importance of our work is that, in contrast to all other similar works that evaluated tissue elasticity under external force, we showed that tissue displacements during a normal breathing cycle, i.e. without the calculation of external forces, provided the needed data to segment the tumor. An investigation of tumor patterns was performed via pixel-wise spatio-temporal features and image-based features, which were used to train a decision forests machine learning method. Both the class probability and feature importance from the decision forests were then incorporated into a graph cut segmentation method. To extend our evaluation, we are currently in active pursuit of acquiring more 4D data containing lung tumors, which has been difficult. A future research direction is to examine the additional use of in-between motion dynamics and extraction of "local velocity curves", which have been successfully used in heart disease discrimination [18].

References

[1] Kanakatte, et al.: A Pilot Study of Automatic Lung Tumor Segmentation from Positron Emission Tomography Images using Standard Uptake Values. IEEE CIISP, 363–368 (2007)

[2] Dizaji, et al.: Evaluation of ultrasound in tissue characterization. In: Proc. EMBEC 1999, vol. 37(1), pp. 666–667 (1999)

[3] Sudhakar, et al.: MR Elastography of Liver Tumors: Preliminary Results. AJR, 2781 (2008)

[4] Dizaji, et al.: Detection of Internal Displacement of Tissues in Ultrasound Images Using Image Registration Technique. In: Proc. IEEE Canadian Conference on Electrical & Computer Engineering, pp. 1145–1148 (2002)

[5] Muthupillai, et al.: Magnetic resonance elastography. Nat. Med. 2, 601–603 (1996)

[6] Rey, et al.: Automatic Detection and Segmentation of Evolving Processes in 3D Medical Images: Application to Multiple Sclerosis. MIA 6(2), 163–179 (2002)

[7] Zhou, Liu: Training cost-sensitive neural networks with methods addressing class imbalance problem. IEEE TKDE 18(1), 63–77 (2006)

[8] Handels, et al.: 4D medical image computing and visualization of lung tumor mobility in spatio-temporal CT image data. International J. Medical Informatics 76, S433–S439 (2007)

[9] Richberg, et al.: Diffeomorphic diffusion registration of lung CT images. In: Medical Image Analysis for the Clinic: A Grand Challenge, MICCAI, pp. 55–62 (2010)

[10] Murphy, et al.: Evaluation of Registration Methods on Thoracic CT: The EMPIRE10 Challenge. IEEE TMI 30(11), 1901–1920 (2011)

[11] van Rikxoort, et al.: Automatic lung segmentation from thoracic computed tomography scans using a hybrid approach with error detection. Medical Physics 36(7), 2934–2947 (2009)

[12] Vercauteren, et al.: Diffeomorphic demons: Efficient non-parametric image registration. Neuroimage 45(1), S61–S72 (2008)

[13] Boykov, et al.: An Experimental Comparison of Min-Cut/Max-Flow Algorithms for Energy Minimization in Vision. IEEE TPAMI 26(9), 1124–1137 (2004)

[14] Plathow, et al.: Measurement of tumor diameter-dependent mobility of lung tumors by dynamic MRI. Radiotherapy and Oncology 73(3), 349–354 (2004)

[15] Cuingnet, et al.: Spatial and anatomical regularization of SVM for brain image analysis. In: NIPS, pp. 460–468 (2010)

[16] Tu, et al.: Automated extraction of the cortical sulci based on a supervised learning approach. IEEE TMI 26(4), 541–552 (2007)

[17] Gu, et al.: Automated delineation of lung tumors from CT images using a single click ensemble segmentation approach. Radiotherapy and Oncology 105(2), 167–173 (2012)

[18] Syeda-Mahmood, Yang: Characterizing normal and abnormal cardiac echo motion patterns. IEEE Computers in Cardiology, 725–728 (2006)

[19] Martin, et al.: Building motion models of lung tumours from cone-beam CT for radiotherapy applications. Physics in Medicine and Biology 58(6), 1809 (2013)

[20] Britton, et al.: Assessment of gross tumor volume regression and motion changes during radiotherapy for non-small-cell lung cancer as measured by four-dimensional computed tomography. Int. J. Radiat. Oncol. Biol. Phys. 68, 1036–1046 (2007)

Improving Probabilistic Image Registration via Reinforcement Learning and Uncertainty Evaluation

Tayebeh Lotfi, Lisa Tang, Shawn Andrews, and Ghassan Hamarneh

Medical Image Analysis Lab., Simon Fraser University, Burnaby, Canada
{tlotfima,lisat,sda56,hamarneh}@sfu.ca

Abstract. One framework for probabilistic image registration involves assigning probability distributions over spatial transformations (e.g. distributions over displacement vectors at each voxel). In this paper, we propose an uncertainty measure for these distributions that examines the actual spatial displacements, thus departing from the classical Shannon entropy-based measures, which examine only the probabilities of these distributions. We show that by incorporating the proposed uncertainty measure, along with features extracted from the input images and intermediate displacement fields, we are able to more accurately predict the pointwise registration errors of an intermediate solution as estimated for a previously unseen input image pair. We utilize the predicted errors to identify regions in the image that are trustworthy and through which we refine the tentative registration solution. Results show that our proposed framework, which incorporates uncertainty estimation and registration error prediction, can improve accuracy of 3D image registrations by about 25%.

1 Introduction

Image registration, the process of bringing images into spatial alignment, is a key step in the analysis of multi-modal image data. Formally, the process involves finding the optimal transformation T that maps a point $\mathbf{v}_i$ in one image I_a to corresponding point $\mathbf{v}_i + T(\mathbf{v}_i)$ in another image I_b. The task is often formulated as an energy minimization problem, e.g.:

$$\underset{T}{\arg\min} \sum_{\mathbf{v}_i \in \Omega} \alpha D\left(I_a(\mathbf{v}_i), I_b\left(\mathbf{v}_i + T(\mathbf{v}_i)\right)\right) + R\left(T(\mathbf{v}_i)\right), \qquad (1)$$

where $\Omega \subset \mathbb{R}^d$ is the image domain, d is the image dimension, D measures the dissimilarity between image I_a and the transformed image I_b, R encourages the regularity of T, and α is a scalar balancing D and R.

Formulating Eq. 1 as a graph labeling problem allows us to use efficient optimizers, such as graph cuts [13], and random walker (RW) [2]. In this work, we advocate the use of random walker optimization as it 1) provides a unique globally optimal solution that corresponds to an optimal spatial transformation, and 2) generates a probabilistic output, which we leverage to evaluate the solution's uncertainty.

In RW-based image registration (RWIR) [2], one samples the solution search space to generate a labelset $\mathcal{L} = \{\ell_1, \ell_2, \cdots, \ell_L\} \in \mathbb{R}^d$ (each label corresponds to a displacement vector). After optimization, one obtains a probabilistic, unity-sum vector

G. Wu et al. (Eds.): MLMI 2013, LNCS 8184, pp. 187–194, 2013.

$\mathcal{P} = \{p_1, \cdots, p_L\}$ at every $\mathbf{v}_i$. Given a probability distribution over the sampled (discrete and finite) space of possible displacements (or spatial transformations), one may calculate the registration uncertainty at $\mathbf{v}_i$ using Shannon's entropy:

$$U_{Shannon}(\mathbf{v}_i) = -\sum_i p_i(\mathbf{v}_i)log_2(p_i(\mathbf{v}_i)). \tag{2}$$

Although it is a natural choice, $U_{Shannon}$ however does not take into account the spatial meaning of displacement labels. For example, if two labels (i.e. two displacement vectors) are both assigned probability 0.5, one would expect the uncertainty to depend on whether these labels were spatially close or far apart, but $U_{Shannon}$ ignores this. Therefore, it is critical to consider the spatial spread of the probability distribution over the displacement vectors. As our **first contribution** in this work, we develop an uncertainty measure tailored specifically for image registration that, in contrast to Eq. 2, takes into account the aforementioned spatial meaning of labels, as we will present in the next section.

Another important challenge in image registration is the evaluation of registration algorithms. Aside from qualitative visual inspection, the direct quantitative approach is to compare the deformation field with the *ground truth* (GT) transformation (at preselected landmark locations), yielding the target registration error (TRE). However, in clinical data, the GT is typically unknown and is hard to collect. To deal with the absence of GT, some methods opted to *estimate* registration accuracy, e.g., by using uncertainty measures as a surrogate for quantitative registration error. For instance, some methods [8,9] collected training data with GT warps (and hence registration error is known) and employed machine learning algorithms to infer registration error for novel data, while others [7,12,11] used the inferred registration errors to improve the registration results. Adopting these research directions, our **second contribution** involves comparing how different uncertainty measures correlate with registration errors as we present in [10]. As our **third contribution**, we propose augmenting image- and deformation-based features with our novel uncertainty measure to add a new source of information that improves registration error prediction, and, for the first time, incorporate them into a probabilistic registration framework to boost its performance.

To this end, we developed a novel *self-reinforcing* registration framework that consists of the following steps: examine the local confidence of T using our novel uncertainty measure; 2) employ random forest training to learn a predictive function f that infers registration errors from a set of features that includes the proposed uncertainty measure; 3) given a tentative solution, employ f to locate regions of high confidence (shown to correlate with low error), and utilize the displacements at those regions to refine the tentative solution in subsequent iterations.

2   Method

Our approach involves a training and testing stage. In the training stage, we learn a regression function f that predicts registration error from a set of features (details later). In the testing stage, we use f to predict the unknown registration error of a probabilistic registration and use locations with low predicted registration errors to steer subsequent registrations. Alg. 1 and Alg. 2 summarize the steps involved in our method.

Algorithm 1. Training procedure	**Algorithm 2.** Testing procedure
Input: Training images $\mathcal{I} = \{I^n, \cdots, I^N\}$, synthetic warps $\mathcal{T} = \{GT^1, \cdots GT^M\}$ **Output:** f $\quad \mathcal{Q} = \emptyset$ $\quad$ **for** n=1 ... N **do** $\quad\quad$ **for** m=1 ... M **do** $\quad\quad\quad I_a = I^n, I_b = I_a \circ GT^m$ $\quad\quad\quad$ Run RWIR on I_a, I_b to obtain $\hat{T}^m$ $\quad\quad\quad$ Compute reg. error to obtain $\mathbf{Y}^m$ $\quad\quad\quad$ Get features $\mathbf{X}^m$ from $I_a, I_b, \hat{T}^m$ $\quad\quad\quad \mathcal{Q} = \mathcal{Q} \bigcup (\mathbf{X}^m, \mathbf{Y}^m)$ $\quad\quad$ **end for** $\quad$ **end for** Learn f from $\mathcal{Q}$ using RRF [1]	**Input:** Novel fixed image I_1, moving image I_2, f learned from Alg. 1, β = num. of iterations **Output:** Final registered image W $\quad$ Run RWIR on I_1 and I_2 to obtain $\hat{T}$ $\quad$ **for** $k = 1 \cdots \beta$ **do** $\quad\quad$ Use f to predict $\hat{y}(\mathbf{v}_i), \forall i \in \Omega$ $\quad\quad$ Obtain a set of seeds S using $\hat{y}$ (Alg. 3) $\quad\quad$ Adjust "data prior" λ [4] using S (Eq. 7) $\quad\quad$ Re-run RWIR using the adjusted λ $\quad$ **end for** $\quad W = I_2 \circ \hat{T}$

2.1 Training Stage

Let there be a pair of images I_a and I_b and their corresponding registration solution $\hat{T}$ obtained by solving Eq. 1. Our first goal is to learn a function f that predicts the registration error y_i at $\mathbf{v}_i$ from a set of K features $\mathbf{f}_i$ extracted from $\hat{T}$, I_a, and I_b at $\mathbf{v}_i$:

$$f(\mathbf{f}_i; \hat{T}, I_a, I_b) = \hat{y}(\mathbf{v}_i) \equiv \hat{y}_i. \qquad (3)$$

We modeled f using regression random forests (RRF) [1]. While other training methods are possible, e.g. support vector machines, we chose random forests because they 1) additionally infer the importance of features, 2) remove outliers with high accuracy, 3) resistant to over-fitting, 4) can be trained efficiently, even when thousands of input features are used, and 5) requires no feature normalization procedures [1].

Data Collection. Our training data $\mathcal{Q}$ of paired input and output matrices is constructed from a set of images $\mathcal{I}$ and synthetically generated warps $\mathcal{T}$. Specifically, for each image $I_a \in \mathcal{I}$ and the m-th warp $GT^m \in \mathcal{T}$, we simulate a pair of misaligned images by generating I_b as $I_a \circ GT^m$. We then deformably register I_a and I_b by solving Eq. 1 to obtain $\hat{T}^m$. Next, at each location i, we extract a set of image-based and deformation-based features $\mathbf{f}_i$ from $\hat{T}^m$, $I_b \circ \hat{T}^m$, and I_a (details later). We then concatenate feature values from all locations to form a feature matrix $\mathbf{X}^m$ that corresponds to the m-th simulation. Finally, we calculate the pointwise registration error of $\hat{T}^m$, i.e. $y(\mathbf{v}_i) = ||\hat{T}^m(\mathbf{v}_i) - GT^m(\mathbf{v}_i)||$, and concatenate y from all locations to form the corresponding output array $\mathbf{Y}^m$. Repeating this procedure over the N images and M warps thus forms our training set.

Our feature set, $\mathcal{F}$, consists of deformation-based and image-based features ($K \leq 105$). We explored 4 sets of **image-based features**: 1) the squared intensity difference between each registered pair; 2) their sum of squared intensity difference (SSD) over patches,

$$SSD_{patch}(\mathbf{v}_i) = \sum_{\mathbf{v}_s \in \mathcal{N}(\mathbf{v}_i)} I_a(\mathbf{v}_s) - I_b \circ GT(\mathbf{v}_s), \tag{4}$$

where $\mathcal{N}$ is the neighborhood of $\mathbf{v}_i$ of size 3^d; 3) their difference in intensity gradient magnitude, and 4) the difference between their MIND descriptors [6]. **Deformation-based features** include the determinant of Jacobian of $\hat{T}$, denoted as J, and our proposed uncertainty measure which we now present.

As motivated in Sec. 1, Shannon's entropy would not take into account the spatial information inherit to the displacement labels, and as we show in [10], it gives unintuitive results in the registration context. In search of alternatives, we explored the option of fitting various continuous probabilistic distributions over the obtained label space prior to standard Shannon's entropy calculation or K-nearest neighbour estimation [10]. A few other definitions were also examined, although all aforementioned options were suboptimal. To this end, we developed a novel uncertainty measure that is defined as the expectation of the registration error given the probabilistic field $\mathcal{P}$ (defined over labels) derived by solving Eq. 1. In particular, we first assume that each ℓ_i is a potential ground truth and so, its expected error is $\mathrm{E}\,[\delta_i] = \sum_j p_j \delta_{ij}$, where δ_i is a random variable for the Euclidean distance to ℓ_i and $\delta_{ij} = \|\ell_j - \ell_i\|$. If the probability of ℓ_i being a ground truth is p_i, then we obtain:

$$U_{exp} = \sum_i p_i\,[\mathrm{E}\,[\delta_i]] = \sum_i p_i \sum_j p_j \|\ell_i - \ell_j\|. \tag{5}$$

Now, if we consider only the maximum *a posteriori* (MAP) label ℓ_{MAP}, then we obtain *its* expected error to the ground truth. We thus propose a measure of registration uncertainty U as:

$$U = \sum_{i=1}^{L} p_i(\|\ell_i - \ell_{MAP}\|). \tag{6}$$

In [10], we show that U exhibits strong correlation with target registration error, and out of all options explored in [10], we find U to be the most applicable for error prediction in registration. In Sec. 3, we will compare our proposed uncertainty measure with Shannon's entropy in the context of registration and their effects on registration error prediction.

Learning f. For ease of training [12], we quantized y into 3 classes:
1) Class 1: $y(\mathbf{v}_i) < 0.1\,y_{max}$ (low error)
2) Class 2: $0.1\,y_{max} \le y(\mathbf{v}_i) \le 0.6\,y_{max}$ (medium error)
3) Class 3: $y(\mathbf{v}_i) > 0.6\,y_{max}$ (high error)
where y_{max} is the maximum registration error of each training trial (and again, y is the known error). We then trained f using RRF of 80 trees.

2.2 Testing Stage

We develop an iterative registration method based on prior learning that steers the registration process towards minimizing registration error as predicted by f. Specifically, for a new pair of images and a tentative registration solution, we extract the set of features

Algorithm 3. Seed-selection

Input: Initial candidate seeds $C = \{c_1, \cdots, c_j, \cdots\}$,
   their predicted registration errors $\{y_{c_1}, \cdots, y_{c_j}, \cdots\}$
Output: Final seeds S
   $S = \{\}$
   while $|S| \leq nSeeds$ **do**
      $c_j = \arg\max_j \{y_{c_j} + \gamma \sum_{m=1}^{|S|} \|c_j - S_m\|\}$
      $S = \{S \bigcup c_j\}$
   end while

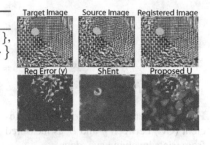

Fig. 1. Textured images. Top: I_1, I_2, W. Bottom: y_i, Shannon's entropy, and proposed U.

presented in Sec. 2.1 and employ f to locate regions with low predicted registration error (class 1). The current solution derived at these locations are highly likely to be valid spatial correspondences and thus are regarded as trustworthy. Our reinforcement-approach reinforces these spatial correspondences and leverages them to influence the solution in the next iteration. We next explain how we locate these confident regions and how their correspondences are reinforced.

Reinforcement. Using terminology from [3,4,5], locations of low predicted error will act as *candidate seeds*, i.e. nodes that will be given preferred spatial correspondences. Given an initial set of locations with low predicted error (as determined by thresholding y), we short-listed them using Alg. 3 such that the final candidates are as spatially distributed as possible.

    Having obtained the candidate seeds S, the next step is to encode them in RWIR. One way is to explicitly enforce them as boundary conditions [5]. However, this assumes that the preferred correspondences are perfect. To relax this assumption, we employ a *soft* approach, where the "data prior" [5], denoted as λ, is adjusted so that the preferred correspondences are encouraged, rather than strictly enforced. Thus, we compute the data prior at $\mathbf{v}_i$ for label l as:

$$\lambda_i^l = \begin{cases} 1 & \text{if } v_i \in S \text{ and } f \text{ predicts error } \hat{y}_i \text{ to be of Class 1} \\ 0 & \text{if } v_i \in S \text{ and } f \text{ predicts error } \hat{y}_i \text{ to be of Class 3} \\ \exp\left(-D_{MIND}(I(\mathbf{v}_i), J(\mathbf{v}_i + \ell_i))\right) & \text{otherwise} \end{cases}$$

(7)

where S is the set of seeds chosen from Alg. 3 and D_{MIND} denotes the Euclidean distance between the MIND descriptors [6] extracted from I and J.

3 Results

Materials. We performed synthetic and real experiments. In the synthetic case, 100 pairs of MRI brain images were used in the training stage. The learned f was then evaluated on 150 image pairs. Image pairs were created by applying random warps to the fixed images. For the real experiments, 90 pairs of $3D$ MRI brain images were registered; evaluation was done based on their registered segmentation maps.

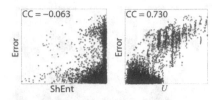

Fig. 2. Scatter plot and correlation coefficient (CC) between y and U as measured from trials involving syn. data

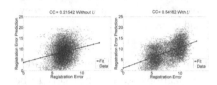

Fig. 3. Scatter plot and CC between real and predicted registration errors (y and $\hat{y}$) when the proposed U uncertainty measure was (a) omitted from, or (b) included in $\mathcal{F}$

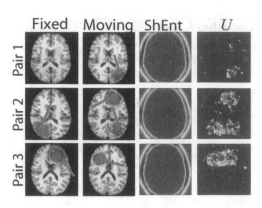

Fig. 4. Ability of U in identifying misregistrations. From left to right: I_1, I_2, ShEnt, and U. Due to presences of tumors, regions with missing correspondences are highly uncertain. While ShEnt has failed to detect regions of high uncertainty in $\hat{T}$, our proposed method reflected the uncertainty in $\hat{T}$ at these regions.

Exp. 1: Usefulness of U. We first examine how this feature correlates with registration error y. For synthetic data, we created a synthetic texture image and corrupted it by adding to it a homogeneous region so that the lack of image features in this region will create ambiguity in the registration solution, thereby increasing uncertainty in this region. Then, we generated a set of moving images by applying synthetic warps to the fixed image. The warps were created by randomly perturbing the control points of a B-spline deformation grid whose displacements magnitude followed $\mathcal{N}(6, 2)$ voxels. We calculated the registration error (y) and U using the derived label probabilities and subsequently, their overall correlations. As shown in Fig. 2, our proposed measure U exhibits much higher correlation with actual error than Shannon's entropy (ShEnt). For real data, we used images from a public database[1] and examined the ability of U in detecting misregistrations caused by missing correspondences (due to the presences of brain tumors). Example results are shown in Fig. 4. Examining the results visually, we find that ShEnt has failed to detect misregistrations caused by the presence of tumor (nor uncertainty of the solution in these regions), while U was able to reflect uncertainty (registration errors) much more effectively. Fig. 1 also shows similar result when we employed synthetically generated textured images.

Exp. 2: U Improves Prediction Accuracy of f. We next examined how the addition of U as feature in $\mathcal{F}$ can improve accuracy of error prediction. For this experiment, we applied a synthetic warp to a target image and registered it to a source image in an attempt to recover the known warp. Fig. 3 shows a scatter plot of the actual (y) and

---

[1] http://www2.imm.dtu.dk/projects/BRATS2012/

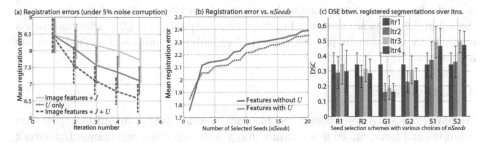

Fig. 5. (a) Registration error over iterations for different feature subsets. It can be seen that the use of image features with J only (green curve) was inferior to use of U alone (red). When all 105 features were used, the reduction was most significant (blue), i.e. as much as by 25%. (b) Inclusion of U always decreased registration error, except when the number of seeds used was inadequate (less than 3). (c) Results of segmentation-based evaluation (Exp. 4). R1 and R2 (G1 and G2) denote addition of 5 and 20 seeds per iteration, respectively.

predicted registration errors ($\hat{y}$). Note that the correlation coefficient between $\hat{y}$ and y was 0.22 when U was omitted from $\mathcal{F}$, but increased to 0.54 when it was included.

Exp. 3: Evaluation of Proposed Learning-Based RWIR. We next examined how our registration algorithm, when incorporated with prior-learning improves registration over iterations. Our evaluation setup was as follows. We employed 40 MRI brain images from the LONI Probabilistic Brain Atlas (LPBA40) dataset[2] where each image is accompanied with an expert's segmentation of 56 brain structures. Then, we constructed training and validation data; the GT warps were created by randomly perturbing the control points of a B-spline deformation grid whose displacement magnitudes followed $N(6; 2)$. This resulted in 250 pairs of synthetically misaligned images with GT registrations. The entire data set was then split into a training set of size 100 and a validation set of size 150, where the former was used to learn and test f, while the latter was used to quantify the registration accuracy achieved by our method as evaluated on unseen image pairs. For reference, we also repeated the trials by training f with different feature subsets. Results are shown in Fig. 5a where we can see that the decrease in registration error is monotonic. Further, we see that the inclusion of U in the feature set improved the error reduction rate. We then examined whether this effect was due to differences in the number of seeds used ($nSeeds$ in Alg. 3). However, from Fig. 5b, we can see that the inclusion of U had almost always led to greater reduction in error, except only when fewer than 3 seeds were used.

Exp. 4: Overall Evaluation on Real Registrations. We next evaluated our proposed method on real registrations using the LPBA40 brain images. Since there is no known GT for these images, we calculated the Dice similarity coefficient (DSC) of the corresponding registered segmentations to evaluate the obtained solutions. For reference, we also compared our proposed uncertainty-based seed-selection strategy (Alg. 3) against other potential alternatives: 1) random seed selection (R), which selects seeds at random, 2) grid-based seed selection (G), which selects seeds at regular interval and

---

[2] http://www.loni.ucla.edu/

mimicks how users choose landmark correspondences by scrolling through slices in the volume. Results are shown in Fig. 5c, where we plotted the DSC after registration obtained by the schemes presented above. Evidently, our proposed method gave the highest final DSC.

4 Conclusions

We have proposed a novel uncertainty measure for evaluating probabilistic registration solutions and incorporated this measure into a *self-reinforcing* registration framework that consists of 1) learning a registration error prediction function and 2) certainty-based seed-selection strategy for reinforcing trusted spatial correspondences in a tentative solution. As future work, we will extend our evaluation experiments with more data and demonstrate applicability of the proposed uncertainty measure in radiation therapy.

Acknowledgements. The authors are grateful to Brian Booth for his input and Natural Sciences and Engineering Research Council and NeuroDevNet for their partial funding.

References

1. Breiman, L.: Bagging predictors. Mach. Learn. 24(2), 123–140 (1996)
2. Cobzas, D., Sen, A.: Random walks for deformable image registration. In: Fichtinger, G., Martel, A., Peters, T. (eds.) MICCAI 2011, Part II. LNCS, vol. 6892, pp. 557–565. Springer, Heidelberg (2011)
3. Couprie, C., Grady, L., Najman, L., Talbot, H.: Power watershed: A unifying graph-based optimization framework. IEEE Trans. Pattern Anal. Mach. Intell. 33(7), 1384–1399 (2011)
4. Grady, L.: Multilabel random walker image segmentation using prior models. In: IEEE CVPR, pp. 763–770 (2005)
5. Grady, L.: Random walks for image segmentation. IEEE Trans. Pattern Anal. Mach. Intell. 28(11), 1768–1783 (2006)
6. Heinrich, M., Jenkinson, M., Bhushan, M., Matin, T., Gleeson, F., Brady, M., Schnabel, J.: MIND: Modality independent neighbourhood descriptor for multi-modal deformable registration. Medical Image Analysis 16(7), 1423–1435 (2012)
7. Kohlberger, T., Singh, V., Alvino, C., Bahlmann, C., Grady, L.: Evaluating segmentation error without ground truth. In: Ayache, N., Delingette, H., Golland, P., Mori, K. (eds.) MICCAI 2012, Part I. LNCS, vol. 7510, pp. 528–536. Springer, Heidelberg (2012)
8. Kybic, J.: Bootstrap resampling for image registration uncertainty estimation without ground truth. IEEE Trans. Image Process. 19(1), 64–73 (2010)
9. Kybic, J., Nieuwenhuis, C.: Bootstrap optical flow confidence and uncertainty measure. Computer Vision and Image Understanding 115(10), 1449–1462 (2011)
10. Lotfi, T.: Uncertainty in probabilistic image registration. Master's thesis, Simon Fraser University, Burnaby, Canada (2013)
11. Muenzing, S., Murphy, K., Ginneken, B., Pluim, J.: Automatic detection of registration errors for quality assessment in medical image registration. In: SPIE Medical Imaging: Image Processing, vol. 7259, pp. 1–9
12. Muenzing, S., van Ginneken, B., Pluim, J.P.W.: DIRBoost: An algorithm for boosting deformable image registration. In: Biomedical Imaging (ISBI), pp. 1339–1342 (2012)
13. Tang, T.W.H., Chung, A.C.S.: Non-rigid image registration using graph-cuts. In: Ayache, N., Ourselin, S., Maeder, A. (eds.) MICCAI 2007, Part I. LNCS, vol. 4791, pp. 916–924. Springer, Heidelberg (2007)

HEp-2 Cell Image Classification:
A Comparative Analysis

Praful Agrawal, Mayank Vatsa, and Richa Singh

Indraprastha Institute of Information Technology, Delhi, India

Abstract. HEp-2 cell image classification is an important and relatively unexplored area of research. This paper presents an experimental analysis of five different categories of feature sets with four different classifiers to determine the best performing combination of features and classifiers. The analysis is performed on the ICIP 2013 Cell Image Classification Contest Training dataset comprising over 13,000 cell images pertaining to six cell classes. The results computed with 10 fold cross validation show that texture features perform the best among all the explored feature sets and the combination of Laws features with SVM yields the highest accuracy.

1 Introduction

Human immune system creates antibodies to fight against infections whereas antinuclear antibodies affect healthy tissues (cell nucleus). Antinuclear Autoantibodies (ANA) test is widely used to determine whether the immune system is developing antibodies or not [1]. Indirect Immunofluorescence (IIF) based ANA test is state-of-the-art due to its high specificity and ability to discriminate the samples belonging to positive, intermediate, and negative classes. In this test, ANAs are detected by a specific pattern among 30 different fluorescence patterns which can be recognized via HEp-2 cells [2]. The process involves manually identifying fluorescence patterns which require visual inspection of slides under fluorescence microscope by highly qualified physicians. Manual evaluation suffers from some limitations such as inter-observer variability and scarcity of highly specialized personnel. The need for automation has been well accepted by the researchers and therefore, recent attempts are made to share HEp-2 cell image classification databases and develop automated algorithms.

HEp-2 cell image classification can be considered as a classical pattern recognition problem where cell patterns can be modeled using an efficient representation and classified using multi-class classification algorithms. Recent research has focused on image based features and standard classification algorithms. Table 1 summarizes some recent techniques for HEp-2 cell image classification. Majority of existing approaches have evaluated their performance using the ICPR 2012 Contest Training Dataset[1] containing approximately 1,400 cell images with positive and intermediate fluorescence intensity.

---

[1] http://mivia.unisa.it/hep2contest/index.shtml

G. Wu et al. (Eds.): MLMI 2013, LNCS 8184, pp. 195–202, 2013.

Table 1. Some recent techniques on HEp-2 cell image classification

	Features	Classifier
Wiliem *et al.* [3], 2013	Dual-region codebook based descriptor	Nearest Convex Hull
Ersoy *et al.* [4], 2012	Shape, gradient, and texture features	Multiview Shareboost
Ghosh & Chaudhary [5], 2012	HOG, ROI, SURF, and texture features	Multiclass SVM
Li *et al.* [6], 2012	LBP, Gabor, DCT, and statistical features	Multiclass Boosting SVM
Iannello *et al.* [7], 2012	SIFT features	Bag Of Visual Words
Ali *et al.* [8], 2012	Contrast based features	kNN
Theodorakopoulos *et al.* [9], 2012	Morphological and LBP features	SVM
Cordelli and Soda [10], 2011	Texture features	MLP, kNN, SVM, and Adaboost
Foggia *et. al.* [11], 2010	Morphological, texture and rectangle features	MLP, Naïve Bayes, kNN, SVM, and Adaboost
Soda & Iannello [12], 2009	Different features specific to each class	Multi-Expert System

The main focus of the paper is to analyze different features and classification approaches for HEp-2 cell image classification. In this research, we broadly categorize the features (corresponding to cell structures and appearances) used in literature under five different categories - Boundary, Descriptor, Shape and Size, Statistical, and Texture Features. Using this categorization, a comparative analysis is performed to understand their underlying discriminative ability across different types of cell patterns. The ability of these feature categories to distinguish among various types of cell patterns is evaluated using four different classifiers[2]. Unlike existing literature where researchers have reported overall classification accuracy, this research reports the performance on *positive* and *intermediate* intensity cell images to compare the complexity of the classification task within each intensity class. For each feature-classifier combination, three classifier models are trained - two pertaining to each intensity class and one for the combined set. The experiments are performed using the ICIP 2013 HEp-2 Cell Image Classification Contest training dataset [13] comprising more than 13,000 cell images. Experimental results suggest that the combination of Laws features and SVM classifier yields a very high classification accuracy.

2   Features and Classifiers for Analysis

A Computer Aided Diagnosis (CAD) system designed for the HEp-2 cell classification from Indirect Immunofluorescence images is based on a well defined

---

[2] To the best of our knowledge, such a categorization and comparative analysis of different types of feature sets is not available in the HEp-2 cell image classification literature.

Fig. 1. Framework of a CAD system for HEp-2 cell classification

procedural model illustrated in Fig. 1. The inputs to a CAD system for HEp-2 classification are IIF images and the corresponding fluorescence intensity class label. Individual HEp-2 cell images are segmented from the IIF image and further categorized into different cell patterns using pattern recognition and machine learning algorithms. The database used and the features and classifiers compared and evaluated in this study are listed in the following subsections.

2.1 HEp-2 Cell Database

ICIP 2013 HEp-2 cell image classification contest training dataset [13] contains 13,596 cell images pertaining to six cell patterns namely *Centromere, Golgi, Homogeneous, Nucleolar, Nuclear Membrane,* and *Speckled*. Cell images are segmented from IIF images pertaining to 83 subjects. For every cell image, there is a mask image of the same size describing the cell boundary in the corresponding cell image. In addition to cell pattern type, the intensity class is also provided for each cell image. In practice, intensity class can either be *Negative, Positive* or *Intermediate*, however the dataset contains images belonging to only *Positive* and *Intermediate* classes. Images from the intermediate intensity class are generally lower in contrast compared to the positive class. The dataset also includes bounding box information for each cell image. Sample images from the dataset are illustrated in Fig. 2 and Table 2 provides the quantitative summary of the dataset.

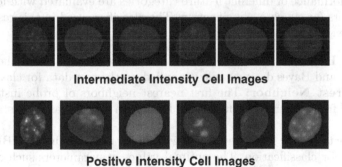

Intermediate Intensity Cell Images

Positive Intensity Cell Images

Fig. 2. Sample images from the ICIP 2013 cell image classification contest training dataset. The cell pattern types of images from left to right - Centromere, Golgi, Homogeneous, Nucleolar, Nuclear Membrane, and Speckled.

2.2 Features and Classifiers

Cell images are first segmented using the given mask images by assigning background intensity as zero in the resulting image. The features widely used in

Table 2. Summary of the ICIP 2013 cell classification contest training dataset

Classes	Centromere	Golgi	Homogeneous	Nucleolar	Nuclear Membrane	Speckled
Intermediate	1363	375	1407	1664	1265	1374
Positive	1378	349	1087	934	943	1457
Total	**2741**	**724**	**2494**	**2598**	**2208**	**2831**

literature are categorized into five general categories of image and object based features: boundary, descriptor, shape and size, statistical, and texture features. Such a categorization represents distinctive characteristics of cell images and also helps in discriminating among different cell patterns. The features extracted and their categorization are presented in Table 3.

Table 3. Features extracted from cell images

Category (length)	Features
Boundary (38)	Perimeter, mean Sobel gradient of boundary pixels, bending energy and 35 spectral energy features derived from FFT of radii vector [14].
HoDesc (221)	LBP and HOG histograms of length 59 and 162 respectively.
Shape and Size (15)	Area, major and minor axis length, eccentricity, orientation, convex area, convex deficiency, solidity, extent, aspect ratio, equivalent diameter, sphericity, compactness, inertiashape, and deviation in centre of mass [14].
Statistical (4)	Mean, standard deviation, skewness, and kurtosis of pixel values.
Texture (211)	65 SGLD [15], 44 GLRL [16], and 102 Laws features [17].

The performance of different feature categories are evaluated with four different classifiers for six class classification. The classifiers used in this research are listed below:

– **Naïve Bayes:** Probability distributions are estimated from the training dataset and Bayes decision rule is applied on the test data for classification.
– k **Nearest Neighbor:** The first nearest neighbors of probe instances are derived from the training data using Euclidean distance as the distance measure.
– **Support Vector Machine:** SVM with linear and non-linear (RBF) kernels is used for classification. The optimal values of parameters such as gamma and cost are estimated in a grid search manner using LIBSVM library [18].
– **Random Decision Forest:** The parameters such as number of trees and forest depth are estimated in a grid search manner.

3   Results and Analysis

Using the ICIP 2013 HEp-2 Cell Image Classification Contest training dataset [13], three subsets of the HEp-2 cell image dataset are considered for experiments:

Positive (P), Intermediate (I), and Combined (C). The subsets are formed based on the fluorescence intensity information available with the dataset. The first two subsets correspond to images from the positive and intermediate intensity class and the third set is the entire dataset containing images with both types of fluorescence intensity. The performance of five different feature categories and four different classifiers are evaluated with 10 fold cross validation on these three data subsets. Mean and standard deviation of accuracy values obtained in 10 folds of cross validation are reported in Table 4 and the key observations are explained below.

Table 4. Comparative results for five feature categories with four different classifiers on three datasets

Classifier		Boundary	Statistical	Shape_Size	Texture	HoDesc
	P	29.65 ± 1.96	86.04 ± 0.89	34.35 ± 1.54	94.89 ± 1.16	70.59 ± 0.78
*k*NN	I	26.83 ± 1.45	76.70 ± 1.36	27.90 ± 1.96	69.12 ± 1.75	50.03 ± 1.38
	C	25.93 ± 1.13	76.29 ± 1.14	28.94 ± 1.35	77.33 ± 1.46	55.08 ± 1.37
	P	26.56 ± 1.88	70.05 ± 2.20	38.27 ± 1.76	56.77 ± 1.48	77.62 ± 2.23
Naïve Bayes	I	23.17 ± 1.20	49.76 ± 1.45	26.24 ± 0.81	33.23 ± 1.91	48.32 ± 1.22
	C	25.47 ± 0.98	54.24 ± 0.97	28.84 ± 1.12	37.24 ± 0.77	44.76 ± 0.98
	P	46.80 ± 1.81	91.38 ± 1.20	51.72 ± 1.99	96.34 ± 0.73	86.56 ± 0.66
RDF	I	45.54 ± 1.47	81.36 ± 1.04	48.28 ± 1.51	86.83 ± 1.48	75.23 ± 1.76
	C	39.75 ± 1.68	83.16 ± 1.11	45.27 ± 1.07	89.02 ± 0.64	77.58 ± 0.99
	P	32.73 ± 4.43	71.31 ± 1.55	33.60 ± 3.37	96.39 ± 0.79	85.95 ± 1.52
SVM-Linear	I	25.44 ± 2.39	41.61 ± 2.07	20.92 ± 2.01	87.96 ± 0.87	76.62 ± 0.80
	C	23.84 ± 1.39	45.56 ± 4.20	20.21 ± 3.70	87.84 ± 1.05	73.89 ± 0.64
	P	40.13 ± 1.47	93.48 ± 1.68	46.60 ± 1.59	**98.06 ± 0.46**	88.26 ± 1.23
SVM-RBF	I	35.11 ± 1.27	75.47 ± 1.38	34.05 ± 1.40	**90.72 ± 1.35**	77.46 ± 1.49
	C	30.17 ± 1.13	79.56 ± 1.22	35.69 ± 0.99	**92.85 ± 0.63**	79.40 ± 0.69

- The intermediate intensity images are generally lower in contrast as compared to positive intensity images. The experiments performed on the three datasets (positive, intermediate, and combined) clearly validate our assertion that the experiments should be conducted independently on images of two intensity classes, positive and intermediate. For instance, the classification accuracy of the best performing combination of texture features and SVM-RBF classifier differs by a significant 8% on positive and intermediate subsets when the classifier is trained independently on both the subsets. Overall results from Table 4 indicate that cell image classification for images pertaining to the intermediate intensity set is difficult as compared to the positive intensity set.
- The results further indicate that cells across different types of cell patterns have similar shape and size thereby increasing the inter-class similarity. On the other hand, grayscale distribution within different cell classes vary significantly thus increasing the inter-class variability. Therefore, the features based on grayscale values such as statistical moments of pixel values, texture features, and histograms of HOG and LBP representations yield better performance for cell image classification than boundary, shape, and size features.

- Texture features outperform all other feature categories by at least 5% for the positive intensity set and 13% for the intermediate intensity set. The second best results are provided by Statistical and HoDesc features using SVM-RBF classifier for positive and intermediate sets respectively. As discussed earlier, though the images pertaining to intermediate intensity set are difficult to categorize, texture features yield significant improvement in classifying these images.
- Among the four classification techniques used for experiments, SVM with RBF kernel yields the highest accuracy for HEp-2 cell image classification. The results of RDF and SVM-RBF are comparable with RDF providing the second best classification accuracy.
- To analyze the performance according to cell classes, the classification accuracy of texture features among different types of cell patterns is analyzed in Fig. 3. It can be observed that the classification performance for positive intensity images is higher than intermediate intensity images among all six cell patterns. Fig. 3 also shows that the cells of Golgi type are the most difficult to identify.

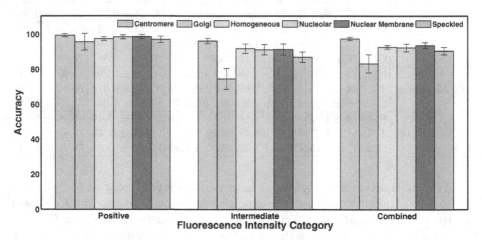

Fig. 3. Accuracies for different cell classes using combination of texture features and SVM classifier with RBF kernel

The above analysis illustrates the impact of different kinds of features for HEp-2 cell image classification. It can be observed from Table 3 that the size of texture and HoDesc features is large. Therefore, the constituent elements of these two features are further analyzed to determine whether any of the elements alone is sufficient for classification. In this research, among several available texture representations such as SGLD (Spatial Gray Level Dependence), GLRL (Gray Level Run Length), wavelet, and Laws features, SGLD, GLRL, and Laws features are used to derive the texture properties of cell images. Among the HoDesc features, HoG and LBP features are analyzed. As shown in Table 5, in case of descriptor based features, HOG and LBP features show similar performance.

Table 5. Comparative analysis of different feature sets used among texture and descriptor based feature categories

Classifier		HoDesc		Texture		
		HOG	LBP	GLRL	Laws	SGLD
kNN	P	70.48 ± 0.82	71.70 ± 2.10	75.16 ± 1.75	93.82 ± 0.67	82.81 ± 1.30
	I	49.38 ± 1.41	56.74 ± 2.02	44.72 ± 1.62	68.21 ± 2.72	45.03 ± 1.32
	C	54.75 ± 1.28	59.79 ± 1.44	54.05 ± 1.58	76.20 ± 0.74	58.02 ± 0.93
Naïve Bayes	P	73.88 ± 1.78	70.15 ± 1.32	50.23 ± 1.54	58.49 ± 1.66	45.67 ± 1.51
	I	47.70 ± 1.57	42.25 ± 1.48	32.88 ± 1.22	34.81 ± 2.99	20.13 ± 1.09
	C	45.60 ± 0.91	38.27 ± 1.09	34.61 ± 0.67	37.83 ± 0.52	28.80 ± 0.72
RDF	P	83.21 ± 1.13	80.22 ± 1.35	82.27 ± 1.87	96.23 ± 0.53	85.33 ± 0.97
	I	69.47 ± 1.13	67.80 ± 1.71	52.32 ± 1.59	85.77 ± 1.35	54.54 ± 2.45
	C	72.36 ± 1.27	70.51 ± 1.00	61.42 ± 1.26	88.81 ± 0.57	63.53 ± 1.77
SVM-Linear	P	81.39 ± 1.51	79.15 ± 1.40	77.23 ± 1.57	94.68 ± 0.75	84.37 ± 1.33
	I	67.83 ± 1.01	62.96 ± 1.52	39.33 ± 1.18	81.06 ± 1.12	49.75 ± 2.98
	C	66.84 ± 1.28	61.24 ± 1.13	47.34 ± 0.81	83.29 ± 1.10	59.66 ± 0.98
SVM-RBF	P	86.30 ± 1.22	84.21 ± 1.47	84.91 ± 1.20	$\mathbf{97.90 \pm 0.71}$	90.81 ± 1.00
	I	73.19 ± 1.50	71.86 ± 1.51	49.96 ± 1.95	$\mathbf{90.49 \pm 1.30}$	58.45 ± 1.28
	C	76.23 ± 1.24	74.39 ± 1.37	61.96 ± 1.24	$\mathbf{92.42 \pm 0.59}$	69.23 ± 1.65

A feature level concatenation of HOG and LBP features helps in further enhancing the classification performance for both positive as well as intermediate intensity classes. On the other hand, comparative results suggest that the accuracy of texture features is primarily attributed to Laws features which not only outperform all other texture features, their performance is significantly higher than any other category of features. The overall analysis shows that the combination of Laws texture features and SVM with RBF kernel yield the best performance to identify the cell patterns in HEp-2 cell images. The combination achieves a classification accuracy of 97.90% and 90.49% for positive and intermediate intensity classes respectively.

4   Conclusion and Future Work

In this research, the features for HEp-2 cell image classification are classified among five broad categories: boundary, shape and size, statistical, texture, and descriptor. This categorization helps in understanding the discriminating properties of HEp-2 cells among six pattern classes, namely, Centromere, Golgi, Homogeneous, Nucleolar, Nuclear Membrane, and Speckled. The performance of feature categories are evaluated using four different classifiers and 10 fold cross validation. The results on the ICIP 2013 HEp-2 Cell Image Classification Contest training dataset show that the texture features yield the best classification performance. The results further demonstrate that within texture features, Laws features alone are sufficient for classification. The comparative results also validate our assertion that the classification results of positive and intermediate intensity cell images should be reported independently. Currently, we are exploring (1) other feature extraction algorithms such as Gabor filters and wavelet transforms and (2) fusion and feature selection paradigms to further enhance the classification accuracy.

References

1. Wiik, A.S., Høier-Madsen, M., Forslid, J., Charles, P., Meyrowitsch, J.: Antinuclear antibodies: a contemporary nomenclature using HEp-2 cells. Journal of Autoimmunity 35(3), 276–290 (2010)
2. NCCLS: Center for disease control - quality assurance for the indirect immunofluorescence test for autoantibodies to nuclear antigen (IF-ANA): Approved guideline. LA2-A 16(11) (1996)
3. Wiliem, A., Wong, Y., Sanderson, C., Hobson, P., Chen, S., Lovell, B.: Classification of human epithelial type 2 cell indirect immunofluoresence images via codebook based descriptors. In: WACV, pp. 95–102 (2013)
4. Ersoy, I., Bunyak, F., Peng, J., Palaniappan, K.: HEp-2 cell classification in IIF images using shareboost. In: ICPR, pp. 3362–3365 (2012)
5. Ghosh, S., Chaudhary, V.: Feature analysis for automatic classification of HEp-2 florescence patterns: Computer-aided diagnosis of auto-immune diseases. In: ICPR, pp. 174–177 (2012)
6. Li, K., Yin, J., Lu, Z., Kong, X., Zhang, R., Liu, W.: Multiclass boosting SVM using different texture features in HEp-2 cell staining pattern classification. In: ICPR, pp. 170–173 (2012)
7. Iannello, G., Onofri, L., Soda, P.: A bag of visual words approach for centromere and cytoplasmic staining pattern classification on HEp-2 images. In: CBMS, pp. 1–6 (2012)
8. Ali, W., Piro, P., Giampaglia, D., Pourcher, T., Barlaud, M.: Biological cells classification using bio-inspired descriptor in a boosting k-NN framework. In: CBMS, pp. 1–6 (2012)
9. Theodorakopoulos, I., Kastaniotis, D., Economou, G., Fotopoulos, S.: HEp-2 cells classification via fusion of morphological and textural features. In: BIBE, pp. 689–694 (2012)
10. Cordelli, E., Soda, P.: Color to grayscale staining pattern representation in IIF. In: CBMS, pp. 1–6 (2011)
11. Foggia, P., Percannella, G., Soda, P., Vento, M.: Early experiences in mitotic cells recognition on HEp-2 slides. In: CBMS, pp. 38–43 (2010)
12. Soda, P., Iannello, G.: Aggregation of classifiers for staining pattern recognition in antinuclear autoantibodies analysis. IEEE TITB 13(3), 322–329 (2009)
13. Hobson, P., Percannella, G., Vento, M., Wiliem, A.: Competition on cells classification by fluorescent image analysis. In: ICIP (2013),
   http://nerone.diiie.unisa.it/contest-icip-2013/index.shtml
14. Boucheron, L.E.: Object- and Spatial-Level Quantitative Analysis of Multispectral Histopathology Images for Detection and Characterization of Cancer. PhD thesis, UCSB (2008)
15. Haralick, R.M., Shanmugam, K., Dinstein, I.: Textural features for image classification. IEEE T-SMC (6), 610–621 (1973)
16. Tang, X.: Texture information in run-length matrices. IEEE TIP 7(11), 1602–1609 (1998)
17. Laws, K.I.: Textured image segmentation. Technical report, USC (1980)
18. Chang, C.C., Lin, C.J.: LIBSVM: A library for support vector machines. ACM T-IST 2(3), 1–27 (2011)

A 2.5D Colon Wall Flattening Model
for CT-Based Virtual Colonoscopy

Huafeng Wang[1,2], Lihong Li[3], Hao Han[1], Rui Shi[4], Bowen Song[1], Hao Peng[4],
Yan Liu[1], Xianfeng Gu[4], Yunhong Wang[5], and Zhengrong Liang[1,*]

[1] Dept. of Radiology, Stony Brook University, Stony Brook, NY 11794, USA
[2] School of Software, Beihang University Of Beijing, China, 10083
[3] Department of Engineering Science & Physics,
City University of New York, College of Staten Island, Staten Island, NY 10314, USA
[4] Dept. of Computer Science, Stony Brook University, Stony Brook, NY 11794, USA
[5] School of Computer Science, Beihang University Of Beijing, China, 10083
jerome.liang@sunysb.edu

Abstract. Conformal mapping for Computed Tomography Colonogra-phy(CTC) provides a two-dimensional (2D) representations for the original three-dimensional (3D) colon wall. Based on the flattening results of the colon, efforts have been devoted toward its applications for some medical uses, such as colon registration, Taniae Coli (TC) detection and Haustral folds segmentation, and so on. Though, the previously-used conformal mapping-based flattening methods can preserve the angle or area on the wall, the 2D flattening result still limits itself to provide more accurate information contained on the original colon wall due to its' lack of the undulating topography. In view of this limitation of the 2D flattening model, a novelty 2.5D approach was proposed in this paper. The new approach was tested for two of the many applications, i.e., the detections of Haustral folds and TCs. Experimental results revealed its validity in these applications.

Keywords: Conformal mapping, 2.5D representation, colon wall, medical imaging, Computed Tomography Colonography.

1 Introduction

According to the recent statistics from American Cancer Society (ACS) [1], colorectal cancer ranks the third most common occurrence of both cancer deaths and new cancer cases for both men and women in the United States. Early detection and removal of colonic polyps prior to their malignant transformation can effectively decrease the incidence of colon cancer [2]. As a new minimally-invasive screening technique, Computed Tomographic Colonography (CTC) or CT-based virtual colonoscopy (VC) has shown several advantages over the traditional optical colonoscopy (OC). In surgical practice, Teniae Coli (TC) and Haustral Folds, are of great significance for assisting physicians to find and analyze polyps in the colon due to their characteristics.

---

* Corresponding author.

G. Wu et al. (Eds.): MLMI 2013, LNCS 8184, pp. 203–210, 2013.
© Springer International Publishing Switzerland 2013

They also play an important role in the colon registration and synchronized virtual navigation of supine and prone CT scans [3]. However, they are often insufficiently observed as a result of the complicated colon structure in CTC. The approach of flattening the 3D wall into 2D image is believed to be much effective for increasing the field of view (FOV) and providing supplementary information to the endoscopic views [4]. Unfortunately, the 2D image will lose or distort some information. Furthermore, the height variances are usually lost, thus preventing examiners from judging the abnormity of tissue. Hence, we developed a 2.5D colon wall flattening model which will best describe not only the whole map of colon but also the details of neighborhood of the components on the colon wall. The rest of this paper is organized as follows. The new colon flattening methodology is presented in Section 2. Two application scenarios with implementation is shown in section 3. Finally, conclusions are drawn in section 4.

2   Method

2.1   Overview of the Pipeline of 2.5D Colon Flattening Model

For the acquired CTC datasets, the first task is to segment the data volume and extract the colon wall as a volumetric mucosa (VM). This is achieved by a statistical maximum a posteriori expectation-maximization (MAP-EM) algorithm [5]. Considering the use of positive-contrast tagging agents to opacify the residual fecal for differentiation of the materials from colon wall, partial volume effects (PVE) became severe and the thickness of the VM varied dramatically. Because there exists PVE in CT scans which make the surface of colon wall more implicit, a levelset based shrinkage method will help to evolve a much better approximated mucosa surface inner the colon wall. In order to extract a polygonal mesh of an iso-surface from the 3D voxels, a marching cube process is introduced into the pipeline. Consequently, a more vividly described colon wall will be presented. In order to build a bridge connecting the 3D wall with the 2.5D morphological map, an inner wall cylinder model will be exploited and a distance map will be created according to the shortest distance map measured between the voxelized points and the given cylindrical surface. Hence, the 2.5D map of colon wall will exhibit geometric features which particularly conserves the original angle and the morphological shape to full extent. Fig 1 illustrates the whole pipeline of the 2.5D flattening model.

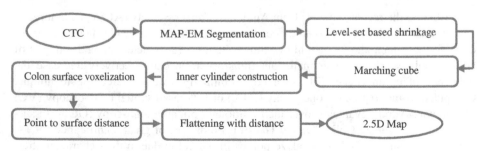

Fig. 1. The pipeline of the new method

2.2   Level-Set Based Shrinkage to Initialize the Layer of Colon Wall(Shrinkage)

The starting layer (SL) is of much importance to describe the contour of the colon wall. We introduce the level set method [6] to retrieve a better SL, from which we build the distance transform to distinguish different topological structures. Compared with other methods, it is able to combine region-based information and edge-based information together, make use of global information and local information simultaneously and control the geometric property of level set function easily. Straightforwardly, it should reside inside the outermost and innermost layers, where the variation of CT intensities across the different layers remains relatively stable. Furthermore, the gradient of image intensity is used to construct the stopping criteria to stop the curve evolution by

$$\phi_t = \delta(\phi) \cdot \frac{\lambda}{1+\|\nabla I\|} \{\alpha_0 A + \alpha_1 B + \alpha_2 C + \alpha_3 \mathrm{div}(\nabla\phi/\|\nabla\phi\|)\} \tag{1}$$

where ϕ is the Lipschitz function, and I represents the image intensity. The two superscripts in and out indicate the regions where $\Phi>0$ and $\Phi\leq0$ respectively, while A, B and C represent the square of the variance of the mean intensity values of voxels in the whole image, the narrow band and the local neighborhood respectively. The notations λ, α_0, α_1, α_2 and α_3 are constants used to control the influence of each term, and ∇ represents the gradient operator. The div($*$) is the curvature of Lipschitz function, which control the smoothness of the zero level set surface.

Once the above evolution procedure stops (Eq. (1) converges), the resulted zero level set surface, where $\Phi_t=0$, indicates a layer between the outermost and innermost layers where the variation of CT intensities changes slightly across different layers. As a result, we will get a series of voxels which represent the SL of the colon wall. Fig.2 illustrates the colon mesh after the marching cube process.

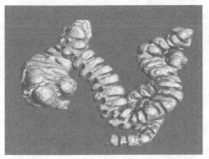

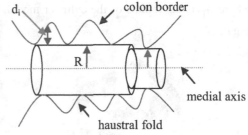

Fig. 2. SL mesh after marching cube   **Fig. 3.** The cylinder model

2.3   Building Distance Map with a Cylinder Model

To build a reliable cylinder model, relying on which we calculate the distance map(as shown in Fig.3), we need to perform two things: (1) determination of the centerline (also known as medial or symmetric axis) inside of the colon lumen; (2) building a radial varying cylinder which is inscribed within the inner wall of the colon lumen. Several methods have been presented for centerline extraction for medical imaging [7]. Combined with the Fast Marching technique [9], an energy minimization formula is given as follows[8],

$$E_{medial-Axis}(C) = \int_{0=C^{-1}(p_0)}^{L=C^{-1}(p_1)} F(C(s))ds \tag{2}$$

where F(x) is a scalar filed, and C=C(s) (*s* being arc length)is the path(traced from two points p_0 and p_1) along which we look for the centerline. What we need to do is to minimize E. In this study, we employed a method to solve a nonlinear hyperbolic partial differential equation [10]. Let $|\nabla T(x)|=F(x)$, then we have,

$$T(x) = \min_{C \in \Gamma(p_0, x)} \left(\int_{0=C^{-1}(p_0)}^{s=C^{-1}(x)} F(C(s))ds \right) \tag{3}$$

where $\Gamma(p_0, x)$ is the set of all paths from p_0 to x. Since the scalar field $T(x)$ represents weighted geodesic distance to point p_0, the weighted geodesic paths are orthogonal to level sets of $T(x)$. Once the field of weighted geodesic distances has been found, the weighted geodesic path of interest is calculated by constructing a path from p_1 oriented as $\nabla T(x)$ in every point. The medial axis is a set of points, $C(\tilde{p})$, $\tilde{p} \in \Omega, \Omega$ stands for the colon object. Then the shortest distance between the points on the medial axis and the vertices on the colon surface ($\partial \Omega$) can be expressed as,

$$\{r_i = \min(d_i) \mid d_i = \sqrt{(\tilde{p}_j - v_i)^2}, \tilde{p}_j \in C(\tilde{p}), v_i \in \partial \Omega\} \tag{4}$$

where r_i is the radials of the cylinder model. a colon inscribed cylinder is shown in Fig 4.

Fig. 4. Illustration of the cylinder of colon(Different colors stands for the varying distance)

This constructed cylinder has its' own surface ($\partial \Omega''$), the Euclidean distance between the vertices on the colon surface and the surface of the cylinder will be further calculated as follows,

$$\{D_i = \min(z_i) \mid z_i = \sqrt{(v_i - l_j)^2}, v_i \in \partial\Omega, l_j \in \partial\Omega''\} \tag{5}$$

where l_j is a vertex on the $\partial\Omega''$, and v_i is a vertex on the $\partial\Omega$. The set of D, named distance map, will be further introduced in the following flattening process.

2.4 Improved Flattening Map Model of Colon Wall

In recent years, a number of methods have been proposed to map the colon surface to a plane or a sphere [11]. For best eliminating the limitations brought by 2D flattening image, we introduce the 2.5D flatten techniques. Given a colon surface Ω (as shown in Fig 2), with boundaries γ_0, γ_1, then we can,

(1) compute a Harmonic function f by solving the Dirichlet problem, such that: $|\Delta f \equiv 0, |f|_{\gamma_0} \equiv 0, f|_{\gamma_1} \equiv 1$, and compute the closed 1-form τ, which denotes :

$$d\tau = 0, \text{ and } \int_{\gamma_0} \tau = 1 \tag{6}$$

where d is the exterior differential operator;
(2) compute a function g: $\Omega \to R$, such that,

$$\xi(\tau + dg) = 0, \text{ and } \xi = *d* \tag{7}$$

where * is the Hodge star operator and $\tau + dg$ is a harmonic 1-form;
(3) let $\omega = \tau + dg$, and calculate the Hodge star of ω, which takes the form

$^*\omega = Cdf$ and C equals to the harmonic energy of f: $C = \int_\Omega |\nabla f|^2$;

(4) select a shortest path γ, which connects γ_0 with γ_1, and slice Ω along γ to get $\overline{\Omega}$. Given a base vertex v_0 ($v_0 \in \overline{\Omega}$), for any vertex $v (v \in \overline{\Omega})$,

$$\varphi(v) = \int_{v_0}^v \omega + \sqrt{-1} * \omega, \tag{8}$$

where φ is the flattening mapping and $\omega + {}^*\omega\sqrt{-1}$ is Holomorphic 1-form.

Along the integration path which may be chosen arbitrarily on $\overline{\Omega}$, we finally got the mapping between any vertex (x,y,z) in 3D and the new vertex(x', y', z')(**Note**: z' equals to the corresponding D_i for vertex (x, y, z)) .

3   Applications

The new 2.5D flattening model can be applied to the following:(1) To improve navigation experience in VC,(2) to help detecting haustral folds on the colon wall, and (3) to find out the taniae coli line of colon. In this paper, we performed two applications: haustral folds detection& segmentation and TC finding.

3.1   Haustral Folds Detection and Segmentation

In previously reported literature, most research methods in the field mainly focused on fold detection, rather than fold segmentation. For example, in [12, 13], folds were detected by thresholding the curvatures in three-dimensional (3D) colon representation, while in [14], the detection task was fulfilled by using a Gabor filter on a 2D unfolded colon representation. A local elevation histogram (LEH) method is proposed for the colonic folds detection or segmentation. The main idea is divided into four steps: (1) dividing the whole flattening colon along the colon wall into several equal parts (experimentally the length of each unit equals to one eighth of the narrowest haustral fold); (2) calculating the average distribution of the elevation(local elevation) along the direction parallel to the walking direction of colon wall; (3) checking the minimum elevation value (MinEv): if (MinEv) is more than the maximum elevation value (MaxEv), then neglect the current part, else if (4) using the split lines (red bold, as shown in Fig.6) to determine which part belongs to haustral folds. It should be noted the threshold (the value on the L) is manually obtained by creating a cutting plane.

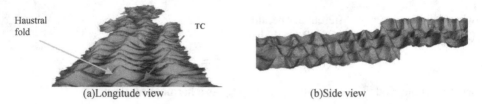

Haustral
fold

TC

(a)Longitude view   (b)Side view

Fig. 5. The 2.5D effects of the flattening model

3.2   Teniae Coli Extraction for Colon

Teniae coli (TC) are three approximately 8-mm-wide longitudinal smooth muscle bands in the colon wall. In previously reported literature, approaches for extraction the Teniae coli can be categorized into two groups, manual drawing and automatic extraction [12, 13, 14]. As far as the automatic approaches to be concerned, most of previous researchers suggested to use curvature filter or gabor filter [14] for surface analysis to get the TC lines on the colon. However, TC usually appear to be with the middle height between the haustra and the haustral folds. Fortunately, this phenomenon can be apparently found in the proposed 2.5D flattened colon (as shown in Fig. 5). Therefore, extracting the TC lines equals to finding the shortest geodesic path on the 2.5 D flattened map. In practice, we can randomly pick up three arbitrary vertices along the top edge of the colon flattened mesh(as shown in Fig.7). Equally, we will choose four vertices at the other end of the colon.

3.3   Evaluation

To evaluate the haustral folds segmentation and the TC extraction, ground truth was established from 15 patient scans by experts' drawing of the fold boundaries. According to the suggestions from experts, a haustral fold would be detected if more than 50% of its area has been detected. As we mentioned before, the maximum elevation value(MEV) needs to be manually determined according to the position of the cutting plane. Experimental result shows that the different case requires different MEV to get the good performance(as shown in Fig.8). In practice, the MEV ranges from 0.28 to 0.51 for the 2.5D flattening results. Fig.8 illustrates the sensitivity which varies with the MEV. The average detection true positive(TP) rate is 93.2%, which is slightly better than the reported in[15]. While for the TC extraction, in most cases, the new approach can draw the approximate TC lines for the colon wall with no much deviation.

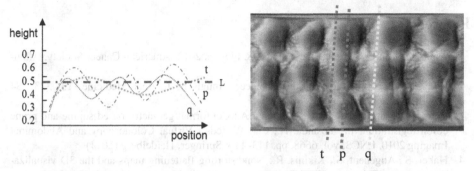

Fig. 6. The smoothed profile lines and an experimental result of colon fold segmentation

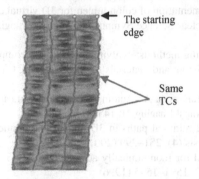

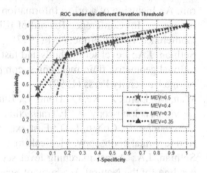

Fig. 7. The result of TC extraction   **Fig. 8.** The ROC under different MEV

4   Conclusion

In this study, we presented a novel 2.5D flattening model to depict the colon wall more comprehensively. The innovation of this work lies in: (1) finding more accurate starting layer of the colon wall and shrink it to single voxel layer for further geometry analysis; (2) presenting a new approach to calculate the approximate undulation of the inner colon wall; (3) building the elevation distance map of the inner colon wall, which can be considered as a new characteristic of the colon wall; (4) coupling with the flattening model to create a completely new view of the colon wall which bring a new vision for colon analysis; (5) providing a new direction for developing approaches for the haustral folds & TC finding based on the new proposed model.

Then, we further applied the 2.5D flattening model for haustral folds detection and segmentation as well as TCs finding. Experimental results have shown the feasibility of the proposed 2.5D flattening model for CT-based virtual colonoscopy. Further validation based on a large database is under progress.

Acknowledgement. This work was partially supported by the NIH/NCI under Grant #CA143111, #CA082402, and the PSC-CUNY award #65230-00 43.

References

1. American Cancer Society: Cancer Facts & Figures 2012. American Cancer Society, Atlanta (2012)
2. Eddy, D.: Screening for colorectal cancer. Annals of Internal Medicine 113, 373–384 (1990)
3. Zeng, W., Marino, J., Gu, X., Kaufman, A.: Conformal geometry based supine and prone colon registration. In: Yoshida, H., Cai, W. (eds.) Virtual Colonoscopy and Abdominal Imaging 2010. LNCS, vol. 6668, pp. 113–119. Springer, Heidelberg (2011)
4. Haker, S., Angenent, S., Kikinis, R.: Nondistorting flattening maps and the 3D visualization of colon CT images. IEEE Transactions on Medical Imaging 19, 665–670 (2000)
5. Liang, Z., Yang, F., Wax, M., Li, J., You, J., Kaufman, A., Hong, L., Li, H., Viswambharan, A.: Inclusion of a priori information in segmentation of colon lumen for 3D virtual colonoscopy. In: Conference Record of IEEE Nuclear Science Symposium-Medical Imaging Conference, Albuquerque, NM (1997)
6. Sethian, J.A.: Level set methods and fast marching methods: evolving interfaces in computational geometry, fluid mechanics, computer vision, and materials science, 2nd edn. Cambridge University Press (1999)
7. Wan, M., Liang, Z., Ke, Q., Hong, L., Bitter, I., Kaufman, A.: Automatic centerline extraction for virtual colonoscopy. IEEE Transactions on Medical Imaging 21, 1450–1460 (2002)
8. Deschamps, T., Cohen, L.D.: Fast extraction of minimal paths in 3D images and application to virtual endoscopy. Medical Image Analysis (4), 281–299 (2001)
9. Sethian, J.A.: A fast marching level set method for monotonically advancing fronts. Proceedings of the Natural Academy of Sciences 93, 1591–1595 (1996)
10. Antiga, L.: Patient-specific modeling of geometry and blood flow in large arteries. PhD thesis, Politecnico di Milano (2003)
11. Hong, W., Gu, X., Qiu, F., Jin, M., Kaufman, A.: Conformal virtual colon flattening. In: Proceedings of the 2006 ACM Symposium on Solid and Physical Modeling, pp. 85–93 (2006)
12. Huang, A., Roy, D.A., Summers, R.M., Franaszek, M., Petrick, N., Choi, J.R., Pickhardt, P.J.: Teniae coli-based circumfe-rential localization system for CT colonography: Feasability study. Radiology 243(2), 551–560 (2007)
13. Lamy, J., Summers, R.M.: Teniæ coli detection from colon surface: Extraction of anatomical markers for virtual colonoscopy. In: Bebis, G., et al. (eds.) ISVC 2007, Part I. LNCS, vol. 4841, pp. 199–207. Springer, Heidelberg (2007)
14. Wei, Z., Yao, J., Wang, S., Summers, R.M.: Teniae coli extraction in human colon for computed tomographic colonography images. In: Yoshida, H., Cai, W. (eds.) Virtual Colonoscopy and Abdominal Imaging 2010. LNCS, vol. 6668, pp. 98–104. Springer, Heidelberg (2011)
15. Zhu, H., Barish, M., Pickhardt, P., Liang, Z.: Haustral fold segmentation with curvature-guided level set evolution. IEEE Trans. Biomed. Engineering 60(2), 321–331 (2013)

Augmenting Auto-context
with Global Geometric Features
for Spinal Cord Segmentation

Jeremy Kawahara[1], Chris McIntosh[1,2], Roger Tam[3], and Ghassan Hamarneh[1]

[1]Medical Image Analysis Lab., Simon Fraser University, Burnaby, Canada
{jkawahar,cmcintos,hamarneh}@sfu.ca
[2]Princess Margaret Cancer Centre, University Health Network, Toronto, Canada
[3]MS/MRI Research Group, University of British Columbia, Vancouver, Canada
roger.tam@ubc.ca

Abstract. Anatomical shape variations are typically difficult to model and parametric or hand-crafted models can lead to ill-fitting segmentations. This difficulty can be addressed with a framework like auto-context, that learns to jointly detect and regularize a segmentation. However, mis-segmentation can still occur when a desired structure, such as the spinal cord, has few locally distinct features. High-level knowledge at a global scale (e.g. an MRI contains a single connected spinal cord) is needed to regularize these candidate segmentations. To encode high-level knowledge, we propose to augment the auto-context framework with global geometric features extracted from the detected candidate shapes. Our classifier then learns these high-level rules and rejects falsely detected shapes. To validate our method we segment the spinal cords from 20 MRI volumes composed of patients with and without multiple sclerosis and demonstrate improvements in accuracy, speed, and manual effort required when compared to state-of-the-art methods.

1 Introduction

Studies of multiple sclerosis (MS) show that spinal cord atrophy strongly contributes to the physical disability of a patient, motivating the need for quantifiable spinal cord measurements to evaluate the progression of pathology and the effectiveness of therapies [8]. Spinal cord segmentation is an important first step to extracting these measurements. However, segmenting the cord is challenging as it has an irregular cross-sectional shape whose signal and diameter change over the length of the cord. The image can be polluted by noise, suffer from motion artefacts, and its boundaries can be poorly defined where the cord contacts the spinal canal wall. When scanned at the most common resolution of 1 mm^3, the cord also contains a high number of partial volume voxels relative to the total size of the cord, which need to be accounted for in order to accurately measure the cord's true shape and volume [10]. Manual segmentation is a challenging and time consuming process that suffers from operator variability, making automated methods desirable. To address these challenges, several approaches have been proposed for automating spinal cord segmentation.

G. Wu et al. (Eds.): MLMI 2013, LNCS 8184, pp. 211–218, 2013.
© Springer International Publishing Switzerland 2013

McIntosh et al. [6] segmented the cord using locally optimal 3D deformable organisms guided by a Hessian-based filter designed to adapt to the spinal cord's varying elliptical and tubular structure. They later extended this approach to use the cord's medial axis (found by a user-guided live-wire method) to guide the spinal crawler's cross-sectional shape fitting [7]. Horsfield et al. [3] fit an active surface model to the spinal cord and had the user specify the cord center-line by placing points on representative slices. Chen et al. [1] used a deformable atlas-based registration combined with a topology preserving classification to fully automate a crisp segmentation of the cord. In previous work [4], we represented the spinal cord's axial shape variations using probabilistic principal component analysis (PCA) and found the globally optimal path in 6D (three spatial and three principal components weights) between two user specified seed points.

Auto-context, proposed by Tu and Bai [11], is a general iterative learning framework used for segmentation that jointly learns the appearance and regularization distributions where the predicted class labels (the context) of the previous iteration are used as input to the current iteration. Auto-context was shown to improve segmentation results [11]; however, if the surrounding local context is incorrect it may re-enforce an incorrect segmentation. This was addressed in the recent work by Kontschieder et al. [5] who used a geodesic distance transform in an auto-context based segmentation approach to incorporate long range spatial context. Similarly, we extend auto-context to learn high-level problem specific information (global context), but rather than considering the geodesic distance, our probability mask represents distinct candidate shapes and encodes their relations to each other to encourage a single connected spinal cord.

Specifically, we propose to extract geometric features (e.g. volume) from the candidate shapes created in each iteration of auto-context where a shape is defined as a distinct region of connected components composed of the same class label. Features from the candidate shapes are extracted and compared with each other to give global information about the other candidate shapes and are included in the auto-context framework. Thus the class label for a specific voxel is conditioned not only on its appearance and surrounding labels, but also on the geometric features of the shape it belongs to relative to other candidate shapes. We demonstrate that augmenting auto-context with global geometric context improves the original auto-context algorithm and results in superior spinal cord segmentations when compared to a more traditional approach with hand-crafted gradient terms and a PCA shape prior.

2   Methods

This section introduces auto-context, describes our global geometric features, explains our auto-context set-up, and outlines the training and testing processes.

Image Segmentation and Auto-context. We can think of image segmentation as a voxel labelling problem where given an image $X = (x_1, \ldots, x_n)$ composed of n voxels, we want to find a set of labels such that each voxel i is assigned a corresponding label, $Y = (y_1, \ldots, y_n)$. The label y_i can take on one of k possible values. Our objective is to find the optimal configuration Y^* out of the possible segmentations Y such that it maximizes the probability given the observed image, $Y^* = \text{argmax}_Y \, p(Y|X)$.

One approach to find Y^* is to apply Bayes' rule with a fixed $p(X)$ to give $p(Y|X) \propto p(X|Y)p(Y)$ where $p(X|Y)$ represents the likelihood of the image given a segmentation, and $p(Y)$ is the probability of that segmentation occurring. Hand-crafted data-terms and/or parametric models with restrictions on complexity and built-in assumptions (e.g. Gaussian) are often used [4,6,7].

Another approach is to directly model $p(Y|X)$. If we assume that the labels $y_i, i = 1, \ldots, n$ are independent and are conditioned only on a small patch of image voxels centred around the ith voxel, denoted as $N(i)$, then this can be modelled by $p(y_i|X_{N(i)})$, where X_i returns the intensities at voxel i. A discriminate model (e.g. decision forest [2]) can be used to learn this distribution; however, it does not consider the class labels of surrounding voxels. One way to model the interdependence of neighbouring labels is with conditional random fields where the class label y_i is dependent on a neighbouring class label y_j [9]. While this more closely approximates the true $p(Y|X)$ it still makes the assumption that each class label y_i is only dependent on a very small neighbourhood.

The auto-context model seeks to condition over a larger area of surrounding class labels to provide more "context" [11]. This is accomplished by introducing an iterative time-step t and training a series of classifiers using the discriminative probability (the classification confidence) map of the previous classification M^{t-1} where $M^t = (m_1^t, \ldots, m_n^t)$. Each vector m_i^t represents the probabilities of voxel i belonging to one of the k possible class labels, $m_i = [p(y_i = 1), \ldots, p(y_i = k)]$. The initial class probability map M^0 is set to have uniform values. At time t, a classifier is trained to predict the true class label y_i given the image patch $X_{N(i)}$ and the context information $M^{t-1}(i)$ where M is centred at voxel i. Once the classifier is trained, the new probability map M^t is used in the next iteration $(t+1)$ and the algorithm repeats until M converges. The final output is a series of learned probability distributions,

$$m_i^t = p^t(y_i|X_{N(i)}, M^{t-1}(i)). \tag{1}$$

In testing, a novel image has the same features extracted and goes through the iterative classification process using the learned probability distributions p^t.

This formulation does not capture high-level information about the entire shape that the pixel belongs to nor does it consider the interaction among other candidate shapes. If we simply increase the size of $N(i)$ we increase the dimensionality of the feature space which can decrease the efficiency of our classifier. Thus this formulation is not well suited to capture high-level knowledge such as that the spinal cord is a single connected structure of a particular size.

Global Geometric Features. We propose to augment auto-context with global geometric features. At iteration t, instead of only using the previous probability map M^{t-1}, we also extract features from the candidate shapes found within M^{t-1} and compare these features to each other to capture global information. More formally, we define a function $C(M, i)$ that takes the maximum a posteriori (MAP) class label of M to form a candidate shape S_q based on the regions of connected component with the same class label, $S_q = C(M, i)$. This divides M into Q distinct non-overlapping connected regions with the same class label, where each distinct region represents a candidate shape S_q (Fig. 1c,g). The shape S_q is composed of indices into the probability map M and the index for voxel i belongs to a single shape, $i \in S_q$.

We define and utilize a single global geometric feature that encourages our method to detect only a single connected spinal cord. For voxel i we extract a feature $f(S_q, M)$ from the shape that i belongs to and compute the ratio between the current and the largest shape feature from the Q candidate shapes,

$$\phi(M, i) = \frac{f(C(M, i), M)}{\max(f(S_1, M), \ldots, f(S_Q, M))}. \tag{2}$$

The feature we extract, $f(S_q, M)$, gives us an indication of the size and label confidence of the component being considered,

$$f(S_q, M) = \sum_{j \in S_q} M(j) \tag{3}$$

where the iterator j sums the probabilities belonging to shape S_q. If $\phi(M, i)$ returns a value of 1, then this indicates that voxel i belongs to the largest probable shape out of all the candidate shapes. We augment the previous auto-context model (1) with our global geometric feature ϕ,

$$m_i^t = p^t(y_i | X_{N(i)}, M_{N(i)}^{t-1}, \phi(M^{t-1}, i)). \tag{4}$$

This model considers *intensity information*, *local context*, and the purposed *global features* about the candidate shapes and the relations between them.

Auto-context Setup and Feature Design. The original auto-context work used probabilistic boosting trees as the discriminate classifier, but other classifiers can be used [11]. We chose to use decision forests for our discriminative model due to their ability to generalize well to unseen data, handle both classification and regression, learn a distribution, and provide a probabilistic output [2]. This probabilistic score m_i is particularly important because it gives us an indication of the probability of being a member of the class by computing the percentage of observations of this class in a tree leaf averaged over all trees.

The neighbourhood of the ith voxel, $N(i)$, is computed using a simple radial pattern where we sample those voxels that are the immediate neighbours (8 in 2D, 26 in 3D) of voxel i and those that are three voxels along the ray away from voxel i (Fig. 1e). This densely samples points close to our ith voxel and sparsely samples voxels further away which helps keep the size of the feature vector relatively small to allow for faster run-times. We use a 52 neighbour 3D version of the neighbourhood shown in Fig. 1e. To compute image appearance

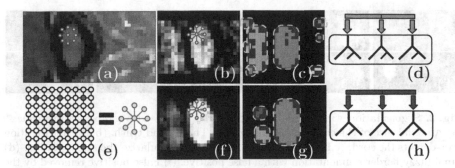

Fig. 1. An outline of our method: (a) The MRI data X. (b) The probability map M^t. (c) The MAP estimate of M produces distinct shapes (*dotted outline*) whose features $\phi(M, i)$ can be extracted. (d) Decision forest trained on a,b,c. (e) The neighbourhood $N(i)$ in 2D. (f) The probability map M^{t+1} produced by d. (g) Shapes computed from f. (h) Decision forest trained on a,f,g.

features we directly sample the neighbourhood intensities. In order to have an invariance to a shift in intensities and to capture the polarity (e.g. dark-to-bright transitions) we divide the intensity of neighbourhood voxels by the intensity of the voxel of interest, $X_{N(i)} = \{\frac{x_1}{x_i}, \dots, \frac{x_{52}}{x_i}\}$.

Training and Testing. Since the two patient groups should not be modelled as samples from a single distribution, we separate the multiple sclerosis (MS) from the non-MS patients to train two different classifiers specifically on the variability found in the two groups. We employ leave-one-out testing.

Our auto-context model is trained based on (4). Our training segmentations have a value of 1 inside the cord, 0 outside the cord, and a partial volume estimate for the cord's boundary. Each decision forest p^t is trained on a subset of this training data (2000 voxels from each volume) split between cord and background samples with the fuzzy border voxels omitted and samples of false positives explicitly included if they exist. To reduce over-fitting, for each training volume V, a separate decision forest that does not include the data from V is trained and used to predict the class membership of V. We repeat this process 5 times as we found that the results generally stabilized without further training (less than 0.01 difference in the mean Jaccard similarity index between consecutive iterations). The training produces a set of 5 trained decision forests, $\{p^1, \dots, p^5\}$.

As our ground truth segmentations have a fuzzy border based on partial volume estimation not modelled by the decision forests, we train a separate regression forest p^r to capture a two pixel thick partial volume border using the same intensity and probability features. It can take up to 6 hrs to fully train our auto-context model on a machine using 4 cores.

In the testing phase, a novel volume is classified by all the trained decision forests, $\{p^1, \dots, p^5\}$, in series. We take the maximum a posterior of our final classified volume M^5 and use the regression forest trained on border partial volumes p^r to produce our final segmentation (Fig. 2d,e).

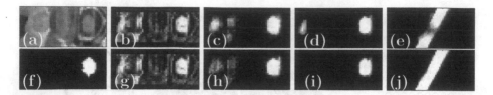

Fig. 2. Segmentation without global features *row 1*, and with global features *row 2*. (a) An axial slice of the cropped spinal cord. (f) The ground truth. (b,g) First iteration over-detects the cord. (c,h) Second iteration begins to regularize the segmentation. (d) Final fuzzy border segmentation with a false positive. (i) False positive removed by the global features. (e) Sagittal plane where weak appearance information splits the cord. (j) Corrected with global features.

3   Results

We validate our method using 20 MRI scans composed of 10 MS patients from a 1.5T scanner and 10 healthy patients from a 3.0T scanner (scans from different studies) with a voxel size of $0.976 \times 0.976 \times 1.000$ mm. Each scan was segmented by an expert who used an in-house method similar to that by Tench et al. [10]. We segment over vertebra C3 - C7 spanning a total of 80 slices.

To capture the partial volume effects (PVE) [10], we use a probabilistic version of the Jaccard index defined in [4] as, $J_{\text{PVE}}(A, G) = \frac{\sum_x \sum_y \min(A(x,y), G(x,y))}{\sum_x \sum_y \max(A(x,y), G(x,y))}$ where A and G are the automated and ground truth segmentations. To highlight our methods improved ability to remove false positives, we compute the Hausdorff distance which measures the furthest distance between the closest points in the two segmentations, $H = \max_{a \in A} (\min_{g \in G} D(a, g))$, where $D(a, g)$ computes the 3D Euclidean distance between points a, g. To measure the similarity between the automated and manual segmentation volumes, we calculate, $Vol_S = 1 - \min(|(|A|_1/|G|_1) - 1|, 1)$ which returns a 0% accuracy if the automated volume overestimates the expert volume by more than 200% [7]. To indicate if our automated method is a useful consistent substitute to the manual method for computing spinal cord volume, we compute the Pearson's correlation coefficient between the volumes of the automated and manual segmentations.

We perform three experiments to validate our method. Our **first experiment**, compares our auto-context augmented with global features method against a segmentation method we previously developed [4]. This previous work modelled the cord using probabilistic PCA and a hand-crafted gradient term. Our new results compare favourably, with a mean J_{PVE} of 0.878 (previous 0.784) for MS and 0.928 (previous 0.832) for non-MS scans, validated over the same dataset. Method [4] had been favourably compared with [6,7] on the same dataset.

Our **second experiment** is done to better understand our improvements and to highlight the problems with restricted parametric models and hand-crafted terms. To examine the effect that the restricted parametric PCA model has on the segmentation, we pass only the *ground truth* data (i.e. the cord is perfectly detected) to be regularized by the PCA model and A* optimizer of [4]. We find that even with the ground truth data, the restricted PCA model produces less accurate J_{PVE} results when compared to our auto-context model (Table 1 - row GT_{PCA}). To show the limitations of hand-crafted terms, we replace the gradient term of [4] with the spinal cord probability map M^1 (trained only on intensity features) as input to be regularized by the PCA model. This improves the segmentation results (Table 1 - row PCA_{M}) over what was originally reported in [4] indicating that the trained classifier is better at detecting the cord.

Our **third experiment** compares auto-context with and without global features. To compare to the approach of Tu and Bai [11], we initially omit the global feature and rely only on the image X and probability maps M as input to the auto-context model to segment the spinal cord (Table 1 - row XM). We then reintroduce the global feature $\phi(M, i)$ and show improved segmentation results (Table 1 - row $XM\phi$). This demonstrates that it is useful to augment auto-context with the global shape feature (i.e. improvement over [11]).

Table 1. GT_{PCA} uses the *ground truth* as input to [4] to demonstrate the best the restricted PCA model can achieve. PCA_{M} uses the spinal cord probability map M^1 as input to the PCA-based method of [4]. XM is auto-context with the image and probability map features. $XM\phi$ is auto-context with the image, probability and global geometric feature. We compute the mean values of the probabilistic Jaccard index ($\overline{J_{\mathrm{PVE}}}$), Hausdorff distance ($\overline{H}$) and area similarity ($\overline{Vol_{\mathrm{S}}}$) in voxels between our automated and ground segmentations over ten MS patients (*left columns*) and ten healthy (non-MS) patients (*right columns*). The Pearson's correlation coefficients (r) and p-values (p) between the automated and the ground truth segmentations are measured.

Case	J_{PVE}	H	Vol_{S}	r	p	J_{PVE}	H	Vol_{S}	r	p
GT_{PCA}	0.853	1.96	98.36	0.997	3×10^{-10}	0.881	1.57	98.97	0.993	9×10^{-9}
PCA_{M}	0.818	2.42	**96.38**	0.931	9×10^{-5}	0.847	2.04	93.65	0.896	4×10^{-4}
XM	0.856	15.35	94.50	0.932	9×10^{-5}	0.916	4.41	97.74	0.939	6×10^{-5}
$XM\phi$	**0.878**	**2.29**	96.32	**0.972**	3×10^{-6}	**0.928**	**1.82**	**98.87**	**0.991**	3×10^{-8}

We note that, once trained, our unoptimized implementation takes under 10 minutes to run for a novel cropped volume while [4] reported run-times between 1 and 5 hours for the same sized volumes. Also, while our method was tested on a cropped volume (Fig. 1a), it did not require any further user-input in contrast to [7,3], and it was capable of capturing the PVE not modelled in [1].

4   Conclusion

We have proposed to augment auto-context with global geometric features that can capture high-level information and relationships between the candidate shapes found within a segmentation. The auto-context approach jointly detects and regularizes a segmentation which allows for a flexible shape space capable of capturing subtle irregularities in the spinal cord. We have demonstrated improvements to accuracy and a lower running time when compared to a recently proposed method. Future work would validate our method over a larger spinal cord dataset with more diverse clinical parameters and investigate the development of other global geometric features.

Acknowledgements. JK, RT, and GH were partially supported by NSERC and Biogen Idec Canada. CM was supported by the Canadian Breast Cancer Foundation and the Canadian Cancer Society Research Institute.

References

1. Chen, M., Carass, A., Cuzzocreo, J., Bazin, P.L., Reich, D.S., Prince, J.L.: Topology preserving automatic segmentation of the spinal cord in magnetic resonance images. In: IEEE ISBI, pp. 1737–1740 (2011)
2. Criminisi, A., Shotton, J., Konukoglu, E.: Decision forests: A unified framework for classification, regression, density estimation, manifold learning and semi-supervised learning. Foundations and Trends® in Computer Graphics and Vision 7(2-3), 81–227 (2011)
3. Horsfield, M.A., Sala, S., Neema, M., Absinta, M., Bakshi, A., Sormani, M.P., Rocca, M.A., Bakshi, R., Filippi, M.: Rapid semi-automatic segmentation of the spinal cord from magnetic resonance images: Application in multiple sclerosis. Neuroimage 50(2), 446–455 (2010)
4. Kawahara, J., McIntosh, C., Tam, R., Hamarneh, G.: Globally optimal spinal cord segmentation using a minimal path in high dimensions. In: IEEE ISBI, pp. 836–839 (2013)
5. Kontschieder, P., Kohli, P., Shotton, J., Criminisi, A.: GeoF: Geodesic forests for learning coupled predictors. In: IEEE CVPR (2013)
6. McIntosh, C., Hamarneh, G.: Spinal crawlers: Deformable organisms for spinal cord segmentation and analysis. In: Larsen, R., Nielsen, M., Sporring, J. (eds.) MICCAI 2006. LNCS, vol. 4190, pp. 808–815. Springer, Heidelberg (2006)
7. McIntosh, C., Hamarneh, G., Toom, M., Tam, R.: Spinal cord segmentation for volume estimation in healthy and multiple sclerosis subjects using crawlers and minimal paths. In: IEEE HISB, pp. 25–31 (2011)
8. Rocca, M., Horsfield, M., Sala, S., Copetti, M., Valsasina, P., Mesaros, S., Martinelli, V., Caputo, D., Stosic-Opincal, T., Drulovic, J., Comi, G., Filippi, M.: A multicenter assessment of cervical cord atrophy among MS clinical phenotypes. Neurology 76(24), 2096–2102 (2011)
9. Szummer, M., Kohli, P., Hoiem, D.: Learning CRFs using graph cuts. In: Forsyth, D., Torr, P., Zisserman, A. (eds.) ECCV 2008, Part II. LNCS, vol. 5303, pp. 582–595. Springer, Heidelberg (2008)
10. Tench, C.R., Morgan, P.S., Constantinescu, C.S.: Measurement of cervical spinal cord cross-sectional area by MRI using edge detection and partial volume correction. J. Magn. Reson. Imaging 21(3), 197–203 (2005)
11. Tu, Z., Bai, X.: Auto-context and its application to high-level vision tasks and 3D brain image segmentation. IEEE TPAMI 32(10), 1744–1757 (2010)

Large-Scale Manifold Learning Using an Adaptive Sparse Neighbor Selection Approach for Brain Tumor Progression Prediction

Loc Tran[1], Frederic McKenzie[2], Jihong Wang[3], and Jiang Li[1]

[1] ECE and [2] MSVE, Old Dominion University, Norfolk, VA
[3] Imaging Physics, University of Texas MD Anderson Cancer Center, Houston, TX

Abstract. Manifold learning performs dimensionality reduction by identifying low-dimensional structures (manifolds) embedded in a high-dim- ensional space. Many algorithms involve an eigenvector or singular value decomposition (SVD) procedure on a similarity matrix of size $n \times n$, where n denotes the number of data samples, making them not scalable to big data. A method to overcome large data set size is to create a manifold with a subset of the original data while embedding the rest into the manifold skeleton. An adequate number of neighbors varies and depends on the geometry of the manifold. Points that contain too few neighbors may not be able to encompass the intrinsic manifold geometry. Conversely, too many neighbors will cause a short circuit in the manifold. To overcome these problems, we introduce a novel adaptive neighbor se- lection approach using ℓ_1 optimization. We show that this neighborhood selection can be useful in creating a more robust manifold in regards to MRI brain tumor data.

1 Introduction

Recent advances in technology make data acquisition a much cheaper process and data sizes are increasing exponentially. Nowadays, data sets usually contain many samples in a very high-dimensional space, making data "big" in both sample size and data dimension. Big data is difficult to store, transmit, visualize and analyze. Dimensionality reduction thus becomes key in reducing a high-dimensional data sets to a low-dimensional space while preserving the inherent structure of the data set. Manifold learning performs dimensionality reduction by identifying low-dimensional structures (manifolds) embedded in a high-dimensional space. Many algorithms involve an eigenvector or singular value decomposition (SVD) procedure on a similarity matrix of size $n \times n$, where n denotes the number of data samples, making them not scalable to big data. As an alternative, low-rank matrix approximation based incremental manifold learning strategies prove to be effective for obtaining near-optimal solutions to the problems [1,2]. In those algorithms, sampling methods are typically used to select a subset of data points as landmarks. A manifold skeleton is then learned using the landmarks. Finally, out-of-bag (remaining) points are inserted into the skeleton by various

G. Wu et al. (Eds.): MLMI 2013, LNCS 8184, pp. 219–226, 2013.

methods such as the Nystrom method, the column-sampling technique or the local embedding scheme [3,4,5]. However, high-dimensional data is known to be sparse and highly structured. Current available algorithms do not consider the structured sparse property of data, which may significantly influence the performance of the low-rank methods. We present a novel adaptive neighbor selection approach using the sparseness property of ℓ_1 optimization and aim to create a brain tumor progression model from MRI data. We improve on the procedure presented by [5] which uses ℓ_2 optimization.

2   Method

2.1   Proposed System

In this study, we focus on multi-dimensional MRI scans of brain tumor patients with a progressed tumor over two time points. In our data set, ten MRI image volumes are obtained for each patient. Thus, each pixel location can be represented as a 10-dimensional feature vector. By considering each pixel of the 256×256 MRI scans as a data point, the total number of data points is roughly 65k. The problem with having a high number of data points is that conventional manifold learning approaches require an $n \times n$ eigendecomposition of a distance matrix. For large values of n, this will become highly computation and memory intensive. An approach to alleviate this issue is to sample points from the large set of features and create a manifold using a smaller subset of features thus resulting in a manifold skeleton. Then the unsampled data points are embedding into the low dimensional space by embedding with local linear embedding (LLE) [6]. Neighborhood selection occurs many times in this approach. Both LLE and many manifold learning approaches require a neighborhood selection step. We introduce an adaptively sparse method of neighbor selection that can be applied directly to current large-scale manifold learning approaches. The system diagram for this method is shown in Fig. 1. In the proposed method, a link between abnormal points and the tumor progression region is found from manifold learning of the multi-dimensional MRI scans. A prediction on tumor growth is then made by selecting regions close to abnormal points in manifold space.

2.2   Sampling

To keep a faithful representation of the original manifold, landmarks should be carefully selected from the original data. Ideally, landmarks should be the smallest subset that can preserve the geometry in the original data. Local curvature variation (LCV) is a sampling method that selects points depending on the curvature level at each point. Intuitively, a manifold's data structure can be preserved effectively by sampling more points from high curvature regions. We assigned an importance value for each of the points by computing the local tangent space variation for it. For each data point in the data set, we found its k-nearest neighbors and performed a local principle component analysis on the

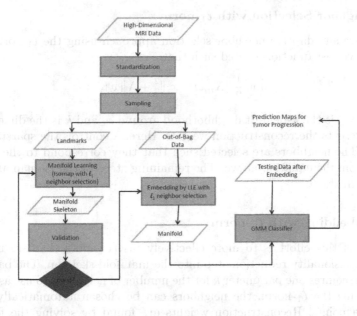

Fig. 1. System diagram

k-nearest neighbors including itself. We then identified the eigenvector (spans the tangent space) corresponding to the largest eigenvalue. For each data point, it has k such eigenvectors and we computed the mean value of angles between its eigenvector and the eigenvectors of all of its k-nearest neighbors. We then normalized the importance values across all data points such that they sum to one. We then sampled the data set to obtain a set of landmarks based on the importance values.

2.3   Dimensionality Reduction

The Isomap method for manifold learning consists of three steps [7]. First, a neighborhood graph is constructed. Second, pairwise distances are calculated through shortest paths from the neighborhood graph. And lastly, Multidimensional Scaling (MDS) converts the pairwise adjacency matrix to a lower dimensional space preserving pairwise geodesic distance. In conventional Isomap, the neighborhood selection is performed with either a ϵ-neighborhood or a k-nearest neighbors approach. The former method will select all points around an ϵ sized neighborhood to be neighbors. The drawback of this approach is that size of ϵ is difficult to determine. Also, some points may not have neighbors within the specified neighborhood and will thus be unconnected in a neighborhood graph. The k-nearest neighbors will choose the closest k points as neighbors of a data point. An adequate value for k varies within the data set depending on the geometry of the manifold. A point with a k value that is too high may result in "leaking". Likewise, a value that is too low will fail to encompass the underlying manifold.

2.4   Neighbor Selection with ℓ_1-norm

We propose an adaptive neighbor selection approach using the ℓ_1-norm. A reconstructive cost function is used such that:

$$\min_{\omega \geq 0} \frac{1}{2} \|X_{n_i}\omega - x_i\|_2^2 + \lambda \|\omega\|_1$$

where X_{n_i} is the k-nearest neighborhood around x_i and k is the dimension of x_i. ω represents the reconstruction weights. Here, λ controls the sparsity of the solution. The neighbors are selected such that they correspond to the nonzero weights from the equation above. The remaining steps of the Isomap algorithm follow normally.

2.5   Embedding with ℓ_1-norm

The goal of this effort is to more effectively insert points that are not used in the dimensionality reduction step into the manifold skeleton. The basic LLE algorithm requires one parameter k for the number of neighbors to use as weights [6]. By using the ℓ_1-norm, the neighbors can be chosen automatically among all n data points. Reconstruction weights are found by solving the following optimization:

$$E\left(W\right) = \sum_i \left(\left| X_i - \sum_{k=1}^n W_{ik}X_k \right|^2 + \lambda \sum_{k=1}^n |W_{ik}|_1 \right)$$

where X_i is the high-dimensional data point. The non-zero weights of W_{ik} correspond to the neighbors selected to make a reconstructive of the point in manifold space. This adaptive approach is expected to be more robust since the number of neighbors is not fixed for each data point. The ℓ_1-norm in the second term promotes sparsity of the solution. This is because most weights calculated from the ℓ_1-norm will be zero. The few neighbors with a nonzero weight, W_{ik}, will be chosen as the landmarks to reconstruct the data in the low dimensional manifold. The λ parameter controls the trade-off between reconstruction error and sparsity of the solution.

One drawback to this is that the localization of neighbors in Euclidean space is not guaranteed. This is because each point in the data set is considered to be a potential neighbor. Another consequence in having a large number of potential neighbors is that the number of nonzero weights could potentially be very high.

In a sense, the ℓ_1-norm has the benefit of having an adaptive number of neighbors while the original method guarantees localization and a maximum number of neighbors. In order to incorporate all of these properties, the ℓ_1 optimization function was then modified to the following:

$$E\left(W\right) = \sum_i \left(\left| X_i - \sum_{k=1}^{k'} W_{ik}X_k \right|^2 + \lambda \sum_{k=1}^{k'} |W_{ik}|_1 \right)$$

The neighbors in this formula are restricted to the k' nearest neighbors of each point. In the implementation, a good value for k' is a few values larger than the expected dimensionality of the manifold. To embed the data point X_i into the lower-dimensional manifold, we reconstructed it in the low-dimensional space as Z_i using the weights W_{rk} derived above

$$Z_i = \sum_k W_{ik} Z_k$$

2.6   Classification

Next, we classify abnormal regions and normal regions using Gaussian Mixture Models (GMM) with Expectation Maximization optimization. Here, we select the landmarks found in the manifold learning step that fall within the known abnormal and normal regions as the training data. The testing data included all other points within those regions. The advantage of using GMM as the classifier is that a probability map can be created where the probability is the likelihood of a sample to be abnormal. The classification can thus be adjusted by a simple thresholding of the probability map to form a growth prediction. Morphological filtering is applied to the classification to extract the largest contiguous block as the final classification region.

3   Experimental Setup

The MRI data of brain tumor patients were collected using various 256×256 2D MRI scans including FLAIR, T1-weighted, post-contrast T1-weighted, T2-weighted, and DTI. Five scalar slices were also computed from the DTI slice including apparent diffusion coefficient (ADC), fractional anisotropy (FA), max-, min-, and middle- eigenvalues, yielding a total of ten image slices for each visit of every patient. Each patient went through a series of scans with an interval of one or two months, and a rigid registration was utilized to align all slices to the

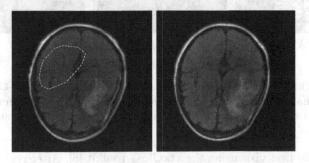

Fig. 2. Original ground truths for Subject 1 where the red region is the labeled abnormal region and the yellow dotted region is the normal region. (Left) Visit 1. (Right) Visit 2 showing a progressed abnormal region.

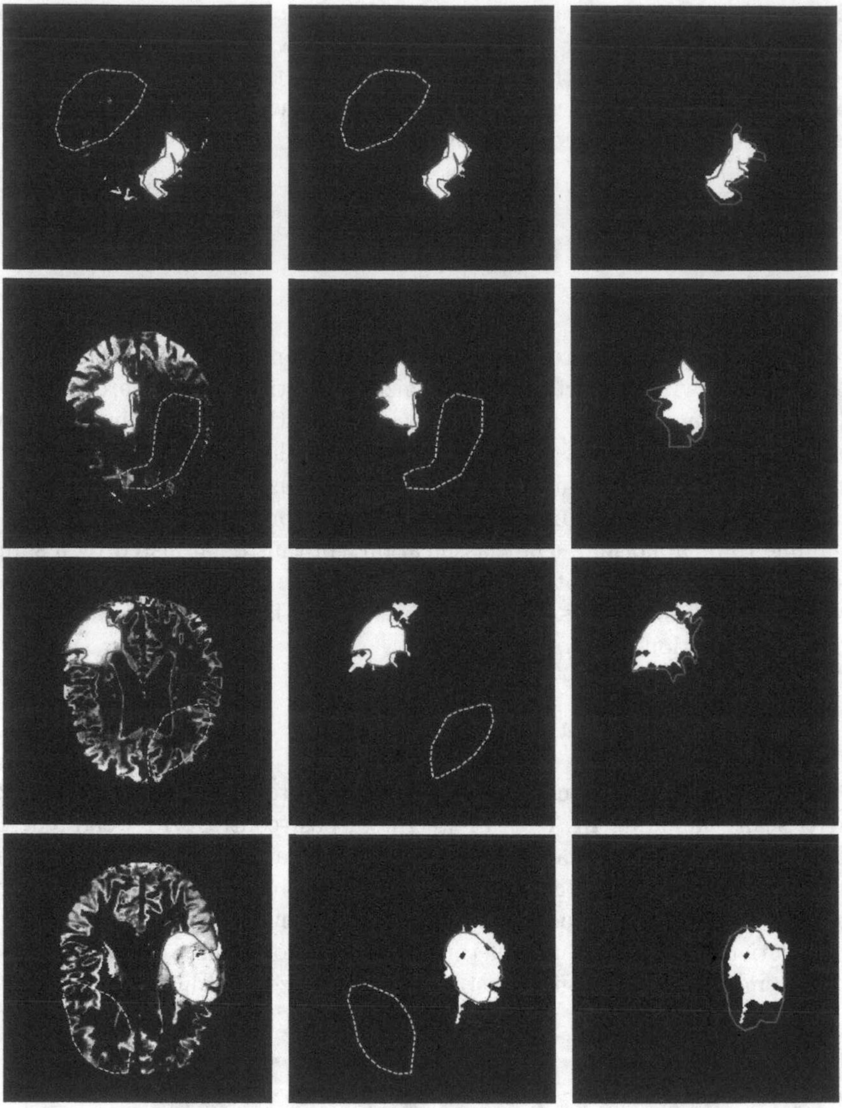

Fig. 3. Results for four subjects. Column A shows the output from the GMM. Column B shows the final classification after thresholding and filtering. Column C shows the classification on the second time point. The rows correspond to different subjects.

DTI slice of the first visit using the vtkCISG toolkit [8]. After registration, each pixel location can be represented by a ten-dimensional data point corresponding to the ten MRI slices. Two visits were selected in this study and denoted as "Visit 1" and "Visit 2" where Visit 2 showed an expanded tumor region. Hyperintensity

Table 1. Results for each subject

	Sensitivity Visit 1	Specificity Visit 1	Sensitivity Visit 2	Precision Visit 2	Average
Subject 1	0.985	1	0.704	0.832	0.880
Subject 2	0.972	1	0.587	0.931	0.872
Subject 3	0.981	1	0.725	0.864	0.893
Subject 4	0.946	1	0.623	0.900	0.867

Table 2. Average results over all subjects compared to other methods

	Sensitivity Visit 1	Specificity Visit 1	Sensitivity Visit 2	Precision Visit 2	Average
Proposed	**0.971**	1	0.659	**0.882**	**0.878**
[5]	0.951	1	0.663	0.781	0.849
PCA	0.945	0.999	0.649	0.473	0.766
Raw data	0.917	0.872	**0.705**	0.617	0.778

regions were defined on the FLAIR scans as abnormal regions. A similarly sized region far away from the abnormal regions was also defined as a highly confident normal region for training purposes. Fig. 2 shows example MRI slices overlaid on the defined tumor and normal regions. In [5], Tran et al. showed progressed tumor regions lie close to abnormal regions in manifold space. We aim to predict the progression of the tumor in Visit 2 from the manifold learned from Visit 1.

4 Results

Fig. 3 shows the results of four subjects. Column A denotes the output of the GMM classifier. Column B shows the final classification region after thresholding and filtering the GMM probability map. Here, the solid red polygon are the marked abnormal regions while the dotted yellow polygon denotes the marked normal regions from Visit 1. Column C show the classification region on the progressed hyperintensive region of Visit 2.

Table 1 show quantitative performance metrics calculated for each subject. The sensitivity measures the ratio between the number of pixels correctly predicted as abnormal versus the total number of marked abnormal pixels. This measure was calculated for both Visit 1 and Visit 2. Specificity is the ratio of the correctly predicted normal tissue samples inside the normal contours. The precision is the number of correctly predicted abnormal pixels divided by the total number of predicted abnormal points. The precision will be 1 if every pixel predicted as abnormal is within the marked abnormal region and conversely, the metric will be low for methods that have an over-estimated tumor region. The precision was calculated only at Visit 2 because the abnormal region was expected to expand between Visit 1 and Visit 2. The average metrics across those four subjects are summarized in Table 2 and compared to three other methods.

The results for Raw are found by directly applying the GMM classifier in the high dimensional space. For PCA, the dimensionality reduction is performed using principal component analysis. Lastly, [5] follows the same procedure as the proposed method while using ℓ_2-norm optimization.

From Table 2, the proposed method outperforms the other methods in terms of average sensitivity, specificity, and precision. This suggests that the ℓ_1 neighborhood selection creates a more robust manifold. While the proposed approach does not have the best Visit 2 sensitivity, this may be attributed to the other methods over-predicting abnormal regions. This results in the other methods having a low precision.

5   Conclusion

We show that a more robust manifold can be achieved using an adaptive neighborhood selection algorithm for large scale manifold learning. The proposed method improves the average classification accuracy of four MRI brain tumor data sets. While we have applied the approach to a specific data set, the general procedure may be easily applied to other nonlinear manifold learning data sets.

References

1. Belabbas, M.-A., Wolfe, P.J.: On landmark selection and sampling in high-dimensional data analysis. Philosophical Transactions of the Royal Society A: Mathematical, Physical and Engineering Sciences 367(1906), 4295–4312 (2009)
2. Zhang, K., Kwok, J.T.: Clustered nystrom method for large scale manifold learning and dimension reduction. Trans. Neur. Netw. 21, 1576–1587 (2010)
3. Deshpande, A., Rademacher, L., Vempala, S., Wang, G.: Matrix approximation and projective clustering via volume sampling. In: Proceedings of the Seventeenth Annual ACM-SIAM Symposium on Discrete Algorithm, SODA 2006, pp. 1117–1126. ACM, New York (2006)
4. Talwalkar, A., Kumar, S., Rowley, H.: Large-scale manifold learning. In: IEEE Conference on Computer Vision and Pattern Recognition, CVPR 2008, pp. 1–8 (2008)
5. Tran, L., et al.: A large-scale manifold learning approach for brain tumor progression prediction. In: Suzuki, K., Wang, F., Shen, D., Yan, P. (eds.) MLMI 2011. LNCS, vol. 7009, pp. 265–272. Springer, Heidelberg (2011)
6. Roweis, S.T., Saul, L.K.: Nonlinear dimensionality reduction by locally linear embedding. Science 290(5500), 2323–2326 (2000)
7. Tenenbaum, J.B., de Silva, V., Langford, J.C.: A Global Geometric Framework for Nonlinear Dimensionality Reduction. Science 290, 2319–2323 (2000)
8. Hartkens, T., Rueckert, D., Schnabel, J.A., Hawkes, D.J., Hill, D.L.G.: Vtk cisg registration toolkit: An open source software package for affine and nonrigid registration of single- and multimodal 3D images. In: Meiler, M., Saupe, D., Kruggel, F., Handels, H., Lehmann, T.M. (eds.) Bildverarbeitung fur die Medizin. CEUR Workshop Proceedings, vol. 56, pp. 409–412. Springer (2002)

Ensemble Universum SVM Learning
for Multimodal Classification of Alzheimer's Disease

Xiaoke Hao and Daoqiang Zhang[*]

Dept. of Computer Science and Engineering,
Nanjing University of Aeronautics and Astronautics, Nanjing 210016, China
dqzhang@nuaa.edu.cn

Abstract. Recently, machine learning methods (e.g., support vector machine (SVM)) have received increasing attentions in neuroimaging-based Alzheimer's disease (AD) classification studies. For classifying AD patients from normal controls (NC), standard SVM trains a classification model from only AD and NC subjects. However, in practice besides AD and NC subjects, there may also exist other subjects such as those with mild cognitive impairment (MCI). In this paper, we investigate the potential of using MCI subjects to aid the identification of AD from NC subjects. Specifically, we propose to use the universum support vector machine (U-SVM) learning by treating MCI subjects as the universum examples that do not belong to either of the classes (i.e., AD and NC) of interest. The idea of U-SVM learning is to separate AD from NC subjects through large margin hyperplane with the universum MCI subjects laying inside the margin borders, which is in accordance with our domain knowledge that MCI is a prodromal stage of AD with cognitive status between NC and AD. Furthermore, we propose ensemble universum SVM learning for multimodal classification by training an individual U-SVM classifier for each modality. Experimental results on the Alzheimer's Disease Neuroimaging Initiative (ADNI) database demonstrate the efficacy of our proposed method.

1 Introduction

Alzheimer's disease (AD) is one of the most common forms of dementia in elderly people worldwide. Early diagnosis of AD is very important for possible delay of the disease. Over the past decades many machine learning methods (e.g., support vector machine (SVM)) have been developed for classification of AD or its prodromal stage, i.e., mild cognitive impairment (MCI), based on either single or multiple modalities of biomarkers [1-3]. However, one challenge in AD classification is that the number of AD patients and normal controls (NC) is usually very limited while the dimensionality of imaging data is quite high, which makes it very difficult to train a robust and powerful AD classifier under the standard SVM framework. On the other hand, besides AD and NC subjects, we may have other domain-related subjects such as those with MCI, a prodromal stage of AD. These subjects may help to build a powerful AD classifier, although their cognitive status may not belong to AD or NC.

---

[*] Corresponding author.

G. Wu et al. (Eds.): MLMI 2013, LNCS 8184, pp. 227–234, 2013.

To address that problem, in this paper we propose to use a new learning technique called universum support vector machine (U-SVM) which classifies AD from NC subjects with the extra help from MCI subjects. It's noteworthy that in some recent neuroimaging-based classification works, some other machine learning techniques including semi-supervised learning and transfer learning have also been used for enhancing the neuroimaging-based classification with subjects from other domains [4, 5]. However, different from semi-supervised learning and transfer learning which use the auxiliary knowledge from the related subjects or domains, universum learning (including U-SVM) aims at employing universum data as contradiction samples that do not belong to either of the classes (i.e., AD and NC) of interest to boost the generalization performance [6]. Although U-SVM has been successful applied for many other applications such as handwritten digits recognition [7], however, to the best of our knowledge it has not been introduced to neuroimaging-based brain disease classification.

In this paper, we investigate the potential of using U-SVM learning to aid identification of AD from NC subjects with MCI subjects as universum data. The objective of exploiting U-SVM learning is to separate AD from NC subjects through large margin hyperplane with the universum MCI subjects laying inside the margin borders, which is in accordance with our domain knowledge that MCI is a prodromal stage of AD with cognitive status between NC and AD. Furthermore, the ensemble learning classifier is adopted to combine individual U-SVM classifiers trained from each modality of biomarkers, including magnetic resonance imaging (MRI), fluorodeoxyglucose positron emission tomography (FDG-PET) and cerebrospinal fluid (CSF), for multimodal classification [8, 9]. The proposed methods are validated on the Alzheimer's Disease Neuroimaging Initiative (ADNI) database.

2   Method

The U-SVM learning aims at employing a portion of the universum data as a priori knowledge to boost generalization performance [6]. To exploit the potential of using MCI subjects to aid classification between AD and NC subjects, we treat MCI subjects as universum data, and the then adopt U-SVM learning to solve the classification problem. In the following sections, we will first introduce the U-SVM method for single-modality classification, and then present the ensemble U-SVM method for multimodal classification.

2.1   Universum Support Vector Machine (U-SVM)

We first compare U-SVM with SVM through an illustration, as shown in Fig. 1. As can be seen from Fig. 1, compared to the standard SVM with solid lines, in U-SVM the universum samples are constrained to fall inside the margin borders with dashed lines. Here in U-SVM we require the universum samples lie inside the margin borders (dashed lines in Fig. 1), because these samples do not belong to either class. In this way, the universum learning achieves a trade-off between explaining training samples using large margin hyperplanes and maximizing the number of contradictions on the universum [7] [10].

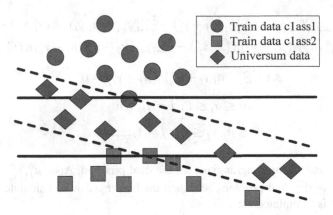

Fig. 1. Two large margin separating hyperplanes on training data

Assume we have n samples with corresponding class labels as $\{x_i, y_i\}_{i=1}^n$, where $x_i \in R^d$ is a sample and $y_i \in \{+1, -1\}$ is the class label (i.e., AD as 1 and NC as -1). Also, assume we have m universum data without corresponding class labels denoted as $\{x_j^*\}_{j=1}^m$, where $x_j^* \in R^d$ is a universum sample without class label (i.e., MCI in this paper). U-SVM tends to make the normal vector orthogonal to the principal direction of the universum data [11], with the following objective function

$$\min_{w,b} R(w,b) = \frac{1}{2}(w \cdot w) + C \sum_{i=1}^n \xi_i + C^* \sum_{j=1}^m \xi_j^*$$

$$\text{s.t.} \quad y_i[(w \cdot x_i) + b] \geq 1 - \xi_i \quad \xi_i \geq 0, i = 1, \dots, n$$

$$|(w \cdot x_j^*) + b| \leq \varepsilon + \xi_j^* \quad \xi_j^* \geq 0, j = 1, \dots, m \qquad (1)$$

where $C, C^* \geq 0$, $\varepsilon \geq 0$, W is the parameter vector of the classifier and b is the bias term. U-SVM augments the objective term $C^* \sum_{j=1}^m \xi_j^*$ and constraint $|(w \cdot x_j^*) + b| \leq \varepsilon + \xi_j^*$ for universum data. The parameters C and C^* control the trade-off between the minimization of errors and the maximization of the number of contradictions. When $C^* = 0$, the U-SVM formulation is reduced to standard SVM. For labeled training data (i.e., AD and NC), we use standard SVM soft-margin loss with slack variables ξ_i. Also, for the universum samples (i.e., MCI) we adopt the ε-insensitive loss as in standard support vector regression with ξ_j^* denoting slack variables for samples from the universum [7].

The solution to the optimization formulation (1) defines the large margin classification hyperplane between AD and NC that incorporates the priori knowledge with MCI into the final model. The decision function in the dual space is constructed by using a kernel matrix $(K(*,*))$ of both the labeled samples and the universum samples [10]. As this optimization problem is convex, the solution can also be computed through the corresponding dual optimization problem with kernel version as:

$$max_{\alpha,\mu,\gamma} \sum_{i=1}^{n} \alpha_i - \varepsilon \sum_{j=1}^{m}(\mu_j + \gamma_j) - \frac{1}{2}\sum_{i,k=1}^{n} \alpha_i \alpha_k y_i y_k K(x_i, x_k) -$$
$$\sum_{i=1}^{n}\sum_{j=1}^{m} \alpha_i y_i(\mu_j - \gamma_j)K(x_i, x_j^*) - \frac{1}{2}\sum_{j,l=1}^{m}(\mu_j - \gamma_j)(\mu_l - \gamma_l)K(x_j^*, x_l^*)$$

$$\text{s.t.} \quad \sum_{i=1}^{n} \alpha_i y_i + \sum_{j=1}^{m}(\mu_j - \gamma_j) = 0$$

$$0 \le \alpha_i \le C, \ i = 1, \dots, n$$

$$0 \le \mu_j, \gamma_j \le C^*, \ j = 1, \dots, m \qquad (2)$$

where μ_j, γ_j and α_i are Lagrangians for the dual problem. Also μ_j^0, γ_j^0 and α_i^0 are the solutions of the dual problem, and then the bias b_0 can be calculated. The decision function is formulated as:

$$f(x) = \text{sgn}(\sum_{i=1}^{n} \alpha_i^0 y_i K(x_i, x) + \sum_{j=1}^{m}(\mu_j^0 - \gamma_j^0)K(x_j^*, x) + b_0) \qquad (3)$$

2.2   Ensemble Universum SVM

A lot of studies have shown that biomarkers from different modalities may have complementary information for discrimination [8, 9]. A common practice in combining different modalities is the concatenation of all features into a longer feature vector.

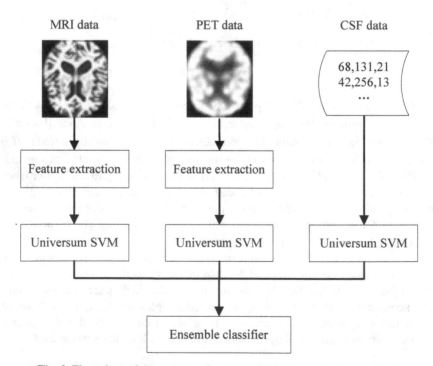

Fig. 2. Flow chart of the proposed Ensemble U-SVM classification method

However, this may be not enough for effective combination of features from different modalities. In this paper, we propose to use ensemble learning [12] to combine complementary information from heterogeneous data.

We give the flow chart of our proposed ensemble U-SVM method for multimodal AD classification in Fig. 2. As can be seen from Fig.2, firstly for each subject we extract features from raw MRI, PET respectively. And then three individual U-SVM classifiers are trained from each different modality using U-SVM. In the procedure of decision-making, for a new unseen testing sample, each of these trained models will have a predication on it, and finally we aggregate all predictions using majority voting strategy to get the final decision.

3   Experiments

In this section, we evaluate the effectiveness of the proposed methods for AD vs. NC classification on the Alzheimer's Disease Neuroimaging Initiative (ADNI) database (www.loni.ucla.edu/ADNI). In our experiments, we use three modalities of data including MRI, PET and CSF data.

3.1   Subjects

The ADNI database contains approximately 200 cognitively normal elderly subjects to be followed for 3 years, 400 subjects with MCI to be followed for 3 years, and 200 subjects with early AD to be followed for 2 years. In this paper, all ADNI baseline subjects with the corresponding MRI, PET, and CSF data are included. This yields a total of 202 subjects, including 51 AD patients, 99 MCI patients, and 52 healthy controls.

Standard image pre-processing is performed for all MRI and PET images, including anterior commissure (AC) - posterior commissure (PC) correction, skull-stripping, removal of cerebellum, and segmentation of structural MR images into three different tissues: grey matter (GM), white matter (WM), and cerebrospinal fluid (CSF). With atlas warping, we can partition each subject image into 93 regions of interests (ROIs). For each of the 93 ROIs, we compute the GM tissue volume from the subject's MRI image. For PET image, we first rigidly align it with its respective MRI image of the same subject, and then compute the average value of PET signals in each ROI. Therefore, for each subject, we can finally obtain totally 93 features from MRI image, other 93 features from PET image, and 3 features ($A\beta 42$, t-tau, and p-tau) from CSF biomarkers. A detailed description on acquiring MRI, PET and CSF data from ADNI as used in this paper can be found at [1].

3.2   Experiment Settings

In the experiment settings, the whole set of subject samples are equally partitioned into 10 subsets, and each time the subject samples within one subset are selected as the testing samples and all remaining subject samples in the other 9 subsets are used for training the models. This process is repeated for 10 times.

Linear kernel is used in SVM and U-SVM after performing a common feature normalization step. For normalization, we first perform a feature-level normalization (i.e., across samples) to make each feature have zero mean and unit standard deviation. Then, we perform a sample-level normalization (i.e., across features) to make each sample have unit L_2 norm.

During U-SVM model parameters selection, note small values of parameter C^* suggest that universum samples have little effect on the final model. So the effectiveness of the universum samples is mainly determined by the values of C and C^* (or their ratio) [7]. To investigate the effect of performance of our multimodality classification method, we test all of their possible parameter values given above by a coarse-grid search through cross validation on training samples.

3.3   Results

We compare U-SVM with standard SVM for both single modality and multimodal cases. Table 1 shows the comparison results achieved by standard SVM and U-SVM methods on different modalities. Note that Table 1 shows the averaged results of 10 independent experiments, given the mean and standard deviation of classification accuracies, sensitivities and specificities. As we can see from Table 1, U-SVM can consistently achieve better accuracy than SVM in all cases, which validates the efficacy of our U-SVM method on using MCI subjects as universum data for helping the classification between AD and NC. Specifically, for multimodal case, our proposed ensemble U-SVM can achieve a classification accuracy of 92.76%, which is better than ensemble SVM that achieve only 92.06%. For other performance measures such as sensitivity and specificity, U-SVM also outperforms SVM in most cases.

The results in Table 1 show the advantages of the proposed ensemble U-SVM in improving classification accuracies. We also perform the significance test using paired t-test at the significance level of 0.95. The corresponding results show that our proposed ensemble U-SVM method is significantly better than all other methods including standard SVM and ensemble SVM. This again validates the efficacy of our proposed method.

Table 1. Comparison of performance measures of SVM and U-SVM for AD vs. NC classification using different modalities. (ACC= Accuracy, SEN=Sensitivity, SPE=Specificity).

Methods	SVM			U-SVM		
	ACC%	SEN%	SPE%	ACC%	SEN%	SPE%
MRI	87.11	82.40	91.77	87.98	84.00	91.91
	±1.24	±1.73	±1.41	±0.87	±1.36	±1.22
PET	86.25	88.20	84.29	86.55	87.60	85.49
	±1.12	±1.46	±1.50	±0.79	±1.12	±1.29
CSF	82.26	82.60	82.00	83.36	83.97	82.86
	±0.57	±0.78	±1.64	±0.84	±0.74	±1.51
Ensemble	92.06	91.37	92.71	92.76	91.57	93.91
	±0.59	±1.06	±1.32	±0.70	±1.03	±0.88

Finally, in Fig. 3, we compare the classification performance of the proposed ensemble U-SVM method for multimodal classification, with respect to different number of MCI subjects as universum data. As we can see from Fig. 3, as the number of universum data (i.e., MCI subjects) increases, the performance of ensemble U-SVM also increases steadily, showing the usefulness of the universum data in improving the performance of AD classification. This further validates the effectiveness of adopting U-SVM learning by considering MCI as universum data, compared with standard SVM learning.

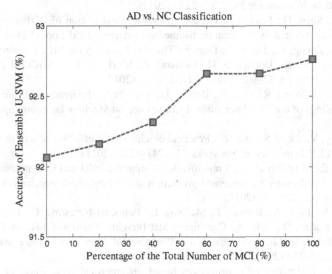

Fig. 3. Average accuracy of Ensemble U-SVM on different numbers of MCI subjects

4 Conclusion

In this paper, we investigate the potential of exploiting MCI subjects that do not belong to either of the classes (AD and NC) of interest to aid the classification between AD and NC subjects. Specifically, we propose to use the universum support vector machine (U-SVM) learning to separate AD from NC subjects through large margin hyperplane with the universum data (i.e., MCI subjects) laying inside the margin borders. Furthermore, we adopt ensemble learning to combine individual U-SVM classifiers trained from each modality. Experimental results on the multimodal imaging data and biological biomarkers from the ADNI database have validated the efficacy of our proposed method.

Acknowledgements. This work was supported in part by SRFDP grant (No. 20123218110009), NUAAFRF grant (No. NE2013105), and JiangsuSF for Distinguished Young Scholar.

References

1. Zhang, D., Wang, Y., Zhou, L., Yuan, H., Shen, D.: Multimodal classification of Alzheimer's disease and mild cognitive impairment. Neuroimage 55, 856–867 (2011)
2. Davatzikos, C., Bhatt, P., Shaw, L., Batmanghelich, K., Trojanowski, J.: Prediction of MCI to AD conversion, via MRI, CSF biomarkers, and pattern classification. Neurobiol. Aging 32, e2322.e19–e2322.e27 (2011)
3. Cho, Y., Seong, J., Jeong, Y., Shin, S.: Individual subject classification for Alzheimer's disease based on incremental learning using a spatial frequency representation of cortical thickness data. Neuroimage 59, 2217–2230 (2012)
4. Zhang, D., Shen, D.: Semi-supervised multimodal classification of Alzheimer's Disease. In: IEEE International Symposium on Biomedical Imaging (ISBI), pp. 1628–1631 (2011)
5. Cheng, B., Zhang, D., Shen, D.: Domain Transfer Learning for MCI Conversion Prediction. In: Ayache, N., Delingette, H., Golland, P., Mori, K. (eds.) MICCAI 2012, Part I. LNCS, vol. 7510, pp. 82–90. Springer, Heidelberg (2012)
6. Weston, J., Collobert, R., Sinz, F., Bottou, L., Vapnik, V.: Inference with the Universum. In: Proceedings of the 23rd International Conference on Machine Learning, pp. 1009–1016 (2006)
7. Cherkassky, V., Dhar, S., Dai, W.: Practical conditions for effectiveness of the Universum learning. IEEE Trans. Neural Networks 22, 1241–1255 (2011)
8. Westman, E., Muehlboeck, J., Simmons, A.: Combining MRI and CSF measures for classification of Alzheimer's disease and prediction of mild cognitive impairment conversion. Neuroimage 62, 229–238 (2012)
9. Walhovd, K., Fjell, A., Brewer, J., McEvoy, L., Fennema-Notestine, C., Hagler, D., Jennings, R., Karow, D., Dale, A.: Combining MR Imaging, Positron-Emission Tomography, and CSF Biomarkers in the Diagnosis and Prognosis of Alzheimer Disease. Am. J. Neuroradiol. 31, 347–354 (2010)
10. Vapnik, V.: Estimation of dependences based on empirical data. Springer, New York (2006)
11. Sinz, F., Chapelle, O., Agarwal, A., Scholkopf, B.: An Analysis of Inference with the Universum. In: Proceedings of the 21st Annual Conference on Neural Information Processing Systems (NIPS), pp. 1–8 (2008)
12. Tan, A., Gilbert, D.: Ensemble machine learning on gene expression data for cancer classification. Appl. Bioinformatics 2, S75–S83 (2003)

Joint Sparse Coding Spatial Pyramid Matching for Classification of Color Blood Cell Image

Jun Shi and Yin Cai

School of Communication and Information Engineering, Shanghai University
junshi@staff.shu.edu.cn

Abstract. In the Automatic recognition of blood cell images, the color blood cell images are usually transformed into grayscale images for feature extraction, which result in losing plenty of useful color information. Although the sparse coding based linear spatial pyramid matching (ScSPM) is popular in grayscale image classification, the sparse coding methods in ScSPM fail to extract color information. In this paper, we proposed a novel joint sparse coding SPM (JScSPM) method by using the joint trained joint codebook. The joint codebook is able to represent the inner color correlation among different color components, and the individual color information of each color channel as well. JScSPM method was then applied to classify color blood cell images. The experimental results showed that the proposed method achieved mean 3.1% and 6.6% improvements on classification accuracy, compared with the majority voting based ScSPM the original ScSPM, respectively.

1   Introduction

The analysis of blood cells in microscope images is one of the most important steps in clinical hematological procedures. Consequently, the image-based automatic counting and classification of blood cells have attracted lots of attention.

In current classification system, the colored blood cell images are usually transformed into grayscale images for further feature extraction, in order to simplify algorithms and reduce the computational complexity. However, plenty of useful color information will be discarded. Furthermore, there are few special designated color feature descriptors for blood cell images.

In recent years, the sparse coding technique has been successfully used in image classification task [1], not only directly as a classifier, but also embedded in the classification framework [2]. The sparse coding based linear spatial pyramid matching (ScSPM) is a popular sparse coding embedded classification method developed on spatial pyramid matching (SPM) [2, 3]. It computes a spatial pyramid image representation with sparse coding instead the vector quantization [2, 3]. The ScSPM and its variations [2, 4, 5] have achieved great success in image classification. The main improvements in ScSPM mainly focus on applying different regularization terms for

G. Wu et al. (Eds.): MLMI 2013, LNCS 8184, pp. 235–242, 2013.

sparse coding [4, 5] instead of adopting new sparse coding paradigm. Furthermore, ScSPM is usually applied to classify grayscale images. When dealing with color images or any other types of vector-valued images, one would either convert it into grayscale image, or process different color channels as separate images and then combine the features at the end. The existing sparse coding methods used in ScSPM fail to consider the inherent correlation among different color components of the vector-based images.

Recently, the joint sparsity model (JSM) for sparse coding has achieved great success in image processing and analysis [6-14]. Among these JSMs, one category (named JSM-1) is very suitable to represent color images, in which all signals share a common sparse component, and meanwhile each individual signal has a sparse innovations component [15]. As different color components have same scenes, there exist common and shared information among them. Therefore, the inter-correlation among RGB channels could be represented by the common sparse component, while the unique portion of each color channel image is characterized by the sparse innovation component. This JSM-1 has been applied to image fusion [6, 7], denoising [14], and restoration [11]. To the best of our knowledge, JSM-1 has not been used in classification framework.

In this paper, we proposed a Joint Sparse Coding SPM (JScSPM) method for the classification of color blood cell images. The joint codebook construction and joint sparse coding are acted as a way to fuse inner-common and individual color information, which makes it easy to extract color descriptor, instead of special designated color features. The main contributions of our work are threefold: (1) we apply the JSM-1 to the classification framework for the recognition task; (2) we propose the joint sparse coding SPM (JScSPM) method with JSM-1 for the classification color image; (3) we apply the JScSPM method to discriminate color blood cell images.

2   Joint Sparse Coding SPM with Joint Sparsity Model

The difference between our JScSPM and the original ScSPM is that a joint sparse coding strategy is adopted to replace the original sparse coding, and it is used to represent color information. See Fig. 1, and the flowchart of joint codebook construction and joint sparse coding is shown in Fig. 2.

In the original ScSPM, let $\mathbf{X}$ be a set of D-dimensional local descriptors extracted from a gray image, i.e. $\mathbf{X} = [x_1, x_2, ..., x_N] \in \mathbf{R}^{D \times N}$. The sparse coding method in ScSPM is to solve the following optimization problem [2]:

$$\arg\min_{\mathbf{C}} \sum_{i=1}^{N} \|x_i - \mathbf{D}\alpha_i\|^2 + \lambda \|\alpha_i\|_{l^1} \quad s.t. \ \|d_k\| \leq 1, \ \forall k = 1, 2, ..., K \quad (1)$$

where $\mathbf{C} = [\alpha_1, \alpha_2, ..., \alpha_N]$ is the set of sparse codes, and $\mathbf{D} = [d_1, d_2, ..., d_K] \in \mathbf{R}^{D \times N}$ is a over-complete codebook trained with the local descriptors of gray image.

Similar to the strategy adopted in above-mentioned JSM-1 [15], all signals are represented as the summation of a common sparse component with a sparse innovation component; that is, for color image,

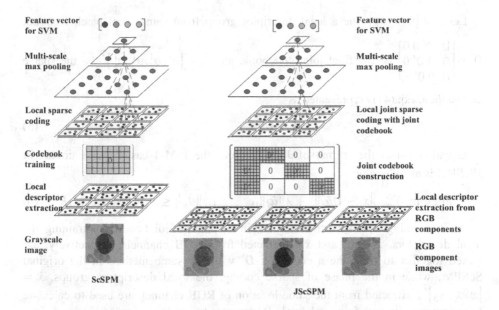

Fig. 1. Comparison of JScSPM and regular ScSPM. The local descriptors are extracted from gray images to train the codebook in ScSPM, while in JScSPM, local descriptors are extracted from RGB color components, respectively, and then used to train and construct joint codebook.

$$\begin{aligned} x_r &= x^c + x_r^l \\ x_g &= x^c + x_g^l \\ x_b &= x^c + x_b^l \end{aligned} \qquad (2)$$

where x_r, x_g, and x_b are the local descriptors of R, G and B channel images, respectively, x^c is the common to all the local descriptors, and x_r^l, x_g^l and x_b^l are the unique portions corresponding to x_r, x_g, and x_b, respectively. Then, they can be represented as

$$\left.\begin{aligned} x_r &= x^c + x_r^l = D'\alpha^c + D'\alpha_r^l \\ x_g &= x^c + x_g^l = D'\alpha^c + D'\alpha_g^l \\ x_b &= x^c + x_b^l = D'\alpha^c + D'\alpha_b^l \end{aligned}\right\} \qquad (3)$$

where D' is the trained codebook with mixed local descriptors extracted from all RGB channel images, α^c is the sparse codes of common sparse component, and α_r^l, α_g^l and α_b^l are the sparse codes of the unique portions corresponding to x_r, x_g, and x_b. Thus, Eq. (3) can be further written as

$$\begin{bmatrix} x_r \\ x_g \\ x_b \end{bmatrix} = \begin{bmatrix} D' & D' & 0 & 0 \\ D' & 0 & D' & 0 \\ D' & 0 & 0 & D' \end{bmatrix} \begin{bmatrix} \alpha^c \\ \alpha_r^l \\ \alpha_g^l \\ \alpha_b^l \end{bmatrix} \qquad (4)$$

where 0 is the zero matrix with the same size of D'.

Let $\tilde{x} = \begin{bmatrix} x_r\ x_g\ x_b \end{bmatrix}^T$ be a local descriptor group from same local patch location,

$\tilde{D} = \begin{bmatrix} D'\ D'\ 0\ 0 \\ D'\ 0\ D'\ 0 \\ D'\ 0\ 0\ D' \end{bmatrix}$ be the final joint codebook, and $\tilde{C} = \begin{bmatrix} \alpha^c, \alpha_r^l, \alpha_g^l, \alpha_b^l \end{bmatrix}^T$ be the sparse

codes, then, Eq. (4) is represented as

$$\tilde{x} = \tilde{D}\tilde{\alpha} \tag{5}$$

Equation (4) is the format of JSM-1. Thus, the JSM-1-based sparse coding in JScSPM is as following:

$$\arg\min_{\tilde{C}} \sum_{i=1}^{N} \left\| \tilde{x}_i - \tilde{D}\tilde{\alpha}_i \right\|^2 + \lambda \|\tilde{\alpha}_i\|_{l^1} \quad s.t.\ \|\tilde{d}_k\| \le 1, \forall k = 1,2,\dots,K \tag{6}$$

As show in Fig. 2, it is worth noting that in the phase of joint codebook training, the local descriptors, x_r, x_g, and x_b, extracted from RGB channels, respectively, are mixed together to train the a codebook $\mathbf{D}'$ with the same method in the original ScSPM; while in the phase of sparse coding, the local descriptors groups, $\tilde{x} = \begin{bmatrix} x_r\ x_g\ x_b \end{bmatrix}^T$, extracted from the same location of RGB channel, are used to calculate joint sparse codes with joint codebook $\tilde{\mathbf{D}}$ generated from $\mathbf{D}'$.

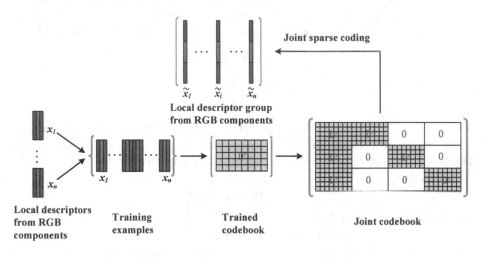

Fig. 2. The flowchart of joint codebook construction and joint sparse coding

To train the codebook and solve the optimization problem in Eq. (6), two approaches were adopted here: the same solution as original ScSPM [2] (named Method-1), and the solution in [6] (named Method-2), which uses K-SVD method [16] to train codebook and orthonormal matching pursuit (OMP) [16] to approximate sparse codes. We refer to [2], [6] and [16] for details of these solutions.

3 Experiment

The ALL_IDB2 database [17], a public image dataset of color peripheral blood samples of normal individuals and leukemic patients, was used to evaluate the proposed JScSPM. There are totally 260 images with the ration of healthy cell to leukemic cell of 1:1. All the images have been cropped to include the region of interest. Figure 3 shows an example of 8 blood cells.

The scale-invariant feature transform (SIFT) descriptors [18] used in the original ScSPM were densely sampled from input images with the patch size of 16×16 pixel and a grid spacing of 6 pixels. The codebook size was fixed as 1024 for all ScSPM methods with training examples of 10000 and 20000, respectively. To estimate the classification performance, the four-fold cross-validation was applied. The ratio of health cell images to leukemic cell images was 1:1 in each fold. It can be observedthat morphologic structure and spatial contextual are different for different types of blood cell images, which make it suitable to adopt spatial pyramid matching algorithms.

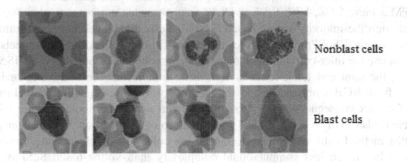

Fig. 3. Example images contained in the ALL_IDB2 dataset with 4 normal white blood cells (nonblast cells) in top row and 4 probable blast cells in bottom row

For comparison, we implemented and evaluated three classes of ScSPM methods, and none have previously been used for the classification of blood cell image.

1) ScSPM: the original ScSPM in [2]. The color blood cell images were transformed into grayscale images for further SIFT feature extraction and image classification.
2) VScSPM: the majority voting based original ScSPM. Three component images were generated from the R, G and B channels of the original color image, and then the original ScSPM was applied to each individual color component image.
3) The final classification result was achieved by majority voting among the three classifiers from each channel.
4) JScSPM: the proposed joint sparse coding SPM.

The joint codebook training and joint sparse code calculations in all these ScSPM methods were approached by Method-1 and Method-2 above-mentioned in Section 2, respectively.

The histogram intersection kernel (HIK) based SVM (HIK-SVM) has been successfully used for the classification of histogram features with better performance than other kernel-based SVMs [19]. Therefore, we choose HIK-SVM over linear SVM in original ScSPM for all these ScSPM methods.

4   Results and Discussion

Table 1 and 2 show the results of ScSPM, VScSPM and JScSPM with method-1 and method-2 solutions, respectively. It can be observed that the results of JScSPM and VScSPM achieve better than ScSPM. This is due to the fact that the color information can help to improve the classification performance. Most importantly, JScSPM achieves the best among three algorithms. The best classification accuracy, sensitivity, specificity and precision from JScSPM are 92.4±8.8%, 89.4±6.8%, 95.5±5.0%, and 95.2±5.6% under method-1 solution with 10000 training examples. Specifically, JScSPM provide mean 3.1%, 1.5%, 4.6% and 4.7% improvements on accuracy, sensitivity, specificity and precision, compared with VScSPM for the overall results. While compared with ScSPM, JScSPM achieve 6.6%, 4.7%, 8.5% and 8.4% improvements, correspondingly.

Although the majority voting based ScSPM method achieves better performance than the original ScSPm, it only votes the classification results of RGB channels, and does not use the inter-correlation among RGB components. In our proposed JScSPM method, the joint codebook contains both the common inner-correlative color information from RGB components and the unique portion of each color channel image. Therefore, the consequent joint sparse codes, from which the pooled feature will be extracted, also include common and individual color information. Consequently, the JScSPM method achieves best performance for color blood cell images. Moreover, JScSPM has much less computational complexity than voting-based ScSPM. It is because VScSPM has to perform ScSPM from RGB channels, respectively.

Table 1. Classification results of different ScSPM methods with method-1 solution (unit: %)

	10000 training examples			
	accuracy	sensitivity	specificity	Precision
ScSPM-1	84.4±6.4	84.1±11.6	84.7±2.1	84.4±3.5
VScSPM-1	88.3±9.1	85.7±14.1	90.9±4.7	90.0±6.3
JScSPM-1	**92.4±8.8**	**89.4±6.8**	**95.5±5.0**	**95.2±5.6**
	20000 training examples			
	accuracy	sensitivity	specificity	Precision
ScSPM-1	87.5±7.2	82.5±12.0	92.4±2.8	91.3±4.1
VScSPM-1	90.5±7.6	**89.5±12.7**	91.6±2.7	91.1±3.9
JScSPM-1	**92.1±5.7**	88.6±6.3	**95.5±5.1**	**95.1±5.6**

Table 2. Classification results of different ScSPM methods with method-2 solution with 15 non-zero elements (unit: %)

	10000 training examples			
	accuracy	sensitivity	specificity	precision
ScSPM-2	80.5±4.8	77.1±8.2	83.9±4.2	82.7±4.4
VScSPM-2	84.0±5.2	79.4±6.0	88.6±4.9	87.4±5.5
JScSPM-2	**88.3±9.3**	**83.4±13.5**	**93.2±5.5**	**92.0±7.2**
	20000 training examples			
	accuracy	sensitivity	specificity	precision
ScSPM-2	82.8±7.3	82.4±11.3	83.2±6.9	83.1±6.5
VScSPM-2	86.3±6.8	**84.1±11.1**	88.5±4.5	87.8±5.1
JScSPM-2	**88.7±9.6**	83.4±15.9	**93.9±4.1**	**92.8±6.0**

In this work, the joint codebook construction and joint sparse coding in JScSPM are acted as a way to extract and fuse color feature, which makes feature extraction easy without special designed color descriptors. Therefore, we only use the grayscale SIFT descriptor, a common feature descriptor in computer vision, and achieve excellent classification performance. In fact, this joint sparse coding with JSM-1 in JScSPM can characterize other information jointly, such as multi-feature, multi-view and vector-valued images. How to realize them will be studied in future work. What's more, we will further improve the performance of JScSPM by combining the other regularization term of sparse coding, such as Laplacian, non-negative sparse coding. At present, the JSM-2 (common sparse supports) is commonly used, which is also named as group sparse representation. We will compare our method with the JSM-2 based SPM in future.

5   Conclusion

In this paper, we proposed a new joint sparse coding SPM method for the classification of color blood cell images. The performance improvement on classification of color blood cell images is demonstrated by comparing with the original ScSPM and voting based ScSPM.

Acknowledgement. This work is partly supported by the Shanghai Municipal Natural Science Foundation (12ZR1410800) and the Innovation Program of Shanghai Municipal Education Commission (13YZ016).

References

1. Cheng, H., Liu, Z.C., Yang, L., Chen, X.W.: Sparse Representation and Learning in Visual Recognition: Theory and Applications. Signal Processing 93, 1408–1425 (2013)
2. Yang, J.C., Yu, K., Gong, Y.H.: Linear Spatial Pyramid Matching Using Sparse Coding for Image Classification. In: IEEE Conference on Computer Vision and Pattern Recognition, pp. 1794–1801 (2009)

 3. Lazebnik, S., Schmid, C., Ponce, J.: Beyond Bags of Features: Spatial Pyramid Matching for Recognizing Natural Scene Categories. In: IEEE Conference on Computer Vision and Pattern Recognition, pp. 2169–2178 (2006)
 4. Gao, S.H., Tsang, I.W.H., Chia, L.T., Zhao, P.L.: Local Features Are Not Lonely-Laplacian Sparse Coding for Image Classification. In: IEEE Conference on Computer Vision and Pattern Recognition, pp. 3555–3561 (2010)
 5. Zhang, C.J., Liu, J., Tian, Q., Xu, C.S., Lu, H.Q., Ma, S.D.: Image Classification by Non-Negative Sparse Coding, Low-Rank and Sparse Decomposition. In: IEEE Conference on Computer Vision and Pattern Recognition, pp. 1673–1680 (2011)
 6. Yu, N.N., Qiu, T.S., Bi, F., Wang, A.Q.: Image Features Extraction and Fusion Based on Joint Sparse Representation. IEEE Journal of Selected Topics in Signal Processing 5, 1074–1082 (2011)
 7. Yin, H.T., Li, S.T.: Multimodal Image Fusion with Joint Sparsity Model. Optical Engineering 50, 1–11 (2011)
 8. Zhang, H.C., Nasrabadi, N.M., Zhang, Y.N., Huang, T.S.: Multi-View Automatic Target Recognition using Joint Sparse Representation. IEEE Transactions on Aerospace and Electronic Systems 48, 2481–2497 (2012)
 9. Yuan, X.T., Liu, X.B., Yan, S.C.: Visual Classification with Multitask Joint Sparse Representation. IEEE Transactions on Image Processing 21, 4349–4360 (2012)
10. Shekhar, S., Patel, V.M., Nasrabadi, N.M., Chellappa, R.: Joint Sparsity-Based Robust Multimodal Biometrics Recognition. In: Fusiello, A., Murino, V., Cucchiara, R. (eds.) ECCV 2012 Ws/Demos, Part III. LNCS, vol. 7585, pp. 365–374. Springer, Heidelberg (2012)
11. Luo, J., Yang, B., Chen, Z.: Color Image Restoration via Extended Joint Sparse Model. In: Liu, C.-L., Zhang, C., Wang, L. (eds.) CCPR 2012. CCIS, vol. 321, pp. 497–504. Springer, Heidelberg (2012)
12. Ramezani, M., Abolmaesumi, P., Marble, K., MacDonald, H., Johnsrude, I.: Joint Sparse Representation of Brain Activity Patterns Related to Perceptual and Cognitive Components of a Speech Comprehension Task. In: 2012 International Workshop on Pattern Recognition in NeuroImaging, pp. 29–32 (2012)
13. Zheng, X.W., Sun, X., Fu, K., Wang, H.Q.: Automatic Annotation of Satellite Images via Multifeature Joint Sparse Coding with Spatial Relation Constrain. IEEE Geoscience and Remote Sensing Letters 10, 652–656 (2013)
14. Yu, N.N., Qiu, T.S., Ren, F.Q.: Denoising for Multiple Image Copies through Joint Sparse Representation. Journal of Mathematical Imaging and Vision 45, 46–54 (2013)
15. Duarte, M.F., Wakin, M.B., Baron, D., Baraniuk, R.G.: Universal Distributed Sensing via Random Projections. In: IEEE International Conference on Information Processing in Sensor Networks, pp. 177–185 (2006)
16. Aharon, M., Elad, M., Bruckstein, A.: K-SVD: An Algorithm for Designing Overcomplete Dictionaries for Sparse Representation. IEEE Transactions on Signal Processing 54, 4311–4322 (2006)
17. Labati, R.D., Piuri, V., Scotti, F.: ALL_IDB web site, The University of Milan, Departement of Information Technology, http://www.dti.unimi.it/fscotti/all
18. Lowe, D.G.: Distinctive Image Features from Scale-Invariant Keypoints. International Journal of Computer Vision 60, 91–110 (2004)
19. Wu, J.: Efficient HIK SVM Learning for Image Classification. IEEE Transactions on Image Processing 21, 4442–4453 (2012)

Multi-task Sparse Classifier for Diagnosis of MCI Conversion to AD with Longitudinal MR Images

Manhua Liu[1], Heung-Il Suk[2], and Dinggang Shen[2]

[1] Department of Instrument Science and Engineering,
Shanghai Jiao Tong University, 200240, China
[2] IDEA Lab, Department of Radiology and BRIC,
University of North Carolina at Chapel Hill, 27599, USA
mhliu@sjtu.edu.cn, {dgshen,heung-il_suk}@med.unc.edu

Abstract. Mild cognitive impairment (MCI) patients are at a high risk of turn-
ing into Alzheimer's disease (AD) within years. But it is known that not all
MCI patients will progress to AD. Therefore, it is of great interest to accurately
diagnose whether a MCI patient will convert to AD (namely MCI converter;
MCI-C) or not (namely MCI non-converter; MCI-NC), for early diagnosis and
proper treatment. In this paper, we propose a multi-task sparse representation
classifier to discriminate between MCI-C and MCI-NC utilizing longitudinal
neuroimaging data. Unlike the previous methods that explicitly combined the
longitudinal information in a feature domain, thus requiring the same number of
measurements in time, the proposed method is not limited to the availability of
the data. Specifically, by means of multi-task learning, we impose a group constraint that the same training samples, ideally belonging to the same class, are
used to represent the longitudinal feature vectors across time points. Then we
utilize a sparse representation classifier for label decision. From a machine
learning perspective, the proposed method can be considered as the combination of the generative and discriminative methods, which are known to be effective in classification enhancement. In our experiments on magnetic resonance
brain images of 349 MCI subjects (164 MCI-C and 185 MCI-NC) from ADNI
database, we demonstrate the validity of the proposed method, which also outperforms the competing methods.

Keywords: MCI diagnosis, longitudinal MR images, multi-task sparse learning, sparse representation classifier.

1 Introduction

Alzheimer's disease (AD), characterized by a progressive impairment of cognitive and
memory functions, is one of the most prevalent neurodegenerative disease in elderly
people. Recent researches have identified that neuroimaging or biological features of
AD patients are also observed in mild cognitive impairment (MCI), which is
thus considered as the prodromal stage of AD. Although it is not unveiled why some
MCI patients convert to AD later (MCI converter; MCI-C) and some do not (MCI

G. Wu et al. (Eds.): MLMI 2013, LNCS 8184, pp. 243–250, 2013.
© Springer International Publishing Switzerland 2013

non-converter; MCI-NC), it is important to correctly classify between them in order for early diagnosis and proper treatment.

For the last decades, many research groups have devoted their efforts for computer-aided AD diagnosis, and recent machine learning-based methods presented promising results in terms of the diagnostic accuracy. However, it still remains challenging for the classification of MCI-C and MCI-NC, and relatively a small number of works have been performed in the literature. For example, Davatzikos et al. analyzed brain atrophy patterns from magnetic resonance imaging (MRI) and cerebrospinal fluid (CSF) biomarkers to predict the short-term conversion to AD [1]. Zhou et al. proposed to utilize inter-regional correlation features from local volumetric measurements in MRI [2]. Although these previous work validated the effectiveness of their methods, they considered only the baseline neuroimaging data in prediction. However, as investigated in recent researches, it is beneficiary to utilize the longitudinal data, which can provide useful information on the pathological progression of disease. For instance, Hinrichs et al. proposed a multi-modality framework for analysis of MCI progression and presented the efficacy of utilizing longitudinal data in their experiment [3]. In [4], the longitudinal cortical thickness changes were also extracted to analyze the development of pathology in AD. In [5], both baseline and longitudinal biomarkers were combined and utilized to predict the future clinical changes of MCI patients.

When considering the availability of longitudinal data due to possible data missing, those methods are very limited since they require every subject to have the same number of data in time, which is not much feasible in practice. Thus, this limitation prevents large amounts of data from being used to build a robust model. To this end, in this paper, we propose a novel method that can efficiently deal with the longitudinal data, each of which may have different number of measurements in time points.

Specifically, we utilize a multi-task sparse representation classifier, which has been successfully used in face recognition [6]. Given longitudinal data, we define a task to represent the neuroimaging features measured at one time point with the training data and thus the representation of all time-point features can be considered as multi-task learning. In our multi-tasking learning, we impose a group constraint that the same training samples, ideally belonging to the same class, are used to represent the longitudinal feature vectors across time points. The rationale behind the proposed method is that patients in a similar time point after being diagnosed as MCI do not necessarily have similar pathological development. We assume, however, that there may exist relations among MCI patients in the pathological development regardless of the time of measurement. That is, neuroimaging features of a MCI patient measured at some months after the baseline can be similar to those of other MCI patients measured at different time points. We evaluate the effectiveness of the proposed method on ADNI dataset.

The rest of this paper is organized as follows. In Section 2, we describe the neuroimaging materials and the preprocessing. The proposed method along with the feature extraction is described in Section 3. We demonstrate the experimental results on the ADNI dataset and compare classification performances with the competing methods in Section 4. In Section 5, we conclude this work and discuss the future work.

2   Materials and Preprocessing

2.1   Materials

In this work, we use the magnetic resonance imaging (MRI) dataset in Alzheimer's Disease Neuroimaging Initiative (ADNI) database (www.loni.ucla.edu/ADNI). The MRI dataset includes standard T1-weighted MR images acquired using volumetric 3D MPRAGE with 1.25×1.25 mm^2 in-plane spatial resolution and 1.2 mm thick sagittal slices. Most of these images were obtained with 1.5T scanners, while a few were acquired from 3T scanners. Detailed information about the MR acquisition procedures is available at the ADNI Web site. In order to evaluate the effectiveness of the proposed method, we use the T1-weighted MR brain image data from 349 MCI patients: 185 MCI non-converters (MCI-NC) and 164 MCI converters (MCI-C). These subjects have a different number of longitudinal imaging data in time points. The maximum number of time points is 5 including baseline, and 6-month, 12-month, 18-month, and 24-month after the baseline. The demographic characteristics of the studied subjects are summarized in Table 1.

Table 1. Demographic characteristics of the studied subjects from ADNI database

Diagnosis	# Subjects	Age	Gender (M/F)	MMSE
MCI-C	164	74.9±6.8	102/65	26.6±1.7
MCI-NC	185	74.9±7.7	158/78	27.3±1.8

2.2   Preprocessing

The MR brain images of multiple time points were preprocessed before performing classification. Specifically, an intensity inhomogeneity on the T1-weighted MR brain images was corrected using nonparametric non-uniform intensity normalization (N3) algorithm [7]. Then, a robust and automated skull stripping method [8] was applied for brain extraction and for cerebellum removal. Each brain image was further segmented into three tissue volumes: gray matter (GM), white matter (WM), and cerebrospinal fluid (CSF). Finally, the segmented brain tissue volumes were warped and registered into a template with 93 manually labeled ROIs [9].

3   Methods

3.1   Feature Extraction

Since it is known that the GM is more related to AD and/or MCI than other tissues, in this work, we extract features from the GM by computing the tissue volumes of 93 ROIs. That is, we have a 93-dimensional feature vector from MR images at a time point. Importantly, with the increasing availability of longitudinal data, the dynamic features that directly describe the temporal changes of GM tissue volumes can also be computed to provide more information about the pathological development. In order to utilize the longitudinal imaging information, we also compute the ratios of GM volumes for each ROI between the baseline and the most recent time point (endline) in measurement, which can further provide a measurement for the severity of the disease. Therefore, besides the GM volumes of 93 ROIs at each time point, we also use these dynamic features as complementary information.

3.2   Multi-task Sparse Representation Classifier

One of the key ideas of the proposed method is that we consider the representation of a target neuroimaging feature vector based on the training data without concerning the time-point of measurement. Unlike the previous methods that explicitly combined the longitudinal information in a feature domain, we consider the information fusion in our sparse representation method implicitly. Therefore, it is not a concern for the availability of data in time, which can be the advantage of the proposed method.

Let $X^k = [X_1^k \cdots X_c^k \cdots X_C^k] \in \Re^{M \times N}$ denote training samples of the k-type feature vector (i.e., GM or dynamic feature vector in our application) over C classes, where $X_c^k = [X_{c1}^k \cdots X_{cn}^k \cdots X_{cN_c}^k] \in \Re^{M \times N_c}$, $X_{cn}^k \in \Re^M$ is the n-th sample of the class c, M is a feature dimension, N_c is the number of training samples of the class c, and $N = N_1 + \cdots N_c + \cdots N_C$. Note that, in the notation, the time-point of a sample is not explicitly specified.

In this paper, we assume that a neuroimaging target k-type feature vector $y_t^k \in \Re^M$ at a time-point t can be represented by a linear combination of the training samples with a l_1-norm constraint as follows:

$$\hat{w}_t^k = \underset{w_t^k}{\mathrm{argmin}} \left\| X^k w_t^k - y_t^k \right\|_2^2 + \lambda \left\| w_t^k \right\|_1 \tag{1}$$

where w_t^k denotes a coefficient vector for the k-type feature vector and λ is a sparsity control parameter. We consider finding the optimal coefficient vector w_t^k as a task. Then, given longitudinal data, the problem of finding the optimal coefficient vectors for the neuroimaging feature vectors across time points can be defined as multi-task learning [10]. It should be emphasized that, in our multi-task learning, we further apply a group constraint that imposes the same training samples, which ideally belong to the same class, to be used to represent longitudinal neuroimaging feature vectors across time. Here, a feature vector at a time point is considered as one group.

$$\hat{W} = \underset{W}{\min} \frac{1}{2} \left(\sum_{k=1}^{2} \sum_{t=1}^{T_k} \left\| X^k w_t^k - y_t^k \right\|_2^2 \right) + \lambda \|W\|_{2,1} \tag{2}$$

where $W = [w_1^1 \cdots w_t^1 \cdots w_{T_1}^1 w_1^2 \cdots w_t^2 \cdots w_{T_2}^2]$ for our case of using two types of feature vectors such as $k \in \{1,2\}$, T_k denotes the number of time points of the k-type feature vector, $\|W\|_{2,1} = \sum_{n=1}^{N} \|W(n)\|_2$ is a l_1-norm of $\|W(n)\|_2$, and $W(n)$ denotes the n-th row of the matrix W. The group regularization in Eq. (2) ensures that the coefficient vectors for different time-points share common training samples for representation.

Here, we should note that the longitudinal information is fused in a representation domain by means of the $l_{2,1}$-norm in multi-task learning. While the representation error for each time-point is computed individually, the regularization term in Eq. (2) has the effect of fusing the longitudinal information by imposing the same training samples to be used across time points, but having different coefficient values. In this approach, we are not limited to the availability of data, from which the previous methods suffer. That is, while the previous methods require subjects of interest to have the same number of time-point data, which is not much feasible in practice, the proposed method is still applicable without concerning the availability of data in building a robust model. This is one of the advantages of the proposed method.

Earlier, Bishop and Julia proposed to combine a generative and a discriminative method to enhance classification accuracy [11]. Motivated by the research, in this work, we combine the multi-task learning method with a sparse representation classifier (SRC) [12]. From a machine learning point of view, the multi-task learning can be considered as a generative method since its main goal is to determine the best linear combination of training samples to represent the target data. Meanwhile, SRC exploits a discriminative nature in determining a class label with the following rule:

$$\hat{c} = \underset{c}{\mathrm{argmin}} \sum_{k=1}^{2} \sum_{t=1}^{T_k} \left\| X_c^k \hat{w}_{t,c}^k - y_t^k \right\|_2 \tag{3}$$

where $X_c^k = \left[X_{c1}^k \cdots X_{cn}^k \cdots X_{cN_c}^k \right] \in \mathfrak{R}^{M \times N_c}$ denotes the training samples of the class c, $\hat{w}_{t,c}^k$ denotes a reduced coefficient vector, whose elements correspond to ones that are associated with the training samples of the c class in $\hat{w}_t^k$, for the k-type neuroimaging feature vector measured at the time-point t. That is, the class label of the test sample is assigned to the class, a linear combination of whose training samples produces the minimum reconstruction errors. In Eq. (2), the class label is determined based on the test data at the available time points, and it does not require that the test samples should have all the time points available.

4   Experimental Results and Analysis

In our experiments, we performed a leave-one-out cross-validation technique. Specifically, one subject was left out for testing and the data of the remaining subjects were used for training. The regularization parameter $\lambda \in [0, 1]$ in Eq. (2) was determined through cross-validation within the training samples with a grid search approach. In order to evaluate the classification performance, we computed the classification accuracy (ACC), the proportion of correctly classified subjects, by taking the average over the experiments. We also considered the sensitivity (SEN), the proportion of MCI-C patients correctly classified, and the specificity (SPEC), the proportion of MCI-NC subjects correctly classified.

We first performed an experiment with only the GM volume features from 93 ROIs and compared the change of classification performance by varying the number of longitudinal data in time points. Table 2 summarizes the classification accuracies according to the availability of the longitudinal data. We can see that the more the longitudinal data are available, the higher the classification accuracy we could consistently obtain with the proposed multi-task sparse representation classifier. Note that the proposed method can successfully deal with the varying number of longitudinal neuroimaging data with no requirement of modification or retraining.

Table 2. Change of the classification performance according to the number of longitudinal neuroimaging data available in time points. (M: months)

Availability of Data	ACC (%)	SEN (%)	SPEC (%)
Baseline (B)	65.6	56.2	**74.0**
B+6M	66.1	61.0	70.8
B+6M+12M	66.6	61.0	71.4
B+6M+12M+18M	67.6	65.3	69.2
B+6M+12M+18M+24M	**68.8**	**68.3**	69.2

In our second experiment, we evaluated the effectiveness of the multi-feature combination with the proposed multi-task SRC. The performance of the proposed multi-task SRC was compared with that of the conventional SRC on different feature types, i.e., GM volumes and GM volume ratios (dynamic features). In case of combining multiple features of multi-time-point GM volumes and GM volume ratios, an ensemble technique was applied for the conventional SRC. Table 3 shows the classification performances of the competing methods. It is clear that the feature combination is effective to enhance the performance utilizing more information available in classification. Furthermore, the proposed multi-task SRC outperforms the competing ensemble SRC in full use of the longitudinal data. We also presented the receiver operating characteristic (ROC) curve in Fig. 1. Based on the ROC curve, we also computed the area under the curve (AUC), which of the proposed method is the largest as shown in Table 3. From these results, we can say that the proposed method is effective in incorporating the longitudinal neuroimaging features measured at multiple time points for brain disease diagnosis.

Table 3. Comparison of the classification performances among the competing methods

Method	Features	ACC (%)	SEN (%)	SPEC (%)	AUC (%)
SRC	Baseline GM volume	65.6	56.2	**74.0**	70.1
SRC	GM volume ratio	62.8	52.4	71.8	64.0
Ensemble SRC	Longitudinal GM volumes + volume ratio	69.1	66.5	71.3	73.3
Multi-task SRC	Longitudinal GM volumes + volume ratio	**71.4**	**71.3**	71.4	**74.6**

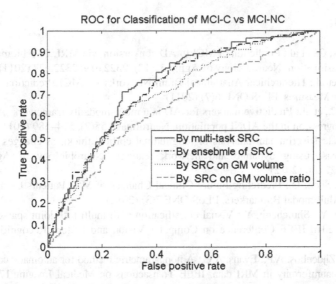

Fig. 1. ROC curves of four classification results with different features and different combination methods

In order for pathological interpretation, we identified the informative features by iteratively adding one ROI at each time and evaluating the change of the classification performance. The ROI with which the maximum improvement was obtained was selected in each time. To sum up, the identified ROIs were hippocampus, entorhinal cortex, parahippocampal gyrus, and amygdala, which coincide with those reported in the literature on AD and/or MCI studies [13, 14].

5   Conclusions

In this paper, we proposed a novel method to identify MCI conversion based on longitudinal neuroimaging data. In order to overcome the problem of the availability of longitudinal data, we proposed to fuse the longitudinal information in a representation domain by means of a multi-task learning and a sparse representation classifier. We also utilized the temporal change of the neuroimaging features with both tissue volumes of brain regions and the ratios of regional volumes between the baseline and endline time points. In our experiments on ADNI database, we validated the effectiveness of the proposed method with the classification accuracy of 71.4% and the sensitivity of 71.3%. While the proposed method exploited the longitudinal information in multi-task learning and sparse representation classifier, it does not take into account the temporal correlations among measurements, which can be helpful to enhance the classification accuracy. Therefore, it would be our forthcoming research issues to efficiently reflect the temporal correlations into our method.

References

1. Davatzikos, C., et al.: Prediction of MCI to AD conversion, via MRI, CSF biomarkers, and pattern classification. Neurobiology of Aging 32(12), 2322.e19–2322.e27 (2011)
2. Zhou, L., et al.: Hierarchical Anatomical Brain Networks for MCI Prediction: Revisiting Volumetric Measures. PLoS ONE 6(7) (2011)
3. Hinrichs, C., et al.: Predictive markers for AD in a multi-modality framework: An analysis of MCI progression in the ADNI population. NeuroImage 55(2), 574–589 (2011)
4. Li, Y., et al.: Discriminant analysis of longitudinal cortical thickness changes in Alzheimer's disease using dynamic and network features. Neurobiology of Aging 33(2), 427.e15–427.e30 (2012)
5. Zhang, D., Shen, D.: Predicting Future Clinical Changes of MCI Patients Using Longitudinal and Multimodal Biomarkers. PLoS ONE 7(3) (2012)
6. Xiao-Tong, Y., Shuicheng, Y.: Visual classification with multi-task joint sparse representation. In: 2010 IEEE Conference on Computer Vision and Pattern Recognition, CVPR (2010)
7. Sled, J.G., Zijdenbos, A.P., Evans, A.C.: A nonparametric method for automatic correction of intensity nonuniformity in MRI data. IEEE Transactions on Medical Imaging 17(1), 87–97 (1998)
8. Wang, Y., Nie, J., Yap, P.-T., Shi, F., Guo, L., Shen, D.: Robust deformable-surface-based skull-stripping for large-scale studies. In: Fichtinger, G., Martel, A., Peters, T. (eds.) MICCAI 2011, Part III. LNCS, vol. 6893, pp. 635–642. Springer, Heidelberg (2011)
9. Kabani, N., et al.: A 3D atlas of the human brain. NeuroImage 7, S717 (1998)
10. Yuan, M., Lin, Y.: Model selection and estimation in regression with grouped variables. Journal of the Royal Statistical Society: Series B (Statistical Methodology) 68(1), 9 (2006)
11. Bishop, C., Lasserre, J.: Generative or Discriminative? Getting the Best of Both Worlds
12. Wright, J., et al.: Robust Face Recognition via Sparse Representation. IEEE Transactions on Pattern Analysis and Machine Intelligence 31(2), 210–227 (2009)
13. Cuingnet, R., et al.: Automatic classification of patients with Alzheimer's disease from structural MRI: A comparison of ten methods using the ADNI database. NeuroImage 56(2), 766–781 (2011)
14. Zhang, D., et al.: Multimodal classification of Alzheimer's disease and mild cognitive impairment. NeuroImage 55(3), 856–867 (2011)

Sparse Multimodal Manifold-Regularized Transfer Learning for MCI Conversion Prediction

Bo Cheng[1,2], Daoqiang Zhang[1,*], Biao Jie[1], and Dinggang Shen[2,*]

[1] Dept. of Computer Science and Engineering,
Nanjing University of Aeronautics and Astronautics, Nanjing 210016, China
[2] Dept. of Radiology and BRIC, University of North Carolina at Chapel Hill, NC 27599
dqzhang@nuaa.edu.cn, dgshen@med.unc.edu

Abstract. Effective prediction of conversion of mild cognitive impairment (MCI) to Alzheimer's disease (AD) is important for early diagnosis of AD, as well as for evaluating AD risk pre-symptomatically. Different from most traditional methods for MCI conversion prediction, in this paper, we propose a novel sparse multimodal manifold-regularized transfer learning classification (SM²TLC) method, which can simultaneously use other related classification tasks (e.g., AD vs. normal controls (NC) classification) and also the unlabeled data for improving the MCI conversion prediction. Our proposed method includes two key components: (1) a criterion based on the maximum mean discrepancy (MMD) for eliminating the negative effect related to the distribution differences between the auxiliary (i.e., AD/NC) and the target (i.e., MCI converters/MCI non-converters) domains, and (2) a sparse semi-supervised manifold-regularized least squares classification method for utilization of unlabeled data. Experimental results on the Alzheimer's Disease Neuroimaging Initiative (ADNI) database show that the proposed method can significantly improve the classification performance between MCI converters and MCI non-converters, compared with the state-of-the-art methods.

1 Introduction

Alzheimer's disease (AD) is the most common type of dementia, which can be characterized by the progressive impairment of neurons and their connections, leading to the loss of cognitive function and the ultimate death. Mild cognitive impairment (MCI) is a prodromal stage of AD, with high likelihood of conversion to AD. Thus, effective prediction of MCI-to-AD conversion is of great significance for early diagnosis of AD and also for evaluating AD risk pre-symptomatically. So far, more and more machine learning methods have been developed for addressing the MCI conversion prediction, i.e., classification between MCI converters (MCI-C) and MCI non-converters (MCI-NC) based on the baseline imaging data [1-6].

One challenge in MCI conversion prediction is the small number of MCI (including both MCI-C and MCI-NC) subjects available for training, while the dimensionality of data is often very high. This makes it very difficult to train a robust and accurate classifier. To address this issue, many advanced machine learning methods have been

---

* Corresponding authors.

G. Wu et al. (Eds.): MLMI 2013, LNCS 8184, pp. 251–259, 2013.

proposed for MCI conversion prediction. For example, Zhang *et al.* used the multi-task learning for joint regression and classification from multimodal data, including magnetic resonance imaging (MRI), fluorodeoxyglucose positron emission tomography (FDG-PET) and cerebrospinal fluid (CSF), achieving an accuracy of 73.9% on classifying between 43 MCI-C and 48 MCI-NC subjects [2]. Cho *et al.* adopted a manifold harmonic transform method using the cortical thickness data, achieving a sensitivity of 63% and a specificity of 76% on 72 MCI-C and 131 MCI-NC subjects [1]. Duchesne *et al.* used the morphological factor method with the MRI data, achieving an accuracy of 72.3% on 20 MCI-C and 29 MCI-NC subjects [5].

On the other hand, some recent studies based on semi-supervised learning (SSL) methods have shown that the task of classifying between MCI-C and MCI-NC is related to the task of classifying between AD and normal controls (NC) [7]. In machine learning community, a new learning methodology called *transfer learning* has been developed to deal with the problems involving cross-domain learning. Unlike SSL, transfer learning does not assume the auxiliary data (i.e., unlabeled data in SSL) have the same distribution as the target data (i.e., labeled data in SSL). Recently, this transfer learning technique has been introduced into medical imaging area. For example, a domain transfer support vector machine (DTSVM) has been used for classification between MCI-C and MCI-NC subjects, showing greatly improved classification performance for MCI conversion prediction with help of AD and NC subjects used as the auxiliary data [8].

In this paper, we propose a novel sparse multimodal manifold-regularized transfer learning classification (SM^{2}TLC) framework for MCI conversion prediction. Specifically, we employ a criterion based on maximum mean discrepancy (MMD) for eliminating the negative effect due to the distribution differences between the auxiliary (AD/NC) and the target (MCI-C/MCI-NC) domains. Then, we combine with the sparse semi-supervised manifold-regularized least squares method for utilization of unlabeled subjects. Our proposed method can be applied to not only the single-modality data, but also the multimodal data. We validate our method on both single-modality and multimodal data, including MRI, FDG-PET and CSF, from the ADNI database.

2   Method

In this section, we introduce our proposed sparse multimodal manifold transfer learning classification method (SM^{2}TLC) for classifying MCI-C from MCI-NC. Specifically, in Section 2.1, we will first introduce a criterion based on the maximum mean discrepancy (MMD) for reducing the mismatch of distributions between the auxiliary (i.e., AD/NC) and the target (i.e., MCI-C/MCI-NC) domains. Then, we will derive the objective function and its corresponding optimization algorithm for the proposed SM^{2}TLC method in Sections 2.2 and 2.3, respectively.

2.1   Maximum Mean Discrepancy (MMD) Criterion

Assume that we have N_A samples with class labels in the auxiliary domain, denoted as $A = \{\mathbf{x}_i^A, y_i^A\}_{i=1}^{N_A}$, where $\mathbf{x}_i^A \in R^d$ is the i-th sample and $y_i^A \in \{+1, -1\}$ is its corresponding class label (i.e., with the AD labeled as 1 and the NC labeled as -1). Also, assume that we have N_T^L *labeled target* samples with class labels, denoted as $T^L = \{x_i^L, y_i^L\}_{i=1}^{N_T^L}$, where $x_i^L \in R^d$ is the i-th sample and $y_i^L \in \{+1, -1\}$ is the corresponding class label (i.e., with the MCI-C labeled as 1 and the MCI-NC labeled as -1). Similarly, we have N_T^U *unlabeled target* samples, denote as $T^U = \{x_i^U\}_{i=1}^{N_T^U}$, where $x_i^U \in R^d$. We use $N_T = N_T^L + N_T^U$ to represent the total number of *target* samples $T = \{T^L \cup T^U\}$. Because of the distribution differences between the auxiliary and the target domains, direct training with samples from the auxiliary domain may degrade the classification performance in another target domain. Therefore, we cannot directly add auxiliary data to target domain for training. To address this issue, we employ a criterion based on the maximum mean discrepancy (MMD) [9, 16]:

$$dist^2(A, T) = tr(\mathbf{KS}) \tag{1}$$

where

$$\mathbf{K} = \begin{bmatrix} \mathbf{K}^{A,A} & \mathbf{K}^{A,T} \\ \mathbf{K}^{T,A} & \mathbf{K}^{T,T} \end{bmatrix} \tag{2}$$

and $\mathbf{S} = \mathbf{ss}^T$, $\mathbf{s} = [\frac{1}{N_A}, ..., \frac{1}{N_A}, \frac{-1}{N_T}, ..., \frac{-1}{N_T}]^T$, and $tr(.)$ is the matrix trace [16]. Here, $\mathbf{K}$ denotes a compound cross-domain kernel matrix over both A and T, with $\mathbf{K}^{A,A} = [k(x_i^A, x_j^A)] \in R^{N_A \times N_A}$, $\mathbf{K}^{T,T} = [k(x_i^T, x_j^T)] \in R^{N_T \times N_T}$, $\mathbf{K}^{A,T} = [k(x_i^A, x_j^T)] \in R^{N_A \times N_T}$, and $\mathbf{K}^{T,A} = [k(x_i^T, x_j^A)] \in R^{N_T \times N_A}$.

2.2 Objective Function of SM²TLC

To explore related auxiliary domains data and the manifold structure of both labeled and unlabeled data from the target domain, we employ the semi-supervised manifold-regularized least squares method [15] and combine the criterion of MMD (i.e., Eq. 1) to design a sparse multimodal manifold-regularized transfer learning classification method (denoted as SM²TLC), which can simultaneously use the multimodal biomarkers for learning a sparse multimodal weight matrix $\mathbf{W}$. To this end, SM²TLC solves the following optimization problem with L_1/L_2-norm regularization:

$$\min_{\mathbf{W}} \frac{1}{M} \sum_{m=1}^{M} (d_m \cdot tr(\mathbf{K}_m \mathbf{S}) + (\mathbf{Y} - \mathbf{J} \mathbf{K}_m \mathbf{w}_m)^T (\mathbf{Y} - \mathbf{J} \mathbf{K}_m \mathbf{w}_m)$$
$$+ \gamma \mathbf{w}_m^T \mathbf{K}_m^T \mathbf{\Lambda}_m \mathbf{K}_m \mathbf{w}_m) + \mu \|\mathbf{W}\|_{2,1} \tag{3}$$

where $\mathbf{Y} = [y_1^A, ..., y_{N_A}^A, y_1^L, ..., y_{N_T^L}^L, 0_1, ..., 0_{N_T^U}]^T$, $\mathbf{K}_m$ is the compound cross-domain kernel matrix defined on the m-th modality according to Eq. 2 and d_m is a nonnegative weight parameter with $\sum_{m=1}^{M} d_m = 1$. And $\mathbf{J} = diag(1, ..., 1, 0, ..., 0)$ is diagonal matrix with the first $N_A + N_T^L$ diagonal entries as 1 and the rest as 0, and $\gamma, \mu > 0$ are the two regularization parameters. Specifically, there are three modalities (e.g., $M = 3$) used in this paper, including MRI, PET and CSF. In Eq. 3, $\mathbf{W} = [\mathbf{w}_1, \mathbf{w}_2, .., \mathbf{w}_M] \in R^{N \times M}$, where $N = N_A + N_T$, is the weight matrix whose i-th row $\mathbf{w}^i$ is the vector of coefficients associated with the i-th training sample across different modalities. It's worth noting that a 'group sparsity' regularization term is used for joint selection of samples across different modalities based on the L_1/L_2-norm, i.e., $\|\mathbf{W}\|_{2,1} = \sum_{i=1}^N \|\mathbf{w}^i\|_2$. Also, Λ_m is the compound cross-domain Laplacian matrix on the m-th modality, which is defined as:

$$\Lambda_m = \begin{bmatrix} \Lambda_m^A & 0 \\ 0 & \Lambda_m^T \end{bmatrix} \tag{4}$$

where $\Lambda_m^A = D_m^A - C_m^A$ and $\Lambda_m^T = D_m^T - C_m^T$ are the Laplacian matrices [15] over the auxiliary domain and the target domain, respectively. Here, $C_m^A = [c_{ij}^A] \in R^{N_A \times N_A}$ and $C_m^T = [c_{ij}^T] \in R^{N_T \times N_T}$ are the similarity matrices that respectively define the similarity of subjects in the auxiliary domain and the target domain, while $D_m^A = [d_{ii}^A] \in R^{N_A \times N_A}$ and $D_m^T = [d_{ii}^T] \in R^{N_T \times N_T}$ are the diagonal matrices with $d_{ii}^A = \sum_j c_{ij}^A$ and $d_{ii}^T = \sum_j c_{ij}^A$. By minimizing Eq. 3, many rows of $\mathbf{W}$ will be zeros, thus we can obtain a sparse solution for $\mathbf{W}$. Then, the decision function $f^*(\mathbf{x})$ for the predicted label in the target domain can be obtained as follows:

$$f^*(\mathbf{x}) = sign\left(\sum_{m=1}^M d_m \mathbf{K}_m^* \mathbf{w}_m^*\right) \tag{5}$$

where we assume that $\mathbf{x} = \{\mathbf{x}_1, \mathbf{x}_2, \dots, \mathbf{x}_M\}$ is a testing sample's multimodal data in the target domain, $\mathbf{K}_m^* = [k(\mathbf{x}_m, \mathbf{x}_m^i)]_{i=1}^N \in R^{1 \times N}$ is the testing sample's kernel vector on the m-th modality (between the testing sample $\mathbf{x}_m$ and the i-th training samples $\mathbf{x}_m^i$ in the cross-domain on the m-th modality), and $\mathbf{W}^* = [\mathbf{w}_1^*, \mathbf{w}_2^*, \dots, \mathbf{w}_M^*]$ is the optimal solution obtained from Eq. 3. Thus, we can get the predicted label $f^*(\mathbf{x})$ for the testing sample $\mathbf{x}$ via the Eq. 5 to compute.

2.3 Optimization Algorithm for SM²TLC

To optimize the problem in Eq. 3, the accelerated gradient descent (AGD) method is employed to solve the optimization problem with L_1/L_2-norm regularization [10]. According to the AGD algorithm, the objective function (denoted as $F(\mathbf{W})$) of Eq. 3 can be separated into a smooth part:

$$G(\mathbf{W}) = \frac{1}{M} \sum_{m=1}^M (d_m \cdot tr(\mathbf{K}_m \mathbf{S}) + (\mathbf{Y} - J\mathbf{K}_m \mathbf{w}_m)^T (\mathbf{Y} - J\mathbf{K}_m \mathbf{w}_m)$$
$$+ \gamma \mathbf{w}_m^T \mathbf{K}_m^T \Lambda_m \mathbf{K}_m \mathbf{w}_m) \tag{6}$$

and a non-smooth part:

$$H(\mathbf{W}) = \mu \|\mathbf{W}\|_{2,1} \tag{7}$$

So, $F(\mathbf{W}) = G(\mathbf{W}) + H(\mathbf{W})$. Then, we define the generalized gradient update step to solve the Eq. 3 as follows:

$$Q_h(\mathbf{W}, \mathbf{W}_t) = G(\mathbf{W}_t) + \langle \mathbf{W} - \mathbf{W}_t, \nabla G(\mathbf{W}_t) \rangle + \frac{h}{2}\|\mathbf{W} - \mathbf{W}_t\|_F^2 + H(\mathbf{W})$$

$$q_h(\mathbf{W}_t) = \arg\min_{\mathbf{W}} Q_h(\mathbf{W}, \mathbf{W}_t) \tag{8}$$

Where $\nabla G(\mathbf{W}_t)$ denotes the gradient of $G(\mathbf{W})$ at point $\mathbf{W}_t$ for the t-th iteration, h is the step size, $\|\cdot\|_F$ denotes the Frobenius norm, and $\langle \mathbf{W} - \mathbf{W}_t, \nabla G(\mathbf{W}_t) \rangle = tr((\mathbf{W} - \mathbf{W}_t)^T \nabla G(\mathbf{W}_t))$ is the matrix inner product. According to [10], the generalized gradient update step of Eq. 8 can be decomposed into N separate subproblems with the gradient mapping update approach. In summary, the AGD algorithm to solve the objective function of Eq. 3 is presented in Algorithm 1.

Algorithm 1. AGD algorithm for SM^{2}TLC

Initialization: $h_0 > 0, \eta > 1, \mathbf{W}_0 \in R^{N \times M}, \bar{\mathbf{W}}_0 = \mathbf{W}_0, h=h_0$ and $\alpha_0 = 1$.

for $t = 0,1,2, \dots$ until convergence of $\mathbf{W}_t$ do:

Set $h = h_t$

While $F\left(q_h(\bar{\mathbf{W}}_t)\right) > Q_h(q_h(\bar{\mathbf{W}}_t), \bar{\mathbf{W}}_t),\qquad h = \eta h$

Set $h_{t+1} = h$ and compute

$\mathbf{W}_{t+1} = \arg\min_{\mathbf{W}} Q_{h_{t+1}}(\mathbf{W}, \bar{\mathbf{W}}_t),\ \alpha_{t+1} = \frac{2}{t+3},\ \beta_{t+1} = \mathbf{W}_{t+1} - \mathbf{W}_t$ and

$\bar{\mathbf{W}}_{t+1} = \mathbf{W}_{t+1} + \frac{1-\alpha_t}{\alpha_t}\alpha_{t+1}\beta_{t+1}$

end for

---

3   Experiments

In this section, we evaluate the effectiveness of our proposed SM^{2}TLC method on multimodal data, including MRI, PET and CSF, from the Alzheimer's disease Neuroimaging Initiative (ADNI) database.

3.1   Experimental Settings

In our experiments, the baseline ADNI subjects with all corresponding MRI, PET, and CSF data are included, which leads to a total of 202 subjects (including 51 AD patients, 99 MCI patients, and 52 normal controls (NC)). For the 99 MCI patients, it includes 43 MCI converters and 56 MCI non-converters. Also, for each of the three modalities, we include another set of data from 153 randomly selected subjects as unlabeled data. We use 51 AD and 52 NC subjects as auxiliary domain, and 99 MCI subjects as target domain.

The same image pre-processing as used in [11] is adopted here. First, we do AC-PC (anterior commissure-posterior commissure) correction on all images using MIPAV software, and then resample the images to $256 \times 256 \times 256$. Automated skull-stripping is performed [12], followed by manual review to ensure clean skull and dura removal. Then the cerebellum is removed based on registration, in which we use a manually labeled cerebellum as template. After intensity inhomogeneity correction (which was done for three times by the N3 algorithm), we use FAST in

FSL to segment the human brain into three different tissues: grey matter (GM), white matter (WM) and Cerebrospinal fluid (CSF). We use HAMMER [13] to do the registration. After registration, we get the subject-labeled image based on the Jacob template, which was manually labeled into 93 ROIs. For each of the 93 ROI regions in the labeled image of one subject, we compute the GM/WM/CSF tissue volumes in this ROI region by combining the segmentation result of this subject. For each subject, we first align the PET image to its respective T1 MR image by affine registration. Then, we get the average intensity of every ROI in the PET image as feature.

To evaluate the performance of different classification methods, we use a 10-fold cross-validation strategy to compute the classification AUC (area under the ROC curve), accuracy, sensitivity, and specificity. In particular, in the target domain, 99 labeled MCI subjects are equally partitioned into 10 subsets, and then one subset is successively selected as the testing samples and all remaining subsets are used for training classifiers. This process is repeated 10 times. The SVM classifier is implemented using the LIBSVM toolbox [14], with a linear kernel and a default value for the parameter C (i.e., $C = 1$). For comparison, LapSVM is also adopted in this paper. LapSVM is a typical semi-supervised learning method based on manifold hypothesis [15]. For LapSVM settings, we use linear kernel, and the Laplacian matrix Λ with N_T nodes are connected using k (i.e., $k=5$) nearest neighbors, and their edge weights are calculated using the *Euclidean* distance among samples. For regularization parameters γ and β, $\gamma, \beta \in \{0.001, 0.01, 0.03, 0.06, 0.09, 0.1, 0.2, 0.4, 0.6, 0.8\}$, they are learned based on the training samples by cross-validation, respectively. In addition, our previous transfer learning based method (i.e., DTSVM) [8] is also included here for comparison. We use both single-modality and multimodal data to evaluate our method. For combining multimodal data in both standard SVM and LapSVM methods and also for computing d_m, we specifically use a multi-kernel combination technique [11], with the weights learned from the training samples through a grid search, using the range from 0 to 1 at a step size of 0.1. Also, for features of each modality, the same feature normalization scheme as used in [11] is adopted here.

3.2 Results

We compare our SM^{2}TLC method with DTSVM [8], LapSVM, and standard SVM (SVM) for both single-modality and multimodal cases. Table 1 shows their classification performance measures on different modalities. Note that Table 1 shows the averaged results of 10 independent experiments. As we can see from Table 1, SM^{2}TLC consistently achieves better results than DTSVM, LapSVM and SVM methods on each performance measure, which validates the efficacy of our SM^{2}TLC method on using AD and NC subjects as auxiliary domains for helping SSL classification. Specifically, for multimodal case, SM^{2}TLC can achieve a classification accuracy of 77.8%, which is significantly better than DTSVM, LapSVM and SVM

Table 1. Comparison of performance measures of SM²TLC, DTSVM, LapSVM, and SVM for MCI-C/MCI-NC classification using different modalities. (ACC= Accuracy, SEN=Sensitivity, SPE= Specificity).

Modality	Methods	ACC %	SEN %	SPE %	AUC
MRI+CSF+PET	SM²TLC	**77.8**	**83.9**	69.8	**0.814**
	DTSVM	69.4	64.3	**73.5**	0.736
	LapSVM	69.1	74.3	62.1	0.751
	SVM	63.8	58.8	67.7	0.683
MRI	SM²TLC	**72.1**	**75.1**	**68.2**	**0.768**
	DTSVM	63.3	59.8	66.0	0.700
	LapSVM	65.9	69.6	61.0	0.686
	SVM	53.9	47.6	57.7	0.554
CSF	SM²TLC	**66.7**	**74.6**	60.5	0.668
	DTSVM	66.2	60.3	**70.8**	**0.701**
	LapSVM	62.1	66.2	56.8	0.660
	SVM	60.8	55.2	65.0	0.647
PET	SM²TLC	**68.1**	**71.5**	63.7	**0.734**
	DTSVM	67.0	59.6	**72.7**	0.732
	LapSVM	61.6	65.7	56.1	0.661
	SVM	58.0	52.1	62.5	0.612

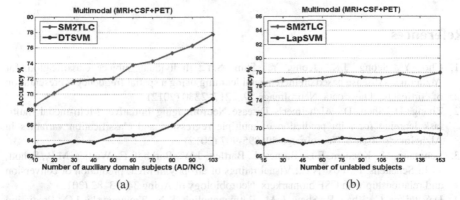

Fig. 1. Comparison of classification accuracy (a) between SM²TLC and DTSVM with respect to the use of different number of subjects in the auxiliary domain, and (b) between SM²TLC and LapSVM with respect to the use of different number of unlabeled subjects

which achieve only 69.4%, 69.1% and 63.8%, respectively. Finally, in Fig. 1, we compare SM²TLC with DTSVM [8] for classification accuracy, with respect to the use of different number of subjects in the auxiliary domain, and compare SM²TLC with LapSVM for classification accuracy with respect to the use of different number of unlabeled subjects, respectively. As we can see from Fig. 1, in most cases, the performance of SM²TLC is significantly better than DTSVM as the number of subjects in the auxiliary domain increases. On the other hand, the performance of SM^2TLC is significantly better than LapSVM as the number of unlabeled subjects increases. These results further validate the efficacy of our proposed SM^2TLC method.

4   Conclusion

This paper addresses the problem of exploiting the use of auxiliary domain data (i.e., AD/NC) and unlabeled subjects for helping classifying MCI converters (MCI-C) from MCI non-converters (MCI-NC). By integrating the criterion based on the maximum mean discrepancy (MMD) and the sparse semi-supervised manifold-regularized least squares classification, we developed a sparse multimodal manifold-regularized transfer learning classification method, namely SM^2TLC, for MCI conversion prediction. Our method does not require the auxiliary domain data and the target domain data to be from the same distribution. Experimental results on the ADNI database validate the efficacy of our proposed method.

Acknowledgements. This work was supported in part by NIH grants EB006733, EB008374, EB009634, and AG041721, SRFDP grant (No. 20123218110009), NUAAFRF grant (No. NE2013105), JiangsuSF for Distinguished Young Scholar, CQESTP grant (Nos. KJ121111, KJ131108), and UNSFA grant (No. KJ2013Z095).

References

1. Cho, Y., Seong, J.K., Jeong, Y., Shin, S.Y.: Individual subject classification for Alzheimer's disease based on incremental learning using a spatial frequency representation of cortical thickness data. NeuroImage 59, 2217–2230 (2012)
2. Zhang, D., Shen, D., Alzheimer's Disease Neuroimaging Initiative: Multi-modal multi-task learning for joint prediction of multiple regression and classification variables in Alzheimer's disease. NeuroImage 59, 895-907 (2012)
3. Lehmann, M., Koedam, E.L., Barnes, J., Bartlett, J.W., Barkhof, F., Wattjes, M.P., Schott, J.M., Scheltens, P., Fox, N.C.: Visual ratings of atrophy in MCI: prediction of conversion and relationship with CSF biomarkers. Neurobiology of Aging 34, 73–82 (2012)
4. Davatzikos, C., Bhatt, P., Shaw, L.M., Batmanghelich, K.N., Trojanowski, J.Q.: Prediction of MCI to AD conversion, via MRI, CSF biomarkers, and pattern classification. Neurobiology of Aging 32, 2322.e19–2322.e27 (2011)
5. Duchesne, S., Mouiha, A.: Morphological factor estimation via high-dimensional reduction: prediction of MCI conversion to probable AD. International Journal of Alzheimer's Disease 2011, 914085 (2011)
6. Cuingnet, R., Gerardin, E., Tessieras, J., Auzias, G., Lehericy, S., Habert, M.O., Chupin, M., Benali, H., Colliot, O.: Automatic classification of patients with Alzheimer's disease from structural MRI: a comparison of ten methods using the ADNI database. NeuroImage 56, 766–781 (2011)
7. Filipovych, R., Davatzikos, C.: Semi-supervised pattern classification of medical images: Application to mild cognitive impairment (MCI). NeuroImage 55(3), 1109–1119 (2011)

8. Cheng, B., Zhang, D., Shen, D.: Domain transfer learning for MCI conversion prediction. In: Ayache, N., Delingette, H., Golland, P., Mori, K. (eds.) MICCAI 2012, Part I. LNCS, vol. 7510, pp. 82–90. Springer, Heidelberg (2012)
9. Borgwardt, K.M., Gretton, A., Rasch, M.J., Kriegel, H.P., Scholkopf, B., Smola, A.J.: Integrating structured biological data by kernel maximum mean discrepancy. Bioinformatics 22, e49–e57 (2006)
10. Chen, X., Pan, W., Kwok, J.T., Carbonell, J.G.: Accelerated gradient method for multi-task sparse learning problem. In: Proceedings Ninth IEEE International Conference on Data Mining, ICDM 2009, pp. 746–751 (2009)
11. Zhang, D., Wang, Y., Zhou, L., Yuan, H., Shen, D.: Multimodal classification of Alzheimer's disease and mild cognitive impairment. NeuroImage 55(3), 856–867 (2011)
12. Wang, Y., Nie, J., Yap, P.-T., Shi, F., Guo, L., Shen, D.: Robust Deformable-Surface-Based Skull-Stripping for Large-Scale Studies. In: Fichtinger, G., Martel, A., Peters, T. (eds.) MICCAI 2011, Part III. LNCS, vol. 6893, pp. 635–642. Springer, Heidelberg (2011)
13. Shen, D., Davatzikos, C.: HAMMER: Hierarchical attribute matching mechanism for elastic registration. IEEE Transactions on Medical Imaging 21, 1421–1439 (2002)
14. Chang, C.C., Lin, C.J.: LIBSVM: a library for support vector machines (2001)
15. Belkin, M., Niyogi, P., Sindhwani, V.: Manifold Regularization: A Geometric Framework for Learning from Labeled and Unlabeled Examples. Journal of Machine Learning Research 7, 2399–2434 (2006)
16. Duan, L., Xu, D., Tsang, I., Xu, D.: Domain Transfer Multiple Kernel Learning. IEEE Transactions on Pattern Analysis and Machine Intelligence 34(3), 465–479 (2012)

Author Index